Duval County Tejanos

An Epic Narrative of Liberty and Democracy

Alfredo E. Cárdenas

Number 9 in the Texas Local Series

University of North Texas Press
Denton, Texas

Permissions:
University of North Texas Press
1155 Union Circle #311336
Denton, TX 76203-5017

The paper used in this book meets the minimum requirements of the
American National Standard for Permanence of Paper for Printed Library
Materials, z39.48.1984. Binding materials have been chosen for durability.

Library of Congress Cataloging-in-Publication Data

Names: Cárdenas, Alfredo E., 1948- author.
Title: Duval County Tejanos : an epic narrative of liberty and democracy /
 Alfredo E. Cárdenas.
Other titles: Texas local series ; no. 9.
Description: Denton, Texas : University of North Texas, [2024] | Series:
 Texas local series ; no. 9 | Includes bibliographical references and index.
Identifiers: LCCN 2024022951 (print) | LCCN 2024022952 (ebook) | ISBN
 9781574419443 (cloth) | ISBN 9781574419542 (ebook)
Subjects: LCSH: Mexican Americans--Texas--Duval County--History. |
 Mexican Americans--Texas--Duval County--Ethnic identity. | Community
 power--Texas--Duval County--History. | Duval County (Tex.)--Social
 conditions. | Duval County (Tex.)--Politics and government. | BISAC:
 HISTORY / United States / State & Local / Southwest (AZ, NM, OK, TX) |
 SOCIAL SCIENCE / Ethnic Studies / American / Hispanic American
 Studies
Classification: LCC F392.D9 C35 2024 (print) | LCC F392.D9 (ebook) |
 DDC 305.868/720730764463--dc23/eng/20240627
LC record available at https://lccn.loc.gov/2024022951
LC ebook record available at https://lccn.loc.gov/2024022952

Duval County Tejanos is Number 9 in the Texas Local Series.

The electronic edition of this book was made possible by the support of the
Vick Family Foundation. Typeset by vPrompt eServices.

To my wife, Genie; my children, Monica and Ryan, Christina and Bobby, Matthew and Jes; and my incredible grandchildren, Joseph, Aurora "Rory," Maya, Hayden, and Leo.

Contents

List of Figures and Tables

Foreword

The history of Mexican Americans (Tejanos) in Duval County spans more than two centuries. In Alfredo E. Cárdenas's survey of that history, people of different origins—immigrants from Spain and Mexico as early as the eighteenth century, joined in the nineteenth century by newcomers from the United States and Europe—descended on land belonging to Indigenous groups, and on that section of the brush country of South Texas sought new beginnings. Frustrating their occupation were numerous problems. During the last half of the nineteenth century, the pioneering Mexicans and Anglos dealt with Indian and bandit attacks, natural disasters, and neglect from Austin's government. Greed and conflicting ideologies—ones rooted in the two people's respective homeland cultures, institutions, and principles—and racial hostility obstructed the orderly process of settlement. Complicating plans for community building were the competitors' political, social, and economic outlooks. Which course—contention or accommodation—would more likely bring about a version of the place left at their point of origin? After fits and starts, accommodation became the preferred alternative for forming and governing the model society each group desired.

To be sure, coexistence functioned along bifurcated lines. Each group harbored ideas on how best to establish the community they visualized. Politically, both groups postured to erect a system of governance, allowing them an advantage in administering county affairs. In free elections citizens would decide who would rule over that apparatus. Anglo merchants, landowners, professionals, and everyday workers vied against their Mexican American counterparts in a contest for financial profit in the economic sector. Socially, Anglo Americans sought to create a place mirroring those of the greater United States, while Tejanos preferred a Mexican and American way of life.

Notwithstanding a political system dominated by an Anglo minority with a nexus to the state capital, Tejanos made advances in their aim to attain an equal and ultimately controlling role in Duval County's development. They served in positions such as constables, justices of the peace, and county commissioners. Demonstrating their political leanings, they supported groups such as the Huaraches and Botas during 1886 and the Catarino Garza movement of 1891–1892. Tejanos advanced the local livestock and cotton industries as ranchers, farmers, and common laborers. Urban dwellers established new businesses, organized churches, created civic clubs, and fostered municipal growth. Throughout the county—whether it was in the ranch, the village, or the town's Mexican district—Tejanos preserved the heritage of their ancestors, practicing old lifeways, customs, and values, perpetuating the mother country's language, observing Mexican holidays such as the Diez y Seis de Septiembre, and generally adding to the South Texas regional aura as a Tejano cultural zone.

As Duval transitioned into the twentieth century, two social-cultural worlds coexisted in the county. While all involved adhered to the American way of life, respected American institutions, and displayed unquestioned loyalty to their country, the Anglo minority lived apart from the syncretic universe of the majority Tejano population. These separated cultural domains served ethnic Mexicans to sustain tradition and reinforce (within their own space) self-assuredness, conviction, and ethnic identity. Therein, Mexican Americans, relying on the resources of their will, dogged determination, and the human instinct for survival, challenged adversity, resisted hardships and poverty, and contrived to fend off racial injustices. Mexicoamericanos pursued life goals in these enclaves, resourcefully adjusting to the changing times and the transformation around them.

Published scholarship on Duval County during the Archie, George, and Archer Parr eras (1912–1975) depicts a scenario wherein bosses used the poor and uneducated Mexican population for personal power and enrichment. But Cárdenas rejoins that Mexicans, continuing their earlier modus vivendi of partnering with the establishment holding political power, forged a mutually beneficial relationship with the Parr minority. Their aim was to continue to attain political parity, full constitutional rights, social standing, and economic independence. Persistent in their goals, they derived benefits from the machine (in the form of county services and welfare assistance), maintained a presence in various political positions, carved out space for entrepreneurial opportunity, and proudly demonstrated their cultural presence in Duval County.

Shared governance was evident in the posts Mexican Americans occupied under the Parrs: county judge, tax collector, county treasurer, sheriff, district judge, county auditor, county commissioners, justices of the peace, constables, school superintendent, teachers, courthouse staff, advisory boards' personnel, and more. Some even colluded as partners in crime with the Parrs, profiting brazenly from the bosses' corruption. Undercurrents of dissent and dissatisfaction with the *patrón*-style arrangement always existed and were energized beginning in the 1950s with the founding of the Freedom Party, the appearance of the Republican Party in the first half of the 1960s, and the challenge of a competing faction from Benavides in the early 1970s, all in which Mexican Americans were involved.

Hardly people to be disincentivized by a "culture of corruption" or bereft of entrepreneurial acumen, *la raza* dominated the commercial sector in Duval. Mexicanos owned or managed eating establishments, gas stations, dry goods and general merchandise stores, barrooms, and barber shops. They held professional positions, including as lawyers, pharmacists, journalists, educators, and real estate agents. Whether Spanish-dominant or bilingual, consumers negotiated business with members of a white-collar class not much different from themselves.

Culturally, Duval County was simultaneously Mexican and American. As in the days of Escandón during the 1750s and the years of the nineteenth century, the primary language in the barrios and *colonias mexicanas* remained Spanish, and old customs and traditions stayed in place. But as in South Texas and the rest of the state, residents were Mexicoamericanos. Their allegiance was to the United States, and their observable involvement (as bilingual and bicultural citizens) in politics and business attests to their ability to function in two worlds.

Several features commend this history of Mexican Americans in Duval County. First, it is Tejano history. Mexican Americans are primary actors in the narrative, conspicuously engaged in the county's politics, business, and society. Subordinated in the chronicle is the Anglo-American minority, heretofore given primary action in much of Duval County scholarship. In Cárdenas's overview of events, Mexicans play an active role in making Duval County a site where the American political structure is accepted, yet heritage is acclaimed.

Second, this is model microhistory, as it fixes laser-like on one specific county unit in South Texas. Notwithstanding its local focus, it is grounded on the most reliable sources: archival materials, Land Office records, census enumerations, tax files, newspapers, and online information. Critical secondary publications buttress the primary raw materials.

Third, the work falls neatly within the thematic contours of the New Social History and the more recent field of Borderlands History. As per components of this latter school, people (in this case of Mexican origin) cross expansive geographic terrains and national borders and begin community building amid existing populations. Conflict or accommodation determines relations. Such processes are evident in Cárdenas's writing: in the case of Duval County, Mexican Americans decided on an arrangement permitting them to cogovern with dominant forces.

Fourth, *Duval County Tejanos* represents another contribution to the exciting and informative scholarship that is unearthing history at the grass-roots level and showing that ordinary people have always had a hand in advancing the general state of life. More to the point, it is an essential corrective to the tenacious story that the Mexican-origin people of Duval were historical objects manipulated for decades by a ring led by corrupt Anglo politicians. In advancing the case that Mexican Americans shared in shaping Duval County's history as coagents, this masterful project overturns that erroneous depiction.

Arnoldo De León
Distinguished Professor of History Emeritus
Angelo State University, San Angelo, Texas

Acknowledgments

For nearly half a century, I have been interested in Duval County's history; during that time, however, my research was sporadic since my profession was not as a historian. God blessed me with a success-filled life that allowed little time off for scholarly investigation, but in my spare time, I kept plowing away.

My career—in antipoverty programs, politics, journalism, government, and the church—was an incredible journey that positively impacted my life and from which I gained many skills for writing this book. They were all "good stops," where I learned about Tejanos' lives in all parts of the state and in many different political, social, and economic settings.

The feeling of "Soy de Duval" ("I'm from Duval") has always been inherent in me, and I dare say in everyone raised in Duval County. The first time I heard it verbalized was when it flowed from the mouth of my good friend and colleague Ernesto González. While "Neto" was the first I heard verbalize the term, it had been our identity for a long time. After the fall of the Parr regime, we both returned to Duval County after achieving professional success in other parts of Texas. We were both dedicated to doing everything we could to move Duval County forward, away from the stench left after the collapse of the Parr political dynasty. But, of course, we were not the only ones with this impulse. Indeed, since George B. Parr's demise, this force spread throughout the county like a modern-day supervaccine protecting everyone from a corrupting political virus, and many of us threw away our masks and went to work, making our ancestors' dreams come true for us and our progeny.

When I arrived on the grounds of St. Mary's University in the winter of 1968, it seemed that those of us from Duval resided in an oasis where the rest of the world lived under different rules, customs, and beliefs. Besides my new college friends from Laredo who shared a similar upbringing, my other Tejano friends identified with *discrimination*, a concept unfamiliar to me. Although I had not experienced discrimination, I soon accepted it as palpable and pervasive. Prejudice was part of the Tejano experience in the inner reaches of Texas. To be clear, I did not encounter this bigotry and unpleasantness at St. Mary's University. The atmosphere at St. Mary's was very welcoming, from both students and professors. But conversations with fellow Tejano students from other parts of Texas and visits to the San Antonio barrios surrounding St. Mary's brought me into firsthand contact with the curse of discrimination. It served to help me appreciate my upbringing in Duval County even more.

Soon my inquisitive nature prompted a desire to learn more about this dynamic of race or ethnic relations. Perhaps Duval County could serve as a model of tolerance for others. Two professors at St. Mary's mainly influenced my desire to learn more about this phenomenon. First was Dr. Bill Crane, a political science professor who taught students to examine both sides of any issue before deciding which fit their sense of right and wrong. This lesson served me well throughout my professional life. Second was Dr. Félix D. Almaráz, whose introductory history course inculcated in me the idea that previous events significantly influenced the present. Before that time I believed history was in the past, over and done with. I, however, lived in the present and wanted to impact the future.

While it took awhile for Dr. Almaraz's lectures—that the past influenced the present—to germinate in my mind, my interest in the overall story of Duval County began in his classroom at St. Mary's University. Working at federal and state agencies in Austin led me to discover the incredible resources available at some of the capital city's archives, where I spent many lunch hours.

Like many other Tejanos of that Chicano era, I felt the best way to achieve change was through politics and government. Despite Dr. Almaráz's prescient observation about the past, I needed time to disabuse the notion that history was blasé and useless to the present. I continued to believe in the power of the options directly in front of me. Unlike my Chicano and Raza Unida contemporaries of the 1960s and early 1970s who were fighting for fundamental rights at the local level, my Duval experience was that we were already independent and in control of politics. The needed change, I felt, was on the state and national stage, so my approach to activism was somewhat conservative in light of the radical course of those Tejanos who were then fighting for fundamental rights I had long taken for granted. In time, barriers to progress in other South Texas communities began to fall, thanks to the efforts of the many activists who chose confrontation over accommodation. But those of us who took a more moderate approach also served as allies to those who eventually came to preside over politics and, astoundingly, became the establishment. We were both right, and both had a role to play.

In 1984 I returned home to Duval County to join the competent and talented staff of County Judge Gilberto Uresti and his committed colleagues on the commissioners court who had inherited the task of rebuilding the county after the downfall of the Parr political machine. Before that time I had valuable experiences in politics, having served on the staffs of Congressman George Bush in his run for the US Senate (1970) and of US Senator John Tower (1975–1976). I also gained valuable experience working with antipoverty groups throughout Texas, such as Model Cities (1971), Community Action (1971–1974), and Legal Aid (1977–1984). Returning to live and work in Duval County was fulfilling and allowed me to reconnect with my roots. Two years later I founded the *Duval County Picture*, a weekly newspaper covering Duval County. Through 1999 I benefited from many enriching experiences as a publisher/editor. Rewarding also was my time with city staff and council members at the city of San Diego, where I had the honor of serving as mayor for two terms (1992–1999).

In 2000 I moved to Austin to work for the Texas comptroller of public accounts as head of the local government assistance division. This opportunity gave me an inside look at Texas's state and local government operations, which served me well in writing this book. After retiring in 2010, I served as managing editor of the *South Texas Catholic*, the diocesan magazine for the Roman Catholic Diocese of Corpus Christi. There I learned firsthand the Catholic church's contributions to Duval County. After retirement I returned to Austin and completed my master of arts in history at Texas State University in San Marcos.

God has blessed me with the friendship of one of the greatest *cronistas* (historians) of the Tejano experience, Arnoldo De León, Distinguished

Professor of History Emeritus at Angelo State University. Professor De León unselfishly guided me along the scholarly publishing process, providing invaluable advice at every step. I will forever be indebted to his friendship and mentoring hand, which is present throughout this work.

Many Texas historians are responsible for giving me the tools to become proficient in researching and recording history. Dr. Almaráz was the first to pique my interest in history during my first year at St. Mary's University in San Antonio in 1968. Many other scholars helped me grow in historical research: Dr. Jesús de la Teja, Dr. Paul Hart, Dr. Andrés Tijerina, Dr. Robert Wooster, and Galen Greaser. Also, avocational historians like myself shared their findings through the years, especially my Duval County friend Homero Vera.

I would be remiss if I did not also extend my appreciation to friends in and from Duval County who, through the years up to the present, have offered me support and help. In particular, the Duval County Historical Commission board members have always served as soundboards and were quick to lend me a helping hand with my research. In addition, many genealogists shared their families' stories and photographs.

My most sincere appreciation goes to the many unnamed archivists and librarians who willingly helped me search for the past. Special thanks to the staff of the Texas State Library and Archives Commission, the Dolph Briscoe Center for American History, the Texas General Land Office Archives, the Benson Latin American Collection, the Texas A&M University–Corpus Christi Special Collections and Archives, and the South Texas Archives of the Jernigan Library at Texas A&M–Kingsville. Also, I extend due acknowledgment and appreciation to the Nueces and Duval County Clerks' offices, the Nueces and Victoria District Clerks staff, the San Diego Independent School District superintendent's office, the Local History Archives at La Retama Central Library in Corpus Christi, the Alicia Salinas City of Alice Public Library, and other depositories containing historical records about Duval County, Texas. All contributed to the final product you hold in your hands, but none of them is responsible for any errors of interpretation or fact, which are the specific domain of the author.

Finally, I would be remiss if I did not extend my most sincere appreciation to the Portal to Texas History at the University of North Texas. In a brief period, it has become an essential archival resource for Texas historians. In addition to its massive and continually growing newspaper collection, which provides vital contemporary information about any Texas era, many other resources, such as maps, rare books, and statutory and court sources, are available electronically at the Portal.

An explanation of terminology might be helpful for the reader. Before the Mexican-American War, residents of the area of the new state of Texas referred to themselves as Mexicanos. When Americans began to arrive in the Trans-Nueces, they called the people living there Mexicans. Before long, both groups started to use uncomplimentary names for each other. Both groups were Americans, but only the newcomers from the United States used that term. The initial residents called themselves Mexicanos or Mexican Americans. According to Merriam-Webster, the term *Tejano* did not gain widespread use until 1958.

Subsequently, historians in Mexican American and Chicano Studies programs began to refer to Mexican Americans (the most commonly used self-describer) as Tejanos. At the same time, terms such as *Hispanics* and *Latinos* gained widespread use in the United States. It was a recognition that many Spanish-speaking citizens from various South and Central American countries and the Caribbean were present in the United States, not only Mexicans. Gradually, many Mexican Americans began self-describing as Tejanos, a cultural descriptor that set them apart from their other Spanish-speaking brethren. They were also proud American citizens but sought to forge their distinctive cultural identity beyond language.

So in this book, in deference to a term that recognizes a distinct culture, I refer to Mexicanos who became American citizens at the end of the Mexican American War as *Tejanos*. The new arrivals from the United States and Europe, representing several cultural and language groups, are called *Americanos*. I will call the Mexican immigrants *Mexicanos*; while the latter two groups shared a broad spectrum of cultural traits, Tejanos embraced distinct differences, not the least of which was bilingualism.

Alfredo E. Cárdenas
Austin, Texas

Preface

In Texas, Duval County evokes Parr, politics, and corruption. Making such a connection is equivalent to hearing the word *Mexican* and immediately thinking lazy, dirty, illegal, and wetback. Yet these reductionist assumptions do not remotely represent Duval County or its Tejano community. Located in the geographic and cultural heart of South Texas—between San Antonio and Brownsville and Corpus Christi and Laredo—Duval County as a place connotes an authentic sense of being Tejano.

While the Archie and George B. Parr political machine, so widely written about, was at the center of the historical narrative during the first half of the twentieth century, it did not define Duval County. The fact is that Duval County shaped and molded Archie Parr's politics. Duval County does not mirror the political principles of the Parrs; the Parrs embraced and corrupted Duval County's electoral past and Tejanos' political aspirations. The politics that the Parrs learned from Duval County were not those of dishonesty but the actuality—in plain sight—that Tejanos had the clear majority and wanted to control their destiny. Corruption was a Parr expediency that Tejanos tolerated as a necessary evil to achieve their aspirations for fair political representation. But make no mistake, while Tejanos may appear to have made a deal with the devil, they enjoyed political and cultural independence much before most of their brothers and sisters in other parts of Texas or the United States.

Duval County Tejanos: An Epic Narrative of Liberty and Democracy accentuates the "significance and meaning of place," much like Monica Perales's monograph *Smeltertown: Making and Remembering a Southwest Border Community* does for that El Paso community.[1] In addition, it showcases Tejanos as historical actors, not bit players. Like Perales's connection to *Smeltertown*, the author of *Duval County Tejanos* has an attachment to Duval County.

What is it about Duval County that influenced and formed the identity of the entire Tejano community in the county? From early on the ambiance in Duval County fostered self-confidence among Tejanos—the notion that they were equal to everyone and could succeed in applying themselves, respected their elders, and recognized and venerated authority but knew when to challenge it if the need arose. Families, neighbors, teachers, elected officials, and people in business inculcated these notions into Duval County residents, as their forebears had instilled in them. Most of them grew up with feelings of independence, of being as capable as others, even if they were Americanos. Self-determination was not something they read about or that teachers put up on the chalkboard; it was as natural as breathing the fresh South Texas air. Confidence in themselves and their identity permeated the community, and when anyone moved away, they transported these traits throughout Texas and the United States. Teachers, coaches, elected officials, judges, mayors, and business owners were Tejanos. Being from Duval County was a statement of self-determination.

Duval County Tejanos is a community study focused on the development of Duval County in the brush country of South Texas as if it were under a microscope. It documents the life of the hardy Mexicano pioneers who first arrived as *pobladores* (settlers) circa 1810. They, and others who followed, established ranchos and villages and played a significant role in the growth of Duval County. This book speaks to the ups and downs of the frontier life of Tejanos and their Americano neighbors. It is a story of the struggle for survival, including the hardships and isolation nature presented and the conflict and violence they saw from *indios bravos* (warlike Native Americans), outlaws, and *los rinches* (Tejano colloquialism for Texas Rangers).

As does much of Tejano historiography, *Duval County Tejanos: An Epic Narrative of Liberty and Democracy* addresses labor, immigration, politics, education, economic development, ranching, culture, "law and order," and other relevant frontier topics. This manuscript combines aspects of New Social History and New Narrative History. James West Davidson urges "literary historians . . . to use the results" of their research "to paint a vivid, yet accurate canvas."[2] This book uses the hues of the county's development efforts to capture the story of Duval County. Moreover, it is distinct because it focuses, laser-like, on one community rather than a larger area. This chronicle is a local history of a South Texas county that contributed significantly to the Tejano identity in that region of the Tejano empire. Finally, it concentrates on Duval County's formational stage when it developed its unique cultural roots.

This work parallels, among others, Omar Valerio-Jiménez's *River of Hope: Forging Identity and Nation in the Rio Grande Borderlands* and Miguel Angel González-Quiroga's *War and Peace on the Rio Grande Frontier: 1830–1880*.[3] It looks at *River of Hope's* Villas del Norte, where Duval County harvested the cultural, political, and social elements distinguishing Tejanos in the Trans-Nueces Region. Moreover, *Duval County Tejanos* chronicles the determined ways pobladores—upon crossing the Rio Grande—made their home miles away from the international border. They met the challenges of the frontier, resisting violence from Native Americans and Americanos, the latter often law enforcement officers who refused to share power. Finally, like *River of Hope*, *Duval County Tejanos* illustrates Tejanos' adjustments in cultural and national identities.

Much like González-Quiroga's *War and Peace on the Rio Grande Frontier*, this book examines a later and much broader aspect of life in the region, among them the social, economic, and political arrangements between Tejanos and Americanos. In addition, *Duval County Tejanos* looks at the lives and contributions of the common folk, including vaqueros, sheep-herders, laborers, priests, teachers, carpenters, cotton pickers, worshipers, and women, as does González-Quiroga's book.

But Valerio-Jiménez's and González-Quiroga's books cover a much broader geographic area than this monograph, as do other older but substantial scholarly works that have an affinity to this book—namely, Armando C. Alonzo's *Tejano Legacy, Rancheros and Settlers in South Texas, 1734–1900*; Arnoldo De León's *The Tejano Community, 1836–1900*; and Andrés Tijerina's *Tejano Empire, Life on the South Texas Ranchos*.[4]

In the 1960s the Chicano and Tejano Studies era was in its infancy. The scholarship on Mexican Americans was still in the hands of historians (most of them Anglo-Americans) with a distorted view of Tejanos. Soon some books on Tejanos began to appear, such as *They Called Them Greasers* and *Anglos and Mexicans in the Making of Texas, 1836–1986*.[5] After these books, others written by Tejano authors continued to embrace an authentic view of their subjects.

Works that have focused exclusively or primarily on Duval County include *Los Chicanos: segregación y educación* by Elena Bilbao and María Antonia Gallart; *Early Tejano Ranching: Daily Life at Ranchos San José and El Fresnillo* by Andrés Sáenz, edited and with an introduction by Andrés Tijerina; and *Turn-of-the-Century Photographs from San Diego, Texas*, by Ana Carolina Castillo Crimm and Sara R. Massey.[6] Bilbao and Gallart's work is a social anthropological study focusing on the educational setting in San Diego, the county seat of Duval County. Ranchos San José and El Fresnillo are also both in Duval County.

Regional presses and individuals have turned out several local South Texas community histories emphasizing Duval County. Worthy of mention are *Father Jaillet: Saddlebag Priest of the Nueces* by Sister Mary Xavier, IWBS; Dorothy Abbott McCoy's *Oil, Mud & Guts: Birth of a Texas Town*; Coleman McCampbell's *Texas Seaport: The Story of the Growth of Corpus Christi and the Coastal Bend Area*; *Llanos Mesteñas: Mustang Plains* by Agnes G. Grimm; and Val W. Lehmann and José Cisneros's *Forgotten Legions: Sheep in the Rio Grande Plain of Texas*.[7] These books cover significant aspects of Duval County, although the county is not their exclusive focus.

Political interest, participation, and the rule of law had always been significant to the people of Duval County and the South Texas border communities. Tejanos had long asserted their rights in the brush country of Duval County, as did the Rio Grande communities of Webb, Zapata, and Starr Counties. In Duval County such expressions manifested as early as 1860 and continued throughout the nineteenth century. In the late 1880s and early 1890s, nearly one hundred years before the Chicano movement blossomed, Duval County Tejanos formed their version of the Raza Unida Party, La Bota. During the last years of the nineteenth century, political unrest was not uncommon as Catarino Garza launched his revolution against Porfirio Díaz from the ranchos in Duval and other South Texas counties. Duval County Tejanos' activism continued into the twentieth century when, in 1915, *los sediciosos* (insurgents) penned *El Plan de San Diego*.

As this monograph shows, the Tejano community in Duval County from its beginning exhibited an unrelenting insistence on exercising the group's political rights and an entitlement to fair representation in their ruling government institutions.

Indeed, Tejanos' political involvement has always been a hallmark of Duval County's history. For example, the first election held in Duval County in 1860, in which Tejanos participated, made such an impact it caught the attention of Governor Sam Houston and the Texas Supreme Court. Also, the first Tejano county judge in Duval County assumed that post in 1892, eighty years before the next neighboring county elected a Tejano judge. Today, every county in the Trans-Nueces, save two, has a Tejano as head of government.

While the Parr contributions to Duval County history are substantial, "their" account does not happen without the epic tale of the Duval Tejanos. The Parrs were two individuals, hardly enough to preside authoritatively over a people numbering in the thousands. Absent the political challenges Duval County Tejanos experienced and confronted directly, the Parrs' history would not exist. To tell the Parr narrative without equal or more significant notation of the Tejanos' participation and contributions—as other books on the Parrs have done—does a disservice to history.

Nevertheless, no history of Duval County would be complete without encompassing the Parr era. However, works specifically focused on the county's machine politics overlook the foundations the Parrs built upon, which were put in place by hardy pioneers in the nineteenth century. For example, the first book on the Parr political dynasty, *The Duke of Duval: The Life and Times of George B. Parr* (Dudley Lynch), focuses on political mischief but fails to capture the full story of Duval County. In *The Fall of the Duke of Duval: A Prosecutor's Journal*, the author, John E. Clark, points out that both Archie and George Parr saw the public treasury as their personal piggy bank. This book captures more recent history but still is not nearly the complete story. And so it goes for other Parr publications, such as *Texas Mutiny: Bullets, Ballots and Boss Rule* (Sheila Allee) and *The Dukes of Duval County: The Parr Family and Texas Politics* (Anthony R. Carrozza).[8] These make for interesting reading on the Parrs but denigrate the Tejanos' role and fail to create a complete account of Duval County.

Unlike these works, which zoom the microscope into one aspect of Duval County's political history under Archie and George Parr, *Duval County Tejanos: An Epic Narrative of Liberty and Democracy* takes a more holistic approach. It reviews the community's beginning under Spanish and Mexican rule. It follows the original pobladores as they moved away from royal and national authorities, distancing themselves from Spain and Mexico's sovereignty and establishing new relationships with other newcomers to South Texas. This unique setting allowed them to fend for themselves and transition into a Tejano identity of self-reliance and individualism. At the same time, they maintained their language, culture, Christian faith, familial structure, and dependence on the land and what it provided for sustenance.

Still, the Parr era is vital to the complete story of the county's history, so the final two chapters of this work look at this period of Duval County. It seeks to fill in the omissions in the Tejano story that earlier Parr books committed, such as Tejanos' long-held desire for political agency. The Parr system permitted Tejanos to fully realize their American citizenship, while the American power structure sought to keep them in secondary citizenship. The original pioneers had struggled against prejudice, a new language and culture, nature's elements, challenges from Native Americans, and the ever-present encounter with outlaws, including the Rangers, who were supposed to protect people, not subdue them by force. To his credit, Archie Parr encouraged the fulfillment of Tejanos' long-held desires for a fair share of political rule.

Duval County Tejanos captures the full breadth of the county's economic development efforts, beginning with nineteenth-century initiatives to build roads, bring in postal services, and establish the railroad and the telegraph. It also reports on establishing new communities, opening new businesses, founding churches and schools, organizing and celebrating social events, and generally fostering a society. Additionally, Tejanos in the Duval County area undertook legal means to retain their land, on which they raised livestock, especially cattle and sheep, and farmed various crops, notably cotton. This book highlights the county's challenges in taming a wild frontier, including dealing with Indians, bandits, the Civil War, revolutionaries, and lawless lawmen. It provides a systemic look at the development of Duval County politics and its critical role in the county's history and identity. Finally, the work notes the Tejanos' community attachment to Duval County. They were part of a region that geographer Daniel Arreola (*Tejano South Texas: A Mexican American Cultural Province*, the University of Texas Press, 2002) describes as "a cultural province."[9] This sense of belonging comprised *la familia, las costumbres, la fe católica, y las comidas* (family, customs, Catholic faith, and cuisine). And we must not leave out *la política* (politics).

Indeed, Tejanos in Duval County were not extras in this historical production. On the contrary, they were engaged in community life: organizing politically, cultivating the county's land, promoting local agriculture and livestock raising, advancing the local economy, building churches, establishing schools, perpetuating patriotic celebrations, and holding various social activities. This involvement in the community gave Tejanos a sense of belonging and identification with the physical environment, local ambiance, history, memory, home, and all the elements that contribute to a group's identity.

Chapter 1

El Principio
(The Beginning),
1800–1848

The history of Duval County should logically start with its enabling legislation. If that were so, Duval County's history began in 1858 when the Texas legislature carved it out of Nueces, Live Oak, and Starr Counties. Its origins can be traced to its political organization in 1876 when the Nueces County Commissioners Court accepted a call from area residents to organize Duval County, and citizens elected the first commissioners court.

However, "the children of the Sun," as the Native Americans called the Spanish explorers, were the first to leave a historical record of Duval County's early history. Between this time and before the legislature's act of 1858, pioneer settlers from Spain and Mexico took control of the region. Later, the Texans claimed the Trans-Nueces. It was these early settlers who gave Duval County its foundational identity.[1]

Los Españoles (The Spaniards)

Europeans' earliest appearance in the Duval County area was in 1533, less than fifty years after Columbus sailed to the New World. In 1528 the Spanish Crown sent Pánfilo de Narváez to explore the coastline from the Rio Grande to the Cape of Florida. Unfortunately, a storm off the Texas coast over-whelmed Narváez's ship, killing him and four hundred of his men.[2]

However, several crew members survived, including Alvar Núñez Cabeza de Vaca. According to historian Bethel Coopwood, Cabeza de Vaca made it to land and, in due time, traveled in Duval County en route to Mexico. Assuming Coopwood is correct—and he makes a persuasive argument—Cabeza de Vaca landed at St. Joseph's Island, situated off the coast of present-day Corpus Christi. The route Cabeza de Vaca took has been a point of contention through the years. Historians hold various theories on the course de Vaca traveled. However, recent studies confirm Coopwood's assertion that de Vaca passed through Duval County, wandering westward to an area where McMullen and Duval Counties meet and where the prickly pear flourished and was very popular among the Indians.[3]

Cabeza de Vaca most likely labeled the natives he met as *indios infideles* (infidels), in keeping with the Spanish caste system. While Cabeza de Vaca identified seventeen tribes—all members of the Coahuiltecan clan—existing in hamlets throughout South Texas, it is unclear which of these seventeen clans, if any, made Duval County their home. During the Spanish settlement period, the Coahuiltecan disappeared by eradication or assimilation. Regrettably, none are left in Duval County or its surroundings to tell their story.

While Cabeza de Vaca may have been the first Spaniard to travel to Duval County, he did not come as a colonizer. It was not until 1746 that the Spanish government decided to settle that part of New Spain, Costa del Seno Mexicano (Gulf Coast Colony, later known as Nuevo Santander), where Texas eventually established Duval County. The Spanish commissioned Don José de Escandón to establish settlements at the Provincia Nuevo Santander in northern Mexico. The area extended from the Río Panuco in Mexico to the Nueces River in Texas.[4]

Although Spaniards had been in the New World for more than 250 years, they had hardly explored the area that Escandón was partially responsible for settling, specifically between the Rio Grande and the Nueces River. The closest active community to northern Nuevo Santander was La Bahía del Espíritu Santo, modern-day Goliad, founded in 1821.

In February 1749 Escandón directed Captain Blas María de la Garza Falcón at Camargo to establish a trail for use by the settlers Escandón hoped to bring into the area. The road went through today's Duval County, where travelers could find water at the Agostadero del Charco Redondo on the Palo Blanco Creek in the Concepción area and a *tinaja*, a natural spring on the San Diego Creek at its intersection with the Tarancahua Creek. Both provided a respite for travelers and their livestock.[5]

Escandón looked to Camargo and Dolores on the Rio Grande as crucial to settling the area across the river. He believed Camargo could facilitate the "transit and communication with the Presidio and Misión de la Bahía del Espíritu Santo." In addition, he thought Dolores "could affect the settling of the Nueces River and lands in-between" up to Presidio La Bahía. In 1750 Escandón dispatched Juan José Vázquez Borrego, who had settled Dolores on the north bank of the Rio Grande above Revilla in Zapata County, to inspect the area north of the Rio Grande, particularly on the Nueces River's south bank. After several trips, Borrego concluded that this region was unsuitable for a settlement.[6]

Borrego's caporal, Antonio Manuel Flores, expressed a different view. On a trip to the area that same year, Flores observed that while the lands between the Rio Grande and Goliad did not have settlers, they were "excellent and provided water." Flores described the road to La Bahía del Espíritu Santo as having "convenient, good, permanent, and proportioned" watering places serving men and beasts. In addition, the cattle raiser indicated that the priests from Zacatecas and their companions frequently traversed the area.[7]

As per some of his observations, Flores was thirty leagues, or seventy-eight miles, from Hacienda Dolores; such a distance would have placed him in Duval County. He may have been in Duval's future county seat of San Diego, at the intersection of the San Diego and Tarancahua Creeks, when he reported finding "a low hill in which two creeks are formed and connect."[8]

Four years later, as 1754 ended, Tomás Sánchez, who had settled ten leagues north of Dolores, asked Escandón to allow him to develop a town on the north bank of the Rio Grande. Escandón agreed but asked Sánchez to look into founding a settlement on the Nueces River. Sánchez dutifully went to the Nueces but, like Borrego, found the area near the Nueces to be unsuitable for a village. So Sánchez received leave to establish a new colony and on May 15, 1755, he founded the municipio of Laredo on the north bank of the Rio Grande.[9]

The consensus of various explorers was that the Nueces Strip was uninhabitable. Unsurprisingly, José Tienda de Cuervo, who inspected Laredo in 1757, considered examining the region "useless." He surmised it was impossible to populate the land because it was heavily wooded, had a low elevation and little water, and was generally "unhealthy." Furthermore, he observed that those who had explored the area suffered from a lack of water, resulting in their horses dying of thirst.[10]

However, Blas María de la Garza Falcón's findings contradicted Tienda de Cuervo and others' appraisal of the region. The same year that Cuervo arrived at his conclusions of the Trans-Nueces, Falcón claimed to have discovered the South Texas coast and extensively explored the south side of the Nueces River, establishing ranches and pastures there. Falcón told the royal inspector that no one knew the Nueces River as well as he did.[11]

For the next four decades, the historical record is silent on Spanish activity in the Duval County region. Then, on May 10, 1805, Francisco Cordente, Julián and Ventura Flores, and Marcelo de Hinojosa, all Villa de Mier residents, empowered Don José Ignacio de Alustiza to represent them before authorities in securing fifteen leagues in a place called San Diego. These four men were of the mold of Antonio Manuel Flores and Blas de la Garza Falcón, who believed in the value of the Nueces Strip.[12]

Over the next fifteen years, Spain made grants for twelve ranchos in Duval County, including San Diego de Arriba, San Diego de Abajo, San Leandro, San Francisco, Palo Blanquito, Palo Blanco, San Rafael de Los Encinos, San Pedro del Charco Redondo, Santa Rosalía, Santa Cruz de la Concepción, Santa María de los Ángeles de Abajo, and Santa María de Los Ángeles de Arriba.[13] The owners of these twelve pieces of land formed the cornerstones of Duval County's ancestral heritage.

Escandón taught the residents in Camargo, Dolores, Laredo, Mier, Revilla, and Reynosa methods of governance that served them for half a century. These practices included relying on themselves, their families, and their neighbors, not the state or national government. In addition, they "abhorred arbitrariness and disorder" and were "lovers of true freedom." These traditions undoubtedly took root in the minds of men and women who first settled in Duval County at the dawn of the nineteenth century. After all, Mier and Camargo were the wellsprings for Duval County pioneers.[14]

Those arriving in the Duval area from the Rio Grande villages during the first quarter of the eighteenth century got "busy night and day in the honest work of the land." The land provided sustenance for their horses, cattle, sheep, goats, mules, and other livestock, nourishing the families living on the properties. The Duval County forefathers understood that their livelihood came from a commitment to the land, not anything or anyone else.[15]

In 1810 while Spain was distracted by a dispute with France, the Catholic priest Miguel Hidalgo y Costilla declared Mexican independence. After a contentious eleven years, Mexico finally achieved its autonomy. As a result, Spain's long and storied history in Texas ended. After 1821 power passed to the new Mexican nation, which ratified Spanish land grants and made additional land bequests in Duval County.

Los Mexicanos

As a new and developing country, Mexico needed more people to help settle its northern reaches. The Mexican Congress in 1824 enabled the state legislatures throughout Mexico to administer its national laws within their jurisdiction. Tamaulipas, the new name for Nuevo Santander, governed the Nueces Strip. On October 28, 1830, the new Tamaulipan government approved a land decree, Law No. 47, acknowledging the advantages of populating the Rio Grande and the Nueces River area. The region already had settlers living in functional ranchos throughout the Nueces Strip, from the Rio Grande Valley to the Coastal Bend and across toward Laredo. Aside from Laredo, no *villas* (villages) existed.[16]

Unlike early authorities under New Spain, the Mexicanos considered the Trans-Nueces a most fertile region. However, the scarcity of people in the northernmost reaches of Tamaulipas contributed to a lack of security for Las Villas del Norte and the hardy rancheros who had ventured into that hinterland. In addition, Tamaulipan officials hoped the new law would encourage colonizers, as they had in Coahuila-Tejas.

However, no foreigners accepted the national government's offer to colonize the area around Duval County or anywhere south of the Nueces River. The nearest such settlement was the McMullen and McGloin concession made in 1828 to the Irish by Coahuila-Tejas in nearby San Patricio, thirteen miles north of present-day Banquete, beyond the Nueces River. Nevertheless, Tamaulipas continued encouraging other landowners south of the Rio Grande to head north to seek fortunes and concurrently enrich the state's coffers.[17]

In 1828 the Mexican government sent 38-year-old General Manuel de Mier y Terán to Texas to assess its natural resources. Terán traveled through parts of South Texas on his return from the Texas-Louisiana border. While he may not have passed through Duval County, he spent some time in the Agua Dulce, San Fernando, and Santa Gertrudis areas in modern-day Nueces, Jim Wells, and Kleberg Counties. In the mid-eighteenth century, Spain called this area, including Duval County, a Wild Horse Desert. It was home to countless wild horses and cattle that fed on copious native grass.

Mier y Terán wrote in his diary that the land was "a continuous plain" and mentioned that the flatlands caused rainwater to collect. In addition, Terán found wild and unbranded livestock flourishing in the area and thought it necessary to post guards over the horses and mules to keep them from running off with the numerous *mesteños* (wild horses). This report confirms that Spaniards and Mexicans had already settled in that region.[18]

The occupation of the northernmost part of Tamaulipas by rancheros between the Rio Grande and the Nueces Rivers continued. However, war clouds developed in the neighboring state of Coahuila-Tejas to the north. Even though the Trans-Nueces was not part of Coahuila-Tejas, the insurrection dragged Tamaulipas into the conflict, and the region between the Nueces River and the Rio Grande faced turmoil and uncertainty.

Following the beginning of Coahuila-Tejas's revolt against Mexico on October 2, 1835, General Valentín Canalizo ordered residents in the Nueces Strip to vacate the territory. In addition, Canalizo threatened anyone found in the area with punishment as a spy. However, quickly developing events made

Canalizo's directive null and void. While the Texans' incursions on the south side of the Nueces River during the rebellion were few, the war north of the Nueces River adversely impacted events between the Nueces River and the Rio Grande. Initially the Mexican government made every effort to "strip" the Nueces Strip of everything of value, including settlers, to deprive the Texans of any pretext to cross the Nueces River in search of loot. However, events north of the Nueces were moving fast, overpowering Mexico's plans and forcing Mexicanos in the Nueces Strip to stay in place.[19]

On October 15, 1835, two weeks after Texas's initial skirmish at Gonzales, the military commander of Tamaulipas, J. M. Guerra, alerted ranchers that Texans had captured Goliad and advised them to proceed with initial plans to evacuate the Nueces Strip. Shortly after that, however, Guerra became aware of the situation on the ground and instructed everyone still on the ranchos to arm themselves, and he supplied them with ammunition.[20]

After his capture at San Jacinto, on April 21, 1836, Mexican General Antonio López de Santa Anna signed the Treaties of Velasco, appearing to exchange the Nueces Strip to Texas for his freedom. In reality these documents were not treaties. One report's name was "Public Agreement," and the other a "secret Treaty." The dictionary definition of a treaty is a written agreement between two or more states signed by authorized representatives and usually ratified by each party's lawmaking authority. Santa Anna was not "duly authorized," nor were the documents "ratified" by the Mexican regime. Moreover, Santa Anna agreed to the treaties under duress while a prisoner.[21]

Since the late eighteenth century, nearly all official Spanish and Mexican documents marked the Nueces River as the boundary between Texas and Nuevo Santander, subsequently Tamaulipas. In addition, most maps of the area, including one drawn by Stephen F. Austin, showed the same demarcation line between Texas and Mexico.[22]

Though the Congress of the Republic of Texas (1836–1845) claimed the Rio Grande as the international boundary, the young republic, for its nine-year duration, could not exert sovereignty over the area. However, Mexico also could not exercise dominion over the Trans-Nueces, and settlers found themselves *en medio* (between) two countries. Consequently, neither the Mexican state of Tamaulipas nor the Republic of Texas controlled the region.[23]

This chaotic situation weakened the Trans-Nueces, opening it to attacks from the Comanche and Lipan Apache, who also claimed the area. The *indios* (Native Americans) raided the ranchos at will. Moreover, in 1836 the rancheros, despite orders to retreat, had to deal with "special Rangers" that Texas Provisional President David G. Burnet sent to the Nueces Strip to round up abandoned cattle to feed the Texan Army. Under this lawlessness three million heads of cattle, sheep, goats, and horses soon ran wild in the region encompassing modern-day Duval County.[24]

After the cessation of hostilities between Mexico and Texas, the Mexicanos dealt with livestock pirates, euphemistically called "cowboys," herding cattle north for personal use or selling in New Orleans. Mexican troops made occasional forays into the region to establish peace, but their attempts proved ineffective. As a result, many rancheros retreated to Las Villas del Norte on the Rio Grande, abandoning their livestock. Among the many ranchos intermittently deserted were San Diego, San Leandro, and Los Ángeles de Abajo in Duval County.[25]

Meanwhile, the Tamaulipas government rejected Texas's claim to the Nueces Strip and continued exercising civil authority over the area. In addition, Tamaulipas resumed populating the region with land grants following the Texas War of Independence. All told, Mexico made five land grants in the Duval County area. These were in addition to those already made by Spain. While Tamaulipas continued to make grants in the area and the new Republic of Texas persisted in claiming sovereignty, another uncertainty erupted in 1840.

Medio-México

Following the Texans' example, a disgruntled group identified with the Federalist movement in Mexico met in Laredo on January 17, 1840, declaring the Republic of the Rio Grande independent from Mexico. The Federalists opposed the concentration of power in a national government. Instead, they preferred more vital state governments closer to the people that could better represent their needs, modeling Escandón's paradigm of Nuevo Santander. The Republic of the Rio Grande sought to detach Tamaulipas, Nuevo León,

Coahuila, Zacatecas, Durango, Chihuahua, and Nuevo México from Mexico. The proposed republic included the northern part of Tamaulipas between the Nueces River and the Rio Grande, which both Mexico and Texas claimed.[26]

Indeed, the insurgents proclaimed Laredo, in this disputed territory, as their capital and named Jesús de Cárdenas the republic's president and Antonio Canales the army's commander. Cárdenas declared that *norteños* (northerners) in Mexico and Texans had "a uniformity of interests" and joined in a fight for liberty. Moreover, Canales was very familiar with the many ranchos in Duval County because he had mapped much of the ranch land as Tamaulipas's state surveyor. Canales soon began a dialogue with Tejanos, with whom he shared a Federalist ideology. Juan Séguin, the Tejano hero of the Texas Revolution, recruited some of his supporters from Texas and joined Canales' army.[27]

Throughout 1840 Federalist leaders engaged in open revolt against Mexico, and much of their early military engagement took place in the South Texas brush country. Their ranks grew to a one-thousand-member army, and they bivouacked at locations such as Lipantitlán and San Patricio.[28] This military build-up prompted the central government in Mexico City to send mounted troops to police the area as far north as the Nueces River, provoking Texas President Mirabeau Lamar to order forces into the region to protect the republic's integrity.[29]

The Federalists were unimpressed with Mexico City's or Lamar's orders and continued their open rebellion. Some three hundred Texans joined General Canales's companies at Lipantitlán, from where they launched a drive to try to take Laredo from the centralist army, most likely traversing Duval County, as the area lay on the Lipantitlán to Laredo route. At about that same time, in the summer of 1840, J. H. Yerby led San Patricio Rangers on killing and stealing raids along the Laredo–Corpus Christi road, traversing Duval County, prompting two hundred Centralist troops under Captain Antonio Ramírez to engage the Rangers repeatedly. Finally, the Texans hightailed it back to the north side of the Nueces River.[30]

Before the end of the year, Mexico's Centralist forces defeated Canales in skirmishes south of the Rio Grande, and the commander surrendered and joined Mexico's army, as did President Cárdenas, much to the chagrin of their followers in the Nueces Strip. Both men later enjoyed political success in Mexico, with Cárdenas serving as governor of Tamaulipas. But, as in times past, the rancheros in South Texas were left to fend for themselves. Although the new Republic of the Rio Grande was short-lived, it left disarray in the region. Whatever law enforcement was present vanished, and brigands moved in to fill the void.[31]

War Clouds Again on the Horizon

On February 28, 1845, the United States Congress voted to admit the Republic of Texas as its twenty-eighth state. Texas voters approved the annexation in October 1845, and statehood became a reality for those Texans who initiated the 1836 rebellion against the Estados Unidos Mexicanos. However, American-born Texans were not the only ones to get their wish. US President James K. Polk and his supporters saw Texas as a way to fulfill their pursuit of "manifest destiny."[32]

Even before the Texans went to the polls to approve annexation, President Polk ordered American troops under General Zachary Taylor to march toward South Texas. The president should have known that setting up a military camp below the Nueces River would provoke Mexico, which continued to claim ownership of the area between the Nueces River and the Rio Grande.[33]

Thus, on July 23, 1845, General Taylor bivouacked at Corpus Christi. A Republic of Texas Ranger company commanded by Lt. W. B. Gray soon joined the American troops; only one Ranger, Ponciano Villareal, was a Tejano. These American forces required mule and horse reinforcements, and the area's rancheros, including from Duval County, were not hesitant to engage this new market. Indeed, by December 1845, area ranchers had provided Taylor's army with three thousand heads of livestock.[34]

Mexico broke diplomatic relations with the United States immediately after Congress annexed Texas in December 1845. Diplomatic efforts to resolve differences over the Texas-Mexico border failed. The president ordered General Taylor to move on to the Rio Grande, which he did, arriving there on March 23, 1846. To Mexico these maneuvers were no less than acts of war. To the rancheros in the future Duval County, it presented a challenge. They were loyal to Mexico, but the American troops were in their midst.[35]

On April 25 General Anastasio Torrejón crossed the Rio Grande twenty-eight miles west of newly established Fort Texas, the American headquarters. Torrejón had 1,600 men under his command. American Captain Seth Thornton and his sixty-three men stumbled upon General Torrejón's troops. Severely outnumbered, the Americans lost eleven men, and the rest surrendered. It was an ignoble confrontation for the American Army.[36]

Later that day General Mariano Arista crossed the river at Matamoros with troops of the Mexican Army and attacked the US troops at Fort Texas. The American Army repulsed Arista. In May the Mexican general launched a follow-up offensive against the Americans at Palo Alto and was defeated again. Then, a few days later, Arista undertook a third offensive against the Americans at Resaca de la Palma, suffering another setback, forcing the Mexican Army's remnants to retreat to the Mexican interior. The Americans then crossed the Rio Grande in pursuit. Finally, in September 1847 the Mexican Army surrendered after a devastating defeat in Mexico City, and treaty negotiations began.[37]

After fifty years of Spanish and Mexican settlement in the Duval County area, the Mexican-American War flipped the lives of Mexicano residents in the region, bringing about a radical change. The American victory in the war beckoned dramatic change for the area and its original settlers. Still, the Mexicanos had title to the land and were intent on remaining and operating their ranchos. Duval County entered a new and long-lasting era featuring Tejanos and Americanos.

Chapter 2

Llegaron Los Americanos (The Americans Arrived), 1848–1860

After the Mexican-American War, the United States and Texas governments immediately began efforts to transplant American political, economic, and social institutions to the Nueces Strip. However, "long before the arrival of foreigners in the area, ranchers and merchants [Spaniards and Mexicans] had begun to tie the vast region together."[1] The Americanos, however, sought to put in motion political plans to improve the infrastructure system, support commerce, and provide the security needed for development. Fortuitously, the dispute over the Nueces Strip had ended, and the way of life in the area became a bit more peaceful.

It took time before the region adapted to its new country. The physical distance between the Tejanos who settled in Duval County and their state and national authorities resulted in weak relations, whether these authorities were Mexicans or Americans.[2]

In 1848, when the United States assumed sovereignty over the Nueces Strip, longtime pioneers—who had lived there since the late eighteenth century—remained in the area, but now as American citizens. Of necessity they had to maneuver between two societies. In addition, the new American residents of Mexican origin had to learn and adjust to new legal rules, a new language, and unfamiliar economic and political structures. Still, unlike Mexican law, which limited rights to property ownership, America also provided the right to land ownership to paisanos. The result was that Tejanos' political identity took on a new wrinkle. Additionally, Tejanos had to deal with Americanos arriving in the region. As González-Quiroga points out, thoughtful Tejanos in South Texas, including Duval County, were concerned with "how to survive and maintain their identity and sense of dignity in the force of the growing American presence and domination."[3]

Tejanos in the Trans-Nueces had dealt with Americanos on a limited basis as traders, but their numbers had increased. These strangers looked different, spoke a foreign language, and seemed determined to take the Tejanos' land. Tejanos, who had struggled against Indians, revolutionaries, and bandits, prepared themselves to defend their property against these new outsiders. Change was most certainly the new standard, but the locals proved robust. They soon adjusted to the new reality.[4]

Finally, the Americanos set out to build a new social order. Juan Mora-Torres points out that 1848 marked "the beginning of the end of [South Texas's] isolation" and was the border's "next stage of territorial development." The new southern boundary at the Rio Grande opened up the region and ended the Nueces Strip's "geographic isolation."[5]

In 1834 the Mexican state of Coahuila-Tejas had created the municipio of San Patricio. After the Trans-Nueces became part of the new American state of Texas in 1846, the region came under the jurisdiction of San Patricio County. That same year, however, the Texas legislature created Nueces County, which covered the vicinity of San Patricio south of the Nueces River, including Duval County. Then, in 1848, the legislature extracted Webb, Starr, and Cameron Counties from Nueces. Folks in Duval County were now under the jurisdictions of Nueces and Starr Counties instead of the municipios of Mier and Camargo.[6]

In the first election held in Nueces County on July 13, 1847, Americano voters dominated. They selected Spaniard José de Alba as chief justice, today referred to as county judge. De Alba was editor of the *Corpus Christi Gazette* and was the only Spanish-surnamed person elected to public office in the county that year. In the early years of American South Texas, Spaniards like de Alba, as white Europeans, were more likely to be elected than mestizo Mexicanos. De Alba's election suggested tipping the hat to Spanish-speaking Americans. However, he died in office following a short illness after serving only six weeks. An Americano replaced de Alba, and Nueces County did not elect a Tejano as county judge for another 150 years. This trend persisted in Nueces County and most of the Trans-Nueces well into the twentieth century.[7]

Developing Infrastructure and Commerce

With a governing structure at Corpus Christi, Nueces County began to address much-needed public infrastructure improvements, including in the area that eventually became Duval County. The development started with roads essential for regional and international trade. Indeed, commerce with Mexico was crucial to the region and demanded a functional road system.

As early as 1835, rancheros living on the frontier from Laredo to Corpus Christi had built a road between these two towns. Later, Henry Kinney improved this path, which crossed through Rancho Los Ángeles in southwestern Duval County, to connect his trading post in Corpus Christi to Laredo. Kinney affixed a plow to a wagon and cleared the Rio Grande trail. In 1848 the Nueces County Commissioners Court named William L. Cavanaugh to lay out the road from Corpus Christi to Laredo as agent and commissioner. Cavanaugh enhanced the road Kinney had laid out.[8]

That same year another Kinney associate, James Manning, surveyed the route from Corpus Christi to Mier, then "a clear and perceptible trail" that extended 145 miles. The roughed-out roadway served until the county cut a permanent road. The trail had an upper branch to Mier and a lower fork to Rio Grande City and Camargo. The paths cut "through a country which [commanded] plenty of water, [abounded] in cattle, deer, and game of all descriptions and everything a traveler [needed] on the road for himself or his animals." This description differed markedly from the portrayal Spanish officials had offered years earlier.[9]

Finally, in July 1850 construction began on a new road from Corpus Christi to Eagle Pass. The route traversed Duval County, north of the Rancho San Diego headquarters. In addition to transporting merchandise, this network of roads facilitated transporting troops. The federal government also used it in distributing mail.[10]

In addition to establishing a governmental structure and a functional transportation hub, the newcomers sought to promote trade and commerce. In the minds of commercial interests at Corpus Christi, South Texas could develop economically through business with Mexico. The most enticing markets were towns in the Rio Grande's proximity, specifically Mier, Guerrero, Laredo, Camargo, and San Fernando in Tamaulipas; Candela and Sabinas in Coahuila; and Agualeguas, Nuevo León. In addition, Corpus Christi's business with Chihuahua and California markets also enticed local merchants.[11]

Corpus Christi's business community launched a protracted advertising campaign to win over Mexican traders. They touted the Corpus Christi roads to Laredo, the Mier-Camargo area, and Eagle Pass as the shortest and most efficient corridors between their trade areas. Cozying up to border commercial interests, Corpus Christi's leaders suggested to the Mexican traders on Mexico's northern border that Corpus Christi was more accessible than markets in Chihuahua. Tariffs, moreover, were far lower. Traders from Mier and Guerrero seemed to be won over by these arguments. One hundred came to Corpus Christi in November 1848 to buy lumber and other supplies valued at $40,000.[12]

Duval County communities like San Diego did not appear to participate in this trade. However, traders likely stopped at ranchos for horses, cattle, and hides. Moreover, Duval County was the midpoint between the border and Corpus Christi and a suitable rest area for men and beasts.

Many early Americano settlers, including Henry Kinney who came to South Texas in 1839, willingly developed friendly relations with the recently transformed citizens from old Mexico. Some married Tejanas. The Tejanos were their neighbors, but more than that, they owned considerable land, were a reliable source of labor, and provided most of the clientele for new business enterprises. Therefore, it was incumbent for the newcomers to be on good terms with the old settlers.

Another key player in Nueces County's effort to modernize the region was John Peoples, publisher of the *Corpus Christi Star*. Peoples also saw Tejanos as an asset and developed the *Star* to appeal to Tejano readers by presenting the news in Spanish via a page entitled *La Estrella*. Also, Spanish-language advertisements peddled everything from groceries to legal services. Every individual appearing on *La Estrella* page was referred to by their Spanish first name, including "Juan" Peoples. His intent for *La Estrella*, Peoples noted, was "to have the Mexican reader up to date with all the great events, all matters that may interest them, publish those laws with which it is necessary for new citizens to become familiar and really provide what they have never had on this border."[13]

Soon wealthy Mexicanos from south of the Rio Grande began to visit Corpus Christi and the surrounding area. The Mexicanos were pleased with their excursion. Others of their kin also found South Texas attractive, moving to the Rio Grande Valley and San Antonio. Many other Mexicanos were reportedly seeking refuge from "debt slavery." The newspaper reminded its readers that the United States had always provided "asylum" and would continue to do so.[14]

Postal Service

Political leaders also hoped to entice newcomers from the United States and were prepared to support the Americanos emigrating to South Texas. Communicating with other places in Texas and the United States was one means of attracting newcomers hoping to stay in touch with families back home. This communication link was also vital to enhancing the area's modernization. While local governments could improve roads, there was nothing they could do about mail delivery.

Even though the Corpus Christi to Laredo road was designated a mail route, postal carriers did not always use it. Indeed, in October 1848 the person in charge of implementing the government's policy was not following the designated plan. Mail riders at times failed to appear. These problems continued from Corpus Christi to the valley for years. Finally, in July 1858 new mail routes increased service along the existing roadways, and it appeared that the government had finally solved the mail delivery problem.[15]

The Continuing Indian Problem

During this period Mexicano landowners on the Nueces Strip, who had relocated to northern Mexico after several Indian raids, began to move back to their ranchos. The Mexicanos believed their new country, the United States, could protect them from Indians. In response to complaints about the Indian problem in South Texas, Governor George T. Woods raised three Ranger companies. However, the governor assigned the Rangers to San Antonio. The strategy was for the Rangers to patrol the area west of San Antonio, cutting off Indians marauding on the Nueces Strip, presumably by keeping them out of the Nueces County area altogether. In June 1849 the governor ordered a Ranger Company stationed in Corpus Christi for a three-month enlistment. Residents gave the gesture a warm reception but expressed their hope to the governor that he would extend the tour of duty for a year.[16]

One problem connected to the Indian raids that the state needed to address in Nueces County, landowners believed, was Americano outlaws conspiring with the Indians. Locals alleged that Americano bandits entered town undetected, spied on the Rangers' movements, and passed intelligence to the Indians. The latter then moved their operations away from the section patrolled by the Rangers and returned when detection diminished.[17]

In June 1849 the governor directed John S. Ford, John J. Grumbles, and Henry Smock to recruit volunteers for the three Ranger companies. The state assigned one of the companies to patrol the hinterland at Barranco Blanco in Duval County. The camp was in Rancho Agua Poquita, some ten miles north of present-day Ramírez. In addition, the Rangers stationed a second unit at Tulosa in modern Kleberg County, with the third detachment sent to Laredo and Brownsville, where they patrolled along the Rio Grande border region. Soon, Ford arrived in Corpus Christi with a force of forty Texas Rangers.[18]

After patrolling a triangular area between Laredo, Fort Ringgold in Rio Grande City, and Corpus Christi, Captain Ford declared "mission accomplished" and prematurely returned to San Antonio. He reported that rancheros had resettled abandoned farms and ranches on the frontier between

Corpus Christi and the Rio Grande. Moreover, the Rangers claimed to have made the roads safe for travelers and merchants.[19]

Shortly after that, in September 1851, Indians began preparing to renew their "death and devastation" from the Nueces River to the Rio Grande. "Again, they can resume their cattle stealing and scalping forays along the whole line of settlements from the farms and ranches above Laredo to Corpus Christi," a San Antonio newspaper warned. Ranger protection had not been sufficient or readily available. Thus, into the 1850s ranchers and traders provided their security.[20]

Banditry

In 1836 the so-called "San Patricio Rangers . . . stole, raided, and murdered and plundered Mexican traders along the Laredo-Corpus Christi Road." Also, American bandits or "white land pirates" frequently robbed Mexican traders from the Rio Grande. However, these outlaws were not the only ones impeding trade, as Mexican bandidos often joined in thievery.[21]

As early as 1846, talk in Mexico was that bandits were abusing traders in the Trans-Nueces with the American Army's cooperation. The *Corpus Christi Gazette* sought to assure all Mexican merchants that they were welcome. The newspaper attempted to convince the Mexicano traders that army enlistees were good men, not brigands. Traders from as far away as Monterrey were in Corpus Christi then, and perhaps the newspaper hoped they would carry its message back to Mexico.[22]

The presence of "many idle men" prone to banditry continued to afflict the area and hamper business development on the sparsely settled frontier. Consequently, as they did with the Indian difficulty, local merchants repeatedly appealed to Austin and Washington to curb lawlessness. And like with the Indian response, the locals were disappointed with the army and Rangers. One idea citizens entertained was to form a civilian posse to address banditry. In addition, business leaders lamented attacks perpetrated upon Mexicanos; those who robbed Mexicanos would steal not only from them but also from Americans. Furthermore, stealing from Mexicanos was a direct affront to local Americanos' sales.

Indian and bandit attacks occasioned not only considerable loss of
life and property but also caused periodic trade disruptions. In addition,
the danger grabbed the media and the public's attention and instilled fear
in frontier dwellers. However, the army's policy of cutting off the Indians
before they reached South Texas and the periodic assignment of Rangers to
the area eventually reduced these heinous forces.

———◦———

American state and national governments seemed more responsive to
Tejanos' concerns than Tamaulipas and Mexico had ever been, but the seats of
government were still distant from the area. Therefore, the Tejanos' "loyalty
remained . . . fluid." Their focus remained with their families, compadres,
and neighbors in the Nueces Strip; Austin and Washington had a ways to go
before they earned the Tejanos' allegiance.[23]

Chapter 3

El Terreno (The Land), 1850–1900

Americano newcomers to South Texas sought to start and build a trade economy. However, the old-time Mexicanos had a more personal stake in the new order: making sure they held on to their land. Duval County Tejanos looked to real estate to sustain their families. Some were fortunate to own property, but most worked on the range. They all, however, depended on the land for their survival.

At the dawn of the nineteenth century, there were no other means of support in the Trans-Nueces other than working livestock. No factories, transportation enterprises, service establishments, or government jobs existed. As a result, people mostly raised cattle, horses, sheep, and other *ganado* (livestock) to provide for their families. While some turned to crop farming in Duval County, they primarily harvested small crops to supplement their families' dietary needs.

However, changing governing authorities from Spanish to Mexican to American presented Tejanos with severe challenges regarding their property. The most significant problem was resolving ownership of Spanish and Mexican land grants. After Texas became a state, Tejanos encountered many issues regarding their properties. First was the loss of records and the difficulty and inability to locate them in Mexico. Second, "South Texas titles were clouded by a confusing variety of title instruments, the vagueness of field notes, overlapping surveys, the failure to fulfill requirements set down in the original grants, and the complications of collective ownership."[1]

Over the years several powers claimed sovereignty over the land in present-day Duval County and the Trans-Nueces. Aside from whatever territorial claims the Indigenous people may have had, the history of the public domain in this area begins with Spain's claim to the New World. Mexico (1821), the Republic of Texas (1836), and the United States (1845) also made assertions of sovereignty. Each ruling authority set out the conditions and processes required to obtain and dispose of land.

Succeeding national and state governments developed precedents for confirming or recognizing land grants made by previous regimes. In the 1850s, after its admission into the American Union, Texas adopted legislation setting out the steps landowners needed to take to confirm claims to Spanish and Mexican property deeds in the Trans-Nueces.[2]

In what became Duval County, the quest for property began in the early 1800s after the availability of acreage in the Camargo and Mier region on the south side of the Rio Grande became depleted. Those wishing to become rancheros ventured farther north from Las Villas del Norte. However, obtaining a perfect title in New Spain was cumbersome, expensive, and challenging. In 1826 Tamaulipas, vested with the authority of Mexico's federal government, adopted laws streamlining the process, enabling the new state to approve more tracts. However, some property owners could not prove their titles before 1836, when the Republic of Texas presumed sovereignty over the area. However, Mexico did not recognize Texas's claim, and Tamaulipas continued to issue deeds.

The annexation of Texas by the United States in 1845 established a process to resolve sovereignty over the area. In 1836, although it exercised no control over the region, the new Republic of Texas claimed territory that historically had been part of Tamaulipas. The Texas assertion was validated when the United States and Mexico signed the Treaty of Guadalupe Hidalgo in 1848 to end the war between the United States and Mexico. However, unlike California, where the American national government assumed jurisdiction over Spanish and Mexican land grants, the state of Texas retained jurisdiction over its public lands because the United States refused to take the debt of the Republic of Texas. Thus, confirmation of the Spanish and Mexican land grants fell to the state.[3]

After independence Texas adopted the English common law system, unfamiliar to Tejanos. Faced with new rules on ownership and forced to navigate them in a language not their own, Tejanos proved resilient. Rancheros saw land proprietorship as crucial to their survival and were willing to take any action to preserve their rights.

Fortunately, perhaps because Duval County was considered a brush country with few water resources and was isolated from access to foreign markets, Americanos did not rush into the county to gobble up land. Still, Duval County Tejanos stood vigilant against the chicanery some Americanos devised of using "their acquaintances with the legal system and their association with friends in high places to rob old Mexican grantees" of their sizable estates. So Tejanos turned to Texas's legal framework to defend their land rights.[4]

While the Treaty of Guadalupe Hidalgo of 1848 gave the new Tejanos citizenship rights, the state provided avenues for rancheros to confirm titles to property they had received from Spain and Mexico. Also aiding Tejanos were Americano judges in the Trans-Nueces who possessed an admirable commitment to the law and justice regarding real estate.[5] Moreover, Article VIII of the Treaty of Guadalupe Hidalgo contained language important to South Texas. It read, in part, "Mexicans now established in territories previously belonging to Mexico, and which remain for the future within the limits of the United States, as defined by the present treaty, shall be free to continue where they now reside, or to remove at any time to the Mexican Republic, retaining the property which they possess in the said territories, or disposing thereof, and removing the proceeds wherever they please, without subject, on this account, to any contribution, tax, or charge whatever."[6]

Article X of the treaty addressed Texas's Spanish and Mexican land grants, including South Texas. However, President James K. Polk directed American negotiators to remove this section from the treaty.

The president's reasoning for deleting this article appeared simple to him. First, Polk stressed that Texas—including South Texas—was part of the United States before the outbreak. In annexing Texas the United States recognized the territorial claims of the Republic of Texas, including the Nueces Strip. Second, the president believed that the US Constitution sufficiently protected land-grant owners regarding property rights. Third, the federal government had no power to dispose of Texas public lands or change the conditions of grants because Texas had been a national entity with laws regarding land.[7]

Emissaries from both countries met at Querétaro, Mexico, in 1848 to clarify the president and the United States Senate's alterations to the treaty. They adopted the Protocol of Querétaro, which stipulated that the American government did not intend to annul Mexican land grants made in Texas until March 2, 1836. This date marked the day Texas declared its independence from Mexico. Of course this assurance did not consider that the Nueces Strip was not yet part of Texas. The Republic of Texas did not proclaim the Rio Grande as its southern boundary until December 19, 1836. The president asserted that the Protocol of Querétaro was unnecessary for the same reasons articulated for removing Article X. Moreover, Polk ignored that Mexico, a sovereign nation, had never recognized the Nueces Strip as part of Texas.[8]

Even before the United States Supreme Court established the legal precedent, in *McKinney v. Saviego*, that the Treaty of Guadalupe Hidalgo provisions did not apply to Texas, the state's legislature adopted measures to protect the "established privileges" of property owners in the Nueces Strip. These laws sought to clarify existing property rights.[9]

Legislation Clarifying Existing Titles

On February 8, 1850, Texas lawmakers approved "an act to provide for the investigation of land titles in certain counties therein named." Under this law, the legislature created a board of commissioners appointed by the governor to (1) investigate the Spanish and Mexican land claims in South Texas and (2) recommend valid land rights for the lawmakers' approval.[10]

Governor Peter Hansborough Bell named William H. Bourland and James B. Miller as commissioners. Bourland was a member of the state legislature, and Miller was a doctor and had been active in politics since the days of Mexican rule over Texas. Thus, the board became known as the Bourland-Miller Commission. The commission could only consider grants made before December 19, 1836, when the Texas Congress designated the Rio Grande as its southern border. As a result, the legislature directed the commission to hold hearings in South Texas, including Nueces and Starr Counties, of which present-day Duval County was a part.[11]

Under rules the legislature codified for the commission, applicants first had to pay a two-dollar fee to initiate the land ratification process. Second, the landowner's claim had to be in English. Third, the required paperwork was to include a complete description of the land, including "boundaries and extent," and a copy of the title or other evidence of rights under which the grantee claimed ownership. Fourth, the statute directed commissioners to investigate claims and report to the legislature whether it should approve or reject them. Finally, the law prohibited claimants from selling the land under review while the legislature determined its final ownership.[12]

Longtime Tejano ranchers, like recently arrived Americano settlers, greeted this process with suspicion. They feared it was a ploy by the legislature to seize their properties and make them available to speculators. On September 4, 1850, while the commission continued its work, legislators sought to reassure landowners by adopting a statute "to confirm certain land titles . . . and to require the commissioner of the General Land Office to issue patents" to the property. The state devised this law to certify the grants the commission initially approved at Laredo. The Webb County surveyor inspected the land and forwarded certified field notes to the General Land Office for final confirmation.[13]

While the legislature's gesture seemed to calm some landowners, the commission encountered unconvinced property titleholders when it returned to Rio Grande City. They engaged in a boycott; no owner was willing to submit the required documents. Duval County landowners with grants in the southern part of the county would have been part of this group.

Frustrated, the commission moved on to Brownsville, where the news of the legislature's approval of the Laredo grants elicited a more favorable response from landowners.[14]

In November 1850, however, the grantees and the commission suffered a severe setback. The steamship *Anson*, which carried documents the commission collected at Brownsville and $800 in fees paid by landowners, sank in the Gulf of Mexico. Commissioner Miller petitioned the legislature to allow the commission to approve, not merely recommend, the grants. The legislature balked at the idea, and "the commissioners found themselves with the utterly unpleasant task of returning to Brownsville again, obligating landowners to procure duplicates and other evidence of the lost titles and documents."[15] The commission then returned to Rio Grande City and Corpus Christi to continue its work. This time the Rio Grande City area landowners capitulated to the law's requirements and participated in the commission's work. In these two cities, commissioners received documentation and heard testimony on most of the Duval County grants.[16]

Once the Bourland-Miller Commission completed its work and submitted recommendations to the legislature, the lawmakers approved yet another measure entitled "An act to relinquish the right of the state to certain lands." The legislation listed all the grants the legislature confirmed, including nine of the ten properties submitted by Duval County rancheros. Since no one from the San Leandro tract attended a hearing to provide the commission with the necessary documentation, the commissioners did not recommend its confirmation.[17]

Bourland-Miller Commission Approved Grants

The Bourland-Miller Commission's earliest property examinations were from southern Duval County at Rio Grande City. Most of these land grants were in Starr County in the 1850s. The boundary between Nueces and Starr Counties ran farther north than the present southern border of Duval County. Los Olmos Creek most likely marked the separation of Nueces and Starr Counties.[18] This area did not become a part of Duval County until 1858, when the legislature created the county.[19]

San Francisco was the first Duval County grant for which the Bourland-Miller Commission recommended confirmation. In August 1809 Francisco Contreras performed a survey for José Juan Manuel de la Garza Falcón's land. On July 6, 1832, the Mexican state of Tamaulipas issued a title to de la Garza Falcón for this ongoing Spanish grant, consisting of four and a half leagues. Laureano Falcón applied for confirmation of this grant to the Bourland-Miller Commission for himself and his coheirs. The commissioners approved ownership after receiving information from witnesses Cirilo Tanguma and Tomás Farías. The informants' testimony, the commissioners said, proved the occupation, forage, and cultivation of the tract before 1836. After the Falcón family had the strip surveyed, Nueces County Clerk H. A. Gilpin, on January 22, 1869, certified the copy and translation of the original Spanish survey and title from Tamaulipas in the Nueces County records.[20]

Palo Blanquito, a grant composed of two leagues of land located west of the present-day Texas Mexican Railroad and north of Realitos, was titled to José Antonio Cuéllar in 1835 by Tamaulipas. Cuéllar had the land surveyed in 1831. Nepomuceno Cuéllar told the Bourland-Miller commissioners that his father, José Antonio, had resided and raised horses, cattle, and sheep at Palo Blanquito since 1825. Ranch hands Luis García, 50, and Antonio Aguilar, 34, supported the son's claim.[21]

Typically, a rancho included several residential structures. The main house on the ranch was called the *casa mayor* (main house); colonists built them of stone but often used caliche blocks called *sillar*. These homes were utilitarian in purpose and had little pretensions of luxury. They were designed and made primarily for protection against the elements, the danger of wild animals, and threats from marauding Indians. The homes had *troneras* (portholes) from where ranch hands fended off attacking *indios* (Indians).[22]

Other smaller lodgings, called jacales, surrounded the main house and provided shelter for vaqueros and other ranch hands who built them from what nature provided. *Postas* (posts) taken from available trees or shrubs, such as mesquite, held up the outside frame. *Cuero crudo* (rawhide) and *barro* (mud) held the walls together. Ranch hands built the *techos* (roofs) of straw or grass common to the area. Dirt floors were commonplace in these makeshift dwellings. Also found in ranchos, such as in the Cuéllar property, were corrals and *tanques de agua* (water tanks).[23]

Between 1836 and 1838, Indian attacks forced Señor José Antonio Cuéllar to abandon his rancho, but he returned and lived on the property until his passing in 1849. Nepomuceno Cuéllar filed a claim with the Bourland-Miller Commission for himself and his siblings. They included Reyes, Jesús, Trinidad, Juanita, and Chapita. The latter sister was deceased but had left two daughters as heirs. To assert his claim to the land, the younger Cuéllar presented substantial evidence, including a survey map drawn on August 18, 1831, a copy of the grant made by Tamaulipas on January 17, 1835, and information that the Mexican state had placed his father in possession of the property on September 8, 1835. Juan Antonio Cuéllar had the tract resurveyed in 1854. Subsequently, Texas issued a patent to the Cuéllar heirs.[24]

Circa 1809 José Marcelo Hinojosa placed a claim before the Spanish authorities for fourteen leagues of land called Palo Blanco. The land was located south of today's Realitos and extended into modern Jim Hogg and Brooks Counties (which at the time were part of Duval County), with Palo Blanco Creek as its southern boundary. At Rio Grande City, witnesses Rafael Ramírez, Justo García, and Ysidro Guerra testified before the Bourland-Miller Commission that Hinojosa had occupied the land since 1809, raised large stock, and cultivated it until 1837. In 1835 Hinojosa, a Mier resident, paid the land's appraised value of three hundred pesos and tendered a petition to Tamaulipas to perfect his title. On December 7, 1835, satisfying the act of possession, Tamaulipas granted Hinojosa "full control and ownership" and formally confirmed his deed. On June 9, 1859, Texas issued a patent for the property.[25]

In addition to the fourteen leagues granted to José Marcelo Hinojosa, witnesses appearing before the Bourland-Miller Commission indicated the Hinojosa claim included two other parcels of five *sitios* (leagues) each. Mexico had initially approved titles to these tracts of five leagues, one each, to Santos García and Diego Hinojosa.[26]

In 1848, two years before the legislature created the Bourland-Miller Commission, the Nueces County Clerk's office recorded copies of a title for five leagues of land that Tamaulipas issued Santos García. The document indicated that after García paid 150 pesos to the state treasury on January 21, 1835, Tamaulipas granted him title to El Charco de Palo Blanco property. The grant was immediately north of Palo Blanco and included Realitos and the surrounding area. The state surveyor, José Antonio Gutiérrez de Lara, surveyed the land on August 19, 1835. Twenty years later, on August 25, 1855, Felipe Cadena, on behalf of the García heirs, provided Nueces County with notarized copies of the original grant issued at Mier in 1835. On June 12, 1856, R. C. Trimble, assisted by Cosme Patillo and Ramón Barrera, performed an official property survey. Finally, on August 23, 1856, the state patented the land for the Santos García heirs.[27]

Another tract in the extreme southern part of Duval County, west of Realitos, was San Rafael de Los Encinos. On January 17, 1835, the governor of Tamaulipas ceded it to Diego Ynojosa. The alcalde completed the title process by putting Ynojosa in possession of the land on December 15, 1835. On June 23, 1856, Trimble, Patillo, and Barrera surveyed the tract, and a month later Texas issued a patent to Diego Ynojosa.[28]

In 1808 Simón Ramírez and his son-in-law, Rafael Ramírez, began the process, under Spain's procedures, to prove the title of two tracts of land of five leagues each, San Pedro del Charco Redondo and Santa Rosalía, respectively. San Pedro del Charco Redondo was between Palo Blanco and Santa Cruz de la Concepción. Santa Rosalía was an out-of-the-way grant directly west of Benavides, halfway to Duval County's border with Webb County. Soon after Spain awarded them the land, the two men took possession and successfully built a large farm. Mexico ultimately ratified the acquisition, and Ysidro Guerra, Antonio Canales Salinas, and José María Flores testified before the Bourland-Miller Commission that landowners operated the farms until 1837. Upon Simón Ramírez's death, his son-in-law assumed ownership by purchase and inheritance. With help from chain carriers Crispín Gonzales and Segundo Garza, Trimble surveyed the land on September 9, 1853, and the state issued patents for the two tracts on August 29, 1856.[29]

After Francisco Cordente paid the Spanish government six hundred silver pesos for the Santa Cruz de la Concepción tract, on August 7, 1809, surveyor Contreras went to the property to survey it. Contreras' survey description yielded details on the *diligencias* (field procedures), including examination, survey, and appraisal, that was part of the title process under Spain.[30] With José Antonio Guerra serving as the presiding judge at the site and José Ignacio Ibáñez and José Hipolito Peña helping as Contreras's assistants, the review got underway on the morning of August 7, 1809.[31]

Contreras and his crew prepared their instruments according to custom by measuring with a *cordel* (string), fifty varas long, with a staff tied at each end. The vara was a unit of land measurement and equaled slightly less than a yard. Contreras began the survey on the west side of the property, at the foot of a hill, known as San Pedro, located in a small grove of mesquite. Next, Contreras directed the survey crew to proceed north with a compass in hand. They extended the cord two hundred times, equaling about a mile and a quarter, where they encountered abundant mesquite near the Laguna de Retamas, which they renamed Mesquite del Cuervo.[32]

At noon the men took a break until Guerra, in charge of the operation, ordered work to resume. Contreras recalibrated his instruments, set up the compass, and had Ibáñez and Peña step off one hundred cords until they arrived at the ranch headquarters. Cordente pointed out to the survey crew that their route bypassed some of the improvements he had already made on his property and asked Guerra to widen the area to include his upgrades. Cordente's revelation that he had already established a headquarters endorses the notion that pioneers from Mier and Camargo had settled the area and staked claims before the start of the granting process.[33]

Contreras and his men, at Guerra's direction, walked off thirty more cords from east to west, arriving at a small mesquite tree, which they used as an identifying marker. Next they measured off four cords south to north, crossing Concepción Creek. Again, large mesquite trees marked that point, and they named it San Francisco de Peña Blanca. Finally, with sunset approaching, they ceased their work for the day.[34]

On August 8, 1809, the survey crew measured 162 cords from west to east, stopping when they came to a hill covered with shrubs. They designated this point with a stick and called it San Amador. Guerra ordered the men to readjust the cord and recalibrate the instruments. The survey crew resumed the work, moving on a north-to-south track and marking the survey's east line. They measured off 100 cords and stopped again at noon. The measuring continued in the afternoon, with the crew walking off 204 cord lengths, coming upon a prairie. They planted a large tree to mark a corner and named it Santa Catarina. At this point, as sunset approached, they suspended the survey until morning.[35]

However, the crew took the day off the following day, August 9, 1809. Resuming on August 10, 1809, the surveyors continued east to west and reached the south boundary at Santa Catarina. They extended the chord 133 times to the starting point at San Pedro de Charco Redondo. The parcel exceeded the four leagues Cordente had purchased because the surveyor included the ranch improvements the landowner had requested. However, Guerra had to survey adjoining land and told Cordente they would discuss the matter on his return and conclude the transaction.[36]

On August 17, 1809, Contreras valued the four leagues for raising large cattle that Cordente wanted at ten pesos per league. The survey also entitled Cordente to two leagues for small livestock and one lot eighty-seven varas square. Cordente paid the royal treasury fifty-five pesos for the land not included in the original acquisition on June 27, 1810, but a few months later, on November 10, 1810, he died in Mier, leaving his estate to his widow.[37]

Then, on May 25, 1829, Don Juan de Borges, a resident of Camargo and the *mandatario general* (attorney/agent) of Doña María Leonarda Liscano, widow of Francisco Cordente, sold to Juan Manuel Ramírez the four leagues in Agostadero de Santa Cruz, also known as Concepción. The land was between the Palo Pinto and Concepción Creeks, about seventy miles north of present-day Rio Grande City.[38]

The Bourland-Miller Commission recommended validating the Santa Cruz de la Concepción based on the testimony of Francisco López Díaz, José María Solís, Antonio García, Agustín García, Apolinario de la Garza, Nicolás García Longoria, and Desiderio Vela. The witnesses confirmed that Francisco Cordente had received, occupied, and possessed the land since 1807. Surveyor

Trimble and chain carriers Agapito Garza and C. Gonzales resurveyed the tract on October 26, 1853. For reasons not apparent in the Texas General Land Office files, Felix Blücher did a second survey in June 1868. Texas finally patented the tract to Juan Manuel Ramírez, Cordente's legal assignee, on March 13, 1869, eighteen years after the Bourland-Miller Commission had recommended its approval.[39]

On July 26, 1836, Tamaulipas granted Vicente Ynojosa five leagues of land known as Las Anacuas. Prudencio García, representing Jesúsa García y Ynojosa (by then deceased), appeared before the Bourland-Miller Commission in Corpus Christi in September 1851. García brought along two witnesses, Gregorio Sáenz and José María Vela, who testified that Ynojosa had settled and worked the land before 1836. Their testimony proved sufficient for the Commission to recommend it for confirmation.[40]

The legislature concurred and included it for approval under the 1852 legislation. On October 19, 20, and 24, 1854, Blücher made field notes of Las Anacuas grant to comply with the legislative requirements. His survey team included Julián Cortés and Refugio Salas. Duval County Surveyor J. M. French resurveyed Las Anacuas from November 25 to December 2, 1879. J. A. Dix and J. J. Dix served as chain carriers. Receipts from the heirs of Vicente Ynojosa indicated they paid property taxes to Nueces County from 1846 to 1883. On June 17, 1886, the state finally deemed the grant "correct for patenting."[41]

Clearing Land Titles in Court

The remaining property owners now turned to district courts to ratify their titles. Under proposals adopted by the legislature in 1860 and 1870, landowners were now to take their claims to the courts. However, judges could only consider grants approved before December 19, 1836.

The 1860 legislation, entitled "An Act to ascertain and adjudicate certain legal claims for land against the state, situated between the Nueces and Rio Grande Rivers," set out the steps people needed to take to confirm their Spanish or Mexican titles. First, landowners had to file a petition in the district court with jurisdiction in the county where they paid their property taxes. Second, they were to file the request at least ten days before the opening day of the court's session. Third, the law required the application to provide "a full description of the land claimed," including its boundaries. Finally, it required evidence of the claimant's "right" to the land, such as a title.[42]

The Fourteenth Judicial District had jurisdiction over cases affecting Duval County. When a plaintiff offered proof of ownership, the district judge was bound to rule for the landowner. Moreover, if the title "would have been matured into a perfect title in the country where it originated," the court could approve the instrument. Judges had the authority to hear cases without a jury. The plaintiffs had the right to appeal to the Texas Supreme Court.[43]

If the district court ruled for the plaintiff, the legislation directed the Texas General Land Office to issue a patent to the original owner or heirs. However, to obtain a patent, claimants had to furnish the land office with a court certificate showing confirmation of the grant and certified field notes of the property's boundaries. Next, the applicant had to prove property taxes were current. Finally, the petitioner had to pay the required court and Land Office costs.[44] As is apparent, it was a complicated and tedious process, especially for the Tejanos, who did not usually deal with life's problems in English. Nevertheless, they took up the challenge; after all, the issues nature presented daily were more demanding.

Perhaps Spain's most iconic grants in Duval County were San Diego de Arriba and San Diego de Abajo. These grants became the focal point for early development, making San Diego the most significant community and the Duval County seat. Julián Flores and his son Ventura petitioned the Spanish government for this property as early as 1805. José Faustino Contreras of San Luis Potosí surveyed the Flores spread on May 5, 1809. On May 30, 1810, the Flores clan paid 184 pesos to the royal treasury in San Luis Potosí and formally petitioned to purchase the land, giving public notice of their intent. They took possession, with a formal ceremony invoking the words "*Corto sácate, arranco yerba, cojo agua, me lavo las manos y tiro la agua a los cuatro vientos sobre la tierra*" (I cut grass, I gather the grass, I get water, I wash my hands, and I throw the water to the four winds over the earth).[45]

Herders for Julián Flores soon occupied Rancho San Diego on the north side of the Creek. Juan Sáenz, whose father was the head herdsman for

Señor Flores, was born on the ranch in 1815 and may well be the first-ever documented birth in Duval County. Sáenz remained at the Flores rancho until 1833, when he turned 18. In 1860 Sáenz testified in court that San Diego de Arriba and San Diego de Abajo's original grantees always occupied and cultivated the land, except whenever the San Diego Creek flooded or Indians threatened their lives.[46]

While most references to the two grants treat them as one, they were separate parcels. Ventura Flores owned the most eastern lands called San Diego de Abajo. His father, Julián, owned the western tract known as San Diego de Arriba. The ranches' two headquarters, one for each grant owner, were next to each other on the creek's north bank, directly across from the San Leandro Rancho.

In the Mexican era, the Flores father and son perfected their Spanish grants under Articles 23 and 26 of Decree No. 42, the colonization law of Tamaulipas. On April 18, 1831, Tamaulipas placed Julián and Ventura Flores in possession of the land. Then, on July 22, 1831, José Santiago de Ynojosa, Mier's mayor, legally completed the title transfer to both grants. But first Ynojosa performed a ceremony marking the traditional act of possession by traveling to San Diego and riding the properties' length and width with Ventura Flores and his brother Jacinto Flores, representing their father, Julián.[47]

While none of the heirs filed a claim with the Bourland-Miller Commission, they took steps to protect their rights. Several years after the Bourland-Miller Commission closed shop and before the state adopted the 1860 law for district court lawsuits, the Flores contracted on November 4–5, 1854, and July 18–20, 1855, with Deputy District Surveyor of the Nueces District Félix Blücher to survey the two grants. Julián Cortes, Refugio Salas, Domingo Escamilla, and Andrés Gonzales assisted Blücher as chain carriers.[48]

While Julián Flores and his wife, María Teresa, had eight children and an adopted son, almost none of his heirs seemed interested in settling on their parents' property. His eldest son Ventura and his wife, María Rafaela, had six heirs, but only María Trinidad, born on November 5, 1819, appeared to take a hands-on interest in the lands. However, in 1860 heirs of the two grantees represented by Ventura's daughter María Trinidad Flores y Pérez availed themselves of the legislation Texas provided. On December 11, 1860, they filed suit against the state in district court to confirm title to their estate. On January 13, 1862, after receiving testimony from Juan Sáenz and Félix Blücher and examining copies of the Mexican title and Blücher's survey, Judge Edmund Davis ruled for the Flores heirs. The judge directed the plaintiff to pay court costs.[49]

José Antonio Gonzales's La Huerta grant was perhaps the most litigated of Duval County's Spanish and Mexican land grants. La Huerta's file at the Texas General Land Office includes a notation that the original documents went "missing as of November 29, 1954." The folder, however, contains copies of 1849 documents that indicate that La Huerta's owners recorded them in Nueces County in January 1849. The county clerk issued a certified copy of La Huerta's survey in Corpus Christi the next month.[50]

The lands, however, were disputed in two cases that reached the appellate courts. First, on January 16, 1885, the Texas Supreme Court ruled on a case involving La Huerta, styled *Ignacio Gonzales et al. v. Gertrudes Chartier*. The heirs of José Antonio Gonzales filed a "trespass to try title" suit in Duval County. The inheritors sought to establish "the boundaries of and quieting title to a tract of land known as La Huerta." The court was silent on the title to La Huerta but dealt with Gertrudes Chartier's failure to pay her share of the costs in bringing the action.[51]

The Travis County District Court upheld the validity of La Huerta's title in *State v. Palacios* in 1912.[52] In this case Texas filed suit for 1,770 acres it believed were outside the boundaries of La Huerta. However, the heirs of the original grantee, represented by José Antonio Gonzales, contended the disputed acreage was within their property. The state asked the Texas Court of Appeals to review the lower court's decision. The state had issued a patent on the land in 1869. The Gonzales heirs claimed ownership under a title given to José Antonio Gonzales by the governor of Tamaulipas on October 15, 1835. After considering the objections raised by the state, the court ruled the Gonzales heirs' title was valid, and the 1,770 acres in question were within the boundaries of the original grant.[53]

On October 15, 1835, Tamaulipas deeded to Dionicio Elizondo the El Señor de la Carrera tract, consisting of two leagues, six *labores* (a unit of measure equivalent to about 177.1 acres), and 891,000 square varas. Tamaulipas declared that the award, located about fifty-five miles southwest of Corpus Christi, was "perfect" and "genuine." The Laredo Road traversed the property at its northern tip, and the Mier Road passed on its southern side. On the northeast corner of the property was the Laguna Traviesa. Blücher surveyed El Señor de la Carrera on September 1, 2, and 4, 1854, with help from Refugio Salas, Nieves García, Rafael L. Salinas, and Albino Canales.[54]

On May 21, 1864, Benito Gonzales García, on behalf of the Elizondo heirs, filed suit in the Fourteenth Judicial District in Nueces County to confirm the land's title under the 1860 act approved by the legislature, and as amended by the Confederate legislature on January 11, 1862. After the Civil War, Texas extended the law on March 30, 1866, when the Convention of the People ratified Ordinance Number 212, preserving the intent of the 1860 legislative initiative.[55]

El Señor de la Carrera owners surveyed the land again on March 12–14 and 16, 1868, to satisfy the law's requirements. Judge E. B. Carpenter presided over a trial on October 31, 1868, and approved the title issued by Tamaulipas but noted that the grant had fifteen labores and 642,000 square varas more than Elizondo paid Tamaulipas. Accordingly, the judge ordered García pay $19.20 to the General Land Office to cover the excess property, plus court costs and the district attorney's fee of $20.00. Based on the judge's decision, the land office patented El Señor de la Carrera to the Elizondo heirs in February 1870.[56]

As previously mentioned, Francisco Cordente and José Marcelo de Ynojosa had applied to Spain for two grants on the south side of San Diego Creek. They chose, instead, other locations in southern Duval County. Juan Sánchez Rosales and José Antonio de la Peña y López then replaced Cordente and Ramírez, respectively, as grantees of land on the San Diego Creek. Unfortunately, Peña y López died before denouncing the San Florentina grant. His son Ygnacio de la Peña, who inherited the property, chose not to complete the grant process for San Florentina; instead, he sought and received a grant in Brooks and Jim Hogg Counties.[57]

Grantee Rosales failed to follow through and yielded his interest in San Leandro to Rafael García Salinas. On March 30, 1810, García Salinas paid 184 pesos into the royal treasury to secure the title and took people to his rancho to improve the land. The ranch's location was at the Tancahua and San Diego Creeks intersection, across the San Diego Creek from Julián and Ventura Flores's spreads. The San Leandro Rancho had fields under cultivation and pens, corrals, stock, and several servants. Unfortunately, as happened to the Flores men, García Salinas was driven out temporarily by frequent flooding of the San Diego Creek and Indian attacks.[58]

Since García Salinas had briefly abandoned the ranch, on April 18, 1831, he paid 296 pesos to Tamaulipas to perfect his San Leandro title. Then, on July 22, 1831, José Santiago de Ynojosa, the mayor of Mier, rode with García Salinas to the four corners of the property and placed him in legal possession.[59]

Representatives of García Salinas had indicated to the Bourland-Miller Commission that they would present witnesses and documentation to prove their San Leandro ownership. However, no one spoke on behalf of García Salinas or his heirs, and the commission disapproved the San Leandro to the legislature. On November 4–5, 1854, Blücher and his crew took San Leandro's measurements. They returned on July 18–20, 1855, and performed a complete survey again. In November 1859 John Levy bought two square leagues of land from the San Leandro and the neighboring La Vaca grant in Nueces County for $1,000. The following year Levy filed a lawsuit against the state under the 1860 act to perfect the San Leandro grant. Judge Davis heard the case in Corpus Christi and returned a favorable ruling for the García Salinas heirs and Levy on January 10, 1862. The state then issued a patent for San Leandro to the García Salinas heirs.[60]

On September 2, 1835, Tamaulipas assessor Antonio Canales surveyed six leagues of land called Agua Poquita for Santos Flores, and nearly a year later, on July 26, 1836, Flores denounced the property. Judge Remigio García of Mier formally placed Flores in possession of the grant on September 24, 1836. The grant's location was on Agua Poquita Creek, a branch of Los Olmos Creek, about sixty-five miles west-southwest of Corpus Christi. The road to Laredo passed through its southern quarter.

The Mier to San Diego trail crossed the property at its southeastern tip. An old map shows the grant's headquarters, Rancho La Felicidad, on the Mier to San Diego road.[61]

A suit styled *John Vale v. The State of Texas*, brought under the 1860 act, confirmed the Agua Poquita grant and eventually led to a patent. As per the Nueces County 1860 Census, Vale lived at Rancho La Felicidad, which he called Rancho Vale. On December 11, 1860, Judge Edmund Davis approved the plaintiff's request in Nueces County District Court. First, however, plaintiff Vale had to pay the General Land Office $131.20, which the heirs still owed Tamaulipas.[62]

In 1808 Trinidad Vela's ancestors took possession of the Santa María de Los Ángeles de Abajo grant located on Arroyo de Los Ángeles thirty-six miles from San Diego. Vela's ancestors denounced the lands in 1810 or 1811 and had houses and pens built. But in 1813 *indios bárbaros* (nomadic Indigenous people who resisted colonization and conversion) ousted Trinidad Vela's ancestors from their ranch. Six years later Indians killed Vela's father and several neighbors. Undeterred by the attacks, the owners of Los Ángeles de Abajo petitioned for their land in the 1820s after Mexico won independence. The Velas had their property surveyed by Antonio Canales.[63]

The district court in Zapata County confirmed the grant in 1861. However, the court's records were "lost, stolen, or destroyed" under Confederate rule. The court reheard the case on October 9, 1879, in *Trinidad Vela v. The State of Texas*. Fortunately for the plaintiffs, their attorney had preserved a copy of the 1861 decision. On October 11, 1879, Judge John Russel reaffirmed the earlier ruling. Texas awarded Vela's heirs a patent on December 2, 1879.[64]

West of Los Ángeles de Abajo was a five-league grant called Santa María de Los Ángeles de Arriba. The land was half in Duval County and half in Webb County. On July 14, 1871, District Judge W. N. Russel heard a case styled *Fernando Uribe and wife v. The State of Texas*, a suit for confirmation of title filed under the 1860 legislation. Uribe's wife, Refugia Arizpe, was the granddaughter of the original grantee. The plaintiffs had initially filed their claim on December 20, 1860, in Zapata County. From the testimony of knowledgeable witnesses, the court determined that on June 5, 1835, Tamaulipas had issued a "genuine and perfect" title for the land to Mariano Arizpe. Unfortunately, as in the Los Ángeles de Abajo case, the Zapata court's records went missing in 1862. Nevertheless, Arizpe convinced the court that he had judicially possessed the land. Moreover, Arizpe and his heirs had held, used, cultivated, paid taxes on, and improved the property, except when the "incursion of Indians, revolution, or civil war" forced them to flee for their safety.[65]

The petitioners had denounced and surveyed the property, as required by law. Moreover, its boundaries were well-known to the public. Judge Russel confirmed the title in the name of Mariano Arizpe and his heirs with the provision that they pay Texas $150, the sum they would have paid Tamaulipas to perfect their title. On February 28, 1874, Felix Blücher, assisted by Manuel Benavides Vela and James McLain, surveyed the tract, and the state issued a patent on July 19, 1881.[66]

On March 22, 1836, Andrés García from Camargo traveled to Ciudad Victoria, the capital of Tamaulipas, to formally claim three leagues of pastures, known as San Andrés, for large stock. On September 15, 1835, Antonio Canales Rosillo surveyed the land, and García paid 300 pesos and twenty-nine granos (96 granos equaled a peso) for the grant. On September 24, 1836, Tamaulipas granted the property of San Andrés to García. Three weeks later, on October 16, 1836, Cayetano López, alcalde of Camargo, traveled to San Andrés and formally proclaimed to García's neighbors that García was the property's legitimate owner.[67]

The San Andrés grant included five leagues about sixty-five miles from Corpus Christi and nineteen miles southwest of San Diego. Two regional roads intersected at Rancho Los Indios on the midwestern side of the grant. Félix A. Blücher surveyed San Andrés on April 30, 1854, and May 21–23, 1861. Helping as chain carriers were Antonio Bermúdez, Cayetano Villarreal, Abram de los Santos, and Cayetano Molina.[68]

On February 14, 1873, the heirs of Andrés García filed suit in Travis County in a case styled *Concepción Garza et al. v. The State of Texas* to confirm title to the land. Other heirs—namely, Rafael García y Garza, Antonio Juan de Dios, Jesús Melona, and Juanita García y Garza—joined the lawsuit.

The court heard the case under the 1870 legislation and ruled for the plaintiffs, awarding them the San Andrés. The state appealed to the Texas Supreme Court, which affirmed the district court's ruling on May 22, 1877. Texas issued a patent for the grant to the heirs of Andrés García on November 6, 1877.[69]

Despite the many challenges they faced, before the close of the nineteenth century, all the original owners in Duval County or their heirs preserved their Spanish and Mexican land grants and, in most instances, retained much of the property. Some families, however, chose to sell parts of their land inheritance to Americanos, such as John Levy and John Vale. On occasion, other exigencies mandated they sell land, but for the most part, this was done on their initiative, not because others outwitted them of their inheritance.

Among the grantees and entrepreneurs settling in Duval County in the first half of the nineteenth century were Julián and Ventura Flores, Rafael García Salinas, José M. de la Garza Falcón, José Antonio Cuéllar, Santos García, Diego Hinojosa, Simón Ramírez, José Marcelo Ynojosa, Santos Flores, Francisco Cordente, José Antonio Gonzales, Dionisio Elizondo, Andrés García, Trinidad Vela, Mariano Arizpe, and Vicente Hinojosa. Unfortunately, they did not live to see the land flourish under the hands of their progeny. Nevertheless, they were the initial founders.

For various reasons it is most likely that these early pioneers split their time between their ranchos in Duval County and their ancestral homes in the Villas del Norte. For one thing, the Duval ranchos existed in an isolated and untamed territory. On the other hand, the villas offered the security of family and church. While providing economic potential, the ranchos suffered from exposure to the *indios bárbaros* and wild elements of nature. They were not places where the early pobladores felt safe raising a family.

While many offspring of the initial pioneers remained in the safe confines of Mier and Camargo, some, like Trinidad Flores, Laureano Falcón, Nepomuceno Cuéllar, José Marcelo Hinojosa, Rafael Ramírez, and their children, risked moving to Duval. Their "shared memory," along with their vaqueros, caporales, mayordomos, and other ranch hands, "influenced the self-perceptions of local people" living in Duval County ranchos.[70]

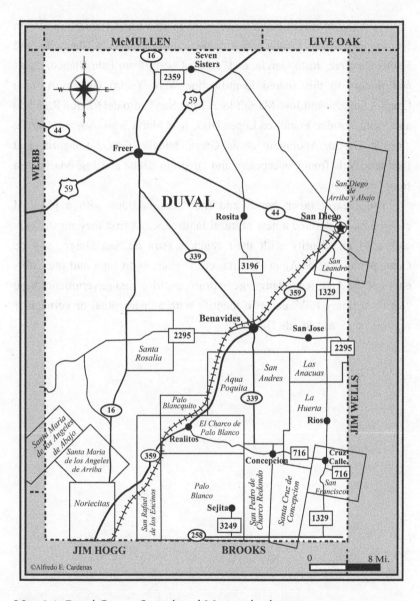

Map 3.1 Duval County Spanish and Mexican land grants.
Note: To give readers a point of reference, the map is superimposed on a current highway map showing cities and communities.

Among these ranch hands were Cirilo Tanguma and Tomás Farías from San Francisco, Luis García and Antonio Aguilar from Palo Blanquito, and Rafael Ramírez, Justo García, and Ysidro Guerra from Palo Blanco. Other contributors to this shared identification were Ysidro Guerra, Antonio Canales Salinas, and José María Flores from San Pedro del Charco Redondo and Santa Rosalía; Francisco López Díaz, José María Solís, Antonio García, Agustín García, Apolinario de la Garza, Nicolás García Longoria, and Desiderio Vela from Concepción; and Gregorio Sáenz and José María Vela from Las Anacuas.

These early ranch hands and their "interactions with a physical environment" defined a new cultural landscape. At first they most likely embraced an identity with their ranchos (soy de San Diego, soy de Concepción, soy de Agua Poquita, etc.). Then, with time and the influences of the Americano language, culture, politics, and government, these "local, ordinary folk" came to identify with a "perceptual or vernacular region," such as "soy de Duval."[71]

Chapter 4

A Second Land Rush

While Spain and Mexico made eighteen land grants to citizens wishing to settle in the Nueces Strip, properties were available only to the upper class. Under their new sovereign, however, ordinary folks qualified for government grants.

In 1836 the Republic of Texas's most valuable asset was its public lands. The newborn republic used this asset to attract more settlers to support the developing nation. Moreover, the republic's Congress utilized the land to pay empresarios, who provided funding to cover the republic's outstanding financial obligations. These underwriters recovered their financial outlay by reselling the land to colonists.

When Texas joined the Union, the legislature continued using land to attract immigrants and secure funds to defray the government's operating expenses. Land grants also helped the state build a tax base to underwrite public services. Whether citizens received the land from the state at no cost or bought it from investors who had acquired it as payment from a public authority, the individual landowners had to pay property taxes on the land, thus adding to the regime's coffers.

After the 1840s Americano arrivals—from different parts of Texas, the United States, and Europe—took advantage of the land acquisition opportunities approved by the Republic of Texas and subsequently by the state. Moreover, as Americanos entered Duval County in the 1860s, they began acquiring land from some Mexicano grantees. However, that was a limited option since most Mexicano heirs held on to their inheritance. But being more familiar with American law and language, Americanos soon began to amass considerable land from the republic and later the state of Texas. While Tejanos in Duval County did not get their fair share of allotments of republic and state lands, they did acquire significant acreage.

How much land the state granted a person depended on various factors: an individual's service in the war for independence, how long the newcomers had been in the state, one's marital status (whether a recipient was the head of a family or an unmarried individual), and various other qualifications. Land-grant programs of the post–Civil War era provided a means for Duval County's landless Tejanos and Americano newcomers to acquire real estate. Texas adopted headright land endowments or constitutional grants patterned after the Spanish and Mexican land administration practices. Eligibility for some headright grants did not require citizenship or a commitment to developing the land, but Texas expected recipients to promise their loyalty.

Headright Grants

Over time the Texas government adopted four types of headright awards. The republic reserved first-class headrights for settlers who came to Coahuila-Tejas before the signing of the Texas Declaration of Independence on March 2, 1836; each head of the household could get one league and one *labor* of land, equaling 4,605.5 acres. In addition, single men could get one-third of a league or 1,476.1 acres. Second-class headrights compensated settlers arriving in the new Republic of Texas between March 2, 1836, and October 1, 1837. Families could receive 1,280 acres and unmarried individuals 640 acres. Third-class headrights were available to persons migrating between October 1, 1837, and January 1, 1840. Again, heads of families got 640 acres and unmarried individuals received 320 acres. Finally, fourth-class headrights were for settlers coming to the Republic of Texas between January 1, 1840, and January 1, 1842, in the exact quantities as third-class headrights plus ten acres allotted for planting.[1]

The state classified first-class headright awards in Duval County as San Patricio Headright Grants. When Texas joined the United States, the area that became Duval County was part of San Patricio County, which the republic organized in 1836. Then, in 1845, when the republic transferred authority to the state, Texas created land districts in each county, including San Patricio, which included the future Duval County. Since the Spanish and Mexican land allotments made in Duval County occurred before the Texas Declaration of Independence, this land came under the San Patricio First Class Headrights Grants classification.[2]

Individuals receiving first-class headrights were entitled to "any vacant and unappropriated public domain" belonging to the Republic of Texas. Based on the notion that Texas claimed the Trans-Nueces as part of the Republic under the Treaty of Velasco (1836), the republic made people north of the Nueces River eligible for land in the future Duval County. Tejanos living south of the Nueces River before the Texas Declaration of Independence also qualified for headrights. They had "arrived in Texas" before March 2, 1836, and under the understanding that the region was part of the republic, they were legally eligible to receive first-class headrights grants. Moreover, the Treaty of Guadalupe Hidalgo, which ended the Mexican-American War, retroactively recognized the Trans-Nueces as part of the Republic of Texas, as the republic had long claimed. Under these circumstances Tejanos met the conditions for land acquisition required by first-class headrights legislation. However, other than the Spaniards and Mexicanos who received land grants from the Spanish crown and the new Mexican Republic, no one living south of the Nueces took advantage of this program since they were unaware of it and saw themselves as citizens of Mexico, not Texas. However, some Texians (American or European arrivals to Texas during years of the republic) did acquire land allotments in Duval County, which muddied the ownership of grants received from Spain and Mexico.

Some individuals who lived north of the Nueces River—including at least one Mexico-Tejano from Bexar County—took advantage of this stipulation and received first-class headright land in Duval County. However, most of the heirs of this land classification later sold it to Duval County residents.

Table 4.1 First- and second-class grants made in Duval County

Date	Patentee	Acreage	Date	Patentee	Acreage
	First Class Grants			*Second Class Grants*	
1876	N. G. Collins	1,107.1	1868	Encarnación García Garza	800.0
1875	N. G. Collins	1,476.0	1873	Encarnación García Pérez	1,280.0
1868	Antonio García Garza	572.0	1875	George Cumberland	1,467.0
1868	Antonio García Garza	572.0	1868	N. G. Collins	1,280.0
1879	N. G. Collins	4,428.4	1875	Edward N. Gray	640.0
1879	N. G. Collins	3,249.0			
1880	Frank W. Schaeffer	1,476.0			
		12,880.5			**3,387.0**

Source: Texas General Land Office.

During the late 1870s, Texas made seven first-class grants in Duval County; N. G. Collins acquired almost half of these tracts, comprising 10,261 acres. Tejano Antonio García Garza obtained two pieces of land totaling 1,144 acres and one second-class grant totaling 800 acres.[3]

In 1845, the Texas Republic's final year, it initiated a new land policy creating preemption grants. If individuals resided on and improved the land for three consecutive years, they were eligible for 320 acres from the republic's unappropriated inventory. After Texas joined the Union in 1845, the state continued the republic's land policies on and off until 1898.[4]

Rewarding Veterans with Land

The republic and the state of Texas issued land grants to compensate military veterans. In Duval County land obtained through this program came from recipients living in other parts of the state and selling it to local buyers. In addition, the republic provided bounty grants to compensate those who served in a military capacity in the Texas War of Independence and enlisted in the army before October 1, 1837. A soldier's time of service determined the amount of land applicants were eligible for; veterans could acquire 320 acres for every three months of service for a maximum of 1,280 acres, equating to a year's tour of duty. The Republic of Texas sometimes rewarded heirs of combatants who died in action 1,280 acres "on the assumption that the fallen soldier would have served for the duration of the war." Texas frontier guards, active between 1838 and 1842, were also included in this benefit by another legislative authorization.[5]

Texas awarded seventeen individuals in Duval County grants for military service to the republic or the state. Not surprisingly, they were all Americanos. But none of them appear to have ever lived in Duval County. Instead, grant recipients passed on their land to heirs who sold it to others who resided in the county, including one Tejano and a Spaniard.[6]

In 1848 Nueces County ratified eight more bounty donations in the future Duval County. Purchases and exchanges of some bounty donation lands became common during the 1860s and 1870s. The republic's Congress made donation grants to soldiers who fought in specific battles, such as the Siege of Béxar and the Battle of San Jacinto. The republic also took care of descendants of Alamo defenders and those executed at Goliad.[7]

Table 4.2 Military grants patented in Duval County

Patentee*	Acreage	Year	Patentee*	Acreage	Year
Bounty Grants			**Donation Grants**		
Lemuel S. Blakey Heirs	960	1847	Asahel C. Holmes	320	1874
J. W. Fannin Heirs	1,920	1847	Asahel C. Holmes	320	1873

(Continues)

Table 4.2 (Continued)

Patentee*	Acreage	Year	Patentee*	Acreage	Year
Bounty Grants			**Donation Grants**		
Swanson Yarbrough	325	1848	William R. Newman	640	1881
Swanson Yarbrough	320	1848	Norman G. Collins	1,280	1882
Charles Bigelow	320	1848	José Vaello	640	1884
George W. Anderson	640	1848	José Vaello	673	1884
D. Watson	320	1848	B. A. Bennett	640	1886
J. E. Duffield Heirs	960	1848	G. Gussett and N. Reynolds	640	1888
Vernon Rhodes	480	1848	Norman G. Collins	345	1885
C. Collins	320	1862	Norman G. Collins	95	1900
Rafael F. Salinas	160	1867	B. A. Bennett	640	1886
George W Hockley	640	1873	James Rudd	1,280	1847
Wiley Martin Heirs	320	1873			
Jesse Harris	160	1873			
Andrew Jackson Bryant's Heirs	640	1873			
John J. and Almond J. Dix	170	1875			
Totals	**8,655**	**16**		**7,513**	**12**
			Grand Total	**16,168**	**28**

Source: Texas General Land Office, Land Grant Search.
*The names are for those who ended up with the land. At times the applicant later sold their award, in whole or in part.

Land Paid for Government Operations

The republic and the state also used loan scrip—certificates issued to financiers who advanced money to the Texas government to cover its operations. These patrons in turn recuperated these advances by selling the land to willing buyers. The McKinney-Williams tract was the earliest loan and sales scrip issued in Duval County. These two individuals, Thomas F. McKinney and Samuel M. Williams, helped finance the Texas Revolution. In 1835 they made a $150,000 loan to the republic to purchase gunpowder and munitions for the Texas army. The republic repaid them with 108,000 acres of land. McKinney and Williams later sold the land to recuperate what they could of their contribution.[8]

Land Grants after the Civil War

Preemption grants proved a boon to Duval County Tejanos from 1875 to 1881. Many took advantage of the opportunity; thus, more Tejanos entered the landed gentry and could provide for their families. At the same time, they contributed to the county's continued economic progress. The state made 153 land allocations in Duval County under provisions of this program; every parcel but two went to Tejanos. At times Americanos purchased land from a Tejano who had fulfilled stipulated requirements and was allowed to sell the property or could not fulfill the grantee obligations. Moreover, their sheer population numbers made Tejanos more likely to qualify and apply for preemption grants.

Table 4.3 Preemption grants made in Duval County

Patentee*	Acreage	Year	Patentee*	Acreage	Year
Santos Balderas	160	1871	Nepomuceno Gutiérrez	160	1878
John C. Cuellar	160	1873	Norman G. Collins (3 grants)	480	1878
Crispín Flores	160	1874	Pedro Caballero	160	1878
Felipe Olvera	160	1874	Placido Benavides	160	1878
Luis Carrillo	160	1874	Trinidad Vela	160	1878
Norberto Salazar	160	1874	Vicente Garza	160	1878
William A. Tinney	160	1874	Victoriano Casas	160	1878
Adolph L. Labbé	160	1875	Antonio García Garza	160	1879
Agustín Balerío	160	1875	Antonio Sánchez	160	1879

(*Continues*)

Table 4.3 (Continued)

Patentee*	Acreage	Year	Patentee*	Acreage	Year
Celestino Benavides	160	1875	Celso Garza	160	1879
Feliciano Serna	160	1875	Eugenio Longoria	160	1879
José Ángel Barrera	160	1875	Eugenio Navarro	160	1879
Matías García	160	1875	Fermín Chapa	160	1879
Miguel Ruiz	160	1875	Francisco Hernández	160	1879
Néstor Garza	160	1875	Genovevo Garza	160	1879
Nicodemus Flores	160	1875	Inez Chapa	160	1879
Pedro Villanueva	160	1875	Jesús Garza	160	1879
Santana Benavides	160	1875	José A. Barrera	160	1879
William A. Tinney	160	1875	Manuel Figueroa	160	1878
Frank C. Gravis	160	1876	José Gutiérrez	160	1879
Hipólito García	160	1876	Ladislao Garza	160	1879
José María Rodríguez	160	1876	Luciano Longoria	160	1879
Juan Garza Gonzales	160	1876	Mónico Garza	160	1879
Melitón Morales	160	1876	Práxedis Sáenz	154.5	1879
Patricio Salinas	160	1876	Santiago Garza	160	1879
Tomás Chapa	160	1876	Severo Sánchez	160	1879
Victoriano Chapa	163.24	1876	Valentín Puig	160	1879
Amado Hinojosa	160	1877	Vicente Vera	160	1879
Antonio Rangel	160	1877	Viviano Longoria	160	1879
Apolonio Hinojosa	160	1877	Gregorio Sánchez	160	1880
Bernardo Almaraz	160	1877	Juan García	160	1880
Brigidio Flores	160	1877	Manuel Ramos	168.4	1880
Cayetano López	160	1877	Bruno Lozano	160	1881
Donaciano Balderas	80	1877	Cesario de los Santos	160	1881
Eugenio Gutiérrez	160	1877	Juan Antonio de los Santos	160	1881
Fabian Favela	160	1877	Juan de los Santos	160	1881

(*Continues*)

Table 4.3 (Continued)

Patentee*	Acreage	Year	Patentee*	Acreage	Year
Faustino Garza	160	1877	Narciso de los Santos Heirs	160	1881
Francisco Flores Gómez	160	1877	Antonio H. Pérez	160	1883
Francisco Seguro Heirs	160	1877	Juan García Yzaguirre	143.67	1883
Guadalupe García	160	1877	R. Salinas	160	1883
Ignacio Balderas	160	1877	Antonio C. Chapa Heirs	160	1884
Jesús Sáenz	40	1877	Guadalupe P. García Heirs	160	1884
José M. Morales	160	1877	Mariano Chapa	160	1884
José María Fuentes	160	1877	Andrés García Ramírez	160	1886
Juan Gonzales	160	1877	Antonio López Heirs	160	1886
Luciano Ramírez	160	1877	Elías Garza	160	1886
Miguel Seguro	160	1877	Juan C. Cuellar	160	1886
Pedro G. García	160	1877	Juan Gonzales	160	1886
Pedro Sáenz	160	1877	Andrés Jiménez	84	1887
Prisciliano Chapa	163.35	1877	F. Morales	160	1887
Ramon García (2 grants)	320	1877	Bruno Garza Heirs	160	1888
Ramon Sepúlveda (2 grants)	320	1877	Francisco Ruiz	160	1889
Santiago Ayala	160	1877	Pedro Caballero	160	1889
Cándido Maldonado	160	1878	Manuel Cantú	68	1890
Cruz Alanis	160	1878	Pablo Hinojosa	160	1890
Gerónimo Maldonado	160	1878	Francisco Cantú	80	1891
Jesús Solís	160	1878	Abran Bazán	153.61	1895
José María Cavazos	160	1878	Anastasio Muñoz	152.8	1895
Juan Antonio Ruiz	160	1878	Andrés Vela	160	1896

(*Continues*)

Table 4.3 (Continued)

Patentee*	Acreage	Year	Patentee*	Acreage	Year
Juan Vásquez	160	1878	Juan Garza (2 grants)	350.55	1900
Leandro Ramírez	160	1878	Macario Muñoz	160	1900
Manuel Cadena	160	1878	Manuel López	118.5	1900

Source: Texas General Land Office, Land Grant Search.
*The names are for those who ended up with the land. At times, the applicant later sold their award, in whole or in part.

Homestead Grants for the Common Folk

In 1870 the state enacted legislation providing for the disposal of public lands through homestead grants. The law provided for "every head of a family who has not a homestead, shall be entitled to one hundred and sixty acres of land out of any part of the public domain as a homestead"; unmarried individuals qualified for eighty acres. Homesteaders had to occupy the property for three years and needed to provide a survey to the General Land Office after a year and prove they lived on the property, and then they could buy it for one dollar per acre.[9]

This law made land ownership available throughout the state. In Duval County 131 residents filed homestead applications, of which the state approved 110; 101, or 92 percent, were Tejanos. They became landowners for the first time, demonstrating that the original Spanish and Mexican *ciudadanos* (citizens) were no longer the only ones who could own property in Duval County.[10]

The tracts Tejanos received averaged 172 acres, large enough to provide for a family. They could now raise cattle or sheep and do some farming. Cotton, corn, sorghum, fruit orchards, and other horticultural products contributed to a family's income and sustenance. In addition, providing for one's loved ones boosted one's self-worth significantly.

Land Built Public Improvements, Railroads

Periodically from 1844 to 1876, Texas enacted legislation allowing internal improvement scrip to finance infrastructure initiatives, such as building railroads. Developers hawked the state's land awards to fund their projects, whether railroad or other ventures.[11] During the height of the land rush (1875–1881), entrepreneurs marketed 766 scrip grants in Duval County, totaling 463,990 acres. Norman Collins acquired 207 tracts totaling 134,212 acres, about a quarter of the scrip sold in Duval County. Other notable land entrepreneurs included John MacKay, Edward N. Gray, Julián Palacios, José María Sáenz, Frank C. Gravis, Charles K. Gravis, Cayetano Ríos, William Hubbard, George Huggins, and Edward Corkill. In all, 162 individuals purchased scrip grants in Duval County, with the top ten buyers acquiring 369,329.2 acres, or 80.1 percent.[12]

In 1854 Texas adopted legislation to specifically encourage building railroads, offering a "specified amount of land . . . for each mile of rail constructed." The 1876 Constitution granted railroad developers "16 sections (640 acres to a section) per mile." Entrepreneurs built numerous railroads throughout the state using this financing.

It is not coincidental that the arrival of the railroad and the explosion of land sales occurred simultaneously. In 1875, when discussions about bringing a railroad to Duval County began, land acquisition from the state, especially the internal improvement scrip, started to surge. The Corpus Christi, San Diego, and Rio Grande Narrow Gauge Railroad Company project was important to Duval County. However, only three county landowners purchased a mere twenty-seven parcels of land. Collins bought twelve properties totaling 7,724.6 acres, Juan López Sáenz procured ten, amounting to 6,494.6 acres, and A. J. and J. J. Dull acquired five tracts of 3,200 acres. All the purchases occurred in 1880 to 1881.[13]

Supporting Public Education

Early on, the Republic of Texas leaders entertained a charitable view of the need for public education and looked at an inexpensive source to finance it; they saw the sale of public land as a means to fund schools. In addition to meeting the need for financing public education, selling public land increased the value of privately owned land, which supplied a vital revenue source from property taxes for years. Finally, it ensured an educated and capable citizenship that could provide competent leadership to the state and local governments.

Texas began to sell school land scrip to fund schools in 1874 and continued through 1905. Duval County benefited greatly from this program. By the end of the nineteenth century, sixty-five individuals in Duval County had acquired 128,192 acres through this program. Of these individual buyers, thirty-eight, or 58 percent, were Americanos, and the remaining 42 percent, or twenty-seven buyers, were Tejanos.[14]

Several Americanos purchased school land in the name of various family members. The Americano-Tejano Gray clan (Edward, Rosa, John, and Stephen) was the most active of these families, acquiring thirty patents totaling 15,905 acres. Edward Gray's spouse, Rosa, was a Tejana. In addition, the highly successful Tejano Cayetano Ríos secured seven grants totaling 3,200 acres.[15]

Distribution of State Land in Duval County

Though not more than 10 percent of the population, Americanos gained 67 percent of the land available in Duval County through the state's scrip programs. On the other hand, making up 90 percent of the people, Tejanos netted 33 percent of all the acreage. These patents, obtained through state land programs, contained 701,052 acres. Of these, 471,577 went to the minority population (i.e., Americanos), and Tejanos (the majority) received 229,475.

Table 4.4 Population, land distribution

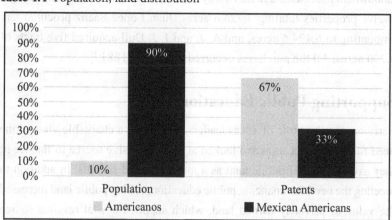

Source: US Census, Texas General Land Office.

During the seven years the railroad was under construction (1875–1881), the number of state land sales in Duval County totaled 764; this amounted to 58 percent of all land sales made during the fifty-three years that public land programs operated during the nineteenth century (1847–1900). Through the seven years of railroad construction, Duval County residents purchased 447,917 acres, or 64 percent, of all state land sold in the county during the nineteenth century.[16]

Table 4.5 Annual distribution of land sales by acre

Year	Acres
1847	11,200.0
1848	9,249.7
1857	640.0
1862	320.0
1867	160.0
1868	7,784.5
1869	6,915.2
1870	2,400.0
1871	6,281.1
1872	5,120.0
1873	14,748.9
1874	7,200.0
1875	39,338.7
1876	1,74,268.2
1877	63,636.5
1878	23,343.1
1879	39,580.1
1880	55,715.4
1881	52,065.4
1882	15,929.0
1883	14,825.2
1884	15,889.5
1885	25,000.7
1886	18,975.6
1887	11,521.0
1888	6,828.0
1889	20,945.0
1890	15,758.0
1891	6,184.0
1892	8,970.0
1893	13,440.0
1894	2,891.6
1895	5,398.4
1896	3,995.0
1897	2,240.0
1898	160.0
1899	1,440.0
1900	723.9

Source: Texas General Land Office.

The land always had a primary place in Duval County. It was an integral part of its history, development, culture, and language—in short, in every aspect of the county's identity. It was not a coincidence that livestock and agriculture thrived during the peak of state land grant sales in Duval County. The land acquisition by farmers and ranchers allowed sheep, cattle, and cotton in Duval County to flourish. The sheep industry appeared to have peaked during this time; simultaneously, cattle raising showed steady growth. Cotton was a mainstay through the end of the century. Through 1874 the county experienced gradual economic growth, and by 1875 it entered an economic boom by introducing the railroad and increasing private land acquisition through the state's scrip and school programs. The availability of land to the landless offered Tejanos an opportunity to partake in the county's development. Moreover, it afforded them more significant economic and political freedom.

Chapter 5

El Ganado Mayor
(Large Livestock)

J ust as the land was the foundation of the Tejano community's existence in the brush country, so was the livestock that they nurtured on their land. Spaniards directly tied the importance of horses and cattle to land value by granting more extensive tracts of land to those wanting to raise *ganado mayor*. Throughout the nineteenth century, land and livestock, especially cattle, were essential to Duval County's economy, leading historian Arnoldo De León to suggest that cattle raising influenced South Texas's "Tejano cultural domination."[1]

Spaniards introduced cattle to New Spain in 1520, Texas in the 1690s, and Duval County at the inception of the nineteenth century. Indeed, the American cattle industry's lexicon comes mainly from the Spanish spoken in the ranchos in Duval County and throughout the Trans-Nueces. Browse through Merriam-Webster and look up vaquero, corral, chaparral, rodeo, and lasso. These are only a few words borrowed from Spanish ranching tradition, and there are many more, including chaps, buckaroo, lariat, bronco, and mustang. Moreover, vaqueros who worked in Duval County ranchos contributed language, ranching techniques, and dress adopted by ranchers elsewhere in Texas and beyond.[2]

Among South Texas colonizers' objectives during the Spanish era was to promote livestock operations between the Nueces River and the Rio Grande, particularly cattle raising. By 1794 herds of cattle numbered eight hundred thousand in the Villas del Norte. At this time *vecinos* (neighbors) began to venture out to the Trans-Nueces area, searching for additional land for their herds, sometimes clandestinely. Initially these efforts involved squatting on royal land, but eventually the crown saw the benefit of an entrada into this region and began to make land grants north of the Rio Grande.[3]

In the early 1800s, Trans-Nueces ranchers could only run a few thousand cattle due to market prices; remuneration for cattle and their byproducts was low and markets were distant, so these early large landowners could not make much money. Another adverse impact on cattle's profit margin was the menace the rancheros faced from Indians; this was a common problem to pobladores who first settled in Duval County in the nineteenth century. By then, peaceful *indios* were virtually extinct. But many of their brethren from the southern Great Plains, including Arizona, New Mexico, Oklahoma, and the South Plains of Texas, frequently raided local ranchos. For decades cattle ranches in what became Duval County—such as Los Ángeles de Abajo, San Diego, and San Leandro—dealt with Indian attacks.[4]

Indians were not the only problem for Duval County rancheros in the region. Between the Texas Revolution and the Mexican-American War, Texian cowboys often made raids, called "cattle hunts," to rustle stock belonging to Mexicano ranchers. Many cattle ran freely on the range and were available for the taking. Some may have been unbranded and grazing on public lands. Mexicanos abandoned them when they left their ranchos due to Indian attacks, joined a Mexican revolutionary group, or enlisted in the Mexican Army to fight revolutionaries or defend the frontier.[5]

But historian Jack Jackson points out in *Los Mesteños* that Americano cowboys intended this extralegal action to drive out Mexicano rancheros from their land and often succeeded, opening the way for Texian land grabbers. As a result, by 1865 no Mexicano ranch owners existed in Karnes, Gonzales, Goliad, Guadalupe, DeWitt, Live Oak, Refugio, San Patricio, or Nueces Counties. Although this was true in modern Nueces County, it failed in the ranchos in the future Duval County, where Jackson notes eleven Mexicano cattle raisers were "clustered at San Diego." Jackson added, "Texas was still a kingdom held together with rawhide."[6]

Ranching in Duval County

In the 1850s Duval County had "much valuable land . . . supposed from the geographers and politicians a desert." In addition to land, Tejanos had extensive water and grazing resources, supporting several sizable prosperous ranchos with large livestock herds.[7] Among these rancheros were Juan Manuel Ramírez (Concepción), Juan Rodríguez (Palo Blanquito), Anastacio García and Guadalupe Guerra (Charco Redondo), Ysidro Guerra (Palo Blanco), and Rafael Izaguirre (Santa Rosalía).[8]

It was not until the 1860 federal census that some data on Duval County's ranchers became available. Of course, this census is a picture in time and captures activities unfolding in the 1850s. Moreover, this data set is sparse because the county was still unorganized. While census takers may have visited some of the county's areas, such as San Diego and Agua Poquita, ascertaining other enumeration districts wherein census takers recorded information exclusive to Duval County is problematic.

Nonetheless, this census for 1860 included eight stock raisers in San Diego, including Juan Sáenz, Antonio García, Edward Gray, Encarnación García, José M. García, Benito Ramos, and Alejos López Pérez and his wife, Trinidad Flores de Pérez. They all experienced prosperity due to the strong economy of the 1850s. The Pérez couple were the wealthiest cattle raisers in San Diego. Alejos Pérez was worth $10,828, including $6,928 in real estate and $3,900 in personal property, most likely livestock. His wife held ranch assets worth $7,828, divided almost equally between land and livestock.[9]

The Nueces County tax rolls for 1860 also shed light on Duval area cattle ranchers. It lists nine cattle owners, most in San Diego, including Antonio de la Garza Flores, with the largest herd numbering five hundred. Also at Rancho San Diego were Antonio Flores García, Trinidad Flores y Pérez, Pablo Pérez, Juan B. Gonzales, and Juan de Dios Pérez. Richard King had a cattle spread on the south side of the creek on the San Leandro grant. John Vale operated

Rancho Esperanza at the Agua Poquita grant, and Feliciano García oversaw Las Anacuas.[10]

From registered brands, the census, and the Nueces County tax rolls, one can account for twenty-three cattle owners living in Duval County in 1860. The census also listed twelve vaqueros, which enumerators called herdsmen. They were Eugenio Alanis, 26; Dionicio Arguijo, 30; Jesús Arguijo, 35; Pablo García, 22; Antonio Gonzales, 47; Juan Hinojosa, 40; Ruperto Longoria, 29; Cándido Maldonado, 39; Mauricio Pérez, 36; Marcos Ruiz, 33; Jesús Sáenz, 18; and Calixto Tovar, 17.

Just as the 1860 Census and tax records reflected the prior decade, so did the 1870 Census for the 1860s. With the 1870 count, the Census Bureau took a more consequential look at Duval County. While the census reported seventy men involved in stock raising, the Nueces County tax rolls only included twenty-two of these seventy men owning cattle in Duval County. Moreover, seven cattle raisers declaring property for taxation did not appear in the census.[11]

The total sum of cattle raisers and herd sizes in Duval County rose significantly between 1860 and 1870, as did the number of vaqueros, increasing from 12 to 120. Mexicanos and Tejanos customarily performed this work. Judging from other household members' names, a couple of vaqueros with Americano surnames appeared to be Tejanos. In addition, the census listed three "stock managers," or caporales, as vaqueros who most likely performed the work for their fathers as suggested by several ranchos with family members in the business.[12]

Cattle Branding

From ancient times livestock owners have branded their animals with identifying marks. Applications of marks or brands were customary in Spain and Portugal. In the fifteenth century, Spain introduced the *Libro de Marcas y Señales* (book of brands). The Spaniards brought cattle branding to the New World, including the Duval County area. Texas continued this practice; however, the state charged counties with registering the brands. Duval County rancheros first recorded their brands with Nueces County and, later, Duval County.[13]

Following the state's requirements for registering livestock, Nueces County began recording brands in 1848. At that time cattlemen in the Duval region who filed their brands in Nueces County included Francisco Flores Gonzales, Santos Flores Gonzales, Juan Sáenz, and Antonio García Flores, all of Rancho San Diego. Also operating out of Rancho San Diego was Pablo Pérez, who had separate brands for his horses and cattle. Alejo Pérez managed cattle herds for Felix A. Blücher and his wife, M. A. Blücher. Other Duval ranchers who recorded brands in Nueces County in 1861 included John Levy, who owned a ranch at San Leandro, south of the San Diego Creek, and Richard Miller, who ran a spread north of San Diego. John Vale operated Rancho Felicidad on the Agua Poquita grant south of San Diego. Tiburcio Ramírez was ranching at Rancho Concepción, and Rafael Hinojosa García and Felis Cadena homesteaded at the same Rancho Palo Blanco.[14]

Table 5.1 Early cattle brands in Duval County

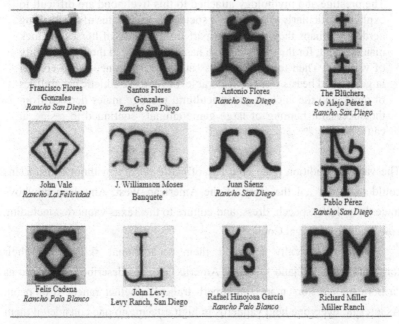

Francisco Flores Gonzales *Rancho San Diego*	Santos Flores Gonzales *Rancho San Diego*	Antonio Flores *Rancho San Diego*	The Blüchers, c/o Alejo Pérez at *Rancho San Diego*
John Vale *Rancho La Felicidad*	J. Williamson Moses Banquete*	Juan Sáenz *Rancho San Diego*	Pablo Pérez *Rancho San Diego*
Felis Cadena *Rancho Palo Blanco*	John Levy Levy Ranch, San Diego	Rafael Hinojosa García *Rancho Palo Blanco*	Richard Miller Miller Ranch

Source: Ranchero (Corpus Christi, TX), January 19, 1861.
*Moses lived in Banquete at this time, but he later moved to Duval County, where he became a prominent citizen.

The Vaqueros

Maintenance of the herds required vaqueros with special skills, temperament, and physical disposition. While one author described vaqueros as "a caste of hired or enslaved laborers," he also pointed out that cattle raising carried a "prestige . . . that, remarkably, extended down even to the unpropertied . . . men who worked the herds or served as overseers." Indeed, Ricardo M. Beasley, who lived among the vaqueros of Duval County in the early twentieth century, said that "to be a vaquero, a man had to be brave and intelligent. They were self-sufficient all the way around."[15]

While ranch owners were in charge of the cattle business, vaqueros tended to the animals, fences, water tanks, and other chores that kept the ranches going. Terry Jordan-Bychkov writes those vaqueros:

> practiced a distinctive way of life, forming a folk community or subculture with its own tools, techniques, jargon, and code of behavior. The prestige and mythology attached to this livelihood are difficult to explain, particularly given the low socioeconomic status of the working herders. Perhaps they derived in part from the use of horses in stock management, for the mounted man has always shared the formidability of warriors. Then too, the prowess and cleverness needed to control large, horned beasts were considerable, beyond the athletic capabilities of most, and the ancient, preagricultural prestige males derived from the successful hunting of large game animals continued to reside in cattle herding.[16]

The vaquero tradition is an epic tale of cattle raising; without it historians could not fully tell the story of the American West. American cowboys trace their skills, speech, dress, and culture to the Texas vaqueros, including cowhands from Duval County.

Vaqueros typically inherited their occupational skills from their forebears. Noted Tejano folklorist Américo Paredes described a vaquero as "a born hunter, horseman, and superb trailer," whether ranchero or peon. As a result, everyone held vaqueros in high esteem; no one considered them "common workers." Consequently, the ranch owner and the vaqueros treated each other respectfully.[17]

Vaqueros' duties involved gathering, herding, trailing, branding cattle, and breaking wild horses. While working on the chaparral, Vaqueros encountered many natural perils, including a harsh land filled with dense undergrowth, spiny shrubs, cacti, and mesquite trees. The cowboys often discovered "wild and belligerent beasts stubbornly resisting capture." Their ponies could buck them off, causing vaqueros to incur "crippling injuries from thorny plants, cat claws, or goring by the longhorns."[18]

As did their ancestors in Spain, who usually signed up for a year and received payment in cash and calves, Duval County vaqueros of the 1850s received six dollars per month, corn rations, and heads of cattle. Indeed, there are reports that this latter form of compensation may have been preferable to vaqueros, undoubtedly allowing them to start their herds in the open range or public lands.[19]

Each vaquero could handle three hundred head of cattle, but in the 1850s, only two ranches in the Duval area stocked more than three hundred beef cattle. In more extensive ranching operations, a caporal oversaw the crew of vaqueros.[20]

Chapter 6

Ranching Resurgence

Because of unsettled times, the cattle business in Texas suffered a downslide during the Civil War and Reconstruction. However, after the conflict it was a golden age for cattle raising. The availability of inexpensive land, access to an open range, a favorable climate for the natural growth of various types of grass, and a surplus of cattle in northern Mexico made restocking herds cheap. These factors helped drive the market to new heights.[1]

Post–Civil War Era Ranching

During this postwar era, rancheros saw the best prices for cattle. A ten-dollar steer in Texas brought thirty-eight to forty dollars in Kansas. Rancheros sold their cattle in Corpus Christi, Rockport, San Antonio, and Brownsville, where the stock was shipped or driven to Kansas and other points in the eastern United States or abroad. At times, buyers from different parts of Texas or the American East came to buy stock from cattlemen at their ranches in the Trans-Nueces. Several meatpackers in the coastal area of South Texas also purchased cattle to process cows, hides, tallows, and pickled beef.[2]

While local buyers and packers provided a marketplace for cattlemen to sell their stock, they did not represent the most lucrative possibilities for sales. Out-of-state buyers offered better opportunities for stock raisers to sell at higher prices, and South Texas was the primary supplier of cattle for out-of-state buyers. Therefore, cattle drives were essential in exposing South Texas cattle raisers to the northern markets.[3]

Neither of the two central cattle trails heading north crossed Duval County, but both skirted the county's eastern and western edges. Rancheros in the Trans-Nueces used several feeder paths to connect to the two major trails. One feeder route was in southern Duval County and traversed northeast, joining the Great Western Trail beyond the Duval County boundary line in modern-day Jim Wells County.

In Duval County vaqueros rounded up *ganado bravo* (wild cattle) grazing in the brush on public lands, branded them, and separated some animals to butcher for food on the trail. The number of livestock in a cattle drive was usually about 2,500. Once the advance got underway in late March, the drovers pushed hard for a week to tire the cattle. Then the cowhands followed the "green grass" north, covering twelve miles per day. The essential crew for a trail drive included the chuck wagon cook, about twelve vaqueros, and a road branding team. On South Texas ranches, vaqueros earned two to five dollars monthly but could make twenty to twenty-five dollars on the drive north.[4]

Three developments helped the cattle business return to profitability and growth. First, the use of barbed wire, invented in 1868, began to spread, especially after 1874, following the introduction of the machine capable of mass-producing the wire. This innovation facilitated fencing and allowed ranchers to protect their herds and grazing grounds.[5] Second, the arrival of the Corpus Christi, San Diego, and Rio Grande Railroad bolstered the cattle trade, opening up markets and thus removing the need to send cattle on long, costly, and dangerous drives to Kansas. Finally, the state's land grant programs expanded the opportunity for new landowners to go into cattle raising. The transformation these new rancheros brought was profound.

The 1880 Census attests to the ranch economy's growth during the 1870s. So did new county tax reports that provided a more accurate picture of the local livestock industry; county employees, familiar with the area and

Fig. 6.1 Rosa Garza García Gray (1831–1917), matriarch of the Gray family.
Family Search, https://www.familysearch.org/tree/person/details/K6SK-RPP.

its people, compiled these reports from data ranchers submitted to the county
for tax purposes; these county tax rolls listed stock raisers' names, herd size,
and the cattle's value. According to county tax rolls, individuals raising
bovine in Duval County increased from 22 in 1870 to 302 by the decade's
end. Total cattle increased from 4,367 to 7,882, or 80 percent. The price per
head more than doubled, going from $3.01 to $6.75. The 302 stock raisers
in the county averaged a modest herd of twenty-six cows. Many individuals
claimed a single animal; many others had less than ten. These latter individuals likely kept a milking cow and a few beeves to feed their families; they
hardly fit the definition of "cattle raiser." Still, local and state governments
were taxing them for cattle ownership. Duval tax data, beginning in 1877,
disclose a steady but robust expansion in the cattle industry. The size of herds
grew 9 percent annually.[6]

Fig. 6.2 Práxedis Tovar García (1839–1920), matron of the influential García family. Courtesy of Eliseo Cadena.

Interestingly, a Tejana was among the top ten cattle raisers. Refugia V. Guerra owned 152 heads of cattle. In *From Out of the Shadows: Mexican Women in Twentieth-Century America*, Vicki Ruiz points out that scholarly works have wrongly relegated Tejanas to "landscape roles." They portray them as "scenery, not as actors." Ruiz notes that women stepped out of society's roles and took on more significant community challenges.[7]

In the nineteenth century, Duval County Tejanas took on responsibilities beyond those that society generally designated to them. For example, Trinidad Flores, Práxedis Tovar García, Refugia V. Guerra, Rosa Garza García Gray, and their *comadres* (formal usage means "godmother," but it can also refer to a female friend or neighbor) played vital roles as cattle raisers and frequently took on other responsibilities equal to their male counterparts.

For example, Trinidad Flores was the lead plaintiff in clearing the San Diego land grant titles. She also played a vital role in subdividing parts of San Diego to provide lots for a town to take form.[8]

Duval County Ranchos

Ranchos remained integral to the local economy in the mid to late 1800s. Duval County "relied strongly on the many ranchos throughout the county [that] raised cattle, horses, mules, and sheep." Also, in 1876 Duval County formally organized and began recording livestock brands. Through 1882 it registered some two hundred brands of livestock operators. Ranchers confirmed their brands in 1878–1882; however, they were likely around much earlier. As can be determined from the number of individuals register-ing cattle with the county tax office, ranchos in Duval were numerous.[9]

In the far northwest part of the county were the Mateo Sendejo Rancho, six miles west of Mendieta Rancho; the John Martin Rancho[10] near Freer; and the Ybañez Rancho. The Labbe and Cibolo Ranchos were farther northwest, as was the Gray Rancho along the San Diego Creek banks. Finally, the Collins and Delamer Ranches were northeast of San Diego. Farther north were the Rancho San José, Becerra Rancho, Los Olmitos Rancho, and others.[11]

West of San Diego were the Rosita, Ruiz, and Soledad Well Ranchos. To the southwest were two Gravis Ranchos, the Oglesby Rancho, two Alaniz Ranchos, and the Ceyades Rancho. Along the railroad the Mesquite and Piedras Pintas Ranchos were north of present-day Benavides,[12] and Placido Benavides's Palo Alto Rancho was adjacent to the town. In addition, the Guajillo, López, and Bandera Ranchos were east of Benavides, and the Hubbard, Murray, Mamsona, and Parilla Ranchos were west of that community.[13]

Other ranchos in the Benavides area during the 1880s were the José Ángel Gonzales Rancho, Glover Rancho, Carrillos Rancho, Rancho de la Muralla, La Gloria Rancho, Rancho Canai, Rancho Aguas Prietas, and Los Horcones. Fifteen miles northwest of Realitos was the Barroneña Ranch, and north of Barroneña were Los Encinos, Chapa, Valderas, and Morris Ranchos.[14]

Farther south, on the east side of the Texas Mexican Railroad, was the Baldwin Rancho and Peña Station. East of Realitos, on the road to Concepción, was the Lewis Ranch and Clovis Rancho. Finally, on the way to Benavides, north of Concepción, was the Sweden Ranch. Other ranchos in the southern part of Duval County included Rancho Las Anaquas, the Florencio Benavides Rancho (formerly Stillman Ranch), and the Hilario Benavides, John Fitch, and Avelino Pérez Ranchos, as well as Rancho San Felipe and Rancho of Juan Salinas.[15]

The 1880 Census listed 141 stock raisers, less than half of the number accounted for by the Duval County tax collector. Precinct One, the extra-territorial area of San Diego, was home to 60 stock raisers, and the town proper had 24 cattlemen. Precinct Two, the Piedras Pintas area, had 57 cattle ranchers. Several factors may have contributed to the discrepancy between the county and the census numbers. First, the census did not include any stock raisers from Precincts Three and Four, the county's most rural area most likely to have livestock. Instead, they may have counted them in the general designation of farmers. A second reason for the difference may be that the county registered small cattle owners who may not have considered themselves cattle raisers and did not identify themselves as such to census takers.[16]

The decennial enumeration included 108 vaqueros in the county, 55 in Precinct One / San Diego, and 53 in Precinct Two. But, once again, the census takers did not tally any vaqueros in Precincts Three and Four.[17]

In 1890 seventy-four ranchers claimed herds with 100 or more cows. The largest cattle raiser was Norman G. Collins, who declared ownership of 3,500 bovines. While constituting only 17 percent of the total ranchers, these seventy-four cattle raisers owned 77 percent of cattle in the county. Tax records again show females raising cattle; Refugia V. Guerra, with a herd of 604, continued to have the largest flock of Tejana cattle raisers.[18]

The most significant change over the ten years was the increase in cattle owners and herd size. According to Duval County's 1890 tax rolls, the number of cattle owners in the 1880s increased to 423 from 302, a 29 percent growth rate. The total cattle in the county had swung up to 40,617 from 7,882. The price for cattle rose auspiciously from 1880 to 1883, almost tripling from $6.75 per head to $16.45.[19] But as it turned out, this was the pinnacle of the

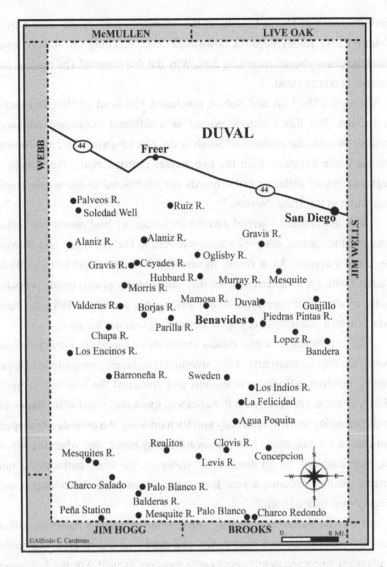

Map 6.1 Ranchos in nineteenth-century Duval County. This map was prepared in 1892 by the Engineer Office of the State of Texas. They left out the area north of what is now SH 44. Some of the ranches omitted included Mateo Sendejo, Mendieta, John Martin, Ybañez, Labbe, Cibolo, Gray, Collins, Delamer, Rancho San José, Cecerra, and Los Olmitos. The map also fails to include other ranchos south of SH 44, including Palo Alto, López, Bandera, José Ángel Gonzales, Glober, Carrillos, Muralla, La Gloria, Canai, Agua Prietas, Los Horcones, Las Anaquas, Florencio Benavides, Hilario Benavides, John Fitch, Avelino Pérez, San Felipe, and Juan Salinas.

cattle business in Duval County in the nineteenth century. In 1884 Duval County cattle values began a downward slide, reaching the lowest level since the county began recording data. Why did this happen? The reasons are somewhat complicated.

Toward 1883 Lott and Nelson purchased 127 head of Hereford cattle in Indiana. But this livestock grazed in a different ecosystem and was unaccustomed to the environs of South Texas. Not long after, Lott and Nelson left the cattle business. Like the two former railroad men, other ranchers began to import different cattle breeds not acclimated to the weather and vegetation in the Trans-Nueces.[20]

With the railroad's arrival and the expansion of land ownership under state grant programs, many newcomers moved to Duval County and entered the cattle business. As a result, the number of cattle quickly multiplied. Coupled with growing sheep herds, they undoubtedly placed undue pressure on the area's native vegetation. And if this was not enough, in 1883, the state experienced a widespread dry spell, portending troubles for pastures.

The experience of cattle raisers statewide undoubtedly impacted their Duval County counterparts. Like livestock producers everywhere, Duval County ranchers fell victim to the ups and downs of the weather. In April 1884 a severe storm occurred at Peña Station, spooking some twelve thousand cattle belonging to Mifflin Kenedy and Richard King. An extended heat spell had caused the animals to become severely dehydrated, and when the storm hit, they scattered "in all directions." However, the freak outburst did not change weather patterns; a year later cattle raisers were "discouraged and gloomy over lack of rain."[21]

In another occurrence, in May 1885, John Fitch said a hailstorm killed three thousand sheep two days earlier and destroyed a corn crop. No doubt it adversely impacted neighboring cattle ranchers as well. For the following two years, severe winter weather blanketed the state. Then, in 1889, a brutal drought returned, killing thousands of cattle due to hunger and thirst.[22]

In late May 1885, Edward N. Gray took 1,899 livestock and 800 horses wherever he could find a market. Three weeks later Duval County cattle raisers shipped more than 15,000 head of cattle from Peña Station due to the drought and declining demand for cattle byproducts.[23]

While cattle were fat in 1886, the market was dull, but it could not dissuade ranchers from selling and seeking a profit. Despite, or perhaps because of, the low prices, cattle raisers were selling. In 1887 beef prices were still fair, but experienced cattle raisers complained that money had never been so scarce in their business. Some ranch operators received offers of eight to ten dollars per head, but no one was selling at those rates. Later that year E. Corkill gathered cattle for transport to the Indian Territory, and Lott and Nelson sent a herd of 225 cattle to Beeville.[24]

Cattle value continued on a downslide, reaching the lowest price of $5.07 per head in 1888. One observer noted that the cattle baron era across the United States ended in 1889. The elite's time may have finished, but the tried and tested rancheros continued in the reputable and trusted business.[25]

Table 6.1 Duval County cattle values, 1880–1889

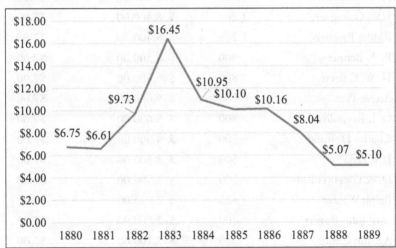

Source: Duval County tax records.

Numbers can best summarize the fate of cattle raising in Duval County in the last decade of the nineteenth century. In 1890 there were seventy-four herds of 100 or more beeves, but this count dropped 68 percent nine years later to only twenty-four. The number of cattle fell from 31,722 to 11,005, or 65 percent. The value of these herds fell 50 percent. The one bright spot was the price, which increased by 37 percent.[26] The number of cattle owners also dropped dramatically, from 424 to 232. Like previous enumerations, the 1900 Census listed 92 ranchers, short of the tax rolls' count. The decennial record included 150 vaqueros, compared to 124 twenty years earlier.[27]

While the northern part of the county got some rain in May 1887, the southern part faced grim straits. Realitos was experiencing a dramatic downturn in cattle herds due to an extended drought. Area ranchers lost a third of their beef in the first three years of the dry spell. In the following four years, cattle raising—which had always been the county's economic backbone—became a disaster, with stockmen losing 85 to 90 percent of their herds.[28]

Table 6.2 Duval County cattle, 1899

Cattleman*	Number of Cattle	Value of Cattle	Value per Head
N. G. Collins	2,000	$14,000.00	$7.00
J. W. Gallagher	1,200	$ 8,400.00	$7.00
Ridder Brothers	1,200	$ 8,400.00	$7.00
B. A. Bennet	900	$ 6,300.00	$7.00
H. W. Garrett	800	$ 5,600.00	$7.00
Archie Parr	800	$ 5,600.00	$7.00
G. J. Reynolds	800	$ 5,600.00	$7.00
Charles Hoffman	700	$ 4,900.00	$7.00
L. P. Peña	500	$ 3,500.00	$7.00
D. & Gregoria Ruiz	500	$ 3,500.00	$7.00
Ralph Welder	425	$ 2,975.00	$7.00
Mrs. Julio Rogers	400	$ 2,800.00	$7.00
Agustín Cantú	300	$ 2,100.00	$7.00
Anastasio Pérez	300	$ 2,100.00	$7.00
Cayetano Ríos	300	$ 2,100.00	$7.00
Nicolas Treviño	300	$ 2,100.00	$7.00
Sinecia Gutiérrez	250	$ 1,750.00	$7.00
C. M. Robinson	250	$ 1,750.00	$7.00
Isidro Benavides	220	$ 1,540.00	$7.00

(*Continues*)

Table 6.2 (Continued)

Cattleman*	Number of Cattle	Value of Cattle	Value per Head
Rufino López	200	$ 1,400.00	$7.00
R. H. McCampbell	200	$ 1,400.00	$7.00
Antonia P. de Hinojosa	150	$ 1,050.00	$7.00
Roque Benavides	110	$ 770.00	$7.00
Neil A. McCampbell	100	$ 700.00	$7.00
Julián Reyes	100	$ 700.00	$7.00
Totals	**13,005**	**$91,035.00**	**Avg. $7.00**

Source: Duval County tax rolls, 1890.
*Only includes cattle owners with one hundred or more.

Nevertheless, some larger operators, such as E. Morris, Archie Parr, W. H. Brooks, George Reynolds, and R. R. Savage, managed to ship cattle to pasture in the Indian Territory. By transporting thousands of cattle from Peña Station and Hebbronville to the Midwest, the Texas Mexican Railroad was the primary beneficiary of the ranchers' troubles. Eventually, the cows were "fattened on Kansas and Missouri corn and sold to eastern consumers." Regrettably, more than two-thirds of the money generated by beef stayed with the railroads that transported them and the grazers and feeders, leaving little for the cattle owners.[29]

Not surprisingly, hundreds of ranchers in the brush country went bankrupt. Some did not have a cow to feed their starving children, an ox to plow the field, or a horse to hunt for the bare necessities.[30] As bad as the rancheros had it, their ranch hands faced even more distressing conditions. On May 11 a train brought corn for distribution among poor people in Duval County. Some 240 individuals benefited from this charity. But the corn did not seem to have reached Realitos, fourteen miles south of Benavides. Two weeks later, reports indicated people were experiencing the worst form of poverty—no food to eat. While some stock raisers sold or slaughtered whatever stock remained to provide for their family's subsistence, their ranch hands were less fortunate. In Realitos, "twenty-two widows with eighty-two children, [were] without . . . food and clothing and thirty-seven able-bodied men" were unemployed and unable to put food on the table or clothes on their 138 children.[31] "Unless we get relief for these starving people, they will either become desperate and lawless criminals or die of hunger," Avelino García observed. So Justice of the Peace Tovar, C. C. Lewis, and other leading citizens asked the rest of the state for help. Among those appealing for support for the Realitos community were N. Gusset, manager of the Realitos Store; stock raisers J. M. Olivares and W. S. and James Gullet; former stock raiser and farmer J. M Wright; one-time cattle raiser Emilio Cadena; storekeeper Santa Anna García; D. F. Gómez, with the railroad; schoolteacher R. W. Cole; and ranch hand H. C. Vitter.[32]

Finally, the business regained footing, recording livestock prices approximating the county's average of $7.37 per head. During the last five years of the century, the value of bovine averaged $7.03 per steer. Cattle-raising operations at the end of the nineteenth century, however, never reached the levels of the mid-1880s when cattle prices were at all-time highs.

Other factors also affected cattle raising in Duval County as the century waned. In the western United States, the buffalo's near extinction by slaughter prompted Midwest farmers to go into cattle raising. Their presence depleted the demand for Texas beef. A weakened market persuaded South Texas ranchers, including some in Duval County, to leave large herds of cattle to graze freely on the range. Moreover, the collapse in demand for sheep attracted sheep raisers to move to cattle raising, thus increasing competition.[33]

One longtime rancher, Pablo Adame, decided he could no longer make a living raising cattle in Duval County, so he sold his land and headed west with his family and livestock. The 53-year-old Adame took his wife, eight children, seven daughters, and a son. Also on the caravan were two sons-in-law. Adame sold a few cattle on the road to feed his family, and he sent the rest of his herd up north in a cattle drive. The family finally settled in Terrell County in West Texas. Others in the same situation likely replicated the Adame family saga.[34]

Prominent ranchers like Archie Parr stuck it out, planting feedstuff for their cattle. Parr cultivated four hundred acres of feed for his herds, hoping to fatten them for shipment to market. S. R. Peters also sowed corn and cane for his animals' upkeep.[35]

In the final analysis, the story of cattle in Duval County is about brave individuals who raised cattle as a source of livelihood for their families. Miguel González-Quiroga observed, "The harsh terrain and adverse climate did not discourage the hardy rancheros who established a thriving community and gave life to the region."[36] One can see evidence of this personal effort by looking at what stock raisers did when cattle raising was not profitable. On such occasions ranchers used their land for farming and planted cotton, corn, sorghum, and other crops.

Chapter 7

Civil War and Reconstruction, 1860–1874

The American Civil War and Reconstruction periods proved erratic to Duval County's early history, stunting economic and governmental development. Ironically, the county's civil society began to take shape during this tragic period. Moreover, the area's population grew in numbers and diversity.

Most of the Americano population chose to side with the South, but a handful chose the Union and had to operate in the fringes. The war pitted friends against friends and temporarily stagnated the once-thriving ranching and cattle industry. In addition, the demands of military service and the needs of the war effort distracted landowners and vaqueros. Finally, the conflict deprived local governments of capable public servants who were tied up fighting for the Confederacy or had gone into exile supporting the Union. While people faced ever-changing demands from the new Confederate government, the war did provide minor financial gains to the Mexicano and Tejano communities. However, these benefits evaporated when hostilities ended.

At the dawn of the Civil War, Duval County was still unorganized and attached to Nueces County for judicial purposes. The county was inhabited almost entirely by Tejanos and Mexicanos who engaged in ranching. The heart of their operations was the land; Tejano *rancheros* in Duval County did not own other human beings. They held no particular animosity against their Black brethren. Moreover, Duval County Tejanos nourished and strengthened their identity based on regionalism. They had never fully embraced aspects of nationalism.

Their ancestors had given Tejanos a state of mind they cherished, embraced, nurtured, and ensured they passed on to their children stronger than they received. The Confederacy did not offer Tejanos more incentive or security than had New Spain or Mexico or suggest anything to change their longstanding commitment to an identity rooted in their land, ranchos, communities, and religion. For the rancheros, staying in or leaving the United States was not urgent; they found themselves in a quandary not of their making.

The War between the States

In Duval County Confederate requirements for military service distracted both landowners and vaqueros. The conflict deprived local governments such as Nueces County of capable public servants; many residents went into exile. Moreover, demands from the new Confederate government at the state and national levels presented an ever-changing challenge to those who remained.

The outbreak of the Civil War called on Tejanos to become Confederates, Southerners, or insurgents; none of the choices made sense or excited long-time residents. Instead, the conflict resembled the constant bickering between brothers they had witnessed in Mexico as one revolutionary group after another rose in arms, ravaging villas and ranchos along the Rio Grande. Most Duval County residents were not interested in what prompted the Americanos to war against each other. What they cared for was the land that provided sustenance for their families.[1]

Confederate stalwarts in Texas and Duval County's brush country correctly perceived Tejanos' indifference to human bondage. Few Tejanos in South Texas had or could afford chattel. Indeed, no indentured individuals were present in Duval County, and most of the county's residents treated Blacks as equals. Thus, Tejanos had no compelling interest in the Americanos' internecine struggle. Many Tejanos shared the sentiments of a group of Tejano abolitionists who repudiated rebel sentiments and sided with the bluecoats.[2]

Such detachment did not sit well with Confederate partisans, however. The *Corpus Christi Ranchero* explicitly, and in crude language, proclaimed, "not only [do Tejanos] consider a nigger equal with themselves, but they . . . court the company of Negroes." Tejanos throughout Texas lacked intolerance toward Blacks, were sympathetic to their plight, and often "helped slaves escape." Confederate conformists claimed such an attitude endangered "the institution of slavery." But Tejanos in Texas, and to a degree in Duval County, mistrusted Americanos who had maltreated Tejanos for years and considered them inferior people, much like they did Blacks. Neither the Union nor the Southern cause made any lasting impression on them; they just wished to stay out of the fight, tend to their ranches, and care for their families.[3]

Oddly, while the Civil War played havoc with the Tejano landholders and Americanos who controlled the political structures under which Tejanos lived, laboring Tejanos fared relatively well. The Civil War provided a modest financial boom to some segments of the Tejano population in South Texas, opening jobs in settlements along the Rio Grande Valley. Tejanos transported goods between Mexican and Texan markets and found a moneymaking source in moving cotton, the Confederacy's financial lifeblood. Their services in transportation and commerce were so critical to the Confederate economy that the South granted these Tejanos waivers from the draft. Tejano freighters employed wooden-wheeled oxen to pull carretas and *vagones* (four-wheeled wagons) drawn by mules. Other well-paying jobs opened up for many Tejanos when Americanos joined the Confederate Army.[4]

Indeed, many Americanos outrightly considered Tejanos to be disloyal to the South. Since their inclusion into South Texas's body politic, Americanos perceived it as un-American for Tejanos to insist on speaking Spanish. Moreover, secessionists did not trust Tejanos, whom they felt had just left "the Anglos to kill one another."[5]

Avoiding Service in the Rebel Army

In November 1861 Nueces County received a request from Confederate higher-ups to adopt an oath of allegiance from all local citizens to the Confederate States of America. The Nueces County Commissioners Court declined, believing it did not have such power. Furthermore, many local officials in South Texas did not favor forcing men in their jurisdiction to join rebel troops. Confederate officers feared that placing towns under martial orders might push the Tejanos to open rebellion and to ask for Union support. Already the number of those avoiding mandatory Confederate conscription was very high. Moreover, some Duval County residents claimed Mexican citizenship and used their birthplace as an excuse not to serve the rebel forces. These perceived disloyalties enraged Confederates.[6]

Desperate Confederate officials sent Tiger Ware to ranchos in the brush country south of the Nueces River to recruit men for the rebel army.[7] At Agua Poquita in Duval County, Ware considered lurking around a watering hole to ensnare potential conscripts, but he only found an elderly Tejana. So in 1863 an enrolling officer for Nueces County, I. W. Engledow, visited Los Olmitos, Concepción, San Diego, Amargosa, and other Duval County–area ranchos to impose draft requirements on Tejanos. However, most men he met avoided conscription by claiming Mexican citizenship. That was not surprising since three out of every four residents in San Diego were born in Mexico.[8]

Support for the Confederacy in Duval County was tepid at best. Never-theless, perhaps at the urging or example of some of their Americano friends who had joined the Confederate Army, several Tejanos did enlist in the Confederate ranks. Some seventy area men signed up for a state troopers' company that Clemente Zapata organized in San Diego in 1862.[9]

At least a quarter of Zapata's company were San Diego residents, and the remaining were from Nueces County communities, including Banquete, Brasanious, Casa Blanca, Palo Blanco, Santa Gertrudes, and Corpus Christi. These men had gone to San Diego to enlist because they viewed the commu-nity as a sanctuary from Americano-bigoted practices. How long these men served in the Confederate Army is unknown, but the rebel desertion rate was very high.[10]

Tejanos Serving Bluecoats

Circa 1863 Tejanos and Mexicanos who had signed up with the rebel army began leaving the Confederate units to join Union forces under the command of Juan Nepomuceno Cortina in the Rio Grande Valley, Cecilio Valerio in the Nueces Strip, and others.[11] For example, Clemente Zapata quit the rebels and joined the Union Army at Zapata County as a captain of the Texas 2nd Cavalry. Colonels John L. Haynes and Edmund J. Davis commanded this mounted unit. Colonel Davis was the district judge who, from 1860 to 1862, ruled in favor of Duval County and South Texas Tejano landowners defending their land grants. Davis's name "was famous in every rancho" in South Texas. Available records do not indicate if Clemente Zapata's San Diego Company followed their commander into the Union cause. However, several men from San Diego served in Union forces, including Juan González of San Diego, who enlisted with the United States Navy and served on the ship *Harriet Lane*, which captured Galveston in October 1862 and fell to the rebels in January 1863.[12]

In 1863 Cecilio Valerio was among thirty-five Mexicanos and Tejanos fighting with the Union Army under Captain James Speed's command. In December Speed's men raided the King Ranch on the Santa Gertrudes, killed Francisco Alvarado, and scattered all the horses at the ranch. Afterward, Valerio, who had a large herd of horses, led a cavalry company of 126 men, including his son, Juan. The company mainly targeted the Confederate cotton trade along the border but occasionally waged guerrilla warfare against the Nueces Strip's rebels. In addition, as a Union officer Cecilio Valerio coordinated with the Union Army on the Rio Grande border and with the Union Navy.[13]

Rebel Operations in the Duval County Area

In 1863 the rebels established several installations in the area. Camp Patterson was a rebel operations headquarters on the San Fernando Creek west of present-day Driscoll in Nueces County. Confederates made plans to "establish a depot and shops at San Diego," where they planned to store twenty days of rations for two thousand men. The rebels also maintained a camp at Barroneño in western Duval County under Lieutenant Colonel Daniel Showalter.[14]

In January 1864 Confederate Colonel John "Rip" Ford, the Rio Grande military district commander, devised a strategy to retake Brownsville from Union forces by mustering Confederate troops at Fort Merrill on the Nueces River banks in southeastern Live Oak County. Then they were to head to San Diego, La Sal del Rey in north-central Hidalgo County, and Brownsville.[15]

Col. Santos Benavides, based in Laredo, advised Ford that going through San Diego was not advisable. Such a trip would render their mounts unserviceable and disable them for active operations. Ford received a similar cautionary note from Major L. M. Rogers. "You cannot imagine how desolate, barren, and desert-like this country is," Rogers wrote to Ford. No vegetation was available for the horses to forage because the area had been under a severe drought. Riders saw "bones of hundreds of livestock piled up in dry water holes."[16] Ford took their advice and decided to march to the Rio Grande from San Antonio to Fort Ewell in La Salle County, farther upriver from Fort Merrill.[17]

First, however, Ford took his troops down the Nueces River and from there to Camp Patterson, arriving in late March. Captain Nolan brought the colonel up to date on recent activities. Nolan's unit, consisting of sixty-two soldiers, had engaged the enemy at Los Patricios within the San Francisco land grant in Duval County. The battlefield straddled the Duval and Nueces County (now Jim Wells County) boundary line. The captain claimed to have "routed" a Union force of 125 men under Cecilio Valerio's command in a "fierce" battle that lasted fifteen minutes. Valerio's men, Nolan said, were armed with Burnsides, revolvers, and sabers. Cecilio Valerio's son, Juan, commanded part of the Union troops, consisting of eighty men. While Nolan claimed to have done short shrift of the enemy, he conceded to Colonel Ford that the Union band had fought "gallantly" with the "fierce battle costing much blood and loss of property."[18]

The battle had proved indecisive, so the Valerio company moved on to Laredo. On their way they raided a ranch ten miles south of San Diego and drove off sixty cattle belonging to the King Ranch. In addition, they hung one of the ranch's vaqueros, named Lucas. Perhaps it was First Corporal Lucas García, a 58-year-old Banquete man serving with the Texas State Troopers in San Diego.[19]

After the war Cecilio Valerio returned to raising horses for some years at La Rosita in Duval County. Before the outbreak of war, Valerio had been a successful rancher in Nueces County with a herd of four hundred horses and mules and the admiration of newly arrived Americano neighbors. However, at the outbreak of hostilities, Valerio likely lost his equine flock to the rebel war effort, which may have prompted him to join the North in the War. In his final years, Valerio returned to Camargo, where he died. Valerio's 36-year-old son, Juan, remained in La Rosita, supporting a family by hauling wool from San Diego to Corpus Christi.[20]

Life away from the War

Duval County's population continued to increase between 1860 and 1870. San Diego's population grew from 271 to 784 residents. Most of this expansion came from Mexicanos, who brought new energy to the Duval County workforce. Recent Mexicano arrivals to the San Diego area totaled 551, up from 202. Tejanos experienced a similar growth pattern, from 68 in 1860 to 219 in 1870. Americanos also began to venture into the brush country.[21] This population growth helped sustain the Duval economy. Large carts arrived daily from Mexico's interior. They came from various points on the Rio Grande, including Guerrero, Camargo, Mier, Rio Grande City, Laredo, and Eagle Pass. They hauled wool and other articles from Mexico and returned with assorted American merchandise.[22]

One individual who sought to profit from this Civil War–era commerce was John Levy, who established a store at Rancho San Leandro on the south side of San Diego Creek. The establishment carried "dry goods, clothing, groceries, cutlery, wines, liquors, and ladies wear." The store had also received commodities from Mexico appropriate for area rancheros, including saddles, headstalls, bridles, morrales, spurs, hair ropes, banders, bits, whips, *chaveras* (protective leggings), and saddle girths. Levy also bought hides, skins, and wool from the local ranchers, paying premium prices in cash.[23]

Other newcomers were involved in the support economy, including five waggoneers or *carreteros* (cart drivers), three carpenters, three tailors, two peddlers, a brick mason, a teamster, a silversmith, one blacksmith, and a musician. One doctor, a schoolteacher, one cook, and a Catholic priest were also new additions to the county's economic vitality during the war and Reconstruction.[24]

On the other hand, several factors adversely impacted the area's ranch economy during the Civil War. As mentioned earlier, a severe drought that began in 1863 lasted two years, taking a toll on Duval County's livestock. Then there were military attacks on the area's ranchos. Union partisans like Cecilio and Juan Valerio raided the ranchos in the region to secure provisions for the Union Army bivouacked along the Mexican border. Many landowners, particularly the Americano ranchers, could not tend to their herds because of their military commitments. Consequently, thousands of unbranded cattle roamed wildly during the Civil War, attracting bandits and rustlers.[25]

By this time, Encarnación García Pérez had entered the retail business in San Diego and, like newcomer Norman Collins, operated a general merchandise store. Collins eventually became the wealthiest individual in Duval County, but in 1860 five Tejanos had more wealth, including Alvino Canales, Alejos Pérez, Pablo Pérez, Santos Moreno, and Jesus García.

Table 7.1 Property values for San Diego in 1860, 1870

	1860	Property Value	1870	Property Value	Growth	Property Value Growth Rate
Americanos	1	$ 5,580	1	$ 4,500	–$ 1,080	**–24.0%**
Tejanos	20	$41,518	35	$78,115	$36,597	**46.9%**
Total	21	$47,098	36	$82,615	$35,517	43.0%

Source: US Census, 1860, 1870.

After 1870 other Americano merchants began to make their way to the growing community of San Diego. Nonetheless, they depended on the Mexicano and Tejano populations as customers at their stores. Unquestionably, San Diego in 1870 was a Tejano town, and Americanos had set their sights on it as a source for economic advancement.

Politics during the Civil War

Tejanos' electoral participation during the Civil War and Reconstruction fluctuated between modest upswings and downward slides. In the January 1861 election, every Nueces County delegate to the Secession Convention received fifty-three votes in Duval County, presumably from Tejanos voting in Precinct Nine in Agua Poquita. Three Tejanos—Jacinto Salinas, Prudencio Azargoita, and Rafael Salinas—served as election clerks. However, none of the delegates were Tejanos. Voting Precinct Ten in San Diego did not report any ballots. Of the 177 members of the Texas Secessionist Assembly, not one was a Tejano, even though this area of Texas had an overwhelming majority of ethnic Mexicanos.[26]

In the second election held in 1861 to determine whether Texas should remain or secede from the Union, voting Precincts Nine and Ten in Duval County did not appear to have cast any votes. On March 24, 1861, in the election to select a state senator and representative, election officials counted 155 votes in Concepción while no voting took place in San Diego. Then, on November 6, 1861, Nueces County held an election to pick electors for the Confederate Congress and decide upon county commissioners. Precinct Nine presiding Judge A. M. Palacios belatedly reported that forty-one people voted. Manuel Salinas and Teodoro Hinojosa served as election clerks. But, once again, San Diego's Precinct Ten seemed not to have held an election.[27]

Since only a handful of Americanos lived in the unorganized county, Tejanos were in command of the electoral process, contributing all the votes from Duval County and overseeing the elections as clerks; however, Americanos secured elective positions. For example, in a referendum on August 4 to select state and local officials, Duval voters chose E. N. Gray as justice of the peace and R. Carter as constable, each with a mere twenty votes. Election judges included Encarnacion García Pérez and C. G. García. Voting Precinct Nine, however, was not open.[28]

In another 1863 election to choose state officials and amend the Texas Constitution, Duval did not return voting results to Nueces County headquarters from either voting precinct. No records of election outcomes from these voting precincts exist in the Nueces County Clerk's office between the war's end in April 1865 and Reconstruction.[29]

Under Reconstruction (1865–1874)

Things were uncertain during the early years of Radical Reconstruction in Texas, with changes from Austin coming down every few months. Moreover, historian Randolph B. Campbell writes that there was "no effort to appeal to Tejanos as a voting bloc. They appear to have been left alone and excluded in political decision-making." The omission of Tejanos in the political life of Duval County was evident, starting with Provisional Texas Governor A. J. Hamilton's appointment of John Dix as chief justice for Nueces County on October 23, 1865. Governor Hamilton appointed those considered loyal to the Union and "willing to support presidential Reconstruction."[30]

An avowed unionist, the 70-year-old Dix had gone into exile after a grand jury indicted him and eight others in absentia for treason. In April 1865 Dix returned to the area after hostilities ended. His coming home may have convinced Governor Hamilton that he could trust Dix to conduct Washington's orders.[31] Dix called a commissioners court meeting at the governor's directives to reorganize the Nueces County government. Unfortunately, Dix's actions as chief justice did not appear favorable to Duval County–area residents. Under Presidential Reconstruction officials, Tejanos' political and civic participation in Nueces County's life deteriorated. The Nueces County Commissioners Court, following Dix's leadership, established five voting precincts; none were in Duval County. In addition, the district judge chose no Tejanos to serve on the grand jury.[32]

To jump-start local governments, on June 18, 1867, county officials launched a voter registration campaign to extend through January 1868. Nueces County registered 261 voters. Among the newly registered voters were 133 Americanos, with the majority being transplants from the North. Also appearing in the new voter list were 88 Tejanos and 48 Freedmen. The formerly enslaved individuals comprised 18 percent of the new voters but had only 8 percent of the population. Tejanos had 34 percent of the registered voters, which underrepresented the 90 percent of the residents.[33]

Edmund J. Davis, the future governor under Radical Reconstruction and seen as a friend by Tejano rancheros, concluded that a "number of Mexicans who are entitled to register failed to do so. As a result, they were universally lost during the war." Davis regretted authorities had omitted Tejanos from the electoral process, denying them "the opportunity to register." Davis believed anti-Tejano forces had spread rumors that the United States intended to make war against Mexico. In so doing the United States would draft Tejanos as soldiers. Chief Justice Dix shared Davis's views, pointing out that while Republicans had a clear majority, a small group of "rowdies and disaffected rebels" and a "trifling newspaper" had stymied Tejano registrations.[34]

In an election held February 10–14, 1868, Nueces County voters approved delegates to a constitutional convention by 119–1. They chose Davis as their convention delegate by a 114–5 vote. Seventy-six percent of the voters were Americanos, and twenty-four were Freedmen. No Tejanos voted.[35] In November 1869 voters cast ballots to ratify the proposed constitution and choose state officials. Guadalupe Cárdenas served as a voter registrar for Nueces County and signed up 280 voters. Fifty-seven percent of those registering were Americanos (seven percent from northern states or newcomers). One-hundred-thirty-eight, or twenty-eight percent, consisted of Tejanos, a considerable underrepresentation of potential voting strength. Seventy-six, or fifteen percent, came from the Freedmen ranks. Once again, Tejanos were underrepresented.[36]

In the race for governor, Republican Davis defeated A. J. Hamilton, a moderate Democrat, with Nueces County providing Davis with a 231–143 margin. However, in the county judge's race, the politically moderate Democrat Milas Polk defeated Dix 144–123. Norman G. Collins won a place on the police court, suggesting that voting occurred in San Diego since Collins was a San Diego merchant and landowner. Under the Texas Constitution of 1869, the county judge position no longer existed. A police court, consisting of five justices of the peace elected by district or precinct, replaced the chief justice and four county commissioners.[37]

In November 1869 the new Nueces County Police Court delineated five new justice precincts, including Precincts Three and Four in San Diego and Concepción, respectively. In May 1870 voters elected Collins as justice of the peace for San Diego. On July 4 the police court named Richard Schubert justice of the peace for Concepción. Two weeks later the police court appointed Charles Roach as constable for Precinct Three in San Diego and Rafael Salinas to the same post in Concepción. Aside from Salinas, the selection process denied Tejanos office.[38]

During Davis's tenure as governor, Tejanos' political involvement was modest, failing to appear in elective office and other important posts. Between 1868 and 1875, Tejanos served only on six grand juries out of sixteen panels. The same men usually participated: Rafael Salinas, for example, received appointments to three grand juries, and Cesario Falcón, Martín Hinojosa, Placido Benavides, and Rafael Gutiérrez served on two grand juries each. Guadalupe Cárdenas, Celestino Tovar, Calixto Gutiérrez, and Ysidro Benavides were others performing grand jury service.[39]

Tejanos, however, were active on several other political fronts as appointees to unelected boards. In 1870 officials named eight Tejanos to the board of prisons, including Eliseo Cantú, Mateo Fuentes, Inocencio Vásquez, Juan Martínez, Reyes Cavazos, Librado Chapa, José María Cadena, and Faustino Ramírez. Also, the Nueces County Police Court called Antonio María Palacios and Encarnación García Pérez to a jury of view, a body created by the Texas Legislature to determine the location and cost of new roads. Since Palacios was from Concepción and Pérez from San Diego, it is safe to assume that the route under consideration was in Duval County. Nueces County authorities also named Falcón and Cárdenas to the board of voter registrars. While these appointments may suggest a degree of Tejanos' participation in Nueces County's civil life, they represent only minimal activity.[40]

Election records from the early 1870s indicate a renewed political involvement of Tejanos in Duval County, which remained attached to Nueces County until 1876. However, the records are incomplete. In the October 1870 election, Collins defeated Frank C. Gravis for the Precinct Three justice of the peace slot 107–87. Even though Collins had previously held the position, officials removed the longtime resident from office for lack of qualifications to hold the post. Available records do not suggest the nature of the rejection. In a special election held to fill the vacancy in May 1871, James O. Luby, known as "the fighting Republican" of South Texas and a

Collins ally, defeated Richard Miller by twenty votes. Voters reelected Luby without opposition in 1873.[41]

Reconstruction in Texas ended in 1874 when Democrat Richard Coke assumed the position of governor in January after defeating Governor Edmund J. Davis in December 1873. In Nueces County Republican Davis, who had close ties to local Tejanos, was victorious by 313–199. Democrats in Nueces County, however, prevailed in all the national and state races while Republicans captured the presiding judge and district clerk's posts. Democrats, however, handily defeated Republicans in two police court contests, and the other two were uncontested. The only Tejano on the ballot was Rafael Salinas, who received only modest support in a losing race for Concepción justice of the peace.[42]

Under another change in state law, Nueces County redrew election precincts and expanded the voting places to seven. New voting boxes were Precincts Six and Seven in San Diego and Concepción, respectively. In the December 2, 1873, general election, voting in Precincts Six and Seven occurred for the first time. Voters cast ballots at Justice of the Peace Luby's office in San Diego, with Collins serving as the election judge. Still, San Diego voting officers did not report votes. In Precinct Seven, seventeen voters cast their ballots at the schoolhouse, where Charles Lege served as the election judge.[43]

While the public records suggest San Diego had no votes, Justice of the Peace Luby submitted claims seeking election officers' compensation. Luby certified payment vouchers tendered for election judges W. B. Lacy, George Hobbs, T. W. Johnson, P. B. Baldesweiler, and special policemen for the election of A. G. Allen and George Pettigrew. All were Americanos in an overwhelmingly Tejano precinct and were newcomers, with none appearing in the 1870 Census for San Diego. Luby also certified payment of $15 for Apolonio Vela, who conveyed the registration books from San Diego to Corpus Christi via Concepción.[44]

———————————————

At the end of Reconstruction, the area south of the Nueces River began looking to resume economic growth. However, the once-thriving ranching operations had suffered from inattention due to preoccupation with the war. In addition, a severe drought had aggravated the ranch economy, and banditry and Indian raids had intensified in the absence of law enforcement and military protection. Nevertheless, the return of peace led to a revival of the cattle- and sheep-raising industries, rejuvenating Tejano rancheros' prospects. In addition, political and civil life also began to make a resurgence.

Chapter 8

A New Social Order

The brush country could be a harsh and unforgiving place. Still, as more and more people moved into the area, it gradually changed with a more significant presence of human influences. Despite many challenges, old-time pioneers and newcomers joined hands to build a faith community, develop schools, improve transportation, and bring commerce to serve their needs.

All these elements were essential for the foundations of a vibrant social order; however, something was missing. Settlers soon started clubs to address the community's needs in many ways, from supporting their churches and enriching culture to providing entertainment, promoting athletic activities, and celebrating families. While these varied activities improve a community, they do not always come without tragedy. Progress and trials characterized life in an area still moving from society's margins to modernity.

During the Civil War and Reconstruction, new forces emerged that defined the county's character for the remainder of the nineteenth century. Newcomers, mostly Union supporters, began to view San Diego and other Duval County areas as prospective places to sink roots. Mexicanos, too, continued migrating into the region. The confluence of these elements sparked growth; the area around Rancho San Diego especially began to experience change. It resembled a town instead of a collection of dispersed ranch headquarters.[1]

San Diego, from Ranchos to Town

Through the years the Flores kin—including José María García Flores, Martiana Pérez de García, Juan Bautista Gonzales, Encarnación García Pérez, and others—settled in the vicinity of Rancho San Diego. By midcentury Trinidad Flores, daughter of Ventura and granddaughter of Julián Flores, the original grantees of San Diego, had established a ranch downstream on the San Diego Creek's north bank, christening it San Remigio. Along with settlers on the south side of San Diego Creek on the San Leandro Rancho, the vicinity's population began to grow.

In March 1853 the first concerted effort to develop a town occurred on the south side of the San Diego Creek. The heirs of Rafael García Salinas, who had assumed ownership of San Leandro and the owners of the adjacent La Vaca grant,[2] sold two square leagues of land to Henry Stadler and Henry Mecklenburger. The sale included trappings and animal stock belonging to the García Salinas heirs. Two years later, on March 26, 1855, Stadler and Mecklenburger agreed that by September 1, 1856, they would perfect the title to the San Leandro and La Vaca grants and incur the cost. Additionally, they contracted to pay all expenses in settling twenty families, giving each family one field of no more than ten acres and a town lot. The two empresarios also agreed to clean the Rancho San Leandro's well and improve the water supply, including deepening the San Diego Creek.[3]

According to J. Williamson Moses, who wrote the earliest history of San Diego, Mecklenburger came to the area and pitched a tent on the south side of the San Diego Creek as his headquarters. He brought Mexican laborers from Starr County and two mayordomos to deepen the creek and build a dam to provide a permanent water supply. The developer then returned to Roma to tend to other businesses, where he died of yellow fever and therefore never came back to establish the town.[4]

At about the same time, William "Peg Leg" Stewart moved to San Diego's vicinity and opened a trading house, or store.[5] The store's primary customers were mustangers and hunters who did a thriving business rounding up wild cattle or killing deer, antelope, and javelinas roaming wild on the mesquite and chaparral along the banks of the San Diego, Tarancahua, and Lagarto Creeks. Stewart also traded hides and pelts for food, clothes, and ammunition. Unfortunately, despite his efforts, Stewart did not succeed at his new enterprise and soon moved his operation to Fort Ewell in La Salle County.[6]

In October 1860 John Levy announced to the Corpus Christi newspaper the *Ranchero* that he had plans to open a store in Rancho San Diego. Levy was not a stranger to town since he had bought two tracts from the San Leandro and La Vaca grants a year before. His 22-year-old daughter was the widow of Henry Mecklenburger, who had committed to developing a community on the San Leandro grant. Sara Mecklenburger inherited her husband's half of the two tracts of land he bought from the García heirs. Then the young widow purchased Stadler's half from his heirs in New York, turned around, and sold the entire tract to her father. True to the spirit of one of the land sales conditions Mecklenburger had with the García heirs, Levy became the plaintiff in the lawsuit that ratified the land's original owner. However, Levy did not fulfill the original owners' requirement that Mecklenburger sign up settlers. Levy soon left San Diego and sold the land to Richard King and Mifflin Kenedy.[7]

With the failure of the two stores, Moses observed that San Diego remained nothing more than a cow and horse town. It remained such until the end of the American Civil War. Before Rancho San Diego could become a city, large landowners had to make parts of their holdings more readily available to the general public. This process involved subdividing land tracts into smaller parcels such as blocks and lots.

On August 21, 1869, the heirs of Julián and Ventura Flores authorized Encarnación García Pérez to establish a town. The lands in play were part of the old San Diego de Arriba and San Diego de Abajo grants. The heirs chose a familiar ally, Corpus Christi attorney Charles Lovenskiold, to advise García Pérez. Signing the document were Antonio García Flores, Juan D. Garza, María Flores González, G. Flores, Santos Flores, Rafael García Flores, Pablo Pérez, Trinidad Flores de Pérez, José María G. Flores, Eduardo G. Flores, and E. García Pérez.[8]

Fig. 8.1 Encarnación García Pérez (1835–1921), patriarch of the prominent García family. Courtesy of Eliseo Cadena.

Six years later, on June 16, 1875, the Nueces County District Court appointed Encarnación García Pérez and Norman Collins as trustees for all land held by heirs of Julian and Ventura Flores, including the town tract of San Diego. They had the property platted and subdivided into blocks and lots and designated two blocks as plazas. Soon Pérez and Collins offered lots for sale in the emerging town. They assured buyers to provide "full and perfect titles." This series of actions set in motion the building of Duval County's future seat of government.[9]

New Missionary Field

The Roman Catholic Church was the first faith community to break ground in Duval County, and in time a couple of Protestant Christian denominations took root. While faithful Jews came to and lived in Duval County, they were not enough to establish a synagogue. However, it was common for all residents to attend each other's church festivals, regardless of religious preferences.[10]

While Tejanos learned aspects of the Catholic faith from childhood, they could not practice it in their isolated ranchos without a priest to provide leadership and direction. Of course, this did not mean Tejanos were utterly ignorant of their Catholic faith. Still, in the absence of priests, Tejana *parteras* (midwives) baptized stillborn babies and those at risk of death. In addition, common-law marriages were prevalent due to the lack of clergy.[11]

During the Spanish and Mexican eras, the seat of the Catholic diocese was in Linares. Parroquia de la Inmaculada Concepción in Mier and Nuestra Señora de Santa Anna at Camargo were the nearest parishes to San Diego. A Franciscan missionary priest from the Villas del Norte may have visited the ranchos around San Diego during the Spanish and Mexican eras, but this would have been infrequent, if at all. Parish priests in northern Mexico were not inclined to go far beyond their small communities.[12]

After Texas became an independent republic, Rome established a church in Texas and raised the vicariate at Galveston in 1840. Seven years later, in 1848, after Texas joined the United States, Pius IX elevated Galveston to the status of a diocese. However, it was not until shortly after that, in the 1850s, that priests of the Missionary Oblates of Mary Immaculate—namely, the Oblates—began to venture into Duval County.[13]

The Oblates began sporadically ministering the sacraments and other devotions to brush country's faithful. Father L. M. Planchet, a diocesan priest at Roma, was the first priest to visit Duval. On December 8, 1858,

Father Planchet witnessed the marriage of Quirino González, widower of the late Francisca Sáenz, with Dorotea Ramírez, legitimate daughter of Antonio Ramírez and Magdalena Garza at Concepción. Isidro García and Jacinta Escobar served as witnesses. The priest recorded the marriage at the Catholic parish in Roma.[14]

In 1864 another diocesan priest from Roma, named Father Antoine Boiras, visited San Diego during the Civil War. Father Boiras, a Frenchman, served throughout South Texas, often at significant risk. Sacramental records show Father Boiras witnessed two marriages in San Diego on November 9, 1864. In the first ceremony, Julián Ureste, son of Guadalupe Ureste and Francisca García, married San Juanita García, daughter of José María García and Martiana Pérez. Francisco García and Juanita Salinas served as *padrinos* (godfathers). In the second wedding, the priest witnessed the sacred sacrament of marriage between Juan Vásquez, a widower, and Guillerma Hernández, the daughter of Paulo Hernández and Mónica Favela. The godparents were Divorció Ramírez and Gertrudis Barrera.[15]

The priest remained in the home of José María García in San Diego for several months. Most likely he also celebrated Mass, which may have been the first in Duval County. Then, on February 16, 1865, at Rancho de los Ramírez, Father Boiras assisted in marrying 39-year-old Apolinario Gonzales, also a widower, to Segunda Mesa, the 14-year-old legitimate daughter of Rafael Mesa and the late Rosa Palacios. The witnesses were Policarpo and Margarita Palacios. Ten days later, on February 26, 1865, at El Rancho de Concepción, the priest witnessed the marriage of Camargo native Ignacio Gonzales, a 37-year-old widower, to Naboría Palacios, 23-year-old daughter of Antonio María Palacios and Refugia Sáenz. The godparents were José María Martínez and Julia Gonzales.[16]

As the smoke was still clearing from the Civil War, a young French priest named Claude Jaillet arrived in San Diego less than a month after landing at Galveston. Father Jaillet, who spoke neither English nor Spanish, reached the small but growing pueblo in early November 1866, entering on horseback with a borrowed missal and a "stolen chalice." A robust norte was blowing, and the priest needed shelter when three Tejanos gave him directions to the home of José María García. The French priest understood them because the Spanish had an affinity for Italian and Latin. Moreover, the priest knew

Fig. 8.2 First Catholic chapel in San Diego. Courtesy of the Mary and Jeff Bell Library Special Collections and Archives, Texas A&M University–Corpus Christi.

García had lodged Father Boiras a few years earlier and expected he would be welcoming. Unsurprisingly, upon realizing Jaillet was a clergyman, García opened the family's home to the priest.[17]

Father Jaillet quickly set off on a goal to build a church. After asking the low-income residents of San Diego for donations and hitting them up twice, the priest raised four hundred dollars but had to contribute three hundred of his own money to build a small chapel that doubled as his home. The Diocese of Galveston dedicated the new sanctuary as a mission church on January 25, 1867. Two weeks after the church's completion, Father Jaillet received word that Bishop Claude Marie Dubuis planned to come down from Galveston to administer the Sacrament of Confirmation. During the visit to the new chapel, the bishop confirmed seventy-nine adults and children.[18]

The arrival of the Catholic Church was one of the first marks of progress for the small community of San Diego. Residents had seen two general stores open and close but had no bank, department stores, school, or city hall—nothing. But now they had a place to celebrate Mass, be baptized, receive communion, get married, and have a priest pray over their departed loved ones. The church undoubtedly became a cornerstone for encouraging community development.[19]

On Christmas almost all of the population of San Diego turned out for Midnight Mass or the *Misa de Gallo*. Due to the enthusiastic attendance, some had to stand outside the chapel. After Mass parishioners enjoyed eggnog and the lighting of firecrackers, including rockets and Roman candles.[20]

The Catholic Church was not the only faith community to come to the new town. In 1874 the M. E. Church South established a mission in San Diego, part of its "Mexican District." Also, by 1877 a Methodist congregation was present in San Diego with Reverend Felipe Córdova in charge. In that year Córdova baptized a young Mexican expatriate named Vicente Hernández. After receiving seminary training in Monterey, Hernández returned to San Diego, where he served as pastor for over fifty years. In 1884, under Hernandez's leadership, the Mexican Methodist congregation in San Diego grew and built a church. Two months later the Reverend A. H. Sutherland came to San Diego to dedicate the house of worship.[21]

A Baptist community might have been present in San Diego by April 16, 1888. According to a newspaper account, "Baptist minister White from Corpus Christi preached to good crowds at Protestant Church."[22]

Early Business Establishments

In 1866, six years after the last attempt to open a store in San Diego, Norman G. Collins followed Levy's steps and relocated to the town from Banquete to establish a retail merchandise store. But unlike Levy, who moved away shortly after arriving, Collins began accumulating land in Duval County and the area extending west and south of Corpus Christi. In time Collins became involved in every significant economic and political matter in Duval County. Soon after, James O. Luby, a would-be entrepreneur who also played a chief role in the county's history, came to San Diego. A native of England, Luby came to town to work as a clerk at the Collins store alongside Manuel Ancira and Charles Hoffman. In 1871, after a failed attempt at operating a store at

Fort Ewell, Luby returned to San Diego and was elected justice of the peace for Nueces County, the equivalent of a county commissioner at that time, launching a distinguished political career.[23]

Ten Americanos resided in San Diego at the decade's end, out of a total population of 784 inhabitants. Collins and spouse Anne Hoffman of Austria, Anne's brother Charles, and 10-year-old Fred Ridder lived in the Collinses' San Diego home. Two other merchants also ventured into retail enterprises in San Diego: E. A. Glover and Charles Roach. The two businessmen lived in the same household with Roach's Mexican wife Concepción and their four children. A store clerk, Robert Berry, also resided with the group. Tejanos Encarnación García Pérez and Manuel Ancira also operated retail establishments in San Diego.[24]

Doctors, Lawyers, and other Professionals

A class of skilled and professional workers also came to the county. Four were practicing law in San Diego, four were doctors, and three were pharmacologists. In addition, two surveyors and two stockbrokers constituted part of Duval County's nascent gentry class. All but one doctor and a pharmacist were Americanos. Another individual who appeared on the 1870 Census but spent little time in the county was Father Adolfo Guichen, who replaced Father Jaillet. The new priest arrived in 1869 but moved to another parish in 1871.[25]

Yet another Americano immigrant in San Diego was George B. Warden, who became the town's first postmaster on July 8, 1867. Luby replaced Warden as postmaster shortly after. Then, on February 6, 1873, the federal government established a second post office at Concepción and named Rafael F. Salinas its first postmaster. Six years later, on May 19, 1879, two more post offices debuted in Duval County: in Borjas Creek with Edward Harvey Caldwell as a postmaster and at Piedras Pintas with Jacob William Toklas as the head. Later that year, on November 24, Fabián Fabela took over the new postal station at Mendieta.[26]

Historian Omar Valerio-Jiménez observed, "Identity formation is a dynamic process subject to multiple interconnecting influences." Such influences affected Tejanos in Duval County, who increasingly interacted with Americanos. Since the area had become part of the United States, Tejanos had employed Americano surveyors and attorneys and, in efforts to prove land ownership, had become familiar with Americano judges. As the presence of Americanos increased, the Tejano identity underwent a perceptible transformation, as is expected whenever two different group identities occupy the same space. Conversely, the Americano identity in South Texas also changed from their contact with Spanish-speaking Catholic Tejanos with unique customs.[27]

Continued Growth

The hub of Duval County society was the budding village of San Diego. In 1875 the town had a population of 1,500. It was thriving economically with some eight to ten stores. Wool warehouses had exported six hundred thousand pounds of wool and two thousand hides. In addition, local retailers and ranch operators had imported two million pounds of merchandise. By the end of 1875, the town expected to do twice as much business. The only other community of any consequence during this period was Concepción. Along with San Diego, Concepción served in the county's early development as one of two voting precincts.[28]

The Mexicano community in Duval County continued its rapid increase after Reconstruction. Continued troubles in Mexico, including the French Intervention in Mexico (1862–1867), accounted for the population jump. However, Duval County and other South Texas counties offered an attractive opportunity for Mexicanos. Most newly arriving immigrants were from rural areas; they were poor people from the countryside, most likely *manos de obra* (manual laborers). Furthermore, they could take advantage of a path to naturalization, at least until the mid-1870s.

Tejanos had first received American citizenship under the Treaty of Guadalupe Hidalgo, which ended the Mexican American War in 1848. The United States and Mexico reaffirmed this right to citizenship with the Naturalization Treaty of 1868. During Reconstruction, Republican state district judges readily honored Mexicanos' naturalization applications.

In 1874, however, the newly elected Democratic Governor Richard Coke replaced all the Republican Reconstruction judges, save one in Robertson County. The new Democratic appointees effectively stopped the approval of naturalization claims.[29]

Also, Tejanos from other parts of Texas found Duval County a welcoming place. With their coming the Tejano population, as enumerated in the 1880 Census, swelled from 41 to 1,948. The Americano population, which started at a meager 37 residents in 1870, increased to 567 in 1880. The source of Americano immigration was quite diverse. Most came from the northern American states and Europe; a few were Southerners.

In 1878, responding to frequent Indian attacks, the federal government sent E Company of the 8th US Cavalry to operate a military post in San Diego, which quartered one hundred temporary residents. In addition to the Army camp in San Diego, there was a Ranger camp of nine men, including eight rangers and a teamster. All were Americanos except for 22-year-old Tejano Paulino Coy and freedman Jack Robertson. Subtracting those transient residents in the army and Ranger camps, the Americano population was 458. Also, the census listed twenty-four formerly enslaved people, or freedmen.[30]

Many newcomers were agricultural workers from Mexico, the United States, or Europe. Duval County, after all, lived off animal husbandry. While horses and cattle were the heart of the local economy before the Civil War, sheepherding became vital to the area's livelihood in the 1870s. Mexicanos who immigrated during that time, the Tejanos already in Duval County, and the arriving Americanos were all familiar with the sheepherding trade. All three groups contributed to the expansion of the industry.

Not surprisingly, leading workers in Duval County as of 1880 were stock raisers, farmers, shepherds, vaqueros, and herders. Some 473 men, including 115 Tejanos, worked as stock raisers and farmers. But, again, Mexicanos dominated this part of the economy.

Working-class jobs also opened up, including in the building trades. For example, in 1880 fifteen stonemasons, four painters, twelve blacksmiths, six silversmiths, and three tinners made their way to Duval County. Other trades that came to Duval County cared for stockmen's needs, including two livery stable operators and six saddlers.

Table 8.1 Agriculture producers in Duval County, 1880

	Mexicanos	*Tejanos*	*Americanos*	*Total*
Stock Raisers	85	96	13	194
Farmers	249	19	11	279
Vaqueros	99	26	2	127
Shepherds	180	44	2	226
Herders	2	0	4	6
Total	**615**	**185**	**32**	**832**

Source: 1880 Census, Duval County.

Note: While the 1880 Census count is from after Reconstruction, it includes those who came to the area during the 1870s.

Several men were employed in transportation, hauling goods and supplies as teamsters, cartmen, dray haulers, waggoners, and freighters. In addition, San Diego was the center of mail distribution routes and a wheel spoke for stagecoaches coming and going to various points. Despite the arrival of the railroad, stagecoaches remained a viable alternative for many, especially those traveling to and from San Antonio and the Rio Grande Valley. Five stagecoach drivers lived in San Diego.[31]

Fourteen county residents made their living as cooks; some served in that capacity at businesses and the rest in households. Sixteen residents conducted what appeared to be a brisk bar or saloon business, including eight bartenders, one a Mexicana. In addition, six individuals worked as draymen, closely tied to the saloon establishments, delivering beer from the breweries.

San Diego's most impressive commercial increase in 1880 was in the retail sector and involved dry goods retailers, grocery stores, bakeries, and meat markets. Retail clerks comprised a visible part of the workforce in these stores, numbering about thirty-seven.

The increase in population engendered other trades related to agricultural fields and the service sector. For example, stores needed processed meat products, so the demand for butchers grew. As a result, eight butchers worked in Duval County. Bakers likewise provided a needed service to the community, and seven individuals operated combination bakery and grocery store businesses. Also, there were two bread vendors.

Fig. 8.3 Duval County's first school. Courtesy of the Mary and Jeff Bell Library Special Collections and Archives, Texas A&M University–Corpus Christi.

The retail business included three printers, five shoemakers, two tailors, a hatter, and three barbers. Nine individuals were musicians. The 1880 Census also listed a few females in the labor pool; most helped support their families from home. Eight were seamstresses, and twenty were laundry workers.

Schools and Education

In addition, Tejano and Americano citizens prioritized education and opened the first school in the county as the end of Reconstruction approached. As of 1873 the San Diego school had one teacher and "as many aides as were needed." At Rancho Piedras Pintas, Tejanos Juan Sáenz donated land on his ranch to Duval County for use as a public school. The *Second Biannual Report of the State Board of Education, 1879–1880*, indicated that 653 schoolchildren between ages 8 and 14 attended the county's schools in six communities. The Board of Education's report also indicated that 498 children were not attending school.[32]

According to the 1880 Census, six of the nine teachers in Duval County were immigrants; the other three were Americano educators. On the other hand, the Board of Education report identified only six teachers working in Duval County in 1880, four males and two females. The discrepancy in the census numbers may be because several Mexicanos operated private schools in the county. The state would not have included these *escuelitas* (little or community schools) in its official record. Clearly, by the end of Reconstruction, Duval County provided children with an education, and students took advantage of this opportunity.[33]

Communication in Rural Country

Newspapers are one of the most valuable mediums to develop and promote a community's growth and character. In addition, newspapers provide historians with an essential tool for charting and documenting a place's early development. Duval County eventually founded its broadsheets, but in its early years, Corpus Christi, Laredo, and San Antonio papers were the primary news providers of the county. Indeed, news organs from throughout the state took great interest in Duval County's development.

The *Corpus Christi Gazette* was one of the earliest newspapers to cover the Duval County communities. It began covering the area in January 1846 and continued coverage until 1881. The *Corpus Christi Star* briefly appeared in 1848–1849 and was, perhaps, the area's only genuinely bilingual newspaper. The *Ranchero* reported news from the vicinity between 1857 and 1862. Two other newspapers were the *Nueces Valley* (1870) and the *Corpus Christi Advertiser* (1876).

Besides the Corpus Christi newspapers, the *Laredo Daily Times*, the *San Antonio Daily Express*, and the *San Antonio Light* were also attentive to San Diego and Duval County life. In addition, San Antonio's Catholic journal, the *Southern Messenger*, frequently commented on Catholic church activities.

Duval County had several early newspapers. Unfortunately, only a few issues are available in regional archives or personal collections. Appearing circa 1871, *La Voz de Duval*, owned by Francisco Gonzales, was perhaps the earliest known newspaper published in Duval County. In 1880 the *San Diego Tribune* began publication in the county seat. That same year, Salvador J. De la Vega of Duval County initiated editing *El Progreso*. Unfortunately, no issues in these newspapers are known to exist. In 1882 the *Bell Punch*, dedicated to woolgrowers, started printing in San Diego every Monday. *El Sordo, Periódico Jocoserio, Político y Aclamador y Paradas*, printed by Francisco Martínez in 1889, was a later entry into the Duval County news business. That same year, F. de P. González published *El Eco Liberal, Periódico Independiente, Orden y Progreso*.[34] W. L. Johnston circulated the *San Diego Sun* from 1891 to 1897.[35]

The use of correspondents was a common practice during this time. The earliest local reporter was Sesom, who wrote for the *San Antonio Express*, *The Galveston Daily News*, and the *Corpus Christi Caller*. Sesom was J. Williamson Moses's last name spelled backward. Moses was a political leader in the county. The *Caller*'s founder, Eli Merriman, covered the Duval County beat using only his initials, E. T. M. Another reporter, whom the readers of the *Corpus Christi Caller* knew as Jeffreys, was Dr. William C. Jefferies, San Diego's first physician. "General" succeeded Jeffries in 1888. The name of the General, who probably was not a military man, is unknown. "K. L." was Kate Luby, an occasional reporter who covered church and community events. Anonymous were Twinkle, Johnson, Lookeron, Athos, and others who briefly wrote for the *Caller*.[36]

This cadre of news gatherers and outlets, and others from throughout the state, is the source of much of what we know of the daily lives of the people who called Duval County home in the nineteenth century. Through this medium, the isolated communities accessed the outside world. Print journalism also provided an outlet for advertising for Duval County merchants, land lawyers, surveyors, and landowners.

People moving into Duval County also needed means to communicate with the outside world. The primary way for this was via the American postal service, as erratic as it may have been in the years of the frontier. In addition, Americanos from established states were familiar with well-developed communication networks, including the telegraph and, to some degree, the newly invented telephone services. These messaging amenities were critical for those engaged in business and set out to ensure Duval County had such conveniences.

Until 1867, when the county's first post office opened in San Diego, the Banquete post office delivered mail to Duval area communities. Also, telegraph lines were most likely strung in 1879 when the train arrived in San Diego.

Then, in March 1883, San Diego postmaster James Luby introduced the telephone. Luby hung wire from the post office to his law practice. "The judge," a newspaper reported, "finds it a great convenience at no expense."[37]

Civic Clubs

Among the organizations contributing to Duval County were social clubs. While most clubs were primarily open to men, they enhanced the general community's yearning for activities outside of business and work. In addition, these organizations' social contact distracted the community from the constant threats from Indians, bandits, and the harsh natural environment. Finally, social clubs provided communitywide opportunities for philanthropic activities.

These various associations included a civic group akin to today's Rotary Club, which met and invited speakers to address its members. In November 1887 Paul Henry was fixing up space over his store for the T. H. M. Club, which the leading citizens of San Diego organized with twenty charter members. Former County Judge James O. Luby served as president, businessman W. B. Croft as vice president, and County Clerk R. B. Glover as secretary-treasurer. The newspaper correspondent Jeffreys confessed not being familiar with the acronym T. H. M. but mockingly offered the moniker "The High Muchamucks" Club. But unfortunately, the newspaper never disclosed the real meaning or purpose of the group. However, the T. H. M. Club did not seem active for long.[38]

In addition, there were several fraternal organizations, including the Knights of Honor, Knights of Pythias, and Woodmen of the World. Membership in the Knights of Honor was open to "acceptable white men of good moral character, who believed in God, were of good bodily health and able to support themselves and their family." The Order of Knights of Pythias is an "international, non-sectarian fraternal order and was the first fraternal order to be chartered by an Act of Congress" at the suggestion of President Abraham Lincoln. The purpose of the Woodmen of the World, founded in 1890, was "to minister to the afflicted to relieve distress; to cast a sheltering arm about the defenseless living [and] to encourage broad charitable views." However, these organizations did not come to Duval County until the late nineteenth century, and little information is available on their activities or membership. In addition, the Tejano community organized the Club Sociedad Mutualista, Hijos de Hidalgo, which had seventy members, with José Elizondo serving as president and Loreto Arguijo as secretary. The *Corpus Christi Caller* credited the club, organized in June 1898, with improving the lives of "our Mexican population."[39]

Sporting Associations

Also, a very active gun club appeared in San Diego. Besides practice shooting, in 1884 the club served at the execution of Refugio Gómez. Between midnight and one o'clock, the Gun Club marched into the jail yard, presumably carrying out guard duty, and positioned itself around the scaffold. Officials hanged Gómez for the murder of Estefan Dimas.[40]

In 1887 the group turned its attention to civic activities, regularly participating in shooting contests. Their first competition was against the San Antonio Gun Club in Corpus Christi on the Fourth of July. After holding several matches, the Gun Club resumed involvement in other community events.[41]

The Gun Club closed an active 1887 tournament on the Monday after Christmas, considering the competition important enough to ask merchants to close down their establishments for that day. The club revealed plans to buy or lease new grounds the following March. Some two weeks following the acquisition of the necessary space, several citizens had already contributed to an effort by the Gun Club to hold shooting matches during the upcoming Cinco de Mayo fiesta. Contributors included F. K. Ridder, E. Martínez, Cayetano Ríos, R. H. Corbett, Antonio Rosales, Mrs. Martinet, Charles Hoffman, W. B. Croft, Paul Henry, J. O. Luby, John Buckley, Peña & Miret, F. Gueydan & Company, and N. G. Collins. As with political involvement, the Gun Club effectively restricted Tejanos from membership, even as they willingly made financial contributions, as they did in politics.[42]

The Trans-Nueces, and particularly Duval County, communities enthusiastically received America's sport of baseball. In the summer of 1887, San Diego organized a baseball team, with Tejanos getting a slight edge in the starting lineup. San Diego promptly challenged Corpus Christi to a game. Corpus Christi's Mysterious squad came to town in September to accept the Uniques' challenge. The inaugural match was played near the Tex-Mex Depot under a cool norther with a threatening cloud occasionally passing overhead. Fans came to see their San Diego team "dressed in elegant suits of dark blue with red stockings and large U on its breast."[43]

The first pitch came shortly after noon. The Uniques team roster included Avelino G. Tovar, pitcher; Darío García, catcher; Arturo García, first base; Loreto Tovar, second base; Felipe Bodet, third base; Thomas Collins, shortstop; Fidel Pérez, left field; J. F. Gravis, center field; and C. K. Gravis, right field. J. Niland served as the umpire, and M. Wolfram kept score. The game ended after seven innings, so the Corpus Christi team would not miss the train. San Diego won its opener 36–10, and manager Frank Feuille boasted that the San Diego boys only warmed up.[44] Catcher García bragged the team "can't be beaten." Tovar got in "twisters" (curve balls) nicely. The contest was close through the fifth inning when San Diego's top of the lineup came to the plate. With two Uniques on base, Pérez powered out a hit "far enough to make a home run." Then Collins split his bat but got a double.[45]

Baseball gained so much popularity that by April 26, 1888, the *Caller* reported San Diego had two baseball teams, the Uniques and the Stars. In the maiden game between the teams, the Uniques prevailed 20–5. Soon, baseball fever spread to the county's rural communities. In April 1889 San Diego boys defeated Espada de Mendieta, a team from the community of Mendieta in northeastern Duval County, 8–6. Then, at the end of April, Concepción and Realitos squared off on the diamond at Concepción, with the Realitos nine taking a very competitive game, 27–25.[46]

In what may have been the first "little league" in San Diego in July 1888, the community organized two boys' baseball teams, the Browns and Mariners. The baseball craze continued to gain momentum, with a couple of "pick-up-nine" squads taking shape. In May 1889 the San Diego baseball club lost 18–3 to a pick-up-nine, giving the excuse for their defeat that players "were tired from the baile." The national pastime was a hit in the brush country.[47]

In 1883 some locals organized a bicycle club in San Diego. However, it does not appear it had much of a future in a country favoring horses, wagons, and a newly arrived railroad.[48]

The Performing Arts

The performing arts were common in Duval County's hinterland; from thespian troops to musical artists to dance lovers, the frontier people's creative genes flowed freely and fully. As early as 1883, theater groups were entertaining crowds in San Diego. In April 1883 the county courthouse was undergoing a temporary metamorphosis. Workers were transforming it from a seat of government to an improvised theater. Also, an amateur thespian group of thirty-one actors was to perform at a church benefit. The San Diego theatrical group staged "The Poor of Mexico," with Señor Salvador de la Vega and his daughter in the lead roles. Later, they gave an encore performance to a smaller crowd. In November 1884 the Monterrey orchestra returning to Mexico from Corpus Christi stopped in San Diego and entertained the locals.[49]

Annual Fiestas

One can hardly imagine Duval County without fiestas. In the 1880s people began hearing the first mention of community festivals. The town generally tied fiestas to patriotic occasions, such as the Fourth of July, Cinco de Mayo, and Diez y Seis de Septiembre. The faith community also observed church feast days. And, of course, these events would not be celebrated without plenty of music and dance.

Although festivities did not always involve dance and music, they were often about fun, frontier style. The first mention of a fiesta in San Diego was on May 13, 1883. The annual festival ran for a few days, and it is safe to assume that this event was the Cinco de Mayo observance. Unfortunately, as sometimes happens at these kinds of festivities, violence occasionally erupted. For example, during the good cheer, two petty burglars from Laredo quarreled, resulting in Refugio Gómez murdering Estefan Dimas.[50]

On the day following Dimas's death, information came to light about the fatal shooting of H. Maas the previous night at Benavides. Some two weeks before the shooting, Hilario Vela, while drunk, allegedly became abusive in the Tokias & Maas store, and Maas demanded Vela leave. Subsequently, Vela met Maas on the fiesta grounds, and the two exchanged hostile remarks. Vela supposedly threatened to kill Maas, but Maas believed he was not in danger. While Maas visited with friends on the fiesta grounds, Vela reportedly placed his pistol against Maas, fired, and escaped. Maas had achieved considerable wealth, and family and friends had him interred in the Corpus Christi Jewish Cemetery.[51]

Americanos and Mexicanos failed to observe their patriotic national holidays for several years during the 1880s. Then, in July 1885, Duval County residents must have felt a tinge of regret for their lack of patriotism. They celebrated the Fourth extravagantly by closing shops, having a glass ball shooting match, and cutting a watermelon.[52]

The following February locals celebrated Washington's Birthday with a big fandango attended by more than five hundred prestigious San Diego residents. Kate Luby, who sent the newspaper an account of the happening, wrote that it was the "most brilliant ball ever witnessed in this county." The San Diego Gun Club, the event's sponsor, did not spare the cost. Luby said that the Gun Club decorated the courthouse, which served as the setting, with mottoes, flowers, and evergreen arrangements. Crossed guns appeared under the wreaths, and American flags with the names of every Gun Club member draped each window. A band performed "soul-stirring" music, and a bounteous supper was served, including cakes, sandwiches, delicacies, and tea or coffee. The community's hoity-toity portrayed historical characters and wore attire appropriate for their parts.[53]

Five months after Washington's Birthday, the community celebrated July Fourth at the main plaza in San Diego with plenty of music, dancing, gambling, cooking, eating, and drinking. Townspeople raised enough funds to enclose and beautify the public square to hold livelier fiestas. Later that year, at Peña Station, Romulo Peña Sr. and several youngsters gave orations during the Diez y Seis de Septiembre celebration. At night, the "city band" played at the public square.[54]

While the Cinco de Mayo celebrations had fallen by the wayside, Benavides's Fourth of July observance saw a small turnout. The only excitement came when the excursion train ran over a cow and "cut off the tail of one of Mrs. Villareal's pigs to the delight of the boys." That was not the case in San Diego, where the Gun Club again assembled a brilliant display, decorating the grounds with American and Texas flags. In addition, Mr. Tibilier raised an Irish flag. A Mexican flag also prompted one observer to note that "no American could be more enthusiastic than were the Mexicans."[55]

In 1888 Don Nasario Peña was in charge of the San Diego Cinco de Mayo celebration, which ran for ten days, from May 5 to 15. The festival opened to a drumbeat, tooting horns, and cannonball fire. Events took place at Long Hall. Organizers decorated the hall with pictures of Mexican patriots General Ignacio Zaragoza, the victor at Puebla on May 5, 1862, President Benito Juárez, and Miguel Hidalgo y Costilla, leader of Mexican Independence from Spain. Event organizers also paid tribute to American President George Washington. Students from the academy, owned by Professor Luis Pueblo, played music and presented speeches and essays. The afternoon program at the plaza grounds consisted of declamations, including an address by Corpus Christi newspaper editor Catarino Garza. Residents went about town with cries of "*Viva Mexico*" and "*Vivan los Mexicanos*." Frenchmen— Mexico's enemies during the conflict of 1862—were figuratively killed all over San Diego, and the opening day continued through the evening, ending with a grand ball.[56]

The ten-day event included Gun Club marches and baseball matches between San Diego, Corpus Christi, and others. Also, participants took part in horse, wheelbarrow, and sack races. A band and a theatrical troupe from Monterrey gave nightly concerts. Attendees enjoyed beer courtesy of the Lone Star Brewery of San Antonio, which donated beer casks for the three days of the Gun Club tourney.[57]

Over in Benavides, the 1888 Cinco de Mayo opened with a twenty-one-gun salute. Fiesta officials raised the US and Mexican flags in the plaza center, with martial music playing and the multitude shouting. The crowds heard a speech about the heroism and courage of Mexican troops.

Mounted on a black horse, the parade's grand marshal led the procession; the Benavides silver cornet band, the community's leaders, and the Benavides Rifle Club followed the procession's honorary leader. Others in the festive line included a uniformed color guard, two benevolent associations, Mexican Army veterans, the Piedras Pintas brass band, and citizens in carriages and on foot. The columns moved along principal streets; all businesses and residences displayed flowers, laurels, and bunting. Finally, the parade stopped at the plaza. A magnificent repast, served upon long tables, included venison, ham, turkey, beef, mutton, and many other entrees, and wine flowed freely. Dance halls were open to the public and guests enjoyed many dances until morning.[58]

As the Cinco de Mayo celebration wound down in San Diego on May 14, the town's children, under the direction of Kate Luby, held a ball to benefit the impoverished Irish tenants evicted due to the Land War in Ireland. "The whole world sympathizes with these oppressed, including San Diego," Luby noted. George Bodet served as treasurer for the event, and Luis Puebla offered his spacious academy hall.[59]

As years passed, community members seemed to have bypassed traditional patriotic commemorations, such as the Fourth of July, Cinco de Mayo, and Diez y Seis de Septiembre, but continued celebrating life. For example, on January 1, 1889, the year started with the San Diego Social Club sponsoring a big New Year's Ball at the Garfield House. While bad weather kept many from attending, "boys went home with girls at 4 a.m."[60]

Indeed, the Duval County fiestas took a slight downturn in 1889; there were no reports on Cinco de Mayo activities or the Fourth of July. But on July 23 the San Diego community announced a fiesta scheduled for August. Perhaps the town's civic leaders planned the fiesta to coincide with the cotton-picking season when everybody had money burning a hole in their pockets. By August 26 farmers brought cotton to the gins, and the party at the plaza was in full bloom.[61]

In San Diego three crews had begun cutting weeds and high grass "growing at that cow pasture dignified by the name plaza." Workers also set up a *lotería* (lottery) stand, refreshment booths, and *carcamán* (chuckle-lock tables). If nothing else, correspondent Vigilanti opined, fiesta promoters got the eyesore of the plaza cleaned up.[62]

Festival activity was quiet for years, but on June 29, 1899, the townspeople of Realitos celebrated the feast day of San Juan Bautista. In blatant sacrilege disregard for the saint, many sordid characters overran the town, including gamblers, smugglers, illicit liquor dealers, and "soiled doves." Hoodlums brandishing .45 Colts to .22 Winchesters made the nights dangerous. In the meantime, the operators of "chuck-luck" lotteries, Monte tables, and other games of chance sanctioned all kinds of misconduct.[63]

A week later, on July 7, 1899, large crowds gathered at one of San Diego's plazas to celebrate the Fourth. Judge Luby donated ammo for a twelve-pound cannon burst. After the train delivered the ammunition, Pedro Cruz, who was in charge of the field gun, fired a twenty-one-gun salute, and the band began to play. A. D. Smith made a short address, and T. E. Noonan from Alice gave "one of his characteristic speeches, logical and eloquent."[64]

On September 22 Benavides commemorated the eighty-ninth anniversary of the Diez y Seis de Septiembre. Numerous residents and merchants from neighboring ranchos and towns participated in the celebration. In addition, the Club Sociedad Mutualista, Hijos de Hidalgo, hosted indoor entertainment. Photographs of Miguel Hidalgo, George Washington, and US and Mexico flags decorated the hall. Outside, wreaths of flowers and evergreens adorned the entrance banisters, as did red and white, green and red, and blue ribbons. The mutualista members and their families enjoyed a free dance at the hall. [65]

After the Civil War, residents of Duval County, both the longtime Mexicanos and Tejanos and the newly arrived Americanos, proceeded with great zeal to ensure their communities kept pace with the rest of the United States. Peace, self-rule, and economic growth made it time to promote a more cultured society.

During the last decades of the nineteenth century, Duval County achieved that level of progress by providing new and growing faith communities to satisfy the soul, social events to fill hearts with joy, and athletic activities to invigorate the body. Duval County was keeping pace with the country's rush to modernity.

Chapter 9

Growing Pains

While Tejanos in Duval County were progressing, they could not let their guard down for the Americanos who had chosen to live among them early on and had adjusted to a Mexicano environment that posed a political and economic challenge. Thus, the desire of Tejanos in the Trans-Nueces to gain full equality and respect occurred amid greed, prejudice, distrust, and suspicion. To be sure, among the newly arriving Americanos, some held no malice and wished to live a Christian life among their new neighbors.

Duval County Tejanos wanted to be part of their new American home, politically and economically. They were fully aware of and closely tied to their ancestral Mexican past. Still, they did not entertain the yearning to return to Mexico or incite insurrection against the United States. The American democratic governmental system afforded them the opportunity for political freedom and economic growth, while Mexico's erratic rule offered neither. Still, growing pains accompanied the improvement of Duval County after Reconstruction.

Among obstacles to county growth during the decades of the 1870s and 1880s were disputes among the county's citizens, disorders from those charged with providing law and order, Indian raids, and bandit attacks. All threatened the peace and impeded progress.

Community Calamities

During those years civil and law enforcement authorities in Duval County had their hands full of various domestic criminal pursuits. First, local authorities in San Diego faced an unusual and tragic development when, in the latter part of May 1873, five schoolchildren in San Diego swallowed sugar laced with strychnine. Police suspected the school's custodian of the deed but had no concrete evidence to arrest him. Dr. J. Williams attended to the victims and said two children would likely recover, suggesting three would not. However, no subsequent reports appeared in the newspapers relative to this misfortune.[1]

Later that year, in September, F. Morgan reportedly shot and killed a shepherd named Santos. The two had argued over cutting out or separating sheep. Santos allegedly took a rock intending to hit Morgan, but a man named McCreary intervened. Santos then took a whip and smacked Morgan on the head, forcing him to the ground. Another shepherd named Pablo Hinojosa stepped in to immobilize Morgan. McCreary pulled Hinojosa off Morgan and pinned him against a corral fence.[2] Meanwhile, Santos reached for Morgan's pistol, grasping it from its holster. Another man at the scene named Fletcher testified that Morgan held on to the barrel, managed to take the gun away from Santos, and then shot the shepherd in the head. Acting as the coroner, Judge Luby again convened a jury of inquest, finding that Morgan's act was self-defense. Jury members included L. D. Harris, W. H. Steele, Jesús Treviño, Leandro Reyna, Francisco González, and Charles S. Murphy.[3]

The same day that Morgan killed Santos, another shepherd named Herculano Martínez, for unknown reasons, shot and killed Joseph Nichols on the Amargosa Road. While Nichols, Martinez's employer, sat on a horse, Martínez reportedly exacted a gunshot to the boss's back and neck. Nichols fell off his mount some twenty yards from where the shooting occurred and two hundred yards from a newly dug grave off the Amargosa Road. The alleged assailant then escaped on horseback. Law enforcement officers went to Concepción, Borjas, and Rosita in search of the suspect, with no success. A one-hundred-dollar reward for Martínez's arrest went uncollected.

Having only recently arrived from England, Nichols came to America to make a new home for his nine children. Ten years later, on June 15, 1884, the Nueces County sheriff finally took Martínez into custody. A final resolution of the case does not appear in subsequent newspaper accounts.[4]

Between Nichols's shooting death and Martínez's arrest, another tragedy—probably of greater interest to the local community—was the fatal gunning down of Rafael Salinas in late October 1879. Salinas was one of Duval County's earliest Tejano political leaders. He was active in the county's public life for almost twenty years, serving in various positions, including justice of the peace, deputy commissioner for hides and animals, supervisor of elections, and Concepción's first postmaster. Before his death, voters had elected Salinas to the first commissioners court in Duval County.

Salinas was returning home from a sheep camp twelve miles from Concepción when an unknown person or persons murdered him. People who lived near Boca Negra's Lake heard four shots fired at about seven in the evening. The next day, while looking for a remuda, Richard Hancock found Salinas's body near the lake. In the absence of Justice of the Peace John Vining, whose responsibility would have been to conduct an inquest, Edward R. Gray and other men rode to the scene to investigate the case. They determined that the killer(s) riddled Salinas's body with four bullets; they found gunpowder burns on Salinas's hat. Horse tracks at the location suggested that five culprits appeared to have dispersed in different directions.[5]

Texas Rangers stationed in San Diego under the command of Captain J. Lee Hall apprehended a suspect near Concepción thought connected to Salinas's murder. The press reported that the man was Salinas's partner in the sheep business, but the newspapers did not name him. As the Rangers transported the alleged killer to the county jail in San Diego, the suspect reportedly "slipped into the mesquital" and escaped. However, on November 5 the body of Florencio Garcia, who was the suspect that had been in custody and alleged to have escaped, was found hanging "to a tree in a dense thicket" a mile west of Concepción. Authorities believed his body had been dangling for about two weeks.[6]

Early Army Harassment

As early as 1841, San Patricio Rangers, a company organized without the consent of the Texas government—and aiming "for the mutual protection of... persons, property and civil and religious liberties"—reportedly attacked, without provocation, eight Mexican traders along the Laredo–Corpus Christi Road, which passed through Duval County. After indiscriminately murdering the individuals, who offered no resistance, they stripped them of their belongings, including horses and cash valued at $1,000.[7]

Five years later, in 1846, even before Americanos had defeated Mexico in the Mexican-American War, talk of the army harassing Mexicanos was an everyday conversation in the brush country of South Texas. The Corpus Christi newspaper tried to assure Mexican merchants the community welcomed their presence and that they could expect decent interaction with their new Americano neighbors. However, fear rested on the shared experiences of traders and fellow campesinos residing in the region surrounding Corpus Christi, and promises of an Americano editor did not ease them.[8]

Detrimental actions against Mexicano traders were only a symptom of Americanos' desire to control the majority Mexican-origin community. To exert their domination on the Nueces Strip, Americanos needed to conquer the locals, and fear was a cheap and accessible weapon. Therefore, it was essential to inflict horror on Mexicanos who lived on American soil. With the right to vote, after all, they could rise politically.

Indian Raids

While settlers contended with Indian attacks from the earliest days, they continued to confront Indian assaults through the Civil War, Reconstruction, and beyond. On September 25, 1870, Kickapoo Indians attacked Rancho San Felipe in Duval County. They killed Thomas Springfield and his wife, absconded with their two small sons, and wounded and left their young daughter behind alongside her parents' corpses. Three years later the Kickapoos returned and launched four separate attacks near San Diego. First, in September 1873, six Indians fell upon Neves Flores and companions near Loma Alta in northern Duval County. The following month the

Indians struck at the Gray Rancho. They killed E. N. Gray's shepherds, his oldest son, Enrique, and his brother-in-law. A posse of 150 pursued the band consisting of thirty Americanos and Indians.[9] Then, at the end of the year, some white men accompanied by Indians returned and killed Flores and fourteen others, including seven *pastores* (shepherds) employed by Toribio Lozano. That same month Indians killed thirty-two people and wounded two at Piedras Pintas.[10]

The last of the Indian raids occurred in April 1878. According to witness accounts, a band of thirty to forty Kickapoo Indians accompanied by several Mexicanos and a couple of Americano outlaws crossed the Rio Grande forty miles north of Laredo. In a letter sent to United States Secretary of State William F. Evarts, a committee of Duval officials and leading citizens described the raids in detail. Conspicuously, no Tejanos were members of the committee.[11]

The Kickapoos and their confederates continued their assault on the ranchos, crossing the county line into Duval County at San Ygnacio, where they killed Frederick B. Moore. The previous night Moore and a cousin, E. Chapman Moore, had spent the night at the Labbe Rancho, some twenty-five miles north of San Diego. The surviving Moore cousin said the two had received "true and kind-hearted French hospitality" from their host before the San Ygnacio attack. Chapman Moore recalled there were four white men in the raiding party.[12]

Twelve miles from Nueces River, close to McMullen County, the raiders targeted Rancho Toribio, where they murdered Vicente Robledo and wounded Tomás Zúniga. Then, on April 18, they changed course and headed to the Rancho Soledad, thirty miles north of San Diego. There they killed Guadalupe Bazán, a nameless shepherd, and his spouse. A small child witnessed the slaughter, telling investigators that the victims' dead "bodies were tied together . . . and swung upon a horse, which was turned loose."[13] The Indians took off to Charco Escondido, a rancho owned by Richard Jordan about thirty miles northwest of San Diego. They killed Jordan's 19-year-old son, John, and an older man named Antonio Valdez. Jordan's other son, Samuel, sought help at the Gravis brothers' ranch six miles east of Charco Escondido.[14]

Frank Gravis had already received a warning of the raid from neighbor Jorge Alaniz, who lived four miles away. Alaniz informed Gravis he was assembling a posse and planned to lead it to Rancho Soledad to find the Indians' trail and track down the perpetrators. Alaniz asked Gravis to round up volunteers and join him. Gravis sent word to Edward Caldwell at Rancho Borjas, informing him of the emergency and asking him to spread the word to other neighbors for help.[15]

From Rancho Muñoz Gravis dispatched a runner to alert the US troops' commanding officer at Camp San Diego of the ongoing crisis and ask the military to pursue the plunderers. Gravis followed up by sending a second note to the army commander about the Indians' direction. Richard Jordan had also given a heads-up to the troops at San Diego via County Judge James O. Luby, who passed the information to the troop commander. The officer in charge replied that the army knew the goings-on and had sent out ten men, "a sufficient force to whip the fifty Indians." Jordan, the bereaved father, stayed at the ranch for twenty-five days and never saw any army troops chasing the raiders.[16]

While the marauders had left Duval County, Gravis and his posse remained in pursuit and finally caught up with the Indians eighteen miles from the Rio Grande. Unfortunately, the army troops from Laredo arrived too late. On April 19, 1878, five days after they began their march of death and destruction, the Indian party crossed into Mexico at Rancho Dolores, twenty-five miles south of Laredo, escaping with an estimated caballada of one hundred horses stolen from the ranchos. When they returned from the pursuit, many men from the neighboring ranchos who had joined Gravis told him stories about the Indians they killed. Unfortunately, the names of most of these courageous individuals, members of the posse, the Mexicano and Tejano ranch hands, and shepherds who died in the raids did not appear in the report to the secretary of state. They remained known to their loved ones and their maker. Duval County Surveyor John Dix lamented the actions, or lack thereof, by the army troops in San Diego and Laredo, expressing more confidence in Texas Rangers than in army troops. Indeed, unlike their counterparts in other parts of the country, according to local organizers' sentiments, the South Texas army troops played an almost inconsequential role in countering the Indian threat.[17] However, the April 1878 incursion was the last major raid by Indians into Duval County. It happened when Indian attacks throughout the United States were diminishing. It marked the end of an era: "Less an elimination of a military threat than an eradication of a way of life."[18]

Banditry

Indians were not the only problem facing residents of Duval County. On Saturday, March 28, 1873, a party of about sixty men stole horses in the upper reaches of Duval County. The bandidos were under the leadership of two well-known outlaws, Alberto Garza—a.k.a. Caballo Blanco—and Atilano Alvarado. Garza had a reputation for banditry in Atascosa County, and Alvarado had built similar notoriety in Mexico. San Diego lawmen José María García Treviño and Apolonio Vela led a posse in pursuit of the horse thieves but failed to capture them.[19]

Garza and Alvarado resurfaced the following week, reportedly leading sixty men on another horse-stealing and cattle-skinning spree. On Sunday, April 6, Garza's band surrounded the Rancho Piedras Pintas south of San Diego, stationing men on all roads leading to the ranch. The bandit leader entered the rancho with seventeen followers and controlled the entire environment. Meanwhile, six Americanos had taken shelter in several of the ranch's homes. Garza threatened to burn the rancho because Eugene Glover and Maurice Levy—among those hiding—had sent word for reinforcements.[20]

Hearing of the danger posed to Piedras Pintas on Monday, April 14, Jasper Clark and James Scott left Banquete and went for San Diego with just eleven men, hoping to increase their numbers as they rode. But only one volunteer joined them. To legitimize the pursuit, Judge Luby provided the vigilantes with warrants to bring Garza in, dead or alive, and gave each one a badge.[21]

The posse left San Diego on Tuesday night for Jorge Alaniz's rancho, thirty miles west of town, reaching it on the morning of April 16. Later that day they set out for Piedras Pintas, some twenty-five miles away. The following morning the party resumed its campaign to find the bandits' camp. Soon the volunteers encountered the outlaws, who opened fire from the brush. In a counterattack Clark's men quickly overtook their adversaries and captured seven horses, including Garza's, still with saddles and bridles. But Garza escaped into the *monte* (the woods). Clark and his men found 655 cattle carcasses in and around the bandits' camp. Neither the posse nor the bandits lost a man in the skirmish.[22]

After a time in the Trans-Nueces rounding up new mounts and confiscated armaments, such as six-shooters, rifles, and plenty of ammunition, the bandit chief and his band returned to Piedras Pintas later that month. Moreover, Garza had the gall to offer to sell two hundred of their hides back to the rancheros and boasted of calling forty men from the Rio Grande communities to join the marauding. Furthermore, he issued a specific threat to Jorge Alaniz, warning that plans were in place to burn his rancho because of the help the Tejano had given the Americanos. Finally, Garza brazenly announced intentions to remain around the area to continue skinning cattle, declared hatred toward the men who took the hides his outlaws had gathered, and promised to deal with those men appropriately.[23]

Nueces and Duval County citizens met at Piedras Pintas on April 23 to devise ways to protect life and property around the Duval area. They designated Martin S. Culver, James F. Scott, and George Alaniz to lead a delegation to Austin and appeal to Governor E. J. Davis and the legislature to implement robust protective measures. The three men carried the petition to the capital, signed by T. H. Clarke, E. A. Glover, Rafael Sáenz, Desiderio Salinas, Felipe Oliveira, José M. Valadez, Rafael Gutiérrez, Leandro Bazán, Nicolas Ybañez, Mariano Garza, Marcial Hinojosa, Apolonio Hinojosa, Francisco Bazán, Ruben Curtis, N. J. Nickerson, Tomás Lerma, Juan Gonzales, José M. Vela, H. B. Glover, William A. Tinney, Calixto Tovar, F. G. Flores, William Hubbard, Máximo Salinas, M. Villarreal, Juan Sáenz, G. Alaniz, J. E. Singleton, Frank Byler, W. W. Wright, Jorge Alaniz, Casimiro Alaniz, Antonio Mireles, E. García Pérez, and Santos Flores.[24]

Garza, in the meantime, retreated to Mexico. However, the killing and skinning of cattle continued in the ranchos near San Diego. Skinners opened a new field of operations near Rancho Trinidad; a half mile from the ranch, vaqueros found fifteen to twenty cattle carcasses stripped of their hides.

Some ten or twelve miles south of San Diego, vaqueros found six dead cows owned by José M. Valadez. Another resident saw one thousand heads of skinned cattle and noted that in the previous week, bandits had slaughtered five thousand livestock."[25]

In the first week of September, a man believed to have been Juan Peña was found hanging from a mesquite tree about two miles from San Diego. Two hides of freshly skinned cows lay near him. In addition, the men who discovered the corpse found tracks of six horses. Since the men identified the body, one can assume Peña was a vaquero tending to the cattle and fell prey to the bandits.[26]

The following week, unknown assailants murdered a man named Hurley from Lagartoville. Authorities said the tragic incident occurred near Concepción, where Hurley had gone to buy sheep. However, law enforcement officers did not believe Hurley's murder was an isolated incident, for in the first week of November 7, ten Mexicano bandits robbed R. Shubert's store in Concepción. Four robbers cased the establishment, and six other Mexicanos joined them to surround the building. Two stood guard at the front door, barring anyone from approaching. After entering the store, the gang threatened Shubert at gunpoint and ordered him to open his safe and surrender the money. The robbers escaped with $2,500 to $3,000 and loaded up on a supply of arms and ammunition.[27]

Authorities in Duval County believed they knew of several organized bands of robbers and murderers operating in the vicinity of Concepción. Two weeks later Shubert learned Mexican authorities had arrested Justo Vela in Camargo and Leonardo Flores in Las Cuevas, Mexico. Without offering proof, law enforcement believed the two men were part of the band of outlaws who robbed the Concepción store.[28]

The good news that the bandit Garza had left the area was short-lived, for in January 1875 he was back in Duval County raiding isolated ranchos. However, the bandit was no longer skinning cattle but rustling horses. Garza had been in self-exile in Mexico, but the demand for mounts in that country lured him back to hunt for equine stock.[29]

Shortly after, in March 1875, reports spread throughout South Texas that "a well-organized band of 150 Mexicans crossed into Texas near Eagle Pass."

They supposedly split into four companies, "bent on plunder." The United States Cavalry stationed at Camp San Diego responded and turned three bandit squads back. At the same time, Hines Clark organized a militia in Duval County to take revenge on those involved in the lawlessness. It did not dawn on Clark that his actions were outside the law. One chronicler of South Texas noted, "No telling how many Mexicans bit the dust" resulting from this revenge, or lawless campaign.[30]

Despite these offensives against plunderers, cattle skinning continued. For example, in September 1875 a group of Mexicano "hide peelers" camped in San Diego's vicinity and, after ten days of illicit labor, returned to Mexico with between four and five hundred hides.[31]

And Then Came the Texas Rangers

In their effort to dominate the region and its local population, ranchers in the Nueces Strip appealed to the state to send a Ranger detachment to South Texas; the Rangers would know what to do. Advancing that the federal government was not meeting its obligation to protect the border, Democratic Governor Richard Coke reactivated the Rangers, which the Republicans had disbanded during Reconstruction. Coke directed them to guard the public's safety. In 1874 the governor dispatched Frontier Rangers under Captain Warren Wallace to Concepción in Duval County. Perhaps someone should have given Governor Coke a geography lesson: Concepción was more than a hundred miles from the Rio Grande border he sought to protect.[32]

The Rangers soon began accusing Mexicanos and Tejanos of banditry and cattle rustling, turning these alleged transgressions into a license to attack Mexicanos indiscriminately. In a story reprinted by the *Daily Express* of San Antonio on August 18, 1874, the Brownsville *Ranchero* saw through the Rangers' actions and denounced them as "organized executioners." The Rangers, the *Ranchero* wrote, were trained to implement the governor's "satanic hate" against fifty thousand Mexicanos and Tejanos in the Trans-Nueces through "barbarous and unconstitutional acts." The San Antonio newspaper had received this information from several leading Starr County and San Diego citizens. However, the newspapers refused to use their names for fear of "exposing them to summary execution" at the hands of *los rinches*.[33]

On July 16, 1874, Wallace's Rangers arrested Ambrosio Monsivais in Concepción on undetermined charges. Captain Wallace ostensibly found Monsivais blameless of baseless complaints and released him. However, Wallace may have done so with the wink of an eye to his Rangers because they promptly disregarded his orders to free Monsivais. Instead, five Rangers severely beat Monsivais, searched his home, and took a carbine and seventy dollars in cash from him. Shortly after, for unspecified reasons, the Rangers apprehended Román Garza and a man named Matías and hung them "until nearly dead." The *rinches* then rode to Rancho Borjas, owned by Francisco Peña, and then to Rancho Barroneña. Then, after resting for a day, the Rangers arrested, again for unknown causes, brothers Antonio and Manuel Treviño and took them about ten miles away from Rancho Borjas and shot them dead.[34]

Next, they detained Peña and took him to Wallace, who promptly released him, as he had done with Monsivais. Following a familiar pattern, the Rangers then terrorized Peña. Fearing for his life, Peña gathered his family and fled across the border. The *Ranchero* described the Rangers' activities as nothing less than a "reign of terror" involving "savage barbarism" and "illegal executions."[35]

In 1880 a Ranger company under Thomas Oglesby's command camped in San Diego. One of the Rangers was a 22-year-old Tejano named Paulino Coy. The name Coy is part of early Texas history; Santos Coy was a pioneer settler who had once served as Nacogdoches's alcalde. Paulino's father, Trinidad Coy, was a Tejano rancher and a scout for the Alamo defenders.[36]

By 1883 Paulino Coy had left the Ranger force, changed badges, and joined the Nueces County Sheriff's Office. Coy had learned some unsavory practices while serving with the Rangers, which he now used on his fellow Tejanos. He received rave reviews from the Americano press but disdain from the Tejano community. Over the next five years, Coy gained the reputation of being a dangerous hombre with a badge and a gun. He was continuously in the Corpus Christi newspaper: stories reported him apprehending outlaws and executing his duties by shooting first and asking questions later.[37]

On December 9, 1883, Coy killed Ezequiel De Los Santos while enforcing a warrant. Two Rangers accompanied Coy when De Los Santos supposedly came out of a house with a pistol and a Bowie knife and opened fire. The law enforcement officers responded in kind, killing De Los Santos. The Corpus Christi newspaper opined that De Los Santos was "a desperate character" while Deputy Sheriff Coy proved "an efficient officer." This incident was the first of several alleged executions credited to the Ranger-trained Coy of suspects in his custody.[38]

A month later, on January 6, 1884, the *Caller* headlined "Coy Gets Another Man." Coy had shot and killed Cristóbal Salinas at a rancho near Concepción. As before, two Rangers accompanied Coy as he sought to arrest Salinas. After capturing two Mexicanos accused of horse theft, Coy and the Rangers came across Salinas, for whom they had a grand jury arrest warrant accusing him of stealing sheep. The suspect reportedly attempted to escape upon learning the law was in pursuit. Salinas allegedly fired at the Rangers, wounding one of them. Coy returned fire and shot Salinas three times. "Everything we have learned of the affair tends to the justification of Coy," the newspaper said, giving the ex-Ranger another pass.[39]

On April 18, 1886, Nueces County Deputies Coy and Del Hoyo left Corpus Christi for Palito Blanco, searching for Andrés Martínez and Pedro Peña, whom rancher Hilario Cruz had accused of stealing his horses. This trip sealed Coy's reputation among Tejanos as an Americano collaborator. It also resulted in one of the most notorious events in the annals of South Texas frontier history.[40]

On April 14, Coy and Del Hoyo went to Martínez's home but did not find him. Even though they suspected Martínez as a horse thief, the deputies left word for Martínez to ride to Collins because they needed him as a "witness." On Friday, April 23, Martínez did as the two officers instructed; he went to Collins to comply with orders. Although asked to act as a witness, Martínez must have worried that something was up because he brought Ireneo López, who was willing to be Martínez's bondsman. Martínez returned to Palito Blanco, accompanied by Constable Juan Juárez, to get a second guarantor for his bond.[41]

Two days later Coy and Deputy Ed Allen went to Palito Blanco and placed Martínez under arrest. Allen transported the prisoner to Collins in a wagon. Accompanying them on horseback were Coy, Del Hoyo, and John Ranahan. They were also ushering José María Cadena, whom they had likewise arrested on suspicion of horse theft; as a source of proof, the party was driving some horses they believed Cadena had stolen. Fermín López traveled along to give Martínez's bond. Martínez and Cadena were taken to Constable Juárez's home in Collins, handcuffed, and left in Juárez's charge. At 3:00 a.m. three masked intruders ostensibly took the constable by surprise, grabbed his pistol, and killed the two prisoners Juárez was guarding.[42]

Coy swiftly moved to form a posse to track down the culprits responsible for assassinating the two cuffed suspects. However, Tejanos saw Coy's call for a posse as a subterfuge to hide his complicity in the murders, so they organized a party of their own to hunt down Coy. In its April 28, 1886, issue, the *San Antonio Express* informed that a large crowd was hunting for Coy and had taken control of Collins.[43] A sizable contingent of "armed Mexicans captured the town; posted sentinels and proceeded to search every house for Coy." But the deputy had, meantime, left for Duval County, presumably in search of Martínez's and Cadena's killers. Martínez's father offered $1,000 for Coy's apprehension, prompting Nueces County Sheriff Whelan to set out to round up the Tejano vigilante leaders, who reportedly lived in Duval County.[44]

But in Duval County a second related injustice involving Tejano victims occurred. The *Fort Worth Daily Gazette* reported on April 29, 1886, that two males had been found dead on the previous Monday, April 26, at Los Indios, a rancho south of San Diego. In addition, the *Gazette* and other newspapers— namely, the *San Antonio Daily Express*—reported that "two Mexican horse thieves had been shot and killed while resisting arrest."[45] "It is probable," the Fort Worth newspaper proclaimed, "that Deputy Sheriffs Coy and Ranahan were the officers who did the work." While the Tejanos threatened Collins's citizens, Coy was "thinning out their ranks," the *Gazette* gloated. The Fort Worth broadsheet joined the *Caller* as a Coy fan club member. "Coy is one of the best and most reliable officers on the border," the *Gazette* wrote. In a stunning revelation, the *Gazette* bragged that Coy had "the reputation of having killed a dozen bad characters."[46]

It turned out that the two individuals who lost their lives at Los Indios, Pedro Peña and Mateo Cadena, had been found hanging. In a candid moment, the *San Antonio Express* correspondent admitted in the newspaper's May 2, 1886, issue that "there are a dozen different versions" of what actually happened at Los Indios and that the newspaper "occasionally" erred. Pedro Peña and Andrés Martínez were suspects in the alleged theft of rancher Hilario Cruz's horses. Mateo Cadena was brother to José María Cadena, who was executed along with Martínez by the still-missing masked men.[47]

Trying to clarify the record, the *Caller* maintained that Coy had nothing to do with the hanging. "If he had, and the thieves were killed while fighting and resisting arrest, it is not a crime that they would have died with a rope around their necks," the *Caller* unashamedly proclaimed. But, of course, it is inconceivable one could take the time to detain and hang someone from a tree while trying to escape. In the end no one paid for the deaths of these four Tejanos, and on May 16, 1886, the *Caller* reported that Deputy Coy, "one of the bravest and most fearless officers on the border," was moving to Zapata County.[48]

While Ranger protégé Coy was leaving Duval County, sheriff's deputies from South Texas met at Los Olmos, located south of Concepción in Duval County. They were purportedly looking for a response to the growing threat posed by disgruntled Mexican soldiers. Elements of Mexico's armed forces had begun to make noises about deposing their president, Porfirio Díaz, whom they believed had taken on a dictatorial character. These rebels from a foreign land looked to South Texas as good training and recruiting grounds for launching their insurrection. Moreover, the deputies believed these Mexico revolutionaries threatened the area's livestock ranches.[49]

Therefore, they petitioned Governor Lawrence Sullivan Ross to station Texas Rangers between Concepción and Rio Grande City. On November 19, under Captain George H. Schmitt's direction, Ranger Company C moved its camp from Laredo to Peña in southern Duval County but soon relocated to Collins to patrol Duval and Nueces Counties. Their stay was inconsequential.[50]

Catarino Garza Advocates for Tejanos

During these challenges with local law enforcement, Texas Rangers, and the US Army, a fiery young Mexicano named Catarino Garza came on the scene, spouting and advocating justice for Tejanos and railing against their treatment as second-rate citizens. The circumstances in which Tejanos lived very much predisposed them to receive encouragement and inspiration from the 29-year-old compañero with a fiery pen and an acerbic tongue. At one point Garza, in his typical oratorical fashion, uttered, "Uno u otro que sea, aquí estoy, dispuesto al sacrificio de mi vida en un pro de la causa que defiendo y defenderé" (One way or the other, here I am, ready to sacrifice my life for the cause that I defend and will continue to defend.) This kind of straight talk attracted and emboldened Tejanos in Duval County and greater South Texas.[51]

During what became known as the Catarino Garza Revolution (1891–1893), uncontrolled and harmful attitudes toward Tejanos produced wanton death and destruction. Indeed, the deadly prejudice against Mexicanos had always existed in South Texas. However, what made this era different was that Tejanos refused to take the abuse any longer and retaliated, in some instances with fatal consequences for Americanos. This disregard for the rights of Tejanos by law enforcement began to grind on their leaders in Duval County.

In May 1888 Tejano leaders from San Diego and the Junta Patriótica de Palito Blanco asked Garza to be the keynote speaker at their Cinco de Mayo celebrations. While a record of Garza's speech is not available for examination, one can reasonably infer that he spoke for the rights of Tejanos and their treatment by Americanos.[52] Soon after his speech at the Cinco de Mayo occasion in San Diego, Garza felt drawn into Duval County politics. His hosts had most likely informed Garza of their efforts to reach political parity with their Americano neighbors. Ethnic relations were already somewhat tense in the region, and Americano residents feared Garza's intent to start a newspaper in San Diego could intensify anxiety.[53] Since its beginnings in Corpus Christi, the tone of Garza's *El Comercio Mexicano*, according to the *Corpus Christi Caller*, had been to "stir up strife between

Americans and Mexicans." As per the *Caller's* point of view, the "best class is crying out against Garza and his paper."[54]

Garza moved to Palito Blanco from Corpus Christi in 1890, shortly after his wedding to Concepción González that summer. A year later, on September 15, 1891, Garza traded his pen for a gun, issued a pronunciamento against Mexican President Porfirio Díaz, and went to war. It was an action that affected the revolutionary and his family at Palito Blanco and significantly impacted South Texas, particularly Duval County.[55]

At least one of Garza's fellow editors disagreed with his aims. On September 26, 1891, less than two weeks after Garza launched his revolution against Díaz, *El Correo* of Laredo argued with Garza's reasoning for the insurgency. Francisco de P. González in *El Eco Liberal, Periódico Independiente, Orden y Progreso*, published in San Diego, had printed Garza's proclamation, which reached the office of *El Correo*. The Laredo organ proclaimed Garza's proposal of overthrowing the Díaz regime "was a dream of madmen, of bums, and of people without jobs." The Laredo publisher declared that "the true revolution is work. . . . Long Live Work! Death to the Revolution."[56]

Garza's relationship with Tejanos in Duval County relied on shared needs and interests. Tejano politicos used Garza's newspaper and oratory to excite the people and inject concern into their Americano political opponents. Garza openly and forthrightly affirmed the Tejano community's struggles. His talk about freedom, equality, fairness, and prejudice—in short, the human condition—was not new to residents of San Diego, Benavides, Concepción, Piedras Pintas, Realitos, Barroneña, La Rosita, and the other rancherias in Duval County. Garza's words were a public acknowledgment of their thoughts, which they had not verbalized effectively as a community. But the Duval County Tejanos did not simply take from Garza; they shared their support with him in volunteers, money, livestock, and protection. Garza based his oratory on the "holy principles of democracy" and professed the government's political ideals should rest "on the rights of the people." Garza's words and ideas certainly rang true in the rural towns of Duval County, whose leaders had been saying this for several years, perhaps not as elegantly or openly.[57]

On or about September 15, 1891, Garza declared open rebellion against Díaz in Mexico, calling on Mexicano compatriots to stand up for the oppressed. Subsequently, two Tejanos, perhaps acting on Garza's call, rode into Realitos with unclear, presumably violent, intentions. Law officers confronted the two, and after a brief clash, the pair left town without anyone hurt. However, on September 18 the two Tejanos returned to Realitos with the same uncertain designs. In the interim, local authorities had called in the Rangers, who did not hesitate to kill the two visitors, Pantaleón Chapa and Santiago Villa.[58]

Meanwhile, the Rangers' action in Realitos riled up folks in San Diego. The *Weekly Times* said Sheriff John Buckley took "every precaution to avoid further bloodshed, and with the assistance of the Rangers, he will no doubt be successful." But perhaps Sheriff Buckley intended to keep the Rangers close so he could keep an eye on their quick draw. Residents of the area in and adjacent to Duval County knew that Buckley was politically on the side of the Tejanos and had a good relationship with Garza.[59]

Many Duval residents joined Garza's revolutionary brigade, "Los Catarinos." The *Aransas Harbor Herald* of October 22, 1891, described Andrés Moreno Nuñez of Concepción as a "typical revolutionist." Nuñez was in Aransas Harbor distributing propaganda for Garza's revolution. The *Herald* may have thought Nuñez typical because the newspaper considered him another Mexican filled with mescal. A US marshal arrested Nuñez for unspecified charges but most likely for violating the American neutrality law.[60]

On January 9, 1892, the US Army established Fort Edward, a mile north of San Diego, under the command of Captain George F. Chase. The post's mission was to patrol the area for Garza's movements. They could patrol east and south of San Diego, primarily in and around Duval County and Palito Blanco, where Garza's in-laws lived and where the revolutionary commander supposedly had headquarters. Another army unit, Troop K, led by Captain George K. Hunter, also made rounds in Duval County.[61]

Garza never lived in Duval County, but he was well known and had many sympathizers. Some seven thousand of the county's eight thousand residents were Tejanos upon whom Garza counted. On the other hand, the media reported, there also lived in Duval County a "better class of people"

who minded their own business and allowed Garza to tend to his. This
category of residents existed in all South Texas counties and was tired of the
agitation peddled by "Mexican malcontents."[62]

On February 2, 1892, information reached Duval County that the Garza
War was real; Garza's followers reportedly killed Rufus Glover, the Duval
County clerk. While scouting the Soledad Wells on the Hubbard Ranch,
Deputy US Marshals Glover, Lino Cuéllar, and Juan Moreno fell victim to
an attack by Los Catarinos. Cuéllar escaped the skirmish and, upon reaching Benavides, gave Justice of the Peace Andrew R. Valls an account of the
assault and then went to a camp of US soldiers in Sweden. Duval County
Deputy S. R. Peters and an army detail headed for the Hubbard rancho,
twenty-five miles north of Benavides, to investigate the tragedy. Glover's
brother Eugene accompanied the party. They found no telling tracks where
the perpetrators had escaped, and the slain scout's death remained on people's
minds. Everyone was determined to find the killer or killers; meanwhile,
the Duval County Grand Jury indicted Eusebio Martínez from San Diego.
In February 1893 army and law enforcement officers cut down Martínez in
Starr County while he "resisted arrest." Newspaper accounts credited him
with the killing of two other men. Martínez left a grieving daughter-in-law
and grandson in San Diego.[63]

An incident believed to be related to the Glover shooting involved the
kidnapping, disappearance, and possible murder of George (Jorge) Alanis in
late March. Alanis was a well-regarded Tejano who always volunteered to
track down bad hombres, including cattle rustlers and Indians. On the night
of March 30, what authorities believed to be outlaws allegedly kidnapped
Alanis with a pretense of business and kidnapped him. The thought was that
the perpetrators had killed Alanis for his quick offer to track down the killers
of Glover and being part of a posse that killed one of the suspected assassins.
However, at the same time, US marshals were searching for and ultimately
arrested Alanis and two hundred other Mexicanos for violation of neutrality
laws. Perhaps the supposed kidnappers were federal officers. Two years prior,
in 1890, Alanis had been one of five Tejanos that provided the bond for newly
elected sheriff and supposed Catarino Garza friend John Buckley. In 1894
Alanis was still providing bonds for Duval County elected officials.

On February 6, in San Diego, Deputy US Marshal E. T. Hall picked up two alleged Garza supporters named T. López and Frank Garza. Hall believed that Duval County citizens—among them, López—were unanimous on how they felt about Catarino Garza. Many openly supported the insurgents and admitted having assisted Garza and his armed forces in avoiding capture.[64]

At about the same time, a reporter embedded himself into a Rangers' company, intending to get a firsthand account of Garza's capture. The correspondent traveled to Clovis Rancho in southern Duval County to join the Rangers. However, after three days of scouting, they had apprehended only one alleged Garza supporter. According to the reporter, their movement in Duval County "was haunted day and night by spies."[65]

With the newsman still in tow, the Rangers moved west to Realitos, capturing another assumed Garza follower. They then set off to Los Ángeles and heard gunfire in the brush. The shooting took them on a wild chase through the chaparral, with the reporter and prisoners having to keep up. Somehow, they got through the pursuit and picked up two more prisoners without losing a man. At Los Ángeles they met up with more Rangers, and almost everyone was convinced, once again, that this time they knew where they could find Garza. But they did not. While sympathetic to the Rangers, the reporter could not withhold noting that the Rangers' "campaign . . . has been crowded so close upon the borders of a comedy."[66]

With little results to show, the army withdrew its troops from the area in March 1892, leaving the Rangers as the primary law enforcement force still pursuing Garza. However, within days the Rangers felt the loss of the army's support. On March 22 Ranger Miguel Martínez came to San Diego with the body of fellow Ranger Robert Doughty, 33 years of age. Los Catarinos stood accused of killing Doughty in a firefight near Bennett's Rancho in southern Duval County. Several years before, on June 4, 1887, Ranger Doughty, the stepson of Francis Gravis, one of San Diego's leading citizens, had received a pardon from President Grover Cleveland for mail robbery.[67]

After withdrawing its troops, the federal government assigned civilian agents in rounding up Garza's Tejano supporters. In March 1892 agents arrested several Tejanos for violating the neutrality laws. Among them were Alejandro González, Garza's father-in-law, and Mauricio González of Palito

Blanco, as well as Duval County residents Jorge Alanis, Francisco Mendoza, Rafael Sáenz, and Albino Canales. Marshals also arrested Alice residents Ramón Moreno and Porfirio Zamora. Some 212 Mexicans, many almost penniless, were arrested for allegedly violating neutrality laws.[68]

In March 1892 State Representative John Dix, a longtime Duval County political leader, offered some hyperbolic advice to the Rangers. Dix, who had served several terms as Duval County surveyor and Democratic Party chair, suggested to the Rangers that some well-placed illicit hangings could send a loud and clear message to Garza's supporters. Dix observed that had the *rinches* strung up Garzista rebels early on and "burnt their possessions long ago, this matter would have ended harsh, hard, and . . . cruel, but it would have saved lives to our country and money to our treasury." Dix wrote that it was the only way "Mexicans could be governed or managed."[69]

Still smarting about Garza's followers killing fellow San Diegoites Glover and Doughty, some Duval Americanos reportedly organized a White Men's Party at the inception of 1892. At about the same time, longtime Duval County political leader James Luby called a public meeting in San Diego for the first week of April 1892 to discuss the continuing violence in their midst.[70] Luby's followers petitioned the governor for more Rangers, as they had done twice previously. In addition, however, Luby's adherents asked if the governor could not get the legislature to okay this measure due to the cost involved if locals could establish a volunteer force at their expense. According to Luby, every Americano in Duval County signed the request. Luby's petition stated, probably correctly, that most of the "Mexican" population in South Texas was sympathetic to Garza. Indeed, more than a few Americanos in Duval County understood that ethnic sentiments drove many Tejanos into Garza's columns.[71]

At about the same time as Luby's gathering, perhaps at the rally, the "better class of people" in Duval County came together to ask the governor for relief from the "Aztec" vote and intended to petition the legislature's special session to adopt the Australian ballot system. The view of political leaders and the media was that people were "tired of Mexicans being allowed to vote by declaring their intention to become American citizens."[72]

A Houston newspaper advocated this voting system for some, not all, voters. "Where unqualified voters abound, and where election lawlessness is most fraudulent, is where even registration . . . would be of little avail." The newspaper said this was the Mexican frontier portion of the state. For years the best citizens protested against "the outrageous corruption practiced in elections . . . and are praying the state come to their aid." So the newspaper explained to that segment of their uninformed readers how the "Aztec vote" worked, as commonly understood: "Several days before the election, large numbers of the lower-class Mexicans are driven to corrals, and there shut-in with a supply of mescal and whisky. This throng is augmented by new flocks, not adverse to the free debauch, until the last moment of voting. Citizenship is no necessary qualification, as only a promise to become a resident, whether attended with any intention of fulfillment . . . will give . . . the candidate the sacred right of suffrage. This mass is marched to the polls and voted to suit the politician in command."[73] The newspaper failed to mention that the "politician in command" often rose from the ranks of the "better class of people," whose motives were no better or different than their political adversaries. To the masses of Tejanos, the advocacy for reform came across as no more than a scheme to deny Tejanos their constitutional rights. Consequently, it pushed them even more toward Garza, who advocated for equality for Tejanos' human and civil rights.

Dix, who advocated the Rangers' lynching of Tejanos, advanced another extreme position for decontaminating the electoral process. He suggested that the willful killing of Mexicans would not be acceptable in the "land of liberty." Still, Rangers could release many Mexicans at the Rio Grande and force them to cross over to Mexico, where the views on execution without due process were more acceptable. "It would have a salutary effect upon this whole country, morally, financially, and politically, and tend to the purification of the ballot," Dix asserted.[74]

Former State Representative and Senator N. G. Collins, who had a good relationship with Tejano leaders and appeared to have a more moderate view of Duval County and South Texas's overall situation, offered counsel to the governor. In February 1892 Collins advised Governor Hogg that if authorities could not stop Garza's activities, the area was on track for a "war of races."[75]

Fig. 9.1 Norman G. Collins (1828–1899) was a prominent citizen and political leader in Duval County. Courtesy of the State Preservation Board, Austin, Texas, Legislative Reference Library of Texas, https://lrl.texas.gov.

Of course the predominant politics were more concerning for Luby, Dix, and their political allies. Even though they had ruled the county for two decades, they were on the verge of being outside looking in and feared the new order could become permanent if not controlled. They must have known they were responsible for the political discontent between Tejanos and Americanos. Sheriff Buckley was the political opponent who appeared to give them the most heartache.

Pablo Longoria, who had served as a soldier in Garza's insurrectionist army but had turned informant for the American Army, confessed to Captain Chase that Sheriff Buckley was always willing to assist Garza in any way the sheriff could. A federal grand jury eventually indicted Buckley for allegedly aiding and abetting Garza's revolutionary activities. But when, in 1892, Sheriff Buckley ran for election with a $2,000 bond over his head for violating US law, Duval County voters reelected him.[76]

In February 1892 a couple of ranch hands from the Carrillo Ranch near Realitos facilitated Catarino Garza's escape, who went "from ranch to ranch in the chaparral" to Cuero. Garza then traveled to Houston, sailed to Cuba and Costa Rica, and eventually arrived in Columbia.[77] Garza left the people of Duval County and South Texas to continue fighting for freedom. The Duval County grand jury reported that the "Garza disturbance" was no more; only "rambling gangs" remained wandering about the county, evading the law.[78]

Garza offered the support Duval County Tejanos needed in their mission to affirm their political and individual rights. Duval County and the surrounding area allowed Catarino Garza to develop his revolutionary intentions. It was a safe zone with welcoming elbow room for Garza's political views as he dealt with Díaz and Tejanos with the Americano political structure in South Texas. While rejecting violence or war, Tejanos in Duval County wanted to secure and ensure their God-given and constitutionally protected rights. Ironically, this era's trauma in Duval County may have set the Tejanos' political efforts back for over a decade. However, the ideas of personal liberty and political rights remained rooted in the Tejano identity and were not to be denied.

The years after the Civil War and Reconstruction produced many challenges for the emerging communities in Duval County. But this era also set the stage for the county's organization and the railroad's arrival. If the land was the bride, the railroad was the groom. The two came together in 1875, and the face and history of Duval County changed forever. The marriage of these two elements encapsulated the county's past and birthed its future.

Moreover, as the end of the nineteenth century approached, Tejanos were poised to assert themselves politically. They had fortified what they had always known: they, too, were citizens of their new country and had every right and expectation to participate in their government. The violent challenges they faced with the Rangers and the rhetoric and example Catarino Garza provided prepared Tejanos for the next step of their political ascendancy.[79]

Chapter 10

Sheep Replace Cattle

The Spaniards who colonized Mexico began raising sheep for wool production as early as the sixteenth century. By the mid-eighteenth century, the wool industry had spread north to the Rio Grande frontier, where the *españoles* raised sheep, goats, cattle, horses, and mules. At this time Spanish sheep outnumbered cattle twenty to one in the Villas del Norte, including the area that is today southern Duval County. At the end of Reconstruction, sheep appeared more pronounced in the chaparral. While sheep had long been present in Duval County, in the 1870s they became a commodity for commercial marketing.[1]

When South Texas entered the Union after the Mexican-American War, there were only 101,000 sheep in the state. At the start of the Civil War, that number had increased to 1,074,000. Then, for various reasons, sheep numbers statewide plunged to 714,000, only to shoot up to 3.6 million after the war ended, making sheep raising a profitable enterprise in the Trans-Nueces, including Duval County.[2]

Ranchers Take Notice of Sheep

The 1880 Census was the first official population enumeration for the newly organized county of Duval. The census provided a count of sheep raisers, who

141

numbered 37. Except for 17-year-old Tejano Modesto Guzmán, all the sheep raisers in Duval County were foreign-born. Twenty-seven (or 73 percent) were Mexicanos, and 9 (or 24 percent) were Americanos who had recently arrived from Europe.[3] Ninety-nine percent of the sheepherders were Spanish speakers, with 43 (or 19 percent) Tejanos and 225 (or 80 percent) Mexicanos. Only 1 Americano and 1 Spaniard were in the shepherding workforce. Nearly half of the 225 shepherds in Duval County were no older than 18. Indeed, one author suggests that sheepherding was often the work of boys and women. At that time the frontier called for all hands on deck to help the family make ends meet. The sparsely settled land, however, posed a danger for adolescents, who were susceptible to kidnapping by Indians. Moreover, disputes between older sheepherders and the herd owners could sometimes turn deadly, placing younger herders at risk.[4]

More than half of the shepherds, 134, made their home in Precinct One, which included San Diego. Sixty lived in Precinct Two, where Benavides was later situated, and 30 in Precincts Three and Four, the county's

Table 10.1 Duval County sheep and goat brands, 1882–1895

Sheep Raiser	Ear Mark	Brand	Location on Animal	Date Registered
Walter W. Meek		=	Nose	March 16, 1892
Rafael A. García		×	Right Cheek	April 1, 1883
Santiago Pamf		ʔ	Left Cheek	May 28, 1883
Santos Medina		ⴄ	Left Jaw	October 20, 1882
Refugia Vela de Guerra		⅄G	Left Jaw	October 20, 1882
Carlos Guerra		⅄	Left Jaw	October 20, 1882
Porfirio Garza		⌂	Left Jaw	October 20, 1882
San Juana Vela		⅄G	Left Jaw	October 20, 1882
María Antonia Jiménez		ℛ	Left Cheek	August 4, 1883
Victoriano Canchola		ʎ	Both Cheeks	October 30, 1883
Marcos Villarreal		⅃⅄	Left Cheek	May 16, 1884
Macaria Muñoz		⊤	Left Ribs	September 19, 1884
Pomposo Perales		J	On the Jaw	September 21, 1885
Jirmet Bayoen		૧	Left Cheek	October 15, 1885
Manuel Longoria		I	Nose	May 6, 1887
Agapito Sáenz		⅃O	Left Jaw	November 6, 1888
Hebbron-Hewlett & Co.		HH	Left Side	May 29, 1890
Hilario Cadena		⊆	Left Jaw	June 6, 1893
Enrique C. Olivares		⌣	Nose	May 30, 1895
N. Gusset		o	Left Jaw	September 19, 1895

Source: Val W. Lehmann and José Cisneros, *Forgotten Legions: Sheep in the Rio Grande Plain of Texas* (El Paso: Texas Western Press, University of Texas at El Paso, 1969).

Concepción-Borjas region. One of the early sheep raisers in Duval was Diego Garza, who, in 1869, owned 2,500 head of sheep and 1,000 head of goats. San Diego shipped 600,000 pounds of wool and 20,000 hides to US markets in 1873.[5]

As a commercial activity in Duval County, sheep raising began emerging as the Civil War currents swirled. The area had a first-rate geographic environment for sheep raising. Livestock entrepreneurs could easily find water for their animals by digging wells and building water tanks. Furthermore, the land was inexpensive, and sheep merchants could buy property for as little as twelve cents an acre. With such advantages sheep husbandry continued to gain importance. By 1867 sheep raising was thriving in Duval County, with more than four hundred thousand sheep and three hundred thousand goats grazing in local ranchos. From 1870 to 1880, sheep raising became the most profitable agricultural market in Duval and Nueces Counties, as more than a million sheep were foraging on the land.[6]

Sheepmen Faced Many Challenges

But sheep raisers dealt with nature's ups and downs daily. For example, in 1874 a fierce storm overwhelmed San Diego, scattering droves of sheep and threatening shepherds who narrowly escaped its fury. W. W. Staples lost 1,500 animals. Then there were droughts. In May 1876 rainfall shortages forced sheep raisers in San Diego to move their flocks to the Nueces River and water holes near the coast. Between Las Borregas and Concepción, 50,000 sheep had to drink water from the area's several watering spots. San Diego and Piedra Pintas had been without rain for months, and many sheep raisers were watering their stocks from wells.[7]

Then there was the menacing danger from Indians and bandits. In October 1876 E. N. Gray of Concepción recounted that Indian raids had prompted many Mexicano sheep raisers to leave the county entirely. The exodus significantly dropped the wool available to ship to San Antonio, where buyers sought Mexican ewes. However, Gray expressed the hope that these sheep raisers would return as soon as they again felt safe. Their presence, Gray said, was vital to the county's future prosperity.[8]

As threatening as these troubles posed to the sheep business, they did not stunt its growth. By the mid-1870s San Diego had emerged as a regional headquarters on the sheep frontier. To kick off the spring clip of 1876, N. G. Collins shipped 3,000 pounds of wool to Corpus Christi. For the fall clip, Collins sold 135,000 pounds of wool. Thus, the recent drought had not entirely impeded the wool business.[9]

In 1877 Duval County tax reports indicated Tejanos dominated the sheep production. The county listed 327,842 sheep valued at $332,872, or $1.02 per head. Ten of the largest herds belonged to Tejanos, namely Manuel B. Vela, 7,700; Rafael Salinas, 7,500; Encarnación Garza, 5,000; Cayetano Ríos, 5,000; Calixto Tovar, 5,000; Encarnación García Pérez, 4,550; José María García Treviño, 4,000; Hilario Leal, 4,000; Pedro Martínez, 4,000; and Rafael Pérez, 4,000. Seven Americanos also owned large herds of sheep, including Gravis Brothers, 7,000; N. G. Collins, 5,000; Hoffman & Collins, 5,000; D. C. Hubbard, 5,000; Richard King, 5,000; Richard Jordan, 4,000; and Charles Roach, 4,000.[10]

While these seventeen men were the largest owners of sheep herds, there were 255 sheep raisers in the county. The average herd numbered 1,286 sheep. The average flock of the seventeen most prominent owners averaged a little more than 5,000 head, while the smaller owners had packs of slightly more than 1,000. These numbers indicate that even individuals of modest means could make a living in this endeavor.[11]

Sheep Raising Begins Downslide

In 1878 Duval County made public lands available as feeding grounds for all breeding stock, not just the large herds of wild cattle and horses that had grazed these pastures in prior years. Woolgrowers preferred the same range, and now they had access to it. It represented, as someone observed, "one extended pasture." The county's move, no doubt, was in response to a trend that must have been obvious.[12]

Nevertheless, from 1877 to 1878, the number of sheep in the county shrank by 21,000, or 6.3 percent. The following year, 1879, the numbers dropped an additional 45,831 heads, a loss in two years of 13.9 percent.

While the county did not have official numbers before 1877, their first year collecting taxes, the trend must have been evident. However, the sheep business remained the county's primary force driving the local economy.

In 1880 Duval County's sheep market made a modest recovery. Some of the more prominent sheep raisers in Duval County at that time included Manuel Vela (12,000), Encarnación García Pérez (10,000), Charles Hoffman (10,000), Cayetano Ríos (10,000), and Hubbard & Company (8,000). Tejanos continued to be dominant in this market. The county tax rolls, however, listed the following figures: Vela (9,800), García Pérez (8,057), Hoffman (7,603), Ríos (6,830), and Hubbard (6,000). Perhaps owners wished to deflate the numbers for tax purposes. However, what was also clear was that the sheep business was the primary livestock commerce in the county.[13]

Trading in wool by 1880 had reached such heights that the *Galveston News* published a daily market report carrying sheep prices from San Diego. Sheep growing became so profitable that railroad builder Uriah Lott joined the action. In 1882 Lott sold his share in the Corpus Christi, San Diego, and Rio Grande Railroad and bought a sheep ranch. J. P. Nelson, who built the railroad with Lott, partnered with him.[14]

In 1883, according to Duval County tax records, Charles Hoffman moved ahead of Manuel Vela as the largest sheep owner in the county, with 9,000 head to Vela's 8,000, prompting the *Corpus Christi Caller* to knight Hoffman as the "sheep King." While the newspaper regarded Hoffman as royalty, many others ranked among the sheep-raising nobility. Based on the figures from previous years, Manuel Vela and Encarnación García Pérez qualified as challengers to Hoffman's crowning since they owned more sheep than Hoffman and for a longer time. Jacinto Guerra could have claimed the honor because he had 100,000 pounds of wool in storage in his warehouse in San Diego.[15]

Nopal Seen as Possible Redeemer for Sheep

In March 1883 P. Gueydan of San Diego noted that sheep raisers in Duval County were using nopal as food for sheep. Gueydan said that he successfully fed nopal to his herd. Poor sheep, Gueydan added, fattened in twelve days, and "they eat with relish." The novel approach involved cutting the prickly pear and then *chamuscando* (searing off) its thorns. Herders then chopped the nopal into small pieces and fed it to the flock. As a result, the sheep had grown used to the nopal diet and subsisted on cacti without needing water.[16]

Later that year, in December, Gueydan announced that sheep raisers had received and tested a machine to cut nopal. However, the device did not yet appear to meet the sheep raisers' expectations, but they hoped to perfect it. The nopal question, Gueydan said, depended entirely on the appropriate machinery that waited for manufacture to reduce the cactus into small pieces. He added that fine-tuning the machinery would greatly benefit all sheep raisers between the Nueces River and the Rio Grande.[17]

In the meantime Gueydan had undertaken another experiment. He found a new way to feed large numbers of sheep by burning the thorns off the nopal over a brush fire and cutting the cactus with large knives. Gueydan surmised that two wagonloads of the plant were enough to feed two thousand sheep. A couple of men could prepare food for several thousand sheep. However, further testing was essential to improving the process for large-scale use. Nevertheless, Gueydan concluded that sheep raisers could fatten poor sheep on the nopal without consuming much water. Moreover, ranchers could save 90 percent of the lambs by feeding nopal to ewes during lambing season, whereas only 60 percent survived without the nopal.[18]

Shearing Seasons

The shearing season was vital for the sheep raisers and the community that depended on the woolly backs for jobs. There were two shearing seasons, one in the spring and another in the fall. Unfortunately, in 1883, before the shearing season commenced, cold conditions contributed to the loss of sheep. No doubt the weather adversely impacted the wool price. Still, sheep shearing started at Duval ranchos, with everyone expecting the clipping to awaken the town's economy. By the end of May, *tasinques* (sheep shearers) had completed the trimming, and the clip was all in. Sheep raisers, however, complained about receiving low prices for the wool.[19]

The fall shearing was soon in full swing in San Diego but was slower than usual due to a drought that had hit the sheep country over the summer, burning the range and drying up water holes. Residents welcomed a shower, hoping it was a sign that the parched weather was ending. Wool, ready for sale and shipment, was coming daily into San Diego.[20]

The 1884 county taxable values report indicates the sheep business took a significant hit. First, the number of sheep in the county continued a steady decline, but the drop was more substantial; from 1877 to 1884, the number of sheep had dropped 46 percent, from 327,842 to 178,637. Then, in September 1884, another dry season disappointed sheep and cattlemen throughout the county. A month later J. T. Murphy, a wool buyer from Laredo, turned up in San Diego to buy sheep, but his prices did not satisfy sheep raisers.[21]

Sheep's Final Decline

The following February 1885, ranchers were facing another wintry, dismal season. Buzzards and strays accounted for significant losses in sheep herds, and a cold spell had claimed much livestock. Merchants were buying plenty of skins and hides. Later that summer another weather calamity befell the county. On the way to his rancho, John Fitch encountered a hailstorm that killed three thousand of his and his neighbors' sheep. When the county gathered numbers for tax purposes, they showed that the sheep population had dropped another fifty thousand.[22]

Even though San Antonio wool buyers paid nineteen cents, two cents more than Corpus Christi, Duval County sheep raisers preferred to take wool to San Diego and sell it to Corpus Christi merchants. Sheepmen more than made up the two cents by incurring fewer transportation costs. Moreover, Corpus Christi traders took fleeces as packed, sacks and all. A San Diego merchant, Juan Puig, reported that fellow ranchers were smiling again even though wool sold at eleven to thirteen cents a pound. The previous spring it had brought eighteen to twenty cents. It was a sign of the times of what was yet to come, but then sheep raisers had a right to be hopeful. As the herds slowly recovered, the sheep increased by five thousand from the county's previous count.[23]

An optimistic sheep raiser tried to stay positive, believing there were more earnings in woolly backs than cattle. One could make more from wool at fifteen to twenty cents per pound than selling cattle at twenty-five dollars a head. He encouraged ranchers not to give up sheep for cattle when bovine prices went "way up" and advised ranchers to reduce their sheep herd to tend to them better. Moreover, cattlemen had to hunt buyers, drive cattle to market, and worry about quarantines, while sheep raisers did not; wool buyers sought the sheep raisers twice a year. Raising sheep, controlling their reproduction, and correctly attending to them yielded satisfactory profits; wool equaled cash. Another advantage of lambs, the sheep raiser added, was the availability of plenty of grass and water to help sheep survive a hard winter. Meanwhile, cattlemen had fat herds, but the market was flat, and they could not sell and make money.[24]

By 1887 people in San Diego felt cheerful despite a drought. Sheep raisers claimed San Diego as the best wool market in South Texas, better than San Antonio. Most clippings sold fast and at fair prices. Corpus Christi and Laredo buyers eagerly came to San Diego to purchase wool. They paid, on average, sixteen cents per pound.[25]

Perhaps sheep raisers were optimistic as the 1887 county livestock tally noted another increase of thirteen thousand sheep. In March 1888 the sheep business still appeared to be making a comeback: N. G. Collins sold five thousand muttons at two dollars a head; Hoffman and Ridder sold their fat sheep for cash; and Shaw and Cleary shipped eight hundred lambs to St. Louis. People kept busy raising and shearing sheep, as well as working crops. Wool began arriving at the Gueydan & Company warehouse with the Albino Canales, J. A. Pérez, and Charles Hoffman clips. Perhaps the optimism was well placed as the 1888 livestock inventory showed an additional twenty thousand sheep.[26]

Unfortunately, the three years of rebound proved misleading. The number of sheep, while increasing, never recovered to the 1884 count. Soon, sheep took a downturn and reached their lowest level in years. This downward spiral in the number of sheep resumed in 1889 and never stabilized. By the end of the century, sheep totaled a mere 7,164, plummeting 98 percent from 1877. By then all the big players had dropped out of the game.[27]

In 1896 Encarnacion García Pérez and his mother-in-law, Trinidad Flores, lost five thousand sheep to a devastating flood at their ranch on the Nueces River. After more than fifty years as leading citizens of Duval County, they returned to Mexico. While his mother-in-law died in Mexico in 1906, García returned to Duval County in 1915 when revolutionary activity consumed all of Mexico.[28]

National Politics and Duval County Sheep

What caused or contributed to this decline in the sheep industry? The issue of free trade and the national taxing policy dominated conversations in those days. The Republican administrations of that era taxed imports at high rates to protect local manufacturers. Many Duval County sheep raisers blamed President Grover Cleveland and the Democrats for opposing the tax because Democrats believed it meant higher consumer costs. Instead, they preferred that goods enter tax free. However, imported wool from Australia and other wool-producing countries competed with American wool, including fleece raised in Duval County, causing prices to plummet. Therefore, Duval County woolgrowers favored the Republican approach to tax imported wool at a high rate.[29]

In 1882 B. W. Johnson established a newspaper in San Diego named the *Bell Punch*, which he dedicated to the woolgrowers' interests. On November 6, 1882, editor Johnson opined that Duval County's sheep raisers deserved legal protection from free trade. The editor wrote that sheep ranchers spent their money at home, and the voters should look out for them. "Ask any successful wool grower, and they will tell you that to succeed, you must be on the saddle or foot day and night; that the harder the weather, the more you are exposed to the wind, and you're living in most instances on black coffee, dried bread, and meat. All year round, they carry their life in their hands," the editor exclaimed.[30]

One modern-day economist describes it this way: "If you were a sheepherder, you wanted tariffs" on wool imports, but "if you were a manufacturer, you wanted cheap wool." Free trade called for the free importation of products, which some believed would adversely affect Duval County's sheep raisers. That is why Editor Johnson called for protection from free trade by imposing taxes on imports.[31]

But the issue was not that simple for everyone. The *Laredo Daily Times* of July 17, 1888, recounted a debate involving local farmer Edward Gray and a Republican who charged the longtime Duval County ranchero with supporting free trade. Gray responded that he had never been an "advocate of a tariff to hold my business up, and I have had sheep for many years and still raise them in Duval County. No, sir, I do not favor taxing the whole people so that a few may become rich. No, sir, I am not quite that low yet, not that selfish."[32]

Democrats blamed the Republican tax policy for the nation's economic woes, although Duval sheep raisers saw it as beneficial. Eventually, Republican President William McKinley, who had championed high tariffs on imports during his time in Congress, acceded to lower import taxes. First, however, the Republican party sought to negotiate reciprocal agreements with other countries. By 1897, when McKinley entered the White House, the sheep economy in Duval County was beyond help.

The decline in sheep raising began shortly after the county's organization in 1876. In 1897 wool protection ended, followed by the disappearance of the sheep industry as a vital cog in the county's economy.

Table 10.2 Duval County sheep numbers, 1877–1899

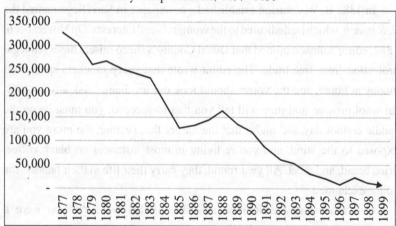

Source: Duval County tax records.

In February 1899 the temperature in the area dropped to 5 degrees Fahrenheit, causing fatal harm to livestock and sealing any hope for a rebound. One man in Santa Cruz lost 800 sheep from a herd of 2,500. The Duval County Commissioners Court acknowledged the end of the era when it approved a 25 percent drop in livestock taxable value, including sheep.[33]

Chapter 11

Treading into Politics

On June 15, 1860, Governor Sam Houston called a special election in the Fourteenth Judicial District, which included Nueces County and, by extension, the future Duval County. The election was to select a judge to fill the vacancy created by the incumbent's death. This election was crucial to Duval County because the new judge would resolve titles to lands in Duval, an issue critical to Tejano landowners.[1]

These rancheros were the guardians of the area's extended families and the people who worked the ranchos. An authentic dynamic, traceable to the Spanish ranch tradition, still existed between the *patrón* and his workers. Rancheros provided jobs and livelihoods for their laboring families, often for more than one generation. The ranchers also served as baptismal *padrinos* and *madrinas* (godmothers) to their employees' children. Moreover, while things were different in Texas regarding individual rights, the political culture of Mexico still lingered in area ranchos. What was beneficial for the ranch owner was advantageous for his ranch hands. So workers exercising voting rights for the first time looked to their *patrones* for direction.

Building a Political Structure

Tejanos needed to back those they believed could help them preserve their way of life. So it was no surprise that the new voters in Duval County came out in large numbers and voted overwhelmingly for the candidate they thought sympathized with the landowners and their best interests.

On Monday, August 6, 1860, Duval County voters participated in the special election Governor Houston had called. At the end of the polling, the turnout in Agua Poquita, south of San Diego, catapulted Duval County into the middle of state politics. Duval County voters cast 313 of 315 votes for one candidate, prompting Houston to throw out the Duval County returns, changing the outcome. Ultimately, the Texas Supreme Court settled the matter, reaching the same conclusion as the governor.[2] It was quite an eye-opening baptism into American politics for Duval County Tejanos. They saw firsthand how the American political and judicial systems worked. Moreover, the election at Agua Poquita helped Tejanos shape their political unity and identity, a character that impacted Duval County throughout its history.

The underlying issue for Duval County voters was protecting their legal rights to the land. The US Supreme Court, in the 1855 case of *McKinney v. Saviego*, had ostensibly clouded the issue of Mexican land titles. However, in February 1860 the Texas Legislature enacted a law giving Duval County landowners another opportunity to ratify their Spanish and Mexican land grants. José Ángel Navarro III from Bexar County, nephew of the venerable Tejano statesman José Antonio Navarro, introduced the bill in the Texas House of Representatives. Nueces County State Senator Forbes N. Britton from Corpus Christi cosponsored it in the Senate.[3]

On February 18, 1860, an anonymous letter from an apparent supporter of Tejanos' land interests appeared in the *Ranchero*, arguing that the law was "a measure of tardy justice to your section of the country." The unidentified newspaper correspondent wrote that legislators voted for the law's passage and demonstrated their friendship with the region. The writer added that lawmakers supported "those who loved justice," adding that "some opponents are devotees at the shrine of ambition." The measure passed the House on a 45–29 vote, with Nueces Representative Henry Kinney voting in favor.[4]

As soon as the legislature adopted the new law, several Tejano landowners in Duval County began to prepare legal suits for filing in the Fourteenth Judicial District. These landowners believed Americanos could help navigate the American legal system to clear their titles. They turned to two men they had employed through the years to help with other land issues. They had hired Prussian-born Felix Blücher to survey their land grants as early as 1854. Blücher was familiar with the owners, and he was with them. In addition, to assist with their land issues, landowners also retained attorney Charles Lovenskiold, a multilingual Dane. Perhaps Tejanos felt an affinity with these two men because, like them, they were not native English speakers and had the accent of foreigners.[5]

The Inaugural Election in Duval County

Governor Houston called a special election for the first week of August 1860 to fill Judge Milton P. Norton's unexpired term. The Fourteenth Judicial District included Bee, Goliad, Karnes, Live Oak, Nueces, Refugio, and San Patricio Counties, an area with slightly less than ten thousand inhabitants. Goliad had the largest population and the highest number of native-born inhabitants. In contrast, Nueces County had the most significant number of voting-age residents and people of foreign birth.[6]

Under the legislature's decree assigning the unorganized counties of Duval and Encinal to Nueces County—for judicial purposes—the Nueces County Commissioners Court created a voting precinct, allowing residents in these two counties to vote in the special election. Accordingly, at a special meeting on July 3, 1860, county commissioners created Precinct Nine for Duval and Encinal Counties. Then, on July 21, 1860, the commissioners court scheduled the election for the first Monday in August 1860, as the governor had decreed.[7]

The voting location for Precinct Nine was at Rancho La Felicidad on the Agua Poquita between San Diego and Los Ángeles. The roads between Corpus Christi, Laredo, San Diego, and Mier crisscrossed the ranch, making it a logical locale for the voting precinct to serve the vast rural region. The Laredo to Corpus Christi road also passed through Los Ángeles, split between Duval and Encinal Counties. The court named John Vale the election judge, but he was not at the ranch on election day, so his mayordomo, Rafael Salinas, took his place.[8]

In late June candidates began filing. Seven men, all attorneys specializing in land issues, expressed interest. Among the candidates was Goliad attorney John F. McKinney, who had unsuccessfully challenged Judge Norton three years earlier and contested the election results because of alleged illegal voting. McKinney's primary challenger was Joseph O'Connor, a fellow Virginian. Among O'Connor's "friends" were Blücher and Lovenskiold, who played a vital role in the election.[9]

Early returns gave O'Connor a substantial lead, primarily from the massive turnout in Nueces County. McKinney closed the gap when votes from the northern counties came in, but his ballots were still considerably short. When voting closed, O'Connor led with a 171-vote margin, 654 to 483. It is unclear why officials did not call a runoff election since neither candidate had a clear majority.[10]

O'Connor received his ostensibly winning margin from the newly created Precinct Nine in Duval County results, which recorded 315 votes, 45.2 percent of the total Nueces County turnout. O'Connor carried Agua Poquita, receiving 313 of the 315 votes cast. Even canceling the Duval County vote, no candidate could claim a majority. McKinney would have ended up with 29.3 percent of the vote, followed closely by L. S. Lawhon with 25.5 percent.[11]

In those years all Nueces County voters, regardless of residence, could vote for any precinct office, just as they did for countywide offices. Therefore, eligible men in Corpus Christi could vote for candidates in the unorganized Duval County running for justice of the peace or constable. In this way men like Blücher, Lovenskiold, and other Americanos from other parts of Nueces County voted at Agua Poquita.[12]

Loser Once Again Cries Foul

As in the previous election for district judge, McKinney claimed cheating. His supporters attacked the legitimacy of the vote from many fronts. They complained that the election announcement did not meet the letter of the law and accused county officials of having surreptitiously established the polling station at Agua Poquita. Nonetheless, despite allegations that the commissioners court created Precinct Nine in secret, voters were in on the secret since Agua Poquita had the largest turnout of any precinct in Nueces County, including Precinct One in the city of Corpus Christi. The allegations made by McKinney backers, however, appeared specious. The Nueces County Commissioners Court had held a special meeting to address the upcoming election two months before, creating a new precinct at Vale's Rancho on the Agua Poquita to facilitate voting in the unorganized counties of Duval and Encinal, and gave notice to all polling stations.[13]

These facts, publicized in the local newspaper, did not satisfy McKinney supporters, and they held meetings throughout the Fourteenth Judicial District. They mailed petitions and affidavits to Governor Houston, asking him to invalidate the election results of Precinct Nine and certify McKinney as the winner. Two attorneys, Foster and Givens, called a meeting in Live Oak County to prevent O'Connor from taking the seat. They claimed the election was "fraudulent owing to the votes of Mexican pelados in Nueces County." McKinney supporters held another protest meeting in Goliad, which alleged the "importation of [300] votes from the Rio Grande and beyond." In Nueces County, "a secret organization" allegedly intended to hang Blücher, O'Connor, Lovenskiold, and County Judge Henry Gilpin.[14]

On October 8, 1860, the *Ranchero* reported that some twenty-six men signed a lengthy petition to the governor, secretary of state, and the attorney general, charging Precinct Nine's returns were illegal and fraudulent. They claimed that "establishing a precinct including voters of all of the unorganized county of Encinal was illegal, and the returns of election from said precinct cannot be received."[15]

Allegations of illegal voting were not the only charges leveled at those associated with Precinct Nine. McKinney loyalists claimed Lovenskiold had urged the legislature to adopt a statute that would upset the status quo. This charge possibly dealt with the land act to help Tejanos clear the title to their grants, a law Lovenskiold supported. It is unlikely that Lovenskiold influenced the passage of the new decree, which applied to a much larger area than his sway in Nueces County. Nevertheless, the petitioners suggested that these charges provoked the worst in the Americano consciousness.[16]

Petitioners, including H. W. Berry, mayor of Corpus Christi, advanced a rumor that Lovenskiold had issued rifles from the militia storehouse to the Mexicanos in San Diego to corrupt voting at Agua Poquita. Governor Houston wrote to reprimand Lovenskiold for misusing the militia arsenal. Lovenskiold responded to Houston on September 14, 1860, informing the governor that such accusations were "false and slanderous" and without foundation. Lovenskiold told Governor Houston that in July, twenty-four rifles and the necessary ammunition were "furnished . . . for the protection of San Diego Rancho, an exposed settlement . . . against threatened attacks by hostile Indians." Moreover, Lovenskiold informed the governor that the rancho was miles from Precinct Nine.[17]

Finally, McKinney advocates claimed that land speculators—led by William G. Hale, Lovenskiold, Blücher, and others—were part of a scheme to manipulate Mexican voters to further personal ambitions. The mention of Hale was no doubt intended to ensure Houston, who had a spiteful history with Hale, took notice. In case Governor Houston did not get the message on Hale's involvement, McKinney reminded the governor he owed McKinney a loan.[18]

Governor Houston Steps In

Houston was sufficiently impressed by the letters and petitions from the protesting counties to postpone a scheduled trip to Washington. On October 15, 1860, the governor and Secretary of State E. W. Cave met in Austin to receive the Fourteenth Judicial District's votes. The governor concluded that a "large portion" of Precinct Nine included by Nueces County was part of Webb County; that the establishment of the precinct, including the voters of all of the unorganized county of Encinal, was illegal; and that "the returns of election from said precinct cannot be received."[19]

The governor also determined Nueces County officials had not established Precinct Nine at a regular Nueces County Commissioners Court term as the law required. Moreover, Houston thought the court had failed to provide public notice of the precinct's establishment when it announced the August election. The Nueces County Commissioners Court's alleged missteps and how election officials had conducted the vote at Precinct Nine convinced the governor that the voting at Precinct Nine was "illegal and fraudulent." Consequently, he and the secretary of state rejected Precinct Nine's returns and declared McKinney the winner.[20]

Houston's action was not received kindly by all. The *State Gazette* in Austin lambasted the governor. "He preferred charges of illegal precincts and went behind the vote of the returning officer," the *Gazette* pointed out, adding that "the law provides that the proper tribunal for this type of case is the district court" in the neighboring judicial district. "We learn, however," the newspaper continued, "that Gov. Houston constituted himself a court to try the case and that the Governor and Ex Officio Judge heard with imperturbable gravity." The newspaper, employing sarcasm, quipped that with the "severe impartiality for which [Houston] is noted, he then decided in favor of his old political friend Col. McKinney." Once again, the *Gazette* reiterated that the law required the adjoining district court to hear the case. "We believe Gov. Houston exercised an arbitrary and unwarrantable power," the paper concluded.[21]

In Corpus Christi the *Ranchero* asked citizens to respect McKinney in his office and simultaneously fight Houston's power grab at every opportunity. It bemoaned rumors that many men were supposedly organizing in northern counties of the Fourteenth Judicial District to "run off every Mexican." Recognizing the vital contribution Tejanos made to the local economy as business owners, consumers, and laborers, the *Ranchero* opined that such an action would be an economic disaster for the area.[22]

Appeal to the Courts

Soon after taking the bench, McKinney found that a cloud hung over his authority, prompting the *Ranchero* to report that the judge could not accomplish much "due to his appointment controversy." In addition, the newspaper reported that O'Connor had filed an election contest in neighboring Victoria County, as the law provided, challenging Governor Houston's action.[23]

The Tejano vote and election uncertainty in Precinct Nine were at the center of controversy in the court case in Victoria's district court in October 1860. O'Connor offered witness testimony that the turnout in Precinct Nine was not extraordinary. First, William L. Rogers testified he had been a resident of Nueces County since 1846 and explained that about five hundred Mexican men lived there. Moreover, "the Mexican voters assembled at Vale's rancho to vote [because] they were impressed with the belief—as I have heard many say—that they would not be permitted to vote at the Banquete where many of them had formerly voted."[24]

Second, Judge Gilpin concurred with Rogers that between five and six hundred "legal Mexican voters" lived within the "old boundaries" of Nueces County. Gilpin informed the court of his familiarity with Spanish and that he had engaged in business and official relations with the Mexican population since 1830. Gilpin said several large ranchos quickly "settling up," such as Agua Poquita, existed in the area. Moreover, the judge declared many Mexicanos had informed Judge Gilpin that they voted in Precinct Nine because they feared "a party opposed to permitting Mexicans to vote" would stop them from voting at other precincts.[25]

O'Connor also offered witnesses that countered the idea that the Nueces County Commissioners Court created Precinct Nine secretively. Furthermore, several people were present when the commissioners court acted on the legislature's directive to include Duval and Encinal Counties for judicial purposes. Perhaps the most glaring weakness in O'Connor's defense was the failure to present firsthand testimony from those who participated at Agua Poquita on election day. O'Connor's attorneys did depose Blücher regarding a map of the area. Still, they entered no depositions or affidavits on the witness stand from Salinas, Lovenskiold, R. Miller, Calixto Tovar, or Antonio de la Garza, all of whom had served as election officials.

McKinney argued that Precinct Nine voters were not qualified to cast ballots because of legal deficiencies involving residence in Mexico or on the Rio Grande, being too young to vote, being deceased, not being present at the polls on election day, and sharing the same name. To bolster his claims, McKinney submitted an affidavit from Rodrigo Ynojosa, purportedly a 52-year-old lifelong resident of Nueces County living in Corpus Christi.

Ynojosa testified on the record, knowing many Mexicanos who lived in South Texas. Although unable to write—having signed with an "X"—Ynojosa nonetheless claimed to have "looked over the list of voters" and recognized more than two hundred names on the electoral roll that were not citizens of the Fourteenth Judicial District. Ynojosa identified forty men who were not eligible to vote in Precinct Nine and said four men were not in the area on election day; five did not live in the district; seven resided in Mexico; eleven lived elsewhere in Texas.[26]

A review of the 1860 Nueces County Census confirms that many of the men Ynojosa singled out as not living in the county may have been legal voters. The same census reveals that Ynojosa might have erred on several calls. For example, the witness testified that José María Gonzales lived in Las Almas, but the census includes a man with the same name living in San Diego. Ynojosa stated Pedro López did not belong in the district, but the census records show a man with that name living in Brasanious in Nueces County. Ynojosa maintained that Ángel Arguijo was a boy of 10. However, the census indicates that a young man by that name lived in San Diego and was 18, perhaps passing for 21. Ynojosa supposed Juan Ramos lived in Mier, but a man by that name also resided in Brasanious. Ynojosa then swore that a voter named Juan Ynojosa might have been his son, but the son was not at the election precinct on that day. However, a voter with the same name lived in San Diego. As a final example, Ynojosa identified Dolores Hinojosa as being a woman. In Mexican naming customs, a man can have a woman's name, such as María, often used as a middle name with José. While not as common, Dolores can also be a man's name, much like Guadalupe and Ventura. The Mexican custom is to name children after Catholic saints: Joseph and Mary (José María), Our Lady of Sorrows (Dolores), and Our Lady of Guadalupe, to name a few.[27]

Chipito Sandoval provided another sworn statement for McKinney along the same lines as Ynojosa. Like Ynojosa, Sandoval could not write. Moreover, Sandoval proclaimed he maintained a lifelong residency at Agua Dulce in Nueces County and claimed to know many Mexicanos in South Texas. However, according to the 1860 Census, the only Sandoval who lived in the area was 40 years old and resided in San Patricio County.[28]

Another individual giving sworn testimony was George W. Foster, who said he had dealt with the people in South Texas for fourteen years and knew many of them. But Foster does not appear in the census; the only Foster in the census was a young man named J. A. Foster, who lived at the home of Esther Mann at Casa Blanca.[29]

It is not difficult to highlight some of the probable mistakes Ynojosa and the others made. For example, more than one man can have the same name, and people with the same name could have lived in Mexico, elsewhere, and Nueces County. But then, two of McKinney's witnesses did not appear in the census for Nueces County. Perhaps they were not home when the census taker came by, and the enumerator overlooked them. Maybe this explains why some Mexicano voters were not in the census. Indeed, it is reasonable to assume that many Mexicanos lived in remote ranches, and census takers did not visit them. Several Mexicanos could have been out on the range or the *brasada* tending to livestock. As O'Connor's witnesses countered, there was no way those men could know every Mexicano in the county and their legal status.[30]

Of the 315 voters on the poll list, 117 (37.1 percent) appeared in the Nueces County Census, including 45 from San Diego and 15 from Agua Poquita. These voters were 82 percent of eligible voters in those two communities. Moreover, of all names from every census place appearing in Nueces County on the poll list, only two men were from San Patricio (also in the Fourteenth Judicial District). Only one individual came from Starr County, which was in another district. These explanations strengthen O'Connor supporters' contention that Tejanos throughout Nueces County saw San Diego as more "Mexican voter-friendly" and traveled to Agua Poquita to ensure their votes counted.[31]

After the election the *Ranchero* advocated adopting a voter registration law to eliminate fraud. The newspaper argued that many Mexicanos had a right to vote and election officials should not arbitrarily disqualify them. Indeed, the editor contended that Mexicanos understood "the principles and wordings of our government, as well as any American."[32]

Before the election, the newspaper noted, everyone made a pitch for the Mexican vote, and "those who get it are satisfied, but those who don't cry fraud and corruption. Those who didn't get this Mexican vote are then, of course, 'immaculate.'" Indeed, O'Connor charged McKinney with paying large sums to obtain "the whole of the votes of the people of Mexican origin." Moreover, O'Connor alleged, "the defendant sought his election to a high judicial station by bribery of voters and by wantonly corrupting the purity of the ballot boxes in contravention of law, good morals, and public policy."[33]

In March 1861 the district court in Victoria ruled for O'Connor, and McKinney promptly appealed the verdict to the Texas Supreme Court. In November 1861 the high court overturned the lower court's decision, reinstating McKinney to the bench. The Supreme Court rejected O'Connor's defense, finding that only a few men, whose names appeared upon the returns as voting, were present at the election. In addition, the court noted that most voters lacked the qualifications to cast ballots. While the court found the witnesses McKinney offered were persuasive, it nonetheless opined, "This evidence [from both parties] is circumstantial for the most part." The court reviewed each deposition, finding that McKinney's testimony contained phrases that the witness "thinks" or "believes" that a specified number of voters were legal. Other witnesses were sure many legitimate Tejano voters could not reside in Nueces County. Not one Tejano voter from Precinct Nine was deposed, interviewed, or cross-examined during any proceedings.[34]

The high court wondered why O'Connor had not brought forth witnesses, such as Blücher and Lovenskiold, who could have attested to what had transpired at Precinct Nine. Their direct firsthand testimony would have been crucial to proving O'Connor's case. This lack of direct evidence troubled the court, which concluded it "must decide the case as we find it." The court did not require those testifying on McKinney's behalf to have the same firsthand knowledge of what had transpired at Agua Poquita. None of McKinney's witnesses acknowledged being at the Precinct Nine voting location on election day. The court, instead, assumed that irregular balloting had led to the results of the August 1860 election; however, it resorted to a somewhat unconventional approach in reaching its decision. The justices employed the "combined knowledge" of all the witnesses, including one of O'Connor's witnesses, to ascertain that no more than ninety votes were valid. This determination raised the "presumption" that the returns from Precinct Nine were fraudulent and false. They concluded, "as a matter of fact, from the evidence" presented at the trial, that McKinney received more "legal votes."[35]

Land Ownership Underscored Election

Why did the voting in Precinct Nine in Duval County yield these results? Why did 313 out of 315 people appear to be of like mind and vote for the same candidate? Clashes between political groups in Nueces County and those in Precinct Nine in 1860 were mainly about the land. Few other issues concerned the old-time settlers. Duval County Mexican land grant holders were vitally interested in ensuring land stayed in Tejanos' hands, and district judges played a vital role in their aspirations.

Lovenskiold and Blücher ensured that Duval County Tejano voters knew McKinney's involvement in Mexicano land cases. It did not help his candidacy that the man who owned the most trespassing grants clouding many Mexican titles in Duval County was named Thomas F. McKinney. Not only did they both have the same last name, but they also shared the same middle initial. Perhaps that association may have raised some concerns from Duval County rancheros.[36]

Tejanos sought out others they trusted to help them protect their lands and safeguard their families and workers. In December 1860 four cases involving land grants in Duval County came before the court. As his election was still in doubt, McKinney recused himself from the court cases and asked Judge Edmund J. Davis of the neighboring Twelfth Judicial District to hear them. The future Reconstructionist governor ruled in favor of the landowners in all four lawsuits.

The court may have thrown out Precinct Nine votes, but Duval County Tejanos achieved their ultimate aim in the courts. Nine of the sixteen original Tejano landowners in Duval County appeared to have voted in the election, and no doubt all sixteen urged their relatives, friends, neighbors, and ranch hands to vote.

The results of Precinct Nine in the 1860 election set the stage for the political future of Duval County. Tejano voters did not base their voting decisions on blind ignorance; instead, they used their overwhelming numbers to influence the election and placed their trust in individuals with whom they had previous business dealings. Such mutually beneficial arrangements helped Tejanos guard their land, which was vital for their economic means, language, customs, and extended family traditions.

Chapter 12

Establishing
a New County

Duval County Tejanos' political prowess withered during the Civil War and Reconstruction. It was not until they again had a stake in an election's results that they returned to the polls in significant numbers. Once Nueces County gave Duval County leave to form a commissioners court, petitioners wasted no time. Before long, Duval County was up and running with a functional local government.

To begin organizing the county, seventy-five citizens living in Duval County petitioned the chief justice of Nueces County for permission. These individuals had to be 21, "bona fide free white male inhabitants," and Texas citizens. In April 1876 N. G. Collins, P. C. Gravis, J. H. Moses, James O. Luby, and others requested such recognition. The Nueces County judge denied the request, questioning whether San Diego was in Duval or Nueces County.[1]

Shortly after, Duval leaders again petitioned the chief justice through Gravis, the Nueces County Commissioner representing their area. The judge tabled the request until the county surveyor could review the county's boundary.[2] Five months later, on September 22, 1876, petitioners were back, but Nueces County tabled the matter a third time, saying the county attorney needed to review the situation.[3]

Fig. 12.1 James O. Luby (1846–1932) was the first county judge of Duval County. Lewis E. Daniell, *Personnel of the Texas State Government: With Sketches of Representative Men of Texas* (San Antonio: Maverick Printing House, 1892).

First Election

Finally, Nueces County called for an election on November 7, 1876, to select Duval County officials and a location for the county seat. The election used existing Nueces County voting precincts in San Diego, Piedras Pintas, Concepción, and Borjas. Election clerks in San Diego were C. K. Gravis, J. A. Murdock, William E. Stanley, A. J. Ayers, and F. G. Tovar. Over in Piedras Pintas, poll workers consisted of Felix Salinas, Esperidión Cuéllar, H. Mass, Isidro Benavides, and C. Stillman. John Vining, Charles K. Moses, Félix del Barrio, Juan Palacios, and Máximo Pérez handled the boxes at Concepción. At Borjas election overseers were José Alejo Pérez, J. C. Cuéllar, Rich Blücher, August Gottlieb, and E. H. Caldwell.[4]

Nearly three hundred voters turned out, comparable to Duval County's voting strength in the 1860 special election for district judge. While the electoral requirements imposed by Presidential Reconstruction were no longer in play, Republican-leaning candidates did well in this initial election. Voters elected James O. Luby, Calixto Tovar, John Dix, Rafael Salinas, and Apolonio Vela, who likely had Republican leanings. Charles Hoffman, Luby's brother-in-law, also might have been a Republican. J. Williamson Moses was married to a Mexicana, suggesting empathy for Republican views on people of color.

Table 12.1 Results of Duval County organizational election, November 7, 1876

Office	San Diego	Piedras Pintas	Concepción	Borjas	Total
County Judge					
James O. Luby	102	31	76	27	236
H. S. Lang	25	32	1	0	58
Total	**127**	**63**	**77**	**27**	**294**
Sheriff					
R. P. Fly	114	61	73	27	275
Sam H. Tinney	13	2	1	0	16
Total	**127**	**63**	**74**	**27**	**291**
County Clerk					
A. R. Valls	119	20	2	10	151
Alfred Moses	7	35	76	18	136
Total	**126**	**55**	**78**	**28**	**287**
Tax Assessor					
Calixto Tovar	101	6	32	26	165
R. B. Glover	25	57	42	2	126
Total	**126**	**63**	**74**	**28**	**291**
Treasurer					
Charles Hoffman	125	56	78	28	287
M. Burks	1	0	0	0	1
Total	**126**	**56**	**78**	**28**	**288**

(*Continues*)

Table 12.1 (Continued)

Office	San Diego	Piedras Pintas	Concepción	Borjas	Total
County Attorney					
J. W. Moses	80	58	78	28	244
C. McGuire	43	5	0	0	48
John G. Bell	2	0	0	0	2
Total	**123**	**63**	**78**	**28**	**292**
Surveyor					
J. C. Caldwell	77	44	3	6	130
John J. Dix	48	19	75	22	164
Total	**125**	**63**	**78**	**28**	**294**
Hides Inspector					
Theodore Lamberton	86	34	61	27	208
Jesús Treviño	34	27	15	0	76
A. Linares	6	2	0	0	8
Total	**126**	**63**	**76**	**27**	**292**
County Seat					
San Diego	118	40	0	0	158
Piedras Pintas	0	2	0	0	2
Concepción	0	0	72	0	72
Borjas	0	0	0	29	29
Total	**118**	**42**	**72**	**29**	**261**
County Commissioner					
F. C. Gravis	124				124
B. W. Toklas		43			43
William Hubbard		20			20
John Vining			38		38
Rafael Salinas			39		39
E. H. Caldwell				26	26
N. S. Lang				4	4
Total	**124**	**63**	**77**	**30**	**294**

(*Continues*)

Table 12.1 (Continued)

Office	San Diego	Piedras Pintas	Concepción	Borjas	Total
Justice of the Peace					
John Humphrey	77				77
B. N. Fletcher	49				49
Eugene A. Glover		18			18
Modesto Garza		45			45
John Vining			78		78
Charles Roach				26	26
Total	**126**	**63**	**78**	**26**	**293**
Constable					
Apolonio Vela	121				121
J. Stansel	1				1
Miguel Martínez		60			60
Peter Skaro			40		40
Jesús Pérez			36		36
Alex Pérez				26	27
Total	**122**	**60**	**76**	**26**	**284**

Source: Nueces County Election Returns, 1858–1876, Nueces County District Clerk.

Americano candidates, who were in the minority, captured all count-ywide posts except the county tax assessor post, which went to Tovar. Two other Tejanos, Jesús Treviño and A. Linares, unsuccessfully contested county-wide offices. In addition, the electorate chose longtime Tejano political activist Rafael Salinas to the commissioners court and Modesto Garza as a justice of the peace. Salinas took his seat by one vote over John Vining. Finally, Tejanos Apolonio Vela, Miguel Martínez, and Alex Pérez took three constable positions. Jesús Pérez lost the fourth constable seat to Peter Skaro by four votes.

In creating Duval County, the legislature decreed that county commis-sioners locate the county seat within ten miles of the county's center. However, there were no communities within this ten-mile range except, perhaps, Piedras Pintas, which was no more than a rancho. Commissioners took the law, which read county seat "may be located by a majority vote anywhere within ten miles of its center," as suggestive rather than mandatory. They reasoned that the law merely suggested the location and left it up to the voters to decide. They chose San Diego in the election held on November 7, 1876.[5]

Getting Down to Business

The new Duval County Commissioners Court held its initial meeting on December 4, 1876, at Judge Luby's store in San Diego, with Luby and Commissioners Gravis and Salinas constituting a quorum. After presenting their election certificates to Nueces County Judge Joseph Fitzsimmons, the commissioners court accepted bonds for Dix of $10,000, provided by N. G. Collins, José María García Treviño, and E. G. Garza. Judge Luby subsequently administered the oath of office to County Clerk A. R. Valls.[6]

Throughout the nineteenth century, Tejanos provided most of the bonds required for an individual to hold office, whether the elected official was Americano or Tejano. From the beginning of the county's formation, it was clear that Tejanos were willing and prepared to support its development with their votes and money. However, they did not serve in public office in numbers anywhere near their population. Nevertheless, Tejanos did not hesitate to show their commitment to playing a vital role in their county with their pocketbooks.

On December 11, 1876, the commissioners court authorized Luby to secure an "iron cage" for a jail. Commissioners also appointed Gravis as "a committee of one" to work with Collins in negotiating with Manuel Ancira to rent his building as a temporary courthouse for twelve months. Finally, they appropriated the first four hundred dollars from the occupation tax to pay for the courthouse's rent, calculated at one hundred dollars quarterly.[7]

At the onset of 1877, at a January 8 meeting, Commissioner B. W. Toklas took his oath and joined the court. Meanwhile, the court rejected the bond of Justice of the Peace of Precinct One Peter Skaro as insufficient. They also declared the offices of Precinct Two Justice of the Peace Miguel Martínez and Constable Modesto Garza vacant because they failed to qualify for those positions. The court replaced Martinez with E. A. Glover, who had lost to Martínez by a better than two-to-one margin. Glover declined, and the court selected Saul H. Tinney.[8] Commissioners approved continuing to maintain roads to Encinal, La Salle, and McMullen Counties, previously established by Nueces County. They also directed the county surveyor to examine routes to San Antonio and Rio Grande City and stake out the first six miles of roads emanating from the county seat in each direction.[9]

On November 15, 1877, the commissioners court engaged in its first controversial issue, fining Sheriff R. R. Fly fifteen dollars for contempt of court. The sheriff had failed to provide a supplemental tax roll the court had requested. Later, the court accepted Fly's resignation. However, political intrigue may have been in the air, as Justice of the Peace John Humphries also tendered his resignation a few days later. The commissioners immediately accepted his resignation and named Humphries the new sheriff and tax collector. Collins, E. G. Pérez, E. G. Garza, José M. G. Treviño, Pablo Pérez, John J. Dix, Gueydan Brothers, Fly, and W. Hubbard guaranteed the $30,000 bonds needed to assume the position. At the same meeting, commissioners appointed P. A. Matteson to fill the justice of the peace position that Humphries vacated.[10]

Commissioners appointed a committee to correspond with architects and iron dealers for a new courthouse and jail. Judge Luby, Collins, and Matteson served on the group. The group was to secure plans and specifications for a thirty-six-by-forty-foot courthouse to cost no more than $4,000 and spend no more than $2,500 for a two-by-six-foot jail or "iron cage." Later, the court added Charles Sullivan and William Hubbard to the newly appointed courthouse and jail committee, accepted a donation of San Diego town lots from Collins to build the new courthouse and jail, and directed Luby to prepare the documents needed to complete the deed transfer.[11]

The court also instructed the road overseer for Precinct One to begin work on the road to Concepción, especially on the San Diego Creek crossing. Roads in other precincts proceeded under Surveyor Dix's direction. Commissioners also appointed five-member juries in each precinct to deal with road development. Their role was to "obtain the assent and signatures of all persons through whose lands any roads were to pass."[12]

Serving on the Precinct One committee were Charles Hoffman, Theodore Lamberton, José M. G. Treviño, Claude Tiblier, and E. García

Pérez. The Precinct Two committee consisted of Isidro Benavides, José María Sáenz, E. A. Glover, Tiburcio Salinas, and Juan Sáenz. The five viewers in Precinct Three were E. N. Gray, Jesús María Palacios, Charles Stillman, Francisco Cadena, and Eduardo G. Hinojosa. Finally, Precinct Four committee members were Richard Jordan, Jesús Sáenz, Santos Balderas, Edward Caldwell, and George Alanis.[13]

Tejanos constituted about twelve (or about 60 percent) of the membership in these important committees, indicating the availability of sufficient numbers of Tejanos capable of serving in the county's administration. Like their willingness to provide sureties for the elected officials, Tejanos were committed to exhibiting a desire and willingness to assist in public endeavors.

In February 1878 Commissioner Rafael Salinas resigned, and the court named Alejos Pérez his replacement. Pérez, however, had to give up his post as constable. Also, that February citizens asked commissioners to delay the construction of a new courthouse and jail. The commissioners "respectfully" told petitioners the committee had already done considerable work and would continue. Instead of stopping the project, the court approved a fifty cents tax on one hundred dollars of valuation for the courthouse.[14]

Duval County Makes Footprint

While the county government was central to its development, other government offices played an important role. In 1878 Duval County got a political boost when voters elected Collins to the House of Representatives for the Seventy-Seventh District. Like many Duval County Republican activists during Reconstruction, Collins had turned Democrat and defeated three Democratic opponents to represent Dimmit, Duval, Frio, Kinney, La Salle, McMullen, Maverick, Nueces, Zavala, and Encinal. Moreover, his appointment to the Agriculture and Stock Raising and the Counties and County Boundaries Committees allowed Collins to help his home county.[15]

In June 1879 the newly created Twenty-Fifth District Court opened in Duval County, with Judge John Russel presiding. The district court brought attorneys, expert witnesses, lawmen, and litigants to San Diego, adding to the town's economy.[16] To serve on grand juries, Judge Russel appointed mostly Americanos. In 1887, for example, Judge Russel named C. K. Gravis, foreman; F. K. Ridder, Julián Palacios, R. R. Savage, J. W. Shaw, William Hebbron, Placido Benavides, G. I. Reynolds, Archie Parr, James Bryden, Fred Frank, and William Hubbard. The jury's membership reflected Americanos' dominance, displaying only token representation by Tejanos. Americanos' supremacy over grand juries persisted well into the next century.[17]

The organization of Duval County in 1876 ushered in a new dynamic that allowed Tejanos and Americanos to chart their destiny. However, they had to tax themselves to pay for the change. Tejanos continued to exhibit interest and ability in the county's affairs, but Americanos maintained control. Such were the demands of growth and progress; much remained to come. Duval County still had a distance to travel, and the train was around the bend.

Chapter 13

Railroad Brings New Prosperity

When the Corpus Christi, San Diego, and Rio Grande Railroad rolled into San Diego in 1879, Duval County residents entered a progressive era of development. The new line made it easier for ranchers to find markets for beef, mutton, hides, wool, and other products. Merchants and ranchers could also import much-needed commodities from American and European outlets. While modernization was a blessing, not everyone saw the railroad on favorable terms: it would also bring Americano newcomers who had their sights on land and thought differently. Old-time residents, mostly Mexicanos, believed the train would threaten their way of life.

Early Interest in Railroad

In early April 1874, before railroad organizers—including San Diego residents N. G. Collins, Frank Davis, and Frank W. Schaeffer—received approval from the state to establish a line, railroad fever was already in the air. Mifflin Kenedy, who owned land and operated a big sheep ranching operation in Duval County, also invested in the railroad idea. However, the participation by Mexicano and Tejano residents was missing, perhaps because no one asked them to donate, even though some were financially able to contribute, or possibly because the local Tejanos were unsure how the project would impact their world.[1]

Chief railroad engineer R. Holub estimated the railroad's cost would be $300,000. Undercapitalized, developers devised a scheme to ask Nueces County voters, including those in Duval, to approve a twenty-year bond issue to cover the entire $300,000. However, locals immediately began complaining, prompting developers to lower their sights and ask for a reduced $200,000. In response, Nueces County officials called for a bond election on August 7, 1874.[2]

Tejanos were not keen on opening their grazing lands to Americano newcomers. Moreover, oral tradition had it that Juan Sáenz at Piedras Pintas did not want the railroad coming through his land for fear it could run over and kill children and cattle. Oxcart haulers, mainly Mexicanos, were also opposed because the railroad would replace their source of livelihood and drive them out of business. Perhaps, in apparent recognition of the potential voting strength of Tejanos, railroad organizers sensed defeat at the polls and asked county officials to call off the election; the Nueces County Commissioners Court complied two weeks before the scheduled voting. However, the word did not get to Duval County election officers, and the balloting proceeded as arranged. According to the Corpus Christi newspaper, fifty-three "Aztecs," as the paper referred to Tejanos, "swam" the Piedras Pintas and San Diego Creeks to show their displeasure for the proposition. "Ox-cart shippers are jubilant over the result of the proposition," the weekly noted.[3]

State Opens Financing for Railroad

On March 13, 1875, the Texas Legislature approved a bill granting legal status to the railroad. In addition, the law authorized the railroad to issue as much as $1 million in capital stock and, if needed, raise an additional $2 million to complete the project. This new cash source made asking for the public's help unnecessary and avoided the voters' likely rejection. Also, on September 18, 1875, the railroad organizers announced that the state had recognized the Corpus Christi, San Diego, and Rio Grande Narrow Gauge Railroad Company as a legal entity.[4]

The law empowered railroad personnel to build, maintain, and operate a railroad and an accompanying telegraph line. The proposal called for the road to begin at Corpus Christi and continue directly to San Diego and then to Eagle Pass, "with a branch from San Diego to a point at or near Laredo." However, the railroad directors decided not to pursue the line to Eagle Pass but to build directly from San Diego to Laredo.[5]

Because Norman G. Collins felt so sure that the railroad project could greatly benefit the area, he contributed $2,500 for the first twenty miles of line. Next, Encarnación García Pérez, whom the Flores heirs had named the San Diego townsite trustee in 1869, asked for Collins's assistance to subdivide the town into blocks and lots. In 1875 Collins hired railroad engineer Holub to survey and subdivide a tract of land in old San Diego, fifty-two miles from Corpus Christi. Pérez and Collins deeded 206 lots for the railroad's use. In the meantime Richard King sold the railroad a one-hundred-foot right-of-way across his land on the south side of the San Diego Creek.[6]

By July 1877 railroad workers, toiling briskly, had laid nine miles of road from Corpus Christi to San Diego. But as the railroad moved farther along, the need for a larger workforce grew. The railroad ran a classified ad seeking fifty "able-bodied" male workers to grade the railway's extension in Duval County and issued a special call for teamsters; the pay offered was twenty-five dollars monthly plus lodgings.[7]

However, building the iron line through the brush presented challenges. Bandits still prowled the area. Indeed, when two inspectors came from Pennsylvania to examine the railroad construction, they faced the danger workers confronted daily. While the railroad's builder Uriah Lott guided the two overseers on rough terrain toward San Diego, they encountered trouble; traveling "along the wilderness . . . shots split the desert air. A band of robbers jumped out of the brush." The bandits quickly "stripped them of all valuables, down to their underwear," and tied the three to a mesquite tree. Lott and the two inspectors freed themselves and went to San Diego, where they must have been quite a sight for residents.[8]

While the railroad inspectors accompanying Lott on the assessment tour may have piqued the curiosity of San Diego residents, the inspectors must also have been taken aback by the oasis their eyes cast upon after traveling through seemingly endless chaparral and arriving in San Diego. The town, said one newspaper, "has more life for a place of its size than any other town in western Texas." The Duval County seat was a "wheel spoke" for mail routes and stagecoaches "coming in from all points" and boasted a new courthouse. "It is generally Mexican in architectural characteristics and three-fourths of its population," the broadsheet observed. San Diego's business center was the plaza, with commercial buildings fronting the square—including some twenty stores in town, three hotels, and several taverns. The Catholic church faced the plaza, while several homes were "scattered promiscuously" throughout the city. An army camp and a Texas Ranger company protected the 1,700 residents in the "city in the woods."[9]

Railroad's Surprising Benefits

It had not taken long for San Diego and Duval County to reap the railroad's benefits. The opening of the railroad gave a new life to the town. Moreover, the Mexicano *carreteros* turned out to be pleasantly surprised by the railroad's coming. They had felt threatened by the railroad. Instead, they found new opportunities in transporting raw products, such as wool, from the remote areas of the county to San Diego for shipment via the train to Corpus Christi and other points. In addition, they hauled merchandise and other goods to the county's more remote communities not in the railroad's path.[10]

By 1880 the Railroad Hotel was open for business in San Diego. It was the place to stay for the many enterprising Americanos looking for a future in the bustling town. In June 1880 saloon keepers Theo Lamberton and Walton Austin, attorney George V. Hale, lumber clerk George W. Stein, and painter Charles Rogers were guests at the Railroad Hotel. Also lodging at the Railroad Hotel were carpenter William Smead; cook William Hawkins; James Morris, a painter; peddler E. E. Delaney; railroad workers James Burns and William Cornelius; and stage drivers William Ramsey and William Ivy. All the hotel's guests were bachelors from every part of the country and Europe, including New York, Illinois, Virginia, Louisiana, Ohio, Pennsylvania, Georgia,

England, Germany, and Ireland. And they all undoubtedly followed the railroad, hoping to chart a new future.[11]

The railroad enterprise, however, continued to face financial challenges. As a result, on June 30, 1881, the Corpus Christi, San Diego, and Rio Grande Narrow Gauge Railroad board of directors filed an amendment to its charter, renaming the line the Texas-Mexican Railroad. At the same time, the board increased its capital to $12 million. Presumably, the directors anticipated the need for this new injection in capital to explore other routes. Indeed, during this period, meetings concerning other railroad projects were frequently held in San Diego. None ever materialized.[12]

Opening the County to New Markets

Merchants shipped many of the county's products along the Texas-Mexican Railroad. In March 1883, after visiting San Diego, a contractor named Shannon showed rock samples picked up at a site where he had seen laborers gathering some seven thousand tons of rock. Railroad workers downloaded the stones six miles west of Corpus Christi and sent them by boat to Aransas Pass for use in "government work." The sandstone rock was ideal for constructing buildings as it was sturdier and cheaper than brick.[13]

A train loaded with cattle was not uncommon on the Texas-Mexican. For example, on August 26, 1883, a train with twenty cars loaded with about 2,500 head of cattle belonging to H. P. Scott left Banquete for San Diego and farther west. Six trains reportedly ran through San Diego daily.[14]

The railroad soon fulfilled its promoters' promises. At the end of the fiscal year of July 31, 1884, the railroad station in San Diego had exported 1,084,051 pounds of wool and 226,227 pounds of hides. By 1888 Duval County reported property assessments that included fifty-eight miles of railroad lines valued at $176,520, fifty-seven miles of telegraph wires valued at $5,717, and $21,605 of rolling stock.[15]

Corpus Christi, Laredo, and San Diego were the main population centers in South Texas outside the Rio Grande Valley. No doubt this was the reason railroad builders laid this route. As the Texas-Mexican Railroad moved west toward the Rio Grande, it generated urban development. Most stimulated by the new line was the long-established community of San Diego. The town chiefly profited because it was the oldest and most significant settlement in Duval County and served as its county seat.

Railroad Promotes New Communities

By the time the railroad arrived, the rancheria of Piedras Pintas was already part of the Duval County political structure, serving as the center of County Precinct Two. It also had a post office and a school. On November 11, 1879, Maas & Toklas, a general merchandise store in Piedras Pintas, had Rufus B. Glover as a clerk. Glover also doubled as postmaster. The establishment undoubtedly counted on the railroad's imminent arrival for its economic success. Indeed, by mid-1880 the rails were only a few miles from Piedras Pintas. By early December 1880, the railroad had set up a construction camp opposite Piedras Pintas at the end of the line.[16]

Unfortunately, the townspeople had initially taken a strong stand against the railroad, and the community's early refusal to cooperate with railroad owners reversed the small town's fortunes. Instead, the rail line found a friendly landowner nearby and rerouted the tracks away from Piedras Pintas.

Profiting from Piedras Pintas's misfortune was a place that came to be known as Benavides. In 1880 Placido Benavides, named after his uncle, the Paul Revere of Texas, permitted the railroad to build a station on his Rancho Palo Alto. The following year Benavides donated eighty acres to bolster the community around the train depot, resulting in a town named in his honor.[17]

Benavides's location was in the middle of the county's livestock-raising region and facilitated the railroad's access to the rest of the county and the outside world. Benavides began to prosper with a "store, depot, market, fandango hall, saloon, restaurant, post office, and new houses" under construction. The community relied on a local windmill for good drinking water. The state stationed a company of Texas Rangers in Benavides. As a result of the railroad's bypassing the community, the Piedras Pintas store of Mass & Toklas moved its operation to Benavides, built a two-story mercantile store, and set up a windmill that watered the trains' engines when they stopped at the Benavides station. The Piedras Pintas post office also relocated to Benavides at about the same time.[18]

By 1887 the new community exhibited an economic boom. New buildings were constantly going up. Adolfo Olivares, employed by the Texas-Mexican Railway, made a house for his father, Apolino Olivares. Postmaster Glover and the railroad's agent named Valverde erected homes close to the railroad eating house, and several smaller residences were also under construction. In addition, the Texas-Mexican Railway established a hotel or eating place. A. L. Muil, a San Diego builder, had finished a Catholic church in Benavides. Four to five stores also went up, and Samuel L. Lewis had plans to build a new schoolhouse. "Business seems to be good," the *Corpus Christi Caller* proclaimed on July 2, 1887. "Benavidites are feeling so large that it is rumored they expect the county seat to be moved there."[19]

The railroad's track soon reached Realitos, where Rufus Glover, who had managed the Maas & Toklas store in Piedras Pintas, contracted with the railroad to provide wood for its engines. Like Piedras Pintas, Realitos was well known to Duval County frontiersmen. According to a familiar story, a passerby reported the area was known as Rancho El Tejón. The ranch owner operated a small eatery for travelers. He served only one combination: picadillo with eggs, *chile pequín* (hot chili pepper hotter than jalapeño sauce), tortillas, and coffee. The plate's price was whatever the man felt like charging, usually *cuatro realitos*, or four bits (fifty cents). This tradition led to him being called Realitos; residents passed the name to the town that grew around his rancho.[20]

Before the railroad's arrival, stagecoaches running to Rio Grande City pulled up at another of the ranchería's hallmarks, a bar operated by a woman who wore a rebozo and sandals. E. F. Hall also managed a stagecoach at the rancho connecting Realitos to Laredo. By the end of 1880, the railroad company had plans to open a small station at Realitos, which had received a post office in 1876 with Charles Shaw as its first postmaster. Shaw also served as justice of the peace.[21]

At the start of 1887, Realitos had become a full-blown railroad station as planned by the Texas-Mexican; the amount of freight handled at the depot weekly attested to the town's growing importance. The station's success prompted a house-building boom.[22] By January 1887 Realitos was also undertaking public improvements. At Ed Corkill's direction, residents drilled a community well for the town, contributing their labor and money. They found water at sixty feet. Community members also uprooted all stumps and cut down brush within the town limits. In February 1887 R. O. Savage sold his store to I. P. Staples. Then, in April, F. Cadena and Company moved its merchandise business from Concepción to Realitos, suggesting that a building boom was underway. The town had welcomed three stores, three hotels and restaurants, two meat markets, and two barbershops—where one could have "your hair powdered al mode Americano." By June 25, 1887, Cadena and Staples were doing a brisk business in town.[23]

As busy as the new railroad kept the town's residents, they still found time to celebrate. The Americanos in Realitos observed San Jacinto Day on April 21, 1887, "as all true Texans should." The Tejano community went all out for Día de San Juan on June 29. Aside from the religious celebration observed at the Catholic church, residents—straying from the spiritual meaning of the day—enjoyed horse racing, cockfighting, and other entertainment activities.[24]

On not such an upbeat note, sheepman Walter Meek, a recent arrival in Duval County, observed, "Everywhere I go, the food brought before me is positively uneatable." He noted that in many of the ranches he visited near Realitos, the people were so impoverished that he felt it inappropriate to ask them to give or sell him something to eat. If they did bring him an offering, it was usually a cup of black coffee and a tortilla. "It is awful to be so poor, and I have great compassion for their distress," Meek wrote in his memoirs.[25]

In April 1887 the Realitos public school closed for lack of funding, and the teacher, Miss Rogers, returned to Corpus Christi. Six months later, however, the school was again operational. By the close of 1887, thirty pupils enrolled in the public school and made progress, with Laura Modd as the new mentor.[26]

On its way to Laredo, the Texas-Mexican line's last stop in Duval County was Hebbronville. Like Benavides, the community came into existence through the help of a landowner. The railroad planned to place a depot at Peña Station on land owned by Lázaro Peña. Before its establishment in 1875, Peña Station was a crucial hub for travelers from the Nueces River to the Rio Grande's border communities in Starr County. Cart haulers moving freight overland by oxen and mules made Peña Station a vital way station. The same was true for stagecoaches, Ranger companies, and army units crisscrossing the area. In addition, entrepreneurs in South Texas considered Peña Station the shortest route to Ringgold Barracks and Rio Grande City from Corpus Christi and San Antonio.[27]

So it was no surprise that the railroad looked upon Peña Station as an ideal place for a depot. In addition, railroad officials planned to extend their line farther south to take advantage of Peña Station's well-known landmark as a crossroads and intended to designate it as an official stop to Laredo. However, like landowners in Piedras Pintas, the Peña family rejected the railroad's offer to purchase part of the land for a townsite. So the Texas-Mexican approached another landowner, James R. Hebbron, with their proposition. Hebbron accepted the offer and worked with the railroad to purchase the necessary land from a local rancher. As a result, the town of Hebbronville came into being within hollering distance of Peña Station.[28]

———————

The Texas Mexican Railroad brought significant change to Duval County. But perhaps the most remarkable change was that it, like its locomotives, set the county's future in motion. Duval County was no longer a place people passed through to the seaport of Corpus Christi or Laredo's inland port. Instead, it was a destination point for many newcomers seeking a better life—both Mexicanos and Americanos.

Chapter 14

When Cotton Was King

During the last quarter of the nineteenth century, 1875–1900, while the United States experienced seven depressions, the Texas and Duval County economies exhibited vitality and adaptability; sheep, cattle raising, and cotton farming anchored and sustained the local economy. Moreover, the arrival of the Texas-Mexican Railway and the land acquisition by numerous previously landless farmers and ranchers insulated Duval County from the economic ups and downs other parts of the nation were experiencing.[1]

While figures are unavailable for Duval County, Texas's cotton production dramatically increased during the last quarter of the nineteenth century. In 1879 Texas farmers produced 802,284 bales of cotton on 2,187,435 acres. By 1900 cotton production across the state had quadrupled to 3,500,000 bales in 7,178,915 acres. While new to the business, Duval County cotton farmers experienced incredible success.[2]

Early Efforts at Commercial Farming in Duval

Perhaps one of the earliest efforts at developing commercial agriculture in Duval County came in 1872 when longtime resident Edward N. Gray began planting fruit trees in his ten-thousand-acre La Gloria Ranch. The ranch, located fourteen miles northwest of San Diego, was bisected by the San Diego Creek. However, the arroyo was unreliable, and Gray depended on four water tanks to nourish his crops.[3]

Gray came to Texas in 1836, during the Texas secession from Mexico, and later joined the American Army fighting in the Mexican-American War. Gray settled in Concepción in 1854, where he operated a frontier store and met his wife, Rosa Garza García; afterward they beget fourteen children. Circa 1868 the couple relocated north to La Gloria. They began to manage a successful ranching operation, raising cattle, horses, oxen, and sheep. La Gloria often served as Gray's laboratory in his desire to launch a successful agricultural enterprise in his adopted county.[4]

As early as 1861, Gray experimented with wheat in the San Diego area. Even though he planted the wheat seeds three weeks later than expected, they yielded good stalks and full heads. In 1872 Gray ordered various fruit trees from New Orleans and planted them, confident they would grow in two years. In 1874, however, Gray picked up his family from La Gloria and returned to Concepción, where their store required attention. When Gray returned to La Gloria seven years later, more than four hundred of his trees had wilted and died, but he did not lose hope. Over the next two years, Gray purchased more than two thousand trees and vines from a Georgia nursery. As a result, in 1883 all the trees flourished and rewarded the persistent farmer with ample fruit. Over time Gray's orchards yielded fruits such as apples, pears, peaches, plums, apricots, nectarines, cherries, figs, Japanese persimmons, grapes, blackberries, raspberries, almonds, English walnuts, and black walnuts.[5]

"I have never irrigated a tree since I planted them," Gray claimed. "I keep them free from weeds and grass and the ground plowed, which is far better than irrigating them." Regrettably, a hailstorm damaged much of Gray's hanging produce. Still, he continued to extoll the plants' hardiness while admitting that he was not a farming expert and that others with more experience could do well in the county's ecosystem. However, Gray continued planting wheat, oats, rye, buckwheat, corn, sweet and Irish potatoes, beans, peas, cotton, barley, and assorted vegetables. Enjoying success with corn, Gray planted four hundred acres, producing seven hundred bushels; by October 1885 Gray's cornstalks generated twelve thousand bushels.[6]

Gray provided the example of vegetable and fruit farming, but other individuals also engaged in agriculture. Farmers in Piedras Pintas likewise planted fruits and vegetables. Paul Henry cultivated cabbage, potatoes, turnips, and carrots near San Diego. Farmers harvested vegetables and fruits widely grown in Duval County. Still, these plants did not become the cash crop that cotton turned out to be.[7]

Beginnings of Cotton in Duval County

Cotton planting spawned a gin in Reynosa as early as the 1830s. Indeed, some eighty-eight "cotton plantations" existed around Matamoros. General Zachary Taylor's soldiers, in 1846, reported cotton growing in the wild on the Rio Grande's banks.[8]

During the Civil War, Confederates considered cotton equivalent to gold; it funded their war effort. At that time cotton was not grown in the Trans-Nueces but passed through the area while transported from Dixie to Mexico and foreign ports. Local *carreteros*, however, received economic benefits from transporting cotton.

Newspapers credited a young Tejano as the chief promoter of cotton in Duval County. According to the *Corpus Christi Caller*, the "introduction of cotton [is] due to efforts of Don Fabián Fabela of San Diego, who has several years of experience in farming."[9] Born in Mexico circa 1845, by 1867–1868, Fabela had received American citizenship, appearing in the Nueces County voter registration rolls. In 1870 Nueces County's census included Fabela, a 25-year-old tailor living in Corpus Christi. He owned real estate valued at five hundred dollars, but by 1878 he had moved to Duval County, where the property tax rolls list the young tailor as owning a 160-acre tract of land appraised at six hundred dollars and a wagon worth thirty dollars. The following year, Fabela received the appointment as the postmaster at Mendieta.[10]

In 1880 Fabela's 160 acres increased in value to $1,080, and he acquired three town lots in San Diego, appraised at $150. By 1885 the thriving wool hat manufacturer owned a second tract of land totaling 1,920 acres, bringing his acreage to 2,080. At this time Fabela started to show an interest in growing cotton.[11]

In 1885 Fabela began "collecting money in San Diego to buy cottonseed to give to the poor who may want to raise a crop." Fabela's labors had distributed—at no cost—"five to six thousand pounds of cottonseed to the *aldeanos* [villagers] of San Diego and small planters to encourage cotton growing." As a result, some farmers decided to give cotton a chance.[12]

With sufficient acreage to plant cotton, landowners used the free seed to produce "experimental fields." These farmers included Placido Benavides, Isidro Benavides, and Vicente Vela, all of the Benavides area. In 1882 Isidro Benavides owned six tracts of land near Benavides, totaling 3,500 acres and valued at $2,340. Placido Benavides held six parcels of land totaling 1,440 acres with a taxable value of $1,480, and Vela had 640 acres valued at $800.[13]

Avelino Pérez planted forty acres of cotton two miles from San Diego. In 1886 Pérez did not declare taxable acreage but had five lots in San Diego valued at $550. While there is no available record showing that Pérez owned land, he owned 330 horses, mules, and 39,390 cattle, so perhaps he planted on a family plot or leased acreage. Pioneer San Diego resident Encarnación García Pérez also gave cotton a try.[14]

Presumably, Fabela was not the only one promoting cotton production. Paul Henry, Frank Gueydan, and others also received credit for encouraging cotton planting. Perhaps it was inadvisable to admit that a Tejano could have launched the cotton interest without Americanos' help.[15]

Growth of Cotton Farming

In February 1887 the Parkman Gin at San Diego processed the county's first bale. It exhibited it as if to say, "There, we told you so" to residents and anyone else who may have expressed skepticism about the endeavor. By October 1887 stacks of cotton bales were awaiting shipment at the train depot in San Diego. The following April cotton fields were everywhere, and someone observed, "Duval County, it can be safely said, is now a cotton belt."[16]

In 1888 Encarnación García Pérez had sixty-four acres planted with cotton, which yielded a bale of cotton per acre. García soon took four bales to be ginned, including the first bale of the picking season. The cotton harvest was a "grand success near San Diego by August." A month later, on September 30, "people saw cotton on all roads leading to San Diego." In October the cotton picking continued, and the Parkman Gin was turning out five-hundred-pound bales every day. By October 1888 growers had picked one hundred bales, and cotton pickers were still on the fields. Two weeks later people noted, "Cotton keeps coming in faster than cotton gins can bale it."[17]

Official information about cotton farmers is not available. Unlike land ownership and livestock, the county tax office did not keep track of land use. As a result, one could discern who owned cattle or sheep but not who was farming cotton or any other crop. Some of the planters' names appeared in the newspapers at times, but those identified were very few and hardly representative of the number of cotton farmers in the county. Many cotton planters were small landowners with as little as 160 acres, but most of the county's land was in the hands of large landowners who mostly raised livestock, such as cattle and sheep.

Some cotton growers in Texas were tenant farmers, also known as sharecroppers, who rented land in exchange for a crop share. Typically, those fortunate to own land worked on credit. They mortgaged their cotton yield and often planted more to cover the loan. Renters or tenants paid the landowner from two-thirds to three-fourths of their harvest. Some South Texas rancheros, including in Duval County, preferred sharecropping agreements with Tejano cotton planters instead of selling to recently arrived Americanos or large land-grabbing neighbors. They wanted to remain in the ranching business but were willing to rent some of their lands to farmers, including their unemployed vaqueros. A few rancheros had as many as fifteen families with whom they shared their land for cotton farming. Tenant farming was a temporary arrangement until livestock prices could improve. Ranchers and cotton growers faced the same challenge; relying on livestock or cotton was no better. Farmers received 22 percent less income from cotton between 1887 and 1890 even though they planted 25 percent more of the crop. Likewise, the value of Duval County's cattle herds dropped 3 percent from 1895 to 1899. So diversification was essential for success in agricultural pursuits.[18]

Cotton Picking

Picking cotton was monotonous, repetitive, back-breaking work. It required dragging a quickly filling burlap bag with a *mecapal* (strap) wrapped around one's shoulder and moving down *surcos*, or rows, of cotton. The pickers hunched low over the plants, pulling cotton from thorny hulls and tossing them in the *costal*, or sack, capable of carrying upward of one hundred pounds. Some pickers plucked the cotton balls from rows on either side simultaneously.

The owner or manager weighed the cotton at the row's end; the cotton picker dumped it into a *traila* (trailer) to transport to the gin in town. Cotton picking occurred when the cotton plants bloomed at the height of the summer heat. Workers got seventy-five cents for every one hundred pounds. Once the picking season was over, migrants and pickers moved north to find work on the cotton fields as far as Eagle Lake in Colorado County. The pay was sometimes not worth the trip, as "every cotton plant has a picker."[19]

But before the field hands could pick cotton, they had to clear the land; this, too, was excruciating work. Ranchers never used their *paisaje* (pastures) for commercial farming, and thus the ground became covered by thick grasses, mesquite, huisache, and other trees and bushes, as well as the excrement of cattle and sheep. So field workers had to *desenraizar*, or uproot, this plant life, which was "back-breaking work," requiring the use of tools, such as a *talache* (mattock) or *hacha* (ax), to remove tree stumps. This work was "intensely physically demanding." The workers got "on their knees and using the hoe side" of the *talache* "cleared litter and dirt from around the roots and turned [the *talache*] to the ax side and cut away the stump." The owner paid five dollars for every acre cleared. Laborers also received wages for any wood salvaged, earning fifty cents for a chord of firewood and varying pay for timber suitable for fencing. Typically, the farmer compensated workers with a weekly allowance of flour, coffee, beans, bacon, rice, and molasses.[20]

While cotton pickers may have seen working at a gin as a plumb job, it was hardly that. It was also back-breaking labor, like picking cotton. Moreover, chores at a gin were repetitive and monotonous, the same routine, day in and day out, every week for six months. First, workers had to unload the cotton from the trailers and then place it on a conveyor belt to pass through the ginning apparatus that separated the seed from the fiber, dried it, and compressed the cotton. The workplace was hot, dusty, noisy, and dangerous. Gin employees manually picked bales weighing five and six hundred pounds off a conveyor belt and loaded them onto horse-drawn trailers for transport to the train station.[21]

Cotton Gins

Cotton farming's emerging success prompted H. W. Parkman, the steam gristmill owner who processed corn, and Frank Gueydan, who owned San Diego's largest mercantile house, to invest in the modern equipment needed for cotton ginning.[22] By 1888 the cotton business in Duval County was so good that a second gin was in the works in San Diego. Workers had completed the E. Martínez Gin by the end of the 1888 first summer cotton-picking season, but the machinery had not arrived. Finally, in August 1889 the E. Martínez Gin opened for business and received its first cotton from Candelario Arredondo from Realitos. About the same time the Martínez Gin was going up in San Diego, in July 1889 H. S. Glover was also building a gin at Benavides.[23]

In September 1899 N. Gusset opened another gin in Duval County. In addition, J. H. Waller was operating the gin in Benavides, which Glover ostensibly opened ten years earlier. Thus, by the end of the century, Duval County had four cotton gins running twenty-four hours a day during the picking season. The need for the four gins was obvious, as the expectation was that more than three thousand bales could come in by the end of the picking season.[24]

When one cotton-picking period finished, anxious farmers began thinking about the following season. At the opening of 1889, farmers expected to plant a large cotton crop based on a good yield the prior year. By mid-summer 1889 second plantings had already started, and cotton crops flourished. Farmers expected four times the production of the previous year. The Parkman Gin had already turned out the season's first bale picked at Dr. L. B. Wright's fields in San Diego and shipped to Galveston, where it arrived the following day.[25]

Cotton Stirs Interest in Duval County

Word of Duval County's success with cotton was spreading far and wide. In November 1889 "five covered wagons containing white movers" were spotted going to Duval County from Grimes County, a distance of some three hundred miles.[26]

Duval County's cotton success stirred interest beyond Texas. Even the cotton gurus in Liverpool, England, lauded Duval County cotton as "the finest in the world." Accordingly, the Liverpool financiers notified their buyers in Galveston and Houston to get all the Duval cotton they could for Liverpool factories to manufacture thread. Duval County farmers and residents received the news with much delight. Duval farmers already had ten thousand acres of cotton in the ground.[27]

In April 1891 Will Johnson sold his interest in the *Yoakum Graphic* to start a newspaper in San Diego. By that summer Johnson was publishing the *San Diego Sun*. Via the *Sun* Johnson had a front-row seat to report why Duval cotton crops always yielded a good harvest despite the slight annual rainfall. For example, on June 7 a farmer in Duval County planted twelve acres of cotton without rain, irrigation, or fertilizing and yielded 22,000 pounds of cottonseed. Moreover, the grower got 19,000 pounds of processed cotton and 7,700 pounds of clean lint. A farmer could harvest two bales per acre with one rainfall at the right time.[28]

One of Duval County's premiere promoters was Encarnación García Pérez, who usually notified newspapers of the first bale coming out of Duval County. On July 5, 1891, García informed the media that the county was ready to ship its initial bale of cotton, grown a few miles outside San Diego and processed by Gusset's gin. In early July 1891, a large delegation from San Diego accompanied the bale on the Texas-Mexican Railroad to Corpus Christi. From there they continued to the Aransas Pass depot, where railroad personnel sent the bale of cotton to Houston three days earlier than the previous year's bundle. The cotton cargo arrived on July 6, weighing 554 pounds.[29]

In July 1891 the *Sun* editor proclaimed that the print media "worldwide" had picked up the word of the first bale. This international publicity about

Duval County cotton attracted prospectors to the county. "When they get here, they will not be disappointed," Editor Johnson declared.[30]

Farmers Take an Interest in Rainmakers

While boasting of their output even without rain, cotton farmers always fell back on the necessity of rain to help their efforts. Many grew other products such as corn and most likely had sheep, cattle, or both, so Duval County farmers and ranchers were interested in getting rain. In 1891 many of the leading ranchers and farmers in the region tried to manipulate Mother Nature to achieve that purpose.

San Diego residents could hardly sleep for three nights in the middle of October 1891 as bombardments exploded through the night. Mexican troops had not crossed the border to pursue Duval County's revolutionary Catarino Garza and his rebels. A foreign enemy did not attack the area; the explosions were part of a rainmaking experiment that captured farmers' and scientists' attention near and far.[31]

Twenty years earlier a fellow named Edward Powers had written a book entitled *War and the Weather* in which he observed that it rained shortly after intense battles involving heavy cannon fire. Edwards hypothesized that the use of explosives could artificially make rain. In 1890 Congress took notice of Powers's idea of "weather modification" and approved $9,000 to pursue this experiment, hopefully for widespread use. Later that year, an initial effort appeared successful in Midland, Texas.[32]

Robert Kleberg of the King Ranch and N. G. Collins of San Diego traveled to Midland to learn what local farmers thought about the experiment. Kleberg and Collins were impressed and invited the rainmakers to South Texas. By this time the experimenters in Midland had spent all the $9,000 approved by Congress, so Kleberg and Collins offered to raise private capital for the effort. They hired John Ellis, a meteorologist from Oberlin College, to replicate the seemingly successful Midland experiment. They brought in an old cannon from the King Ranch and, with the army's help, set up their equipment on the Collins Ranch, a few miles northeast of San Diego.[33] The pseudoscientists chose San Diego due to its location on the railroad and because a hot, dry spell had afflicted the area for several months. They called the encampment Camp Edward Powers to honor the individual who fathered rainmaking theory using explosives.[34]

After two weeks of preparation and waiting for the most suitable time, the rainmakers began firing off explosives in the early morning of October 16. They lit the explosives at night to prevent the daytime winds from affecting the discharge. They detonated explosives every five minutes for several hours and continued for several days. Many spectators came from San Diego and the surrounding communities. As the rainmakers set off the explosives, the onlookers huddled at the center of the base camp.[35]

Judge J. O. Luby observed the blasts from an iron bridge spanning 153 feet across San Diego Creek. Although made of iron and two and a half miles from Camp Edward Powers, the bridge shook with every boom. Twenty-seven miles away at the headquarters of the King Ranch, the bombardment awakened Kleberg, who climbed to the roof of the ranch head-quarters and said he felt the structure rattle with each detonation. The *Kineños* (King Ranch cowboys) watched the fireworks like the Fourth of July or Diez y Seis de Septiembre. Ellis, the meteorologist, climbed into a balloon and rose into the heavens to check the clouds. The soldiers, meanwhile, filled small balls with powder and soaked them in nitroglycerin.[36]

Finally, after days of waiting, some dark clouds appeared overhead, and on Ellis's orders, soldiers released balloons filled with sulfuric acid gas and exploded them with the cannon. The blasts caused a stir in town, and a discharge was so close that it leveled the soldiers' tents. It began raining by nightfall, and the dry grass below sprang back to life. It rained about half an inch in an hour. Then, shortly after five in the morning, a north wind blew the cumulus clouds away, and the rains stopped. With the experimentation concluded, the soldiers took down the camp and returned home. Ellis and the rest of the rainmakers reported to Washington and others that the testing had been successful.[37]

Residents also praised the venture; however, the principal backers of the project were not as effusive. Kleberg agreed the rain probably resulted from the explosions but remained cautious and offered that more work was needed before the process was proven. On the other hand, Collins told the press he did not think the bombing had caused the rain, prompting Ellis to reply that they could not have convinced Collins had it rained gold on his neighbor's land if it had not fallen on his property. As years passed, atmospheric scientists concluded that Collins was right; the explosions had nothing to do with the rain.[38]

Duval County Records First Bale Nine Years Straight

After the excitement ended, Duval County folks returned to those things that affected their daily lives, such as planting and picking cotton. Duval County was not part of the cotton belt, but it had come in with the state's first bale since it began to bale cotton. Starting with the Wright bale in 1889, Duval County farmers had a streak of the first bales in Texas through 1897. Duval County's first cotton bale in 1890 came in at 620 pounds and went to Galveston. Duval County sent the first 1891 bale to Houston with great fanfare, and the streak continued when the first 1892 bale shipped to Houston. The following year, 1893, F. Gueydan of San Diego turned in the first bale, breaking the "world's record by several days."[39]

The cotton industry continued to grow over the years. In 1894 Duval County increased cotton production by 25 percent. The cotton already looked good, but some believed the county could produce five to seven thousand bales if it got good rain. So it was not a great surprise to local planters that their first bale of 1894 again claimed first place in the state. Julián Palacios cultivated the first bale ginned in the United States that year and the earliest bale of cotton ever processed in the history of the United States. The Waller Gin in Benavides baled Palacios's cotton. Palacios farmed in Concepción and had one of "the finest and largest farms in that portion of the state [and] over 400 acres in cotton" production.[40] "San Diego beats the South, as Usual," blared the headline in Brownsville's newspaper on July 13, 1895. As he frequently did, Encarnación García Pérez notified the media of the first bale's processing, owned by Leon Pons. The community joined the exultation, decorating the bale with red, white, and blue ribbons, and Pons accompanied it to Galveston.[41]

On July 18, 1895, the Hallettsville newspaper lamented Duval County's continued success. "What's wrong with this portion of Texas," the newspaper asked, claiming that from 1886 to 1888, Dewitt County had furnished Texas's first bale, but since 1889, Duval County had taken the lead.[42] Other newspapers, however, challenged the Hallettsville editors, including the *Corpus Christi Caller*. "The matter is simply this; you are not in it anymore," the *Caller* proclaimed in its columns. In its defense and hinting at sour grapes, the *Herald* countered that the methods used to determine what qualified as the first bale in recent years were questionable.[43]

The following year (1896), folks in Dewitt County must have felt a sting when the press again proclaimed that Duval County had produced the first bale of cotton. Next, on July 3, 1896, Duval County Treasurer Phillip Bodet brought in the first bale a few miles outside San Diego. The San Diego Gin & Mill, under the management of T. García, baled the cotton. As had become customary, the community saw the bale off with great fanfare.[44]

In February 1896 the Brownsville newspaper shared a report from the *San Diego Sun* giving much credit to the success of cotton farming in Duval County to water availability at various localities. Moreover, the county sat over an artisan belt with water near the surface where a farmer could easily extract and use it for irrigation. Yet despite these proclamations by Duval's hometown newspaper, the county lost about half its usual cotton harvest due to a severe drought.[45]

The extended absence of rain caused a water shortage, prompting local farmers to work harder for a good cotton crop. During March and April 1897, Duval cotton farmers increased the acreage dedicated to cotton. As a result, they expected the biggest cotton crop in the county's history. Not surprisingly, Duval County again took "the honors . . . for the first bale of cotton." On June 24 Brownsville's news organ confirmed that Duval County had shipped the first bale to market. "Southwest Texas should be proud of that county," the newspaper wrote.[46]

The county won the title for so many years that those who kept tabs began to downplay the achievement. Instead, interest shifted to the number of bales and the price. Based on the cotton passing through San Diego streets in July, the gins were gearing up for a busy time. Still, the farmers feared the season might not meet earlier expectations unless it rained soon. Fortunately, God answered the farmers' prayers; Duval County received five inches of rain at the end of August 1897, ensuring a successful cotton season. By that time Duval had already processed five hundred bales of cotton.

Signs of Cotton's Decline

One reason for the county's success in cotton farming was the nature of the cotton-growing season: South Texas planting could begin earlier than northern counties in the state. In 1898 Duval County cotton farmers started three weeks earlier than usual, but the season did not develop as expected. A dry season must have ruined the cotton crop, because Duval County did not deliver the first bale in Texas for the first time in nine years. Another sign of the setback was an advertisement in the *Houston Daily Post* of June 5, 1898, that one of Duval's four cotton gins was for sale.

In February 1899 Duval County farmers planted countless cotton seeds, believing a recent freeze had wiped out the boll weevil, opening the way for a large, healthy cotton crop. Moreover, there was an excess supply of farmworkers in the county, which growers could have at low wages. A drought replaced the early freeze, prompting Duval County farmers to place less acreage into cotton cultivation. The dry spell was short-lived; by late May most of the cotton planted looked very well. Two months later farmers were still hurting from a lack of rain, and the situation could worsen unless it rained soon. The farmers' prayer for rain received an answer three days later, on July 27. Farmers believed the crop would be the best if the rain did not trigger worms to infest the cotton. While the crop did not turn out to be the best, it was not a disaster either. Benavides shipped 110 bales, more than double the previous year's amount, and San Diego gins processed 600 bales. While farmers salvaged the crop, it was not enough to merit the first bale.[47]

After an exciting ride for nine years, cotton in Duval County began to level off. It continued to play a role in the area's cotton economy for several more years, but the glory days were in the past.

Chapter 15

La Política, Revisited

Duval County Tejanos continued to be concerned with the influx of Americanos well after the Civil War. It alarmed them that Americanos were cementing their political influence out of proportion to their numbers. Duval County had been and continued to be a majority ethnic Tejano population. In the 1870s Tejanos pursued organized politics to attain fairness and acquire political power corresponding to their population advantage. Cognizant of their political potential, as demonstrated in the 1860 election, Tejanos in the last decades of the nineteenth century set in motion a strategy to claim what they saw as their rightful place in the community's political structure.

Early Electoral Consequences

The county's organizational election in 1876 revealed Americano dominance at the polls. All countywide offices but one went to Americano candidates, but Tejanos did secure five precinct-level positions. Voters selected Calixto Tovar as county treasurer, making him the first Tejano elected to a county-wide post in Duval. Tovar was the son of Trinidad Flores, who played a vital role in the county's development, including leading the charge to confirm ownership of the San Diego land grants and subdividing San Diego to make it a city. Flores's daughter, Práxedis, was married to Encarnacion García Pérez, another Tejano leader in the community. As a woman, Trinidad Flores did not have the right to vote or run for office but exercised power behind the scenes and through her family.

On November 5, 1878, Duval County held a second election to choose county officers. Again, the results closely paralleled those of 1876, and a significant undercurrent of unfairness became evident. While Tejanos continued to have an overwhelming majority in the population, their underrepresentation in the Duval County halls of power did not reflect their numerical standing. The Tejano leadership either had not figured out the political dynamics or did not feel ready to take the reins of government.[1]

Frank C. Gravis replaced County Treasurer Calixto Tovar, the only Tejano to hold a countywide office. Rafael Salinas, the only Tejano on the commissioners court, had resigned earlier that year, and Edward R. Gray replaced him, thus shutting out Tejanos from the county's governing court. Finally, Herman Maas took the justice of the peace slot from Modesto Garza. As of 1878 only three Tejano constables served at the bottom of the county government's governing structure.

Table 15.1 Duval County election results, 1878

Official	Office
James O. Luby	County Judge
Andrew R. Valls	County/District Clerk
Henry S. Lang	County Attorney
Eugene Glover	Sheriff/Tax Collector
Frank C. Gravis	County Tax Assessor
Charles Hoffman	County Treasurer
Theodore Lamberton	Inspector of Hides & Animals
Asa M. French	Surveyor
Charles K. Gravis	Commissioner, Precinct One
P. Arnold Mattsson	Justice of the Peace, Precinct One
Peter Skaro	Constable, Precinct One
P. W. Toklas	Commissioner, Precinct Two

(Continues)

Table 15.1 (Continued)

Official	Office
Herman Mass	Justice of the Peace, Precinct Two
Alejos Pérez	Constable, Precinct Two
Edward R. Gray	Commissioner, Precinct Three
Jonathan Vining	Justice of the Peace, Precinct Three
George Palacios	Constable, Precinct Three
E. H. Caldwell	Commissioner, Precinct Four
Charles Roach	Justice of the Peace, Precinct Four
Francisco López	Constable, Precinct Four

Source: Duval County Commissioners Court minutes, December 3, 1878.

In the 1880 general election, Tejanos rebounded from their 1878 losses. While they still held no countywide office, Julian Palacios regained a seat on the commissioners court. Moreover, Tejanos Zenobio Cuéllar and Manuel Garza Díaz secured two justice of the peace positions. Camilo García, Abraham Santos Cruz, and Antonio Rangel retained the three constable badges. Finally, two Spanish-surnamed individuals, Andrew R. Valls and Juan Puig, won countywide races as county clerk and inspector of hides and animals, respectively. They were not Tejanos but Spaniards, as Europeans were more palatable to the Americano power structure.[2]

In 1882, two years after his reelection, Luby resigned, and his law partner Edward S. Atkinson, who had only come to Duval County two years earlier in 1880, assumed his office. The following year Atkinson also resigned, and J. W. Moses replaced him. Moses, married to a Tejana, prevailed in his race for county judge in 1884, but Tejanos failed to gain any seats. Underrepresentation continued for years, and concern festered among Tejanos as time passed, presenting the Duval County community with ongoing challenges.[3]

Table 15.2 Duval County election results, 1880

Official	Office
James O. Luby	County Judge
Andrew R. Valls	County and District Clerk
George R. Hale	County Attorney

(Continues)

Table 15.2 (Continued)

Official	Office
M. C. Spann	County Treasurer
John J. Dix	County Surveyor
Lafayette L. Wright	Sheriff and Tax Collector
Juan Puig	Inspector of Hides and Animals
Frank Curly Gravis	Assessor of Taxes
Norman G. Collins	County Commissioner, Precinct One
William Hubbard	County Commissioner, Precinct Two
Julian Palacios	County Commissioner, Precinct Three
Charles Roach	County Commissioner, Precinct Four
James Arnold Mattison	Justice of the Peace, Precinct One
Zenobio Cuéllar	Justice of the Peace, Precinct Two
George W. Davidson	Justice of the Peace, Precinct Three
Charles Roach	Justice of the Peace, Precinct Four
Manuel Garza Díaz	Justice of the Peace, Precinct Five
Charles Hutchinson	Constable, Precinct One
Camilo García	Constable, Precinct Two
Richard Hancock	Constable, Precinct Three
Abraham Santos Cruz	Constable, Precinct Four
Antonio Rangel	Constable, Precinct Five

Source: Texas Secretary of State, Election Returns, Duval County, 1880, Box 2-12/591, TSLAC.

Signs of Disunity

At the opening of 1884, President Chester A. Arthur appointed Judge James O. Luby the customs collector position at Brownsville, and he was soon off to the Rio Grande Valley.[4] Luby's absence from the county created a political vacuum. Despite his Republican affiliation, the Democrats in Duval County had elected him as county judge in three consecutive elections. But with his departure Democrats fell into in-fighting, and two years later local politics came apart at the seams.

On June 30, 1886, a complete rupture occurred at the Duval County Democratic County Convention. The dispute started when Chairman John Dix named E. N. Gray, C. K. Gravis, and J. W. Shaw to the Credentials Committee. Dix ruled out of order a motion to elect a temporary chairman. Gray stepped down from the committee, claiming it "was stacked 2–1," with Gravis and Shaw against him. M. C. Spann motioned that Dix name delegates to the Credential Committee from each precinct, which the chairman promptly ruled out of order. Spann asked the convention delegates to vote on the question, and Dix rebuffed him again.[5]

Chairman Dix declared that the meeting's purpose was to select delegates to the state convention in Galveston. In addition, the gathering was also to pick delegates to represent the party at the Seventh Congressional District Convention in Victoria, the Twenty-Seventh Senatorial District Convention slated in Cotulla, and the Eighty-Third State Representative Convention, site yet to be determined.[6]

Gray, "in a somewhat elaborate speech," refused to serve on the Credential Committee, declaring, "While the matter was cut and dried, it was clear it was a put-up job." Dix countered that it was a convention of Democrats, not of two opposing sides. Gray and his supporters walked out, leading the *Corpus Christi Caller* to report, in a somewhat partisan tone, that "so-called Democrats bolted the convention and left the house with cheers from the delegates who remained, together with shouts of 'get out you mugwumps' and 'bolters,' 'Republicans' and 'traitors.'"[7]

Those remaining named John D. Cleary as temporary secretary. Dix proceeded with his stated program, appointing E. A. Glover and C. G. Ramírez delegates to the state convention, with L. P. Bryant as an alternate. C. K. Gravis and J. W. Shaw were to attend the congressional convention; L. L. Wright and F. C. Gravis, the senatorial convention; and L. L. Wright, J. D. Cleary, C. L. Coyner, J. H. Reynolds, W. H. Simmons, F. C. Gravis, R. B. Glover, and Tomás Ramón delegates to the state representative convention. Again, only two Tejanos received recognition.[8]

Dix also named various committees, including a Committee of Permanent Organization consisting of E. A. Gallagher, F. C. Gravis, and W. H. Simmons. In addition, the Committee of Basis of Representation included C. L. Coyner, R. B. Glover, and L. P. Bryant. Furthermore, George H. Reynolds, Ramón, and Bryant served on the Resolutions Committee. Still, only one Tejano received a committee assignment.[9]

Finally, the remaining courthouse delegates chose Dix, Cleary, Bryant (Precinct One), E. A. Glover (Precinct Two), O. S. Watson (Precinct Three), C. E. Bownes (Precinct Four), and Agustín Cantú (Precinct Five) to form the Executive Committee. Again, a lone Tejano received recognition on the Executive Committee. Before adjourning, the regular Democrats at the Courthouse Convention denounced the bolters. Three Tejanos were all the "Democratic Party" could muster for its leadership positions.[10]

Thirty-eight delegates had walked out with Gray and marched to the schoolhouse, organizing an alternative convention. Of the thirty-eight, twenty-two (more than half) were Tejanos. A. R. Valls, secretary of the Democratic Executive Committee, called the meeting to order. Delegates quickly elected Spann as temporary chairman and A. J. Ayers as temporary secretary. The delegates then voted for Gray, E. Chamberlain, Julián Palacios, Zenobio Cuéllar, and H. Garrett to serve on a Credentials Committee. Despite their majority, Tejanos were outmaneuvered and could not muster more representation than their courthouse counterparts.[11]

The committee recognized Gray, Spann, Chamberlain, and John Buckley as delegates from Precinct One. Precinct Two representatives were Placido Benavides, Valls, Florencio Salinas, Nicolás Molina, Ventura Flores, Ysidro Benavides, Vicente Vera, Cuéllar, and Agustine Canales. Delegates from Precinct Three included Cesario Guajardo, Saturnino Vera, Francisco Furras, Florencio Palacios, Theodore Lamberton, Pérez, Juan Leal, Charles Stillman, and Julián Palacios. As delegates from Precinct Four were Ayers, James Gullet. F. K. Ridder, and M. C. Díaz, and Theodore Weidenmuller served from Precinct Five.[12]

Chairman Spann then named himself and Chamberlain delegates to the state convention; N. G. Collins, George Bodet, and Buckley to the congressional convention; Ridder, Palacios, and Charles Hoffman to the senatorial convention; and Gray, Placido Benavides, and Stillman to the representative convention. Finally, the group selected an Executive Committee composed of Spann, chairman; Valls, secretary; Precinct One, Gray; Precinct Two, Placido Benavides; Precinct Three, Ayers; Precinct Four Palacios; and Precinct Five, Ridder. Tejanos did not do much better than they did in the courthouse confab, even though they were the majority. They had a way to go to be able to maneuver party politics.[13]

Finally, the delegates approved a resolution that the Courthouse Convention, from which they had split, only had representatives from part of Precinct

One and had issued no credentials from Precinct Two. Buckley moved that the convention issue certificates to Precinct Two individuals, thus affirming that Precinct Two's meeting, held June 22, was legal and exposing the wrong the Courthouse Convention had committed to disenfranchise voters from Precinct Two. The motion carried unanimously. The schoolhouse group asserted that they represented 463 of the 640 votes in the county.[14]

Interestingly, County Judge Moses was nowhere in this entanglement. Each faction claimed three elected officials. In addition to Dix, the elected surveyor, Sheriff Wright, and County and District Clerk Glover sided with the regulars. County Treasurer Bodet, Tax Assessor Buckley, and County Commissioner Chamberlin left with the protesters. Only three Tejanos remained with the regular Democrats, while twenty-two left for the schoolhouse.

Huaraches y Botas

By the fall of 1886, campaigning for the general election went into high gear. The two Democratic factions each fielded a ticket. On October 22, 1886, the establishment Democrats held a political rally at Peña with a "professional vocalist" addressing supporters in Spanish. Candidates for this group were called the Wright Party, after Sheriff L. L. Wright, or the Huarache Party.[15] Their opponents, who had bolted the Democratic Convention, were called the Bota (boot) or Luby Party.[16]

The Huarache and Bota classifications first made their appearance in Laredo in 1884. The *Laredo Daily Times* explained the split as "the parties are simply the outs and ins." One historian describes the Huaraches as "Republican in faith" that "appealed to the plebian class" and "sought support from the common people." Another writer refers to them as "reformers," which included prominent Mexican Democrats and Anglo Republicans. One author depicted the Botas as the "self-styled Democrats, mainly composed of the aristocratic element, but with a proletariat following." They were considered the "opposition" party, the outs. These descriptions do not precisely fit Duval County's situation, perhaps because the scholars saw these factions through a present-day lens.[17]

While historians may have varying views on these factions, it is important not to view them from a twenty-first-century prism. For example, modern-day Republicans ostensibly represent the rich and Democrats the poor. Still, the nineteenth-century reality was that the Republicans, who had freed enslaved African Americans, were seen as champions of people of color or the oppressed. Democrats represented the established, entrenched, xenophobic power structure, especially in Dixie.

As indicated earlier, Tejanos had walked out of the Democratic Convention in much greater numbers than had stayed. The Duval County Bota Party leaders included well-known Republicans, such as James O. Luby, N. G. Collins, Charles Hoffman, Charles Stillman, and Julián Palacios. Ironically, they epitomized the insiders in Duval County. Perhaps they had walked out of the convention because the Democratic leadership had tried to wrest control of their party from Republican interlopers.

Moreover, Judge Luby, the Republican leader in Duval County, provided the alternative tag for the Bota Party. In Duval County both sides were Democrats, and each had its share of insiders. But as with the Blue and Red factions in Brownsville, "local issues remained of greater importance in determining party membership than national questions."[18]

While the Duval County parties presumably did not represent any political alliance, social group, or economic class, the Botas were also known as the Mexican Texans Party. So the Botas did indeed stand for something; they stood up for the Tejanos. The political maxim that "all politics is local" was confirmed in Duval County; elections turned not on party label but on how well those in office performed. Locally, this meant how well politicos met their Tejano constituents' needs.[19]

The *Caller* wrote that the Huaraches were not into mudslinging; instead, the party "praised their opponents, in the highest manner." Two weeks before the election, the newspaper repeated its assessment that although the electioneering was "very warm," no one expected problems; it was a contest between friends. Still, the Laredo editor bemoaned rumors that violence could arise between the two groups. This fear was undoubtedly raised by a confrontation between Huaraches and Botas in Laredo earlier that year, which resulted in thirty-five deaths.[20]

Duval County politicians predicted voters would cast over one thousand votes in the general election. After another rally in Realitos, the Huaraches were confident in the outcome and asserted they had "a surplus of scalps." The Bota Party reportedly had not yet appeared in that part of the county. The two parties seemed equally split, and election gatherings bespoke a tight outcome. Still, law enforcement authorities were taking no chances. Privates McNamara and Picket, Texas Rangers stationed in Laredo, went to Benavides to keep order on election day. They arrested Juan García and Phil Villegas for carrying weapons and Pedro Benavides and Alejandro Cantú for assault to kill and murder.[21]

The election went on without incident; both political groups had insisted their supporters abstain from consuming alcohol. San Diego's saloons remained closed on election day, including at night after the polls closed. Botas hosted a big dance in Benavides and Huaraches in Realitos. Voter turnout numbered 1,212. Razor-thin margins decided all races (voting at the Peña precinct was one of the county's closest, with the Botas winning by five votes). Each party won five seats; the Botas won a firm hold of the commissioners court, while the Huaraches took more countywide offices. Luby had recently returned from his assignment at Brownsville and took the county judge's seat for the Botas. At the same time, George Bodet won the county treasurer position and John Caldwell, county surveyor. Huarache countywide winners were L. L. Wright, sheriff; F. C. Gravis, county assessor; R. B. Glover, county and district clerk; and W. B. Austin, inspector of hides and animals.[22]

F. Ridder, Pedro Eznal, and W. M. Hebron gained county commissioners seats, giving the Botas a clear majority on the commissioners court. Ed Corkill was the only Huarache on the commissioners court. Tejanos did not do exceptionally well with either group. Bota Party member Eznal was the only Tejano to win office; Huaraches elected no Tejanos. The turnout produced twice the votes that it had two years prior. Luby was returned to the county judge seat because two Huaraches ran against him, splitting the vote and resulting in a Luby win by a mere twenty-vote margin. Huarache leader L. L. Wright defeated Bota candidate John Buckley by "fifty-odd" votes. Both were Democrats. The county's ballot for statewide candidates showed it to be a Democratic county, with the party's candidates winning by a margin of 1,168 to 36 for Republican candidates.[23]

The Volatile 1888 Election

Duval County Democratic Chairman F. C. Gravis called a precinct convention to meet on June 9, 1888, to select delegates to the county convention and choose county officers of the Democratic party. Moreover, the county convention would elect representatives to state, senatorial, and representative meetings.[24]

On June 14, Democrats gathered for the Precinct One Convention and elected Gravis precinct chairman and R. B. Glover as secretary. In addition to Gravis and Glover, they picked delegates to the county convention, including George Bodet, Harry Reynolds, L. L. Wright, C. K. Gravis, J. W. Wright, N. G. Collins, E. N. Gray, L. B. Wright, Charles Hoffman, C. L. Coyner, F. D. Perrenot, Joe Shaw, John D. Cleary, Antonio Rosales, Juan Puig, M. Corrigan, E. Martínez, and L. Levy. Once again, the Americano power structure continued to slight Tejanos, with only two selected as delegates.[25]

At the county convention, delegates picked J. W. Wright as Duval County Democratic Executive Committee chairman and George Bodet secretary; Bodet, Collins, F. K. Ridder, and L. L. Wright were to represent the Duval County Democrats at the state convention. Delegates to the senatorial convention were R. B. Glover, L. L. Wright, R. R. Savage, G. H Reynolds, and A. R. Valls. John Buckley, J. J. Dix, E. N. Gray, J. W. Wright, E. Corkill, L. Levy, John Puig, and F. C. Gravis would attend the state representative convention. Once again, Democrats did not select Tejanos to participate in conventions outside the county.[26]

It appeared that the dissidents from the 1886 county convention had gotten right with the Wright faction of the Democratic party. Collins, Gray, Hoffman, and Buckley were among the defectors now back under the party tent. While the Americano Democrats had patched their differences from the 1886 Democratic Party split, little had changed for Tejanos; they were still on the outside looking in. But Tejanos spent no time moping about the process that left them out. A month later, on July 17, Tejanos called a meeting in San Diego to organize a political party.[27]

Tejanos Try to Go It on Their Own

Tejano Botas met at the Garfield House in San Diego on July 17, 1888, to organize for the November voting. The confab caused Americanos to pause, as they were now outside looking in—literally, through the Garfield House's windows—and listening to speeches in Spanish. Meeting attendees selected delegates to gather in Concepción in August to nominate candidates for the November election. There was an understandable dissatisfaction among Tejanos regarding the management of county and public affairs. The *Corpus Christi Caller* opined that Tejanos were making a grave mistake. Glaringly overlooking its reporting, the newspaper declared Americanos had never organized to deprive Tejanos of holding office or voting. The newspaper failed to note that Americanos had complete control of the Democratic organization, excluding Tejanos at their most recent convention and refusing to meaningfully include them in elective office for a decade.[28]

Attendees at the meeting in Concepción no doubt were intimately familiar with the political climate in Duval County. They did not need the *Caller's* correspondent lecturing them. They knew the numbers of those who served in public office and that Tejanos had inadequate representation. Tejanos had won only two countywide offices in the ten years since the county's organization, a paltry 4 percent of countywide officials elected. They had fared somewhat better in precinct offices, claiming 43 percent, but most were as constables, the lowest elected county position. Still, Americanos had almost completely shut them out of the more influential elected positions, even though Tejanos comprised an overwhelming majority of the population.

Table 15.3 Duval County elected officials by ethnicity, 1876–1886

Election Year	Countywide Offices		Precinct Offices		Total Officials	
	Americanos	Tejanos	Americanos	Tejanos	Americanos	Tejanos
1876*	7	1	7	3	14	4
1878	8	0	5	3	13	3

(Continues)

Table 15.3 (Continued)

Election Year	Countywide Offices		Precinct Offices		Total Officials	
	Americanos	Tejanos	Americanos	Tejanos	Americanos	Tejanos
1880	9	0	9	3	18	3
1882**	7	1	9	4	16	5
1884	9	0	4	7	13	7
1886	9	0	5	9	12	9
Total	49	2	39	29	86	31

Source: Duval County Commissioners Court Minutes, Book A, "Election Returns," Secretary of State, RG 30, Series 84, Duval County, TSLAC.
*Andrew R. Valls, a Louisianan of Spanish parents, was the county clerk but not counted as a Tejano. As a result, the only Tejano elected to countywide office was County Assessor Calixto Tovar.
**Two Spaniards held countywide office, Valls and Inspector of Hides Juan Puig.

Tejanos convened a meeting in August 1888 at Concepción to nominate candidates for various county offices. But Americanos appeared to have co-opted the gathering. Attendees selected Julián Palacios as chairman and W. L. Hebbron as secretary. Palacios then chose A. J. Ayres, John Buckley, J. Alanis, Juan Zardenta, and Hipolito Cantú to a business committee that established the number of votes communities were entitled to in the group's business. San Diego got nine votes, Benavides six, Concepción five, Rosita four, and Peña two.[29]

However, as always, Americanos were nominated to the primo offices. The committee selected J. W. Parkman for county judge, John Buckley for sheriff, William A. Tinney for county and district clerk, Avelino García for assessor, Juan Puig for treasurer, J. C. Caldwell for surveyor, Vidal García for inspector of hides and animals, J. W. Moses for county attorney, R. H. Corbet for commissioner for Precinct One, Juan Zardenta for commissioner for Precinct Two, Charles Stillman for commissioner for Precinct Three, and W. L. Hebbron for commissioner for Precinct Four.[30]

Nothing had changed as Americanos dominated the slate in what was supposed to have been a convention to nominate Tejanos for the upcoming November 1888 election. Interestingly, many 1886 bolters and Bota candidates, while attending the Democrat County Convention, chose to run on the Mexican

Texan or Bota Party. Still, many Tejanos voiced they could not support the ticket, and others discussed holding another convention to select a truly Tejano ticket. Also, the word spread that some candidates would not run.[31]

The Bota lineup slightly changed before the November voting got underway; Julián Palacios replaced Parkman at the top of the ticket. However, political observers noted this was a strong ticket with the support of the Tejano population. "Unless incumbents, which I understand are candidates for reelection, spend a good deal of money for manipulating votes, there is a strong probability that the ticket will be elected," wrote the correspondent to the *Laredo Daily Times*.[32]

Surprisingly, James O. Luby, who had given the Bota adherents their name, now led the opposition Huarache ticket as their nominee for county judge. Other Huarache candidates included L. L. Wright, sheriff; R. B. Glover, district and county clerk; C. L. Coyner, county attorney; George Bodet, treasurer; F. C. Gravis, tax assessor; J. J. Dix, surveyor; and W. B. Huston, inspector of hides and animals. "Tejanos need not apply," seemed the writing on the wall. The number of *maromeros*[33] was enough to make voters' heads spin. By mid-September, election fever was in the air, and a political pandemic was coming to San Diego and the county. Big turnouts of Bota and Huarache voters attended rallies at Concepción, Mendieta, and La Rosita on Diez y Seis de Septiembre. The election was gaining intensity, but speculation was that whoever won would do so by a razor-thin vote.[34]

The upcoming election was all everyone talked about; the parties were simply the outs and ins, with Democrats and Republicans on both sides. Some voters expressed the desire for change and pushed the idea that some sort of rotation, akin to modern-day term limits in elected offices, was desirable. Others felt that if incumbents were doing their job, they should remain in office.

Violence Raises Its Ugly Face

Politics began to get warm three days before voting. Partisans were everywhere shouting "*¡Viva la Bota!*" or "*¡Viva el Huarache!*" The Botas held a large rally in San Diego at El Ranchero, a large building where the crowd overflowed into the streets. Manuel Garza Díaz, a candidate for justice of the peace, and Juan Puig, the Botas' candidate for county treasurer, rallied the crowd by denying rumors published by Francisco P. de González in *El Clarín* that they were withdrawing from the race. Instead, they proclaimed they were firm Bota supporters who were not dropping out of the race.[35]

After Fred G. García gave an eloquent, lengthy speech at El Ranchero, a band led Bota supporters in a street parade complete with torches and banners. When they passed *El Clarín*, Editor González exited his office with a six-shooter in hand and struck one or two of the youngsters, shouting "¡*Viva la Bota!*" and himself countering with "¡*Viva el Huarache!*" Older boys wrestled the pistol from him, making him holler, "¡*Viva la Bota!*" Finally, they told him to stay "cool," especially in a hot climate, since he appeared somewhat nervous.[36]

On October 20, at about sundown, Atanacio Gómez, a tailor in San Diego, walked into Encarnación Yzaguirre's barbershop on the old plaza as Editor González was putting on his coat after getting a shave. As he came in, Gómez cried out loudly that he did not understand why people were allowed to carry guns in San Diego. González dared Gómez to report him. Gómez accused González of punching his boy with a pistol the previous evening. Gómez challenged González to a fistfight and opened his vest to show the editor he was unarmed. As both men walked out of the barbershop, González said he had no desire to engage in fisticuffs.[37]

At the door, however, González stopped, turned, and drew a .32-American five-shooter. Gómez advanced upon González, struck him with one hand, and grabbed the pistol with the other. As they fought the gun discharged, shooting Gómez in the heart, killing him instantly. William L. Rogers, a bystander, then jumped González and caught the hand holding the pistol, to which González replied, "Let me go, or I will shoot you." A deputy arrived, took the firearm, arrested González, and took him to jail. A double guard was placed on González as talk spread throughout the town that Bota supporters would lynch him. González was a Huarache and Gómez a Bota.[38]

People settled down after Rogers, Ignacio Gauna, Manuel Prados, and Dr. L. B. Wright conducted an inquest of the incident and determined that the shooting was not political. González's friends said he was a small chap, while Gómez was a big man, so they contended that González, acting in self-defense, accidentally triggered the gun. Gómez's six children (Ynes, 16; Bernardo, 13; Joséfa, 12; Fidela, 11; Juan, 9; and an infant) were left orphaned as his wife, reportedly the daughter of one of San Diego's founders, had died several months before.[39]

Election Aftermath

After the voting the commissioners court certified the results and reported them to the secretary of state. Mirroring earlier shenanigans that denied Tejanos political posts, the court took a questionable route to arrive at the winners. Still, nothing had changed.

Days after the election, Juan Zardenta, a candidate for Duval County commissioner, wrote to his brother Romulo in Laredo that the Bota Democratic ticket had won the election in Duval County. Julián Palacios was elected county judge over James Luby. Others elected, according to Zardenta, were W. Tinney, county clerk; Alvino G. Tovar, county treasurer; John Buckley, sheriff; and himself as county commissioner for Precinct Two. Huaraches had elected two commissioners and the Bota two commissioners, but with the Bota County Judge Palacios, the Bota had a majority. In addition, Zardenta informed his brother that rumors of a tie between Buckley and Wright in the race for sheriff were wrong.[40]

Zardenta's report proved premature, as the Duval County Commissioners Court, which had a Huarache majority, threw out more than 400 votes on a technicality. The commissioners court met on November 13 and opened the precinct returns to canvass the election. By a 3–2 vote, the commissioners court threw out all 245 ballots from Precinct Two in Benavides and 187 votes in Precinct Five in Los Julios (La Rosita). Because the election judges failed to indicate the total number of votes cast in their precinct as per state law, the court said it could not approve them. Instead, election officials noted the total votes received by each candidate. Still, the court claimed that election officers failed to include a total for all ballots cast in their respective precincts. Bota Commissioners William Hebbron and Pedro Eznal voted to accept the results submitted by election officials, but Huarache Commissioners Edward Corkill and F. H. Ridder voted no. Finally, perhaps smarting from the Botas' selection of Palacios as the county judge candidate, Judge Luby voted to throw out all votes from the two precincts, totaling 432 ballots.[41]

Foreseeing legal challenges brought on by their actions, the Huaraches hired attorney John S. McCampbell to represent them. Meanwhile, the Botas smelled a problem and engaged J. O. Nicholson of Laredo to advise them. As the commissioners court discussed its options, Nicholson pointed out that the statutes the court alluded to were directory, not mandatory. McCampbell, representing R. B. Glover, F. C. Gravis, and L. L. Wright, questioned Nicholson's assertion.[42]

An appeal to the district court appeared inevitable. Meanwhile, the incumbents remained in office. Moreover, the Bota contingent anticipated a lengthy legal battle since the Huaraches had supported District Judge John C. Russel in the election. The Botas had thrown their support to the judge's opponent. Two years earlier, a similar case occurred in Starr County, and the political reprobates remained in office until the legal challenge reached the Supreme Court, which reversed their shenanigans.[43]

On December 5 the county commissioners met to approve the newly elected officers' bonds, but they still had one more card to play. The court rejected the bond of Bota County Commissioner Charles Stillman, who had won the Precinct Three seat. Ostensibly, according to the Huaraches, Stillman was not a citizen. Though Stillman was born in Matamoros, he came to the United States at 2 and served as Duval County commissioner from 1884 to 1886. Moreover, Luby had named him the presiding judge for the Concepción box. If Stillman was not a citizen, a newspaper asked, should that voting box be invalidated? Stillman and County Attorney Coyner wrote to Texas Attorney General James S. Hogg to clarify the problem. Through an assistant Hogg demurred, writing to Stillman that he had no authority in the matter.[44]

Election Decided in Court

The community took some time off for the Christmas holidays, but politics and the November election soon returned to the forefront with all its unpleasant questions. The Bota partisans moved to file a challenge in district court. On January 9, 1889, District Judge Russell empaneled a grand jury to investigate the election and any possible illegal voting that may have occurred. Judge Russell named N. G. Collins, Luby's political godfather, foreman. The *Dallas Morning News* expected fifty to sixty indictments and lamented that a "lame election law will no doubt send many a poor Mexican to the state prison." Anticipating foul play from the grand jury, La Bota charged that Republicans had imported voters from Nueces County, Starr County, and Mexico to vote for the Huarache slate. While both factions were adherents to the Democratic Party, since Republican Luby was at the head of the Huaraches, it may have prompted the reference to them as Republicans.[45]

At the same district court session, the Bota candidates filed quo warranto proceedings against the county judge, county attorney, county clerk, sheriff, assessor, county surveyor, and hides and animals inspector. A quo warranto is a writ issued by a court formally requiring somebody to state by what authority they are acting or holding a position. The Bota plaintiffs also asked in the quo warranto for a change of venue. The incumbents did not object, and the case went to Corpus Christi. The *Dallas Morning News* wryly reported, "They [Bota candidates] claim they were elected by a majority of their fellow citizens and at the same time claim they cannot get a fair trial from their people."[46]

On January 16, 1889, between district court sessions, authorities arrested newly elected Precinct Two Commissioner Juan Zardenta for allegedly illegally voting because he was not a citizen. However, Zardenta provided proof of citizenship and proof he had lived in the precinct the required number of days before the election.[47]

After granting a change of venue to Corpus Christi, the district court set January 21 to hear the Duval County election case. While Attorney General Hogg had been reticent about involving himself in the Stillman controversy, he did not hesitate to intercede on behalf of John Buckley, the Bota candidate for sheriff. Buckley applied for leave to file information alleging the Huarache incumbent sheriff "usurped, intruded, and is unlawfully holding the office of sheriff and tax collector." The attorney general claimed that the Duval County Commissioners Court had canvassed the votes improperly by excluding voting Precincts One and Five and giving Wright 418 votes to Buckley's 330. By counting Precincts One and Five, the election would have resulted in each candidate for sheriff receiving 590 votes. The record does not explain why the attorney general interceded only for candidate Buckley and not for Stillman—perhaps because the rejection of ballots from Benavides and La Rosita had not affected Stillman's race.[48]

Moreover, Hogg asserted, ballots in Precincts One, Three, Four, and Six had been "fraudulently counted because they included votes cast by persons not entitled as qualified voters." The reasons for the disqualification of voters were numerous: perhaps they lived in another county or had not lived in the county for the required six months. Or maybe they were convicted felons, a Mexican citizen, not 21 years of age, or not a state resident for twelve months. The attorney general claimed that these voters—all but eight were Tejanos—were disqualified on the above-stated grounds. The Botas, or Mexican Texans Party, seemed to be seeking to disqualify their own Tejano backers. Disqualifying these voters would yield a tally of Buckley, 590, and Wright, 555.[49]

On March 27, 1890, District Judge Russell ruled that the law was with the Bota candidate Buckley, and the judge removed Wright from office. Wright appealed to the Texas Supreme Court. The court summarily dismissed the appeal on June 28, 1890, and required "the ouster" of Wright while ruling that Buckley "recover said office of Sheriff and Tax Collector of said County of Duval." Moreover, the high court ordered that Wright and his sureties, George Bodet, C. Tibilier, and A. Rosales, pay all costs. The court sided with Buckley, but no other Bota candidate was party to the lawsuit. The Supreme Court was silent on whether the other Bota candidates would also assume their Huarache opponents' positions.[50]

On July 30, in what may have seemed anticlimactic to John Buckley, the Duval County Commissioners Court entered the Supreme Court's decision into the official record. "Therefore," the minutes read, "in pursuance of and obedience to the . . . honorable district court of Nueces County, Texas, it is . . . ordered, adjudged, and decreed that John Buckley . . . is . . . elected to the office of Sheriff and Tax Collector of Duval County." All that remained was for Buckley to deliver the required $30,000 in bonds of office, which Tejanos Agapito Sáenz, Saturnino Vera, Jorge Alanis, Ysidro Benavides, Anastasio Pérez, and José María G. Treviño provided.[51]

Tejanos Began to Make Inroads

Up to 1890 Democrats held the upper hand in Duval County politics. That year Republicans gained a slight edge in Duval County politics and held on to that advantage until 1906.[52] Available records, however, do not indicate which official was Republican or Democrat, only revealing who won what office. Still, this suggests that Tejanos, affiliated with the Bota Party, had Republican leanings. All the Tejanos but one that attended the Republican County Convention saw success at the polls, including G. D. García, Manuel Rogers, and Julian Palacios, who held public office during this time. Agustín Cantú did not seek public office but actively provided bonds for those elected, whether Republicans or Democrats.

Nevertheless, political lines were not crystal clear. Loyalties reflected friendship, social, and business connections. And they could sway from one election to another. In 1890 the Bota party—born out of Tejanos' desire to gain a fair share of Duval County elected ranks—won the most significant share of Duval County offices.

Table 15.4 Duval County election results, 1890–1894

Office	1890	1892	1894
County Judge	J. Williamson Moses	Francisco García	S. H. Woods
County/District Clerk	William Tinney	William Tinney	William Tinney
County Attorney	Charles L. Coyner	Charles L. Coyner	Charles L. Coyner
Sheriff/Tax Collector	John Buckley	John Buckley	John Buckley
County Tax Assessor	Pedro Eznal	Pedro Eznal	Pedro Eznal
County Treasurer	George Bodet	George Bodet	George Bodet
Inspector of Hides and Animals	Vidal García	Loreto M. García	
County Surveyor	Charles S. Gunter	Charles S. Gunter	Charles S. Gunter
Commissioner, Precinct One	Guadalupe D. García	Guadalupe D. García	Guadalupe D. García

(*Continues*)

Table 15.4 (Continued)

Office	1890	1892	1894
Justice of the Peace, Precinct One	W. L. Rogers	C. D. Gunter	James F. Mount
Constable, Precinct One	Pablo Cardona	John Larcade	John Larcade
Commissioner, Precinct Two	Charles Stillman	Charles Stillman	Charles Stillman
Justice of the Peace, Precinct Two	A. R. Valls	Tomás Romano	Tomás Romano
Constable, Precinct Two		Clemente Reyna	C. Oliveira*
Commissioner, Precinct Three		George Reynolds	F. K. Ridder
Justice of the Peace, Precinct Three			
Constable, Precinct Three	Gregorio Morales		
Commissioner, Precinct Four	F. K. Ridder	F. K. Ridder	William Hebbron
Justice of the Peace, Precinct Four			
Constable, Precinct Four			
Justice of the Peace, Precinct Five	Manuel Garza Díaz	Charles Shaw	Manuel Garza Díaz
Justice of the Peace, Precinct Six			Antonio Rangel*
Constable, Precinct Five		Eusebio Salinas	
Constable, Precinct Six			

Source: Texas Secretary of State, Election Returns, Duval County, 1890, 1892, 1894.
*Not qualified to hold office.

The next opportunity for the two political parties to show their political muscle was in 1892. Unfortunately, there is little documentation on the Bota or Huarache Parties. Still, the political year got underway in May when County Democratic Chairman Charles L. Coyner called the county convention for May 25 at the county courthouse.[53]

At the May 25 conference, the delegates selected Coyner as secretary. As was usual in politics in those years, of the twenty envoys picked for the several conventions, only one, M. L Valverde, was a Tejano. Other representatives were L. Levy, Charles Hoffman, J. W. Shaw, John D. Cleary, W. A. Tinney, C. S. Gunter, C. L. Coyner, A. Beecher, F. C. Gravis, W. C. Benendis, N. G. Collins, E, N. Gray, George Bodet, J. M. Wright, S. H., Woods, Ben Reaves, G. H. Reynolds, John Buckley, and Leofalo Benendis. All twenty delegates voted to support Grover Cleveland for president and split evenly in the governor's race, giving ten votes to George Clark and ten to James S. Hogg. The Democratic division of 1886 had dissipated, but Tejanos' concerns about fair participation remained a nagging challenge.[54]

As the general election approached, Governor Hogg's people were wheeling and dealing for votes in the streets of San Diego. Hogg carried Duval with little resistance on election day, netting 435 votes to his opponent's 176 and a third-party candidate getting 4 votes.[55]

The First Tejano County Judge

County Judge J. Williamson Moses took ill and resigned in 1892. The commissioners court named Francisco García as Moses's successor. That same year Judge García won the county judge's seat, becoming the first Tejano to win the office outright. There is, of course, no royalty in Duval County, but García's family came close to being that. He was the eldest son of Encarnacion García and Práxedis Tovar García. Práxedis's mother and Francisco García's grandmother was the venerable Trinidad Flores, who also played a crucial role in almost every transitional moment of the county's formative history. His maternal great-grandfather, Ventura Flores, and great-great-grandfather, Julián Flores, were the original landowners in San Diego.

Other countywide winners included W. A. Tinney, county and district clerk; John Buckley, sheriff and tax collector; C. L. Coyner, county attorney; Pedro Eznal, tax assessor; George Bodet, treasurer; C. S. Gunter, county surveyor; and Loreto M. García, inspector of hides and animals. Tejanos won three of the eight countywide offices. It was an improvement, but Tejanos still had a way to go.[56]

Fig. 15.1 F. Garcia Tovar (1857–1912), first Tejano judge in Duval County. Courtesy of Eliseo Cadena.

Francisco García was the first Tejano elected county judge south of the Nueces River, outside Webb County. Fellow Tejanos must have felt incredibly proud, and three of them, E. G. Pérez, Eduardo Flores, and S. García Pérez, stepped up to sign the new judge's surety. Víctor G. Elizondo, Gregorio Ruiz, and Julián Ureste provided Assessor Pedro Eznal's surety.[57]

On January 30, 1892, longtime Duval County political leader Judge J. W. Moses died at his home in San Diego. Although Moses had suffered from paralysis and loss of voice, the judge continued writing until the day before his passing. Six months later, on June 27, Moses's successor, County Judge García, resigned for unspecified reasons. The commissioners court accepted his resignation and named S. H. Woods his replacement.[58]

Archie Parr Enters the Political Scene

In June 1894 Archie Parr debuted in state and national politics. In a "sort of a keynote" address to the Duval County Democratic convention, Parr asked for approval of a resolution asking the county's representative to the Texas Legislature to vote for longtime South Texas political boss James Wells to the US Senate over incumbent Roger Q. Mills. Parr told the delegates meeting in San Diego that Wells should win with "a hip and a hurrah." The area's state representative was also the editor of the *Caller* and said to count on his vote. But the rest of the state was not in tune with Parr's suggested choice.[59]

For Duval County the more severe business was the local elections, shaping into quite an event with a crowded race in the county judge's contest. Six candidates sought the post. Another three were vying for sheriff, "and a full complement of candidates" sought various other offices. As a result, political observers expected tight races in November. Most politicians thought this might be the most hotly contested local election in the county's short history.[60]

The Bota and Huarache Parties called a truce the week before the election in deference to longtime Congressman W. H. Crain, who was campaigning for the Seventh US Congressional District. First, Crain made a three-hour speech in San Diego in which "he handled his opponents without gloves." Democrats from all over the county and Corpus Christi were present. Then, Crain left on the morning train for Benavides for a talk. Despite this effort, when the votes came in, Crain received a thrashing in Duval County, losing to V. Welden by nearly a two-to-one margin, 625–316. Welden was an independent Democrat running with Republican support. Nevertheless, despite his poor showing in Duval County, Crain won reelection.[61]

While the newspapers and state politicians were interested in the higher-level races, the people settled on their leaders in Duval. County Judge S. H. Woods won the election to his appointed seat, and Sheriff and Tax Collector John Buckley won reelection. Voters elected others to countywide positions, including County Attorney C. L. Coyner, County/District Clerk John S. Tinney, County Assessor Pedro Eznal, and County Treasurer George

Bodet. Elected members of the commissioners court included G. D. García, Precinct One; F. Stillman, Precinct Two; F. K. Ridder, Precinct Three; and John Hebbron, Precinct Four. Other precinct officers elected on November 7 were justices of the peace James F. Mount and Tomás Almaraz for Precincts One and Two, respectively.[62]

Tejanos, as had become the pattern, mainly provided the financial backing for the required sureties. In 1894 those reaching into their pockets to ensure the county's elected officials were fiscally responsible included Nazario Peña, John Hebbron, Manuel V. Chapa, Francisco Peña Hinojosa, J. M. G. Treviño, Thomas Schaeffer, Antonio Rosales, Juan Puig, A. Parker, Charles Stillman, Manuel Rogers, A. Becker, Jorge Alanis, Julián Ureste, Nazario Peña, Cayetano Ríos, F. K. Ridder, Agustín Cantú, José María G. Treviño, E. Martínez, Fernando López, C. Hoffman, G. D. García, Sylvestre Cuéllar, Isidro Benavides, and José Vaello. Nineteen Tejanos outnumbered the five Americanos sureties, a four-to-one margin. As for the elected officials, the ratio was nearly reversed, with ten Americanos serving in an electoral office while only three Tejanos achieved that level of recognition.[63]

In odd-numbered years Duval County politicians took some time off from the stresses of political life. But not entirely. In April 1895, for example, the commissioners court designated polling places for future elections and named election judges for each location: for Precinct One in San Diego, R. H. Corbett; for Precinct Two in Benavides, S. R. Peters; for Precinct Three in Concepción, Crescencio Leal; Hebbronville's Precinct Four, H. W. Garrett; Precinct Five at Palito Blanco, A. J. Rider; and Jerry Downs at Realitos, Precinct Six.[64]

On April 17 Judge Woods resigned, and the court replaced him with County Attorney Coyner. However, before making Coyner's appointment, commissioners, on a motion by Commissioner F. K. Ridder and seconded by G. D. García, lowered the judge's salary from five hundred dollars to three hundred dollars. Ridder and García then proposed that the court discontinue the current salary for a county attorney, and the motion passed unanimously. The following month, on May 13, N. Peña, Antonio Rosales, A. Becker, and J. Puig put up the bond needed by Coyner to qualify for the judge's seat, and he promptly took his oath of office.[65]

As 1896 rolled in, politics again began to get serious. Duval County Republicans held a convention at San Diego on February 13 to select delegates to the congressional convention slated for Cuero on March 3–4 and the state party convention in Austin on March 24. The group elected James O. Luby and William Hebbron as interim chair and secretary. The delegates named C. Tibilier and Frank Feuille to represent them at state and congressional conventions. Luby then appointed W. W. Meek, James F. Mount, and Feuille to draft resolutions on the group's "sense of the convention on the issues of the day."[66]

Up to this time, Republicans had remained in the background. Luby was the only one frequently recognized as a Republican. Still, after their February 17 county convention, they kept the momentum going and organized the Blaine Republican Club of Duval County. The group drew Republicans from throughout Duval County, including Luby, Tibilier (elected president), Meek, A. L. Muil, Frank Feuille, G. D. García, P. A. Bodet, J. F. Mount, Manuel Rogers, Julián Palacios, William Hebbron, Luther Gillet, and Agustín Cantú.[67]

On March 22, 1896, Duval County Democrats selected J. W. Shaw as executive committee chair and B. Coopwood Jr. as secretary. Delegates chose Shaw, John D. Cleary, and Archie Parr to attend the Corpus Christi convention on March 24. Benavides delegates dominated the convention's decisions, while San Diego and Realitos "were not in it."[68]

At an organizational meeting in San Diego on June 12, Democrats selected F. Gravis as chairman and Cleary as secretary for the subsequent two years. In addition, the group approved several resolutions submitted to the state convention to express Duval County's views. One declaration in particular directly impacted Duval County's Tejano voters. The Duval Democrats declared that "it is a tenet of the Democratic party to require 'full' citizenship as a condition precedent to exercising the right to suffrage."[69]

The March 22, 1896, convention directed state senatorial and representative convention envoys to cast their ballots "condemning any change in the present state constitution, prescribing, the qualification of voter." Also, the convention directed the delegates to vote against any legislative initiative considering such an amendment. No doubt, the right kind of people were applauding from the sidelines.[70]

The convention delegates selected C. L. Coyner, N. Robinson, and E. N. Gray to represent Duval County Democrats at the state gathering in Fort Worth. Moreover, they sent C. F. Stillman, Parr, Cleary, A. R. Valls, and S. R. Peters to the state convention in Austin, who selected delegates to the National Democratic Convention in Chicago. Parr, Shaw, and Cleary were to attend the congressional district convention in Corpus Christi. Finally, Shaw and Parr were selected to go to the state senatorial convention, and R. H. Corbit, Cleary, and F. C. Gravis represented Duval County at the state representative convention. Not surprisingly, the party failed to select a Tejano Democrat Party member to represent them at any convention. Perhaps Parr, who went on to champion the Tejano electorate, might have willingly given up one of his three convention assignments for a fellow Democrat with a Spanish surname; it was not to be.[71]

In the national election of November, Democrat fortunes, or perhaps misfortunes, sent a muddled message. Republican William McKinley overwhelmed Democrat William Jennings Bryan in Duval County by a whopping 782–355 votes in the presidential race. McKinley was the favorite of sheep growers in the county. Jerome C. Kerby, Populist Party candidate for governor, embarrassed Democrat Governor Culberson in Duval County with a 786–355 majority. Republican congressional candidate Grass turned back incumbent Democrat Congressman Kleberg, 763–454. In the state Senate race, Duval voters, who had preferred Republican candidates, chose Democrat Atlee over Tejano Republican Hinojosa, 715–526. Local candidates did well as Democrats, but Duval County showed a robust Republican leaning at the state and national levels.[72]

Determining where local officials fell in party affiliation and ideology is problematic. Candidates did not run as Democrats and Republicans but as Botas and Huaraches. Distinguishing allegiance to either of the county parties is also perilous since individuals frequently switched political affiliations out of convenience. Moreover, while results for the upper-level races are available from newspaper accounts, no such information for local races is available in the sources consulted; they merely reported the winners. Finally, the Duval County Commissioners Court had a relatively loose and odd manner of accepting election results. Its members did not list candidates by the office they contested or provide votes received. They merely indicated in their minutes that the returns for each voting precinct were "received, examined, approved and estimated."

Nevertheless, Duval County conducted national, state, and local elections in November 1896. Since both Republicans and Democrats also held local conventions earlier that year, the political affiliation of some county officials was discernible by the party meetings they attended. Democrat Coyner, who had replaced Judge Woods after he resigned as county judge, won the position outright. H. Reid, H. Becker, and Josephine Rosales provided his bonds. Another Democrat, Bethel Coopwood, was elected county attorney; his bond providers were N. Peña and H. Pecker. Yet another Democrat, William A. Tinney, was voted in as county clerk. Again, Becker and A. H. Pérez provided his bonds. Democrat M. Corrigan replaced Sheriff John Buckley, who had held the post for six years. Sometime later, one of Buckley's sons recalled his father "going into tirades against the 'white trash of the town,'" accusing them of voter fraud and intimidating Tejanos, resulting in his defeat. Still, three Tejanos—Agustín Cantú, Anastasio Pérez, and Isidro Benavides—served as Corrigan's sureties.[73]

While Tejanos were progressing by winning more electoral positions, they continued showing their grasp of the American political system by financially supporting elected candidates. Voters selected Arturo D. García as county assessor, and Anastasio Pérez, Agustín Cantú, and Eduardo Flores provided García's bonds. Julian Palacios, who appeared to be the lone Republican elected to countywide office, won the county treasurer seat. His sureties included A. Y. Villarreal, E. E. Cadena, L. P. Peña, and Anastasio Pérez. Archie Parr voted to reject Palacios's bonds, which would prevent the Republican from serving as county treasurer. Parr's was a single negative vote, and Palacios took his seat as treasurer. Carl Gunter, as surveyor, filled the final countywide office. No information was available about his guarantors or his political affiliation.[74]

Charles Hoffman won for county commissioner for Precinct One, and F. K. Ridder and Isidro Benavides provided his bond. Democrat Parr took the post of county commissioner, Precinct Two with Manuel Rogers and J. D. Cleary serving as his sureties. Since his fellow Democratic commissioners

Hoffman and Parr provided his bond, Precinct Four County Commissioner F. K. Ridder was most likely a Democrat.[75]

Voters elected four justices of the peace in the November 1896 voting. They included James F. Mount, Precinct One; A. García (who resigned at the same meeting because the commissioners did not accept his bonds), Precinct Two; Hayes Dix, Precinct Three; and Manuel G. Díaz, Precinct Five. Two constables, John Larcade, Precinct One, and Hipólito Garza, Precinct Two, were also elected.[76]

As the interest moved to the 1898 general election, Republicans reportedly practiced dirty tricks. Presumably, Republicans printed an election sample ballot labeled "Democratic Ticket." But instead of Democratic Congressman Rudolph Kleberg's name, political rascals replaced his name with that of his Republican opponent, B. L. Crouch. All the other names on the ballot had the names of the Democratic candidates for the various positions. Democrats bellowed that the Republican shenanigans were misleading voters, "especially the Mexican voters who are rushed to the polls under the influence of liquor and cast their illegitimate votes, in many instances not allowed to look at their tickets."[77]

At the local level, S. H. Woods, who in 1893 had replaced Francisco García as county judge but later resigned, was again elected county judge. A. Becher and N. Peña served as Woods's sureties, as they had in 1893. Charles Coyner, elected county judge in 1896, returned to his previous post as county attorney. Other countywide winners included Pedro Eznal, county clerk; M. Corrigan, sheriff; Arturo D. García, assessor; Julián Palacios, treasurer; and John J. Dix, surveyor.[78]

The court did not approve Palacios's sureties because it appeared that some of those providing his bonds were nonresidents. The court gave Palacios until January 10, 1899, to file a new bond, which he did on the date specified, to the court's satisfaction, and his election was certified. Sureties included Antonio G. Villarreal, Isidro Benavides, Hilario Pérez, Jesús Sáenz, Emilio Cadena, and Gregorio Ruiz.[79]

The commissioners who took their seats in 1898 were Archie Parr, Precinct Two; H. W. Garrett, Precinct Three; and F. K. Ridder, Precinct Four. Later, on March 21, 1899, County Judge Woods informed the secretary of state that J. D. Cleary qualified to be commissioner of Precinct One.[80]

Two justices of the peace took their oath of office, Andrew R. Valls, Precinct Two, and Manuel G. Díaz, Precinct Five. Also, the court approved two constables: Candelario Sáenz, Precinct One, and Hipólito Garza, Precinct Five. Finally, the court rejected the bond from Santiago San Miguel, who had won the constable, Precinct Four, position.[81]

No political news came from Duval County in 1899. But on April 4, 1900, Duval Democrats met in San Diego for their county convention. Chairman Archie Parr called the meeting to order, and delegates promptly named J. W. Shaw interim chair and Hayes Dix secretary. Next, the caucus tagged Cleary and F. K. Ridder as delegates to the state nominating convention and directed them, along with Parr, to pick delegates to the national confab. Delegates to the congressional convention were Parr, Shaw, W. W. McCampbell, Cleary, and Manuel Rogers. Senatorial convention delegates included Ridder, Cleary, Pedro Eznal, Parr, Woods, and C. M. Robinson. Finally, the state representative gathering delegates were Hoffman, C. K. Gravis, S. R. Peters, Parr, B. Hubbard, Hayes Dix, and W. F. D. Van Norte, P. P. Price, and Shaw. The convention's final action involved naming precinct chairs, including Woods, Precinct One; Peters, Precinct Two; S. C. Navarre, Precinct Three; H. W. Garett, Precinct Four; A. J. Ridder, Precinct Five; and J. A. Vining, Precinct Six. Once again, the Duval County Democratic Party snookered Tejanos, only acknowledging Pedro Eznal and Manuel Rogers.[82]

Voters elected seven countywide officers at the November general election in 1900, including Woods, county judge; Eznal, county and district clerk; W. W. McCampbell, county attorney; Rogers, sheriff and tax collector; Cleary, assessor; Arturo García, treasurer; and J. J. Dix, county surveyor.[83]

Table 15.5 Duval County election results, 1896–1900

Office	1896	1898	1900
County Judge	Charles L. Coyner	S. H. Woods	S. H. Woods
County / District Clerk	William Tinney	Pedro Eznal	Pedro Eznal
County Attorney	Bethel Coopwood	Charles L. Coyner	W. W. McCampbell

(*Continues*)

Table 15.5 (Continued)

Office	1896	1898	1900
Sheriff / Tax Collector	M. Corrigan	M. Corrigan	Manuel Rogers
County Tax Assessor	Arturo D. García	Arturo D. García	John Cleary
County Treasurer	Julian Palacios	Julian Palacios	Arturo García
Inspector of Hides and Animals		Loreto M. García	
County Surveyor	Charles S. Gunter	J. J. Dix	J. J. Dix
Commissioner, Precinct One	Charles Hoffman	Charles Hoffman	Charles Hoffman
Justice of the Peace, Precinct One	James Mount	James Mount	James F. Mount**
Constable, Precinct One	John Larcade	Candelario Sáenz	Antonio Anguiano
Commissioner, Precinct Two	Archie Parr	Archie Parr	Archie Parr
Justice of the Peace, Precinct Two	A. García*	A. R. Valls	
Constable, Precinct Two	Hipólito Cantú		
Commissioner, Precinct Three		George Reynolds	H. W. Garrett
Justice of the Peace, Precinct Three	Hayes Dix	A. W. Tobin	
Constable, Precinct Three		Anacleto Sáenz	
Commissioner, Precinct Four	F. K. Ridder	F. K. Ridder	F. K. Ridder
Justice of the Peace, Precinct Four		Alonzo Montalvo	Manuel Garza Díaz
Constable, Precinct Four		Santiago San Miguel	Hipolito Garza
Justice of the Peace, Precinct Five	Manuel Garza Díaz	Manuel Garza Díaz	

(Continues)

Table 15.5 (Continued)

Office	1896	1898	1900
Justice of the Peace, Precinct Six		Rafael Arredondo	Charles Shaw
Constable, Precinct Five		Hipólito Cantú	
Constable, Precinct Six		Santana García	

Source: Texas Secretary of State, Election Returns, Duval County, 1896, 1898, 1900.
*He resigned because the commissioners court refused his bond. Andrew R. Valls replaced him.
**Mount died before assuming office and the commissioners court replaced him with Juan de Alcala on December 6, 1900.

On November 12, 1900, the commissioners court certified the results of the November general election and acknowledged other county officers, including county commissioners: Charles Hoffman, Precinct One; Archie Parr, Precinct Two; H. W. Garrett, Precinct Three; and F. K. Ridder, Precinct Four. Elected justices of the peace included Juan de Alcala, Precinct One; M. G. Díaz, Precinct Five; and Charles Shaw, Precinct Six. Elected constables were Antonio Anguiano, Precinct One; and Hipólito Garza, Precinct Five.[84]

Tejanos ended the nineteenth century with three countywide offices and a couple of justices of the peace and constable posts. No Tejanos were sitting on the county commissioners court, where all policy decisions developed. As had become the trend, Tejanos actively backed surety bonds for those elected to office. In 1900 Tejanos provided twenty-one of the thirty-seven bonds, or 57 percent, while Americanos offered sixteen.

----•◦•----

Political change was in the air as the nineteenth century closed. Since Duval County's organization, the old political guard continued to rule, but its power was fading, and new players were hitting their stride. Before 1900 Duval County had no clear political boss; no one in the league of James Powers or James Wells, the Valley's longtime political bosses. Still, there were clear signs that Archie Parr was establishing the foundation for a prominent political future; he was a county commissioner and took a direct interest in other politicians' careers, often acting as surety for them. Moreover, Parr was very active in party politics.

Though lacking a clear political leader, the Tejanos were not without options. Tejanos were active behind the scenes through the end of the century, posting bonds for most elected officials. At the close of the century, three of the seven countywide elected officials were Tejanos, clearly indicating that things were changing. But the Tejanos' most valuable resource still was their sheer numbers and prospective voter strength. At the close of the century, they gained ground in both.

Table 15.6 Duval County voting age population, 1900

Precinct	Voter eligible Americanos	Voter eligible Tejanos	Total Voting Age Population
1	84	439	523
2	18	369	387
3	2	194	196
4	12	140	152
5	16	289	305
6	8	145	153
Total	140	1,576	1,716
Percent	8.16%	91.84%	100%

Source: US Census of Duval County, 1900.

While Americano politicians had co-opted the 1888 effort to form a Tejano political party in Duval County, the idea of organizing such a party never waned. Instead, it took another decade, several more violent deaths, and the political ascendancy of Archie Parr before Tejanos in Duval County achieved inevitable dominance at the polls.

Chapter 16

Dawn of a New Century

The political atmosphere that prevailed in the nineteenth century intensified in the twentieth century as Tejanos pushed forward their agenda of assuming a political role consistent with their numbers. By the end of the first decade, Tejanos reached a meaningful share of political power. At the same time, new faces more willing to share in the power structure, both politically and economically, replaced old Americano leaders. Therefore, a dramatic change came in Duval County's political and social systems at the start of the second decade of the twentieth century.

Land Remained Central to Duval County Life

In the nineteenth century, Tejanos ratified their Spanish and Mexican land grants. They also obtained smaller tracts from the Republic and the state of Texas. However, as time passed, some Tejanos saw a need to sell their property to Americanos; many were absentee landowners who generally proved to be less accommodating than the early Americano pioneers. While land and what it produced continued to be the heart and soul of Duval County's Tejano life in the early twentieth century, it was no longer the dominant force of dependence. At times Tejanos' reliance on land for sustenance proved erratic.

233

First, to make dependence on land uncertain, the state took steps to reclaim some of the acreage it had granted. For example, it sought to regain title to 9,133 acres of land originally part of the Diego Ynojosa San Rafael de Los Encinos grant in southern Duval County, west of Realitos. However, in March 1906 the Third Court of Civil Appeals rejected the state's effort. The property involved two tracts that the original landholders had sold to J. M. Corrigan and Thomas B. Dunn. In a separate case six years later, in 1912, Julian Palacios from Concepción held on to 1,700 acres the state had also tried to reclaim. Once again, the courts ruled for the landowner.[1]

At the dawn of the twentieth century, residents and nonresidents evenly divided the land in Duval County. Residents claimed 430,840 acres, and nonresidents got 430,394 acres. Respectively, this land was valued at $571,469 for residents and $460,394 for nonresidents. This latter group often identified themselves as "taxpayers" when challenging Duval County Commissioners Court actions on property assessments. This terminology was important when these nonresidents, thus nonvoters, challenged the county's efforts in court. In 1917, for instance, some one hundred taxpayers, about 70 percent Americanos, appealed to the Texas Legislature with a tract entitled "Has the Average Citizen of Duval County a White Man's Chance?" The absentee landowners sought to block Duval County voting citizens' efforts to divide the county into two entities. Also, another proposal would have given the Duval County Commissioners Court additional powers to tax property.[2]

A cursory examination of the 1910 Census failed to find any aggrieved Americano petitioners living in Duval County. Also missing were Corrigan and Dunn, the Americanos who owned the Diego Ynojosa San Rafael de Los Encinos grant the state had challenged earlier. The two had acquired land from Tejano owners; however, neither appears in the 1910 or 1920 Duval County Census, suggesting they were absentee landowners.

A second force making Tejanos' reliance on land erratic was promoters wishing to acquire land for marketing to outsiders. On August 28, 1908, the *Corpus Christi Weekly Caller* reported that C. W. Hahl was advertising land for sale in the Rosita Valley. According to the newspaper, Hahl purchased eighteen thousand acres from San Diego resident Manuel Rogers. Two years earlier the biethnic Gray family, prominent in the nineteenth century, had sold twenty-six thousand acres of La Gloria Ranch to buyers planning to subdivide the land into small tracts and recruit farmers from Missouri.[3]

In 1909 a group from Oklahoma and Kansas going by the name of the Gulf Coast Land and Townsite Company bought 55,800 acres between Benavides and Realitos from railroad builders Lott and Nelson for speculation in commercial farming. This effort, as indicated in the March 20, 1908, issue of the *Caller*, was intended to attract Americano commercial farmers to Duval County by replicating the successful strategy employed by promoters in the Rio Grande Valley. Unfortunately for the speculators, the initiative was a monumental disappointment. The group subdivided the land and advertised its availability extensively in national magazines. After receiving no takers, they admitted defeat and sold the entire property to the Driscoll group out of Corpus Christi.[4]

With the discovery of oil at Piedras Pintas and later in the northwest part of the county, land sales became commonplace in Duval County. Most of this activity focused on purchasing or leasing land in and around the various oil fields then springing up in the county. This pursuit led to significant land sales and leasing, mainly by Tejanos but some by Americanos. All told, 150,000 acres were under lease in the vicinity, and more were under negotiation.[5]

Agriculture Staggered Out of the Nineteenth Century

At the end of the nineteenth century, the ranching business in Duval County was in a depression. There were no longer any large cattle herds present as in the past. As 1900 debuted, ranchers only owned 16,369 heads of cattle: the beeves appraised at $114,555, or $7 per head. According to the 1900 Census, 27 stock raisers and 127 farmers made their living as agriculturalists in the county. Of the cattle raisers, 23 percent were Americanos, and Tejanos accounted for the remaining 77 percent. However, 96 percent of the farmers were Tejanos, and 4 percent were Americanos.[6]

Only a few nineteenth-century stock raisers and farmers remained in the twentieth century, including Placido Benavides, John J. Dix, Julian

Palacios, and Archie Parr. No doubt, descendants of some of the early ranching pioneers were still tending to their ancestors' land. At 2,000 head the largest cattle herd belonged to the N. G. Collins Estate. The owner of the next largest cattle herd of cattle was J. W. Gallagher, with 1,200. B. A. Bennet's herd numbered 900; H. W. Garret, G. J. Reynolds, and Parr each owned 800 heads, while Charles Hoffman had 700. No Tejano made the list of top cattle owners.

Also, a drought dried up water wells, causing panic among livestock producers. Moreover, in June 1901, the county commissioners, meeting as the Board of Equalization, reduced valuations of cattle from $12 to $7. Cattle were not the only livestock whose worth declined; horses and mules dropped from $15 to $10 per head, and sheep and goats went from $1 to 75¢ per head.[7]

Five years later the cattle business in Duval County still seemed to be spiraling downward. Grass-fed cattle weighed an average of 856 pounds and got only $3. One year later, fifteen carloads of cake-fed steers at the Fort Worth stockyards brought an offer of $4.75 a head, which the Duval County owner turned down. By 1912 cattle prices seemed to be increasing, with Duval steers weighing slightly more than 1,000 pounds, bringing in from $5.80 to $6.55 a head at the National Stock Yards in Illinois.[8]

Low prices were not the cattlemen's only concerns. Cattle theft was an ongoing enterprise in some quarters of Duval County. Law enforcement officers arrested four men in 1915 for stealing seventeen head of cattle from local rancher Julio Cantú.[9]

Sheep raising was not in better straits than cattle ranching, fading as a viable livestock investment. Duval County, "once the greatest sheep growing portion of the state," by 1900 was down to a mere 7,164 sheep and sold for $1.31 per head. Unlike cattle, the largest sheep herds belonged exclusively to Tejanos and one Tejana. Mariano Serna had the largest flock at 1,700, followed by María Vaello, who had 1,500. Other notable sheep herds belonged to Cesario García, owner of 475 sheep; Agapito Sáenz, with a flock of 400 sheep; Saturnino Vera, who owned 350 woolly backs; and Nepomuceno Cantú, Perfecto Mendoza, and Ambrosio Sendejó, who each ran herds of 300 sheep. Their holdings account for 75 percent of all sheep in the county. Goats were doing more than twice as good as sheep, with 17,190, valued at the same price per head.[10]

Cotton, the third leg of the Duval County farming stool, began the new century on a relatively strong peg. In January 1900, "considerable cotton [was] planted," and farmers expected the best yield in five years. John J. Dix cultivated corn and cotton, while Frank Barton, José Vaello, and James Muller each harvested 100 acres of cotton. Many others also depended on a cotton crop. By September cotton farmers like Archie Parr, who owned 200 acres of cotton land, sent "wagon upon wagon of cotton" to San Diego gins for baling, as did other Benavides area farmers. San Diego paid $2.60–$2.75 per bale, while Benavides balers only paid $2.50.[11]

In 1905 farmers harvested 5,080 bales in Duval County. San Diego gins processed 3,178 bales, Benavides 744, and the Realitos baler 708. Moreover, 200 bales were waiting ginning, and 200 bales more were still unpicked. Seven years later, in 1912, Duval County produced 11,000 bales of cotton. By the 1920s the area from San Diego to Corpus Christi was one of the "most important cotton-producing areas of the state." Still, as a practical matter, cotton was no longer the revenue source it once had been in Duval County's economy.[12]

Black Gold Makes Appearance in Duval County

As the twentieth century unfolded, much of the talk in Duval County surrounded the prospects of oil at Piedras Pintas. As early as 1855, Juan Sáenz, who had settled the area years before, found that his water wells yielded saltwater. On one occasion, at eighteen to twenty feet, he struck oil. Sáenz remembered that as a child in Mexico, he had observed people in his village using oil as grease for wagon wheels, so he put his find to that use. During the Civil War, oxen-pulled caravans traveling to and from the Mexican border stopped at his rancho and loaded supplies and oil, which they used to lubricate the wagon wheels. Piedras Pintas's old-timers recalled a time when their neighborhood was a well-known gathering place for Mexican carretas that transported merchandise between the Rio Grande, Corpus Christi, and other commercial centers in South Texas. They converged at Piedras Pintas because of its reputation as a place providing grease for their wagon axles.[13]

By 1885 word of oil in Piedras Pintas had circulated for some time. The possibility that the Piedras Pintas Creek was the source of a kerosene reservoir was encouraged because the creek was dry most of the year except in spots where springs replenished a pool. The water had a strong taste of sulfur. Applying a lit match to cotton moistened by the spring water would cause it to burn with a blue flame. People believed the area contained a kerosene reservoir, but no one had investigated the possibility.[14]

Three years later, in 1888, W. L. Mandel of New York entered into a contract with William A. Tinney and the heirs of Juan Saénz to provide machinery to develop resources of the Piedras Pintas oil vein. Mandel committed to completing the work within a year, but no evidence exists that he implemented the plan. Early in 1900, however, newspapers across the state began to report that "good quality petroleum" had been discovered at Piedras Pintas at sixty feet in "paying quantity." Tinney was the principal owner of the producing wells, and his neighbors leased adjoining lands for oil speculators. Notably, all this activity predated Spindletop, often mentioned as the first discovery of oil in Texas.[15]

In 1901 oil prospectors leased several thousand acres in Duval and neighboring counties, and another oil driller made his way to Duval County. As the summer approached, H. Keller, a pioneer oil prospector and a believer in the Duval County oil field, began drilling a well at Duval Station, a proposed community on the railroad near Piedras Pintas, sixty-three miles west of Corpus Christi. It was one of the largest plants of its kind in the state. At forty-five feet a mixture of oil and water increased in volume, suggesting it came from the bottom up, not the sides. At sixty-five feet the lubricant from the well was burning, and the flame was visible for miles.[16]

Former County Judge James O. Luby reported he had oil from Piedras Pintas tested at the University of Texas, and the results showed Piedras Pintas oil was the best in the state. Oil activity continued apace, prompting County Clerk Eznal to add several employees to keep up with land speculators. Among the fortune hunters was Standard Oil Company, which was said to be "gobbling up" land in Duval County.[17]

Piedras Pintas continued to pump oil for seven years. Oil producers laid a pipeline from Piedras Pintas to the Texas-Mexican railroad depot, a half-mile distance. Carloads of oil went to Kingsville and Laredo. Piedras Pintas oil fueled the Corpus Christi Ice and Electric Company and the Lone Star Ice Company in Corpus Christi.[18]

The Piedras Pintas oil fields soon began to decline due to legal suits among partners and other setbacks. However, Duval County's oil industry soon saw a second and more substantial wave of production. In 1920 oil exploration spread to the west and north of the original fields at Piedras Pintas. Oil rigs sprouted up eight miles west of Benavides, north of San Diego, close to the McMullen County line, and fourteen miles northwest of San Diego. Oilmen secured numerous leases and drilled many wells in Duval County. "The county was never in better condition," wrote E. T. Merriman in the *Corpus Christi Caller.*[19]

During the 1920s several oil fields sprang up in northwestern Duval County, including the Government Wells field that gave birth to the community of Freer. During the thirties, despite the Great Depression, Duval County saw its most remarkable growth, primarily due to the oil fields.[20]

The energy industry modernized Duval County and began to play an essential role in its future. With the advent of vehicles equipped with internal combustion engines, cars replaced wagons, trucks supplanted horses, and tractors took the place of plows. In addition, other energy products, such as natural gas and uranium, were uncovered later in the twentieth century and became part of the county's energy economy.

Duval County Continued to be Tejano Dominated

The differences in population makeup between Tejanos and Americanos account for why Duval County departed from what evolved in other parts of the Trans-Nueces. The numbers of Americanos in Duval County never rose to a strength that gave them a dominant position vis-à-vis Tejanos; Americanos at no time had the numbers to overpower, manage, and maintain control over the political, economic, and social segments without input from Tejanos. This fact was evident to everyone in the county by the earliest decades of the twentieth century.

In 1880 the US Census included the newly organized county of Duval for the first time. The county's population stood at 5,732. After steadily climbing to 8,883 at the end of the century, the count slipped to 8,186 in 1920. As a result, the number of Tejanos dropped from 7,862 to 7,342, a 7 percent slippage, but they still made up 90 percent of the residents. Some historians suggest that the Mexican Revolution (1910–1920), as well as a locally inspired irredentist guerrilla war—El Plan de San Diego (1915–1917)—and the military draft imposed during World War I, contributed to the departure of Mexicanos and Tejanos from Duval County. However, the primary factor for the population loss was a more straightforward explanation—the creation of Jim Hogg County. In 1913 the Texas Legislature created Jim Hogg County with the Duval County community of Hebbronville as its county seat and only community. In 1920 the first census for Jim Hogg County numbered 744 residents, of whom 717, or 96 percent, were Tejanos. This fact accounted for more than the 520 Tejano population loss in Duval County.

During the 1910s many Americano pioneers left Duval due to political changes. Despite this departure, many other Americanos chasing their fortune in black gold (after the discovery of oil in Duval County in 1900) replaced the nineteenth-century Americano settlers. As of 1900 only 563 Americanos lived in Duval County, but by 1920 that number grew 33 percent to 838. However, they remained only 10 percent of the county's population.

Table 16.1 Duval County population, 1880–2000

Source: US Census, 1880–2000.

Tejanos Continued Political March

As the majority, Duval County Tejanos continued to assert their right to cogovern. In 1888 they had first openly declared their intentions of taking a fair share of the political pie. During the first decade of the twentieth century, they made noticeable advances. Tejanos then shared control of the commissioners court with Americanos, with an equal number of commissioners each biennial term. In addition, Tejano justices of the peace outnumbered Americanos fourteen to six, and Tejanos held every constable office. Beginning in the second decade of the twentieth century, Tejanos occupied every countywide office except county judge and county attorney and continued to exert political influence for many years. Eventually, in the final quarter of the century, Tejanos assumed complete control of politics, government, and their pursued destiny.

Two tragedies early in the twentieth century set the stage for what occurred politically over the next sixty years. Unfortunately, these deadly events came at the cost of innocent blood and gave rise to an unholy political alliance that embodied Duval County for over half a century.

Late in the evening of December 20, 1907, the Democratic political leader John D. Cleary, 49, was dining with two individuals at a San Diego restaurant. It was a raucous night, as many in the community had started celebrating Christmas early, with fireworks exploding throughout the town. Suddenly, a shotgun blast struck Cleary from behind. The pellets came from outside the restaurant through an open door, and eight struck Cleary as he sat on a stool having dinner. It was dark, and no one saw the shooter. And due to the noise from the fireworks throughout town, no one heard the blast. Sheriff's deputies and Texas Rangers did not appear at the scene for several hours.[21]

The *Corpus Christi Caller* immediately made a shameless assumption. Its reporter suggested that the "deadly work is not that of a white man" because the "act of shooting from a hiding place, an unsuspecting and unprepared man and the premeditation displayed, the subject having purposely armed himself with a shotgun and watched for an opportunity to get the advantage of his victim, would lead an average man to believe that Cleary met his death

Table 16.2 Duval County elected officials, 1900–1910

	1900	1902	1904	1906	1908	1910
County Judge	S. H. Woods	S. H. Woods	S. H. Woods	S. H. Woods	S. H. Woods	S. H. Woods
County Clerk	Pedro Eznal	Pedro Eznal	Pedro Eznal	Pedro Eznal	Pedro Eznal	Pedro Eznal
County Attorney	W. W. McCampbell	John George	John O. Luby	W. W. McCampbell	W. W. McCampbell	W. W. McCampbell
Treasurer	A. D. García	Julián Palacios	Julián Palacios	Clemente García	Crisóforo Hinojosa	Lino García
Surveyor	J. J. Dix			Hayes Dix	Hayes Dix	M. A. Muñoz
Sheriff	Manuel Rogers	Manuel Rogers	Manuel Rogers	C. K. Gravis	A. W. Tobin*	A. W. Tobin
Tax Assessor	John D. Cleary	John D. Cleary	John D. Cleary	John D. Cleary	Clemente García	Clemente García
Commissioner, Precinct One	Charles Hoffman	Charles Hoffman	Charles Hoffman	Eliseo Martínez	D. C. Warne	J. W. Shaw
Commissioner, Precinct Two	Archie Parr	Archie Parr	Clemente García	Crisóforo Hinojosa	Archie Parr	Archie Parr
Commissioner, Precinct Three	H. W. Garrett	C. T. Stillman	C. T. Stillman	A. J. Ayers	A. J. Ayers	Filiberto Peña
Commissioner, Precinct Four	F. K. Ridder	M. G. Diaz	M. G. Diaz	M. G. Diaz	N. Couling	M. G. Diaz
Justice of the Peace, Precinct One	Juan. D. Alcalá	Clark Lewis	Juan D. Alcalá	Juan D. Alcalá	R. M. González	A. C. Lewis
Justice of the Peace, Precinct Two			S. R. Peters			W. A. Tinney
Justice of the Peace, Precinct Three	M. G. Diaz		Julián P. Rivera		Victoriano Leal	S. C. Navarro

(Continues)

Table 16.2 (Continued)

	1900	1902	1904	1906	1908	1910
Justice of the Peace, Precinct Four	Charles Shaw		J. A. Roach			
Justice of the Peace, Precinct Five				Feliciano Cantú	Filiberto Peña	Feliciano Cantú
Justice of the Peace, Precinct Six				Rafael Arredondo	Pablo Treviño	
Constable, Precinct One	Antonio Anguiano	Antonio Anguiano	Antonio Anguiano	Antonio Anguiano	Rafael Arredondo	
Constable, Precinct Two	Hipólito Garza	Antonio Anguiano	José Palacios		Aurelio Alemán	Aurelio Alemán
Constable, Precinct Three			Liborio Barrera	Fortunato Martínez	Santiago San Miguel	Crescencio Oliveira
Constable, Precinct Four					Casimiro Lozano	Mauricio Palacios
Constable, Precinct Five						
Constable, Precinct Six						

Source: Secretary of State Election Returns, TSLAC.
*These men had Americano surnames but were Tejanos.

at the hands of a Mexican." It was a shocking observation but regrettably reflective of most Americanos' viewpoint.[22]

Sheriff Charles K. Gravis, who had won the position on the Independent ticket the previous year, asked Texas Rangers to help investigate the case. The Rangers pursued two theories as to the cause of the shooting. The first assumption was the county tax collector's race held in November 1906, contested in court and resolved for Cleary. That made Vidal García, Cleary's Republican opponent in the last election, a suspect, for he had launched a lawsuit against Cleary and was trying to overturn the election. Probably the fact that García operated a saloon added to the suspicion. The Rangers, however, most likely abandoned this theory of the crime because García was pursuing his differences with Cleary through the courts. Moreover, García was not the only defeated candidate challenging the election results. C. F. Stillman was also contesting his loss to Sheriff Gravis, W. L. Rogers questioned his defeat by Pedro Eznal, and Julian Palacios doubted his setback to County Treasurer Clemente García.[23]

The second premise for the shooting dealt with a civil lawsuit between Cleary and a disgruntled partner. Cleary had recently entered an oil deal with T. J. Lawson and his son, Jeff, but the agreement had gone astray. Texas Rangers believed the two Lawson men were responsible for Cleary's death and charged them with conspiracy to murder. The Rangers, however, were inclined to agree with the prevailing thought among the Americano community, as expressed in the Corpus Christi newspaper, that a Mexican had to be involved since the shooting was a cowardly act executed from behind the victim. With Vidal García removed from suspicion, they chose as their fall guy former Constable Candelario Sáenz but did not explain their reasons for accusing him. Relying on circumstantial evidence, the grand jury gave the Lawsons a pass and indicted Sáenz for murder. But Sáenz hired a formidable litigation team, Texas Lieutenant Governor A. B. Davidson and Attorney John H. Bailey from Cuero, who had the state dismiss charges against Sáenz. No one ever paid for Cleary's death.[24]

However, this episode foreshadowed forthcoming changes in Duval County; indeed, there soon occurred a transition of political power from Republican to Democrat. In the 1906 election, Cleary had led the Democratic ticket in which Tejano Democrats gained three seats on the commissioners court, giving them the majority on the court for the first time since the county's organization thirty years earlier. Tejanos won two countywide offices and every justice of the peace and constable seat contested that year. However, the change was short-lived; in 1908 Tejanos lost all three commissioners positions to Americanos, including the Benavides seat to Archie Parr. The 1910 election saw Tejanos regain two commissioners seats and five countywide offices. Tejanos seemed determined to keep moving forward and continue making political gains.

While the ongoing political transition—from Republican to Democrat and Americanos to Tejanos—was still unfolding, a second tragic event triggered a seismic change in the Duval County political fulcrum. On May 18, 1912, San Diego voters began filing to the polls to determine whether they should incorporate their city. The morning's calm exploded when, on the courthouse grounds, three Americanos shot and killed three Tejanos.[25]

As the polls opened, former Sheriff Charles K. Gravis, Frank Robinson, and Dr. S. H. Roberts—the latter ignoring his pledge as a doctor to "first, do no harm"—shot and killed three Tejano leaders, Candelario Sáenz, Antonio Anguiano, and Pedro Eznal, on the courthouse grounds. Gravis, who had run on the Cleary Independent ticket along with Eznal and Anguiano, had partially served a two-year term as sheriff in 1906 before resigning and being replaced by Tejano Antonio W. Tobin. It is unclear why Gravis fell out with his former running mates. Robinson and his brother, Neil, were active in Democratic politics. Dr. Roberts was a newcomer to the county and may have been unaware of the seriousness of the political situation. Contemporary accounts of the shooting appear biased and unreliable. However, 12-year-old Walter Meek Jr. provided his recollections of the day sixty years later.[26]

Young Meek recalled having hotcakes at home, located a block south of the courthouse, when he heard seven gunshots. He jumped out of his chair and ran to the courthouse, remembering his father had said the previous night that they were having an election the following day. Approaching the courthouse, young Meek stumbled on a body lying on the street. He recognized it as that of his neighbor, Candelario Sáenz, who was still alive, and it followed the young boy visually as he walked away. Sáenz's

Fig. 16.1 Pedro Eznal (1859–1912) was assassinated on courthouse grounds in 1912. Courtesy of Graciela Treviño Gonzalez.

pistol was lying next to him. Ten yards farther down, young Meek saw two more bodies. He did not recognize Anguiano because he did not know him, but the victim's gun was still in his hand. Eznal, whom the boy knew, was dead, and there was no gun near him.[27]

Meek witnessed the three shooters standing back-to-back, scanning the gathering crowd. The impressionable boy watched as Sheriff Tobin approached the armed men and informed them they were under arrest, to which Gravis responded, "We don't give a damn if we are." The sheriff told them they had to give up their guns, and Gravis once again replied, "Like hell we will." Meanwhile, the Meek boy learned his father, W. W. Meek, had gone to the train depot to wire for help. Hearing this, the boy hurried home to assure his mother that his father was okay. On his return he noticed a handkerchief covering Sáenz's face and Father Bard giving the deceased his last rites. The following day the young Meek watched through "slits in closed shutters" as three mule-drawn wagons, each carrying a corpse, passed by his home, followed by "every male Mexican in town and the surrounding countryside . . . in an ugly mood."[28]

Tejano men who had come out to vote kept watch on the Americano shooters who had moved to the Charles Hoffman house for protection. In the meantime, neighboring Jim Wells County Sheriff King Hinnant responded to a call for help with a large posse of thirty-two "Americans" on automobiles making their way to San Diego. Also, Charles Hoffman and W. W. Meek received a telegram from Kingsville that a train with a passenger car full of armed men was ready if needed. It was unlikely that Sheriff Tobin would have asked for help from outsiders, but things had calmed down by the time the Alice vigilantes arrived. Still, Hinnant and twelve of his band escorted the three Americano executioners to safety in the Nueces County Jail.[29]

Tejanos Get Help from Archie Parr

The incorporation referendum of May 18, 1912, went down to defeat. It was a bittersweet victory for those opposing the incorporation of San Diego. Three Tejano families lost loved ones. It was a loss felt throughout the Tejano community. As *La Libertad* proclaimed, it was a dark day in the community's history. The price for the Americano opponents of incorporation was giving birth to a political dynasty composed of the majority Tejano community led by Archie Parr, a rancher from the Tejano community of Benavides who held a long association with Tejanos on a personal level. Parr had been active in county politics as a staunch Democrat for twenty years. Following the tragedy on the Duval County Courthouse grounds, Parr formed a partnership with the Tejano community that effectively neutralized the old Americano power structure, ensuring they would never regain the political dominance of the county. It was an opportunity for Tejanos to gain control of the political reigns in Duval County, but to do so they consented to partner with Archie Parr.[30]

Parr had not been particularly sympathetic to Tejanos' political cause during his early years in Duval County politics when he had served as county commissioner and delegate to Democratic conventions. On several occasions he challenged the bonds and eligibility of Tejanos, who had won countywide offices, most likely because they were Republicans. Moreover, as the Benavides county commissioner from 1896 to 1900, he never advocated for Tejanos to represent the Democratic Party at party conventions. Though the two had been very close during Parr's early rise in Democratic Party politics, it was somewhat surprising that Parr joined John D. Cleary in spearheading the Democrats' 1906 victory over the Republicans, which yielded a Tejano majority on the commissioners court. Two years later, however, Parr unseated one of those Tejanos, Crisóforo Hinojosa. Nevertheless, having seen Cleary's success working with Tejanos, Parr picked up the deceased man's banner as party leader.[31] From 1900 to 1908, while he took a sabbatical from elective office, Parr also may have realized that Tejanos had the numbers to win every election easily, especially after the results of the 1906 election.

After dispatching his family to safety in Corpus Christi following the shooting of May 18, 1912, Parr made his way to San Diego on the first train. Once there the elected county commissioner for Benavides offered his help to the Tejano community, counseling citizens to refrain from responding in kind; vengeance would be a mistake, he advised.

On June 12 the Duval County Grand Jury charged each accused Americano with three counts of murder. Judge Hopkins tagged each defendant with a $15,000 bond and, on his motion, moved the case to Austin. However, the Travis County criminal docket was too crowded, and the court retransferred the case to Richmond, an Americano community in Fort Bend County, southwest of Houston. In October 1914 a jury of their peers, no doubt all Americanos, tried the three executioners. After the trial Presiding Judge Norman G. Kittrell instructed the jury to return a not-guilty verdict. The jury dutifully obeyed. Judge Kittrell told the defendants, "Gentlemen, if I had my way, I'd give you all Winchesters and tell you to go back and finish the job."[32]

Unsurprisingly, the Tejano population in Duval County saw the acquittal of the three Americanos for the death of three Tejanos on the courthouse grounds as yet another travesty of justice, a transgression demanding a transformation, a change that could only come about if Tejanos acquired clout politically. Tejanos had already held and managed public offices. Still, incumbency had not been sufficient to effect real change; to carry out actual justice required coalition building with Americanos, but one influenced by Tejanos. Archie Parr proposed such a partnership. In Parr's most recent action—counseling them to refrain from violence in response to the acquittal of the three alleged assassins—Tejanos saw an Americano sympathetic to their causes; he showed them his willingness to stand with them against the Americanos who had managed to manipulate Tejanos for many years. So they entered a *convenio politico*, or political agreement, with Parr to continue marching ahead to ensure an equitable destiny.[33]

For his part Parr moved forward speedily to consolidate his partnership with the Tejano community. He was willing to gamble on his political future with them. As a result of Parr's actions, *La Libertad* publisher F. de P. González, presciently observed in the newspaper's August 3, 1912, issue, "While Parr lives, the people will be loyal to him, and they will not lose. They will enjoy triumph after triumph until all citizens of the county come together under the banner of Parr's party."

Two months later, Editor González observed that the history of San Diego from 1876 to 1908 had existed in "unqualified harmony." González may have been too optimistic, for Americano prejudice had laid under the surface. From the beginning of Duval County politics, the wealthy, mostly Americanos, had manipulated control of the county government with money as their principal ally. Some Tejanos had acceded to such an arrangement by receiving favors, others were in debt to the wealthy, and others gave their support out of friendship and mutual respect. But many Tejanos who remained outside of the power structure that was in control saw Americanos as personal enemies who failed to acknowledge that Tejanos had the same yearning for freedom and power with which to control their destiny. Moreover, a new generation of Tejanos took the political lead in 1912. The lamentable actions of that day in May came from Americanos' failure to acknowledge these differences and wants.

"What can we expect from a political party that has its genesis in spilling Mexican blood?" González asked. There is no doubt that many of his Tejano compatriots took note. They moved forward arm in arm with Parr, turned the political table upside down, acquired considerable influence over the politics in Duval County, and set their eyes on the future.[34]

Chapter 17

The Tejano-Parr Alliance

rchie Parr inherited his father's DNA, but his mother's family—the Givenses—was responsible for his upbringing. Parr's mother, Sarah Pamela Givens, and his uncle, John Slye Givens, were instrumental in forming the future Duke of Duval's individual qualities. From them he acquired the nature that his early Duval County friend Walter Meek described as "one of the few men in Texas whom I have never heard swear and is also free of many small vices so general and common here [Duval County]."[1] However much Meek admired his friend's polite manners, the two became political foes later in life, and Parr the politician was often at political odds with his erstwhile acquaintance.

Archie Parr's Early Years

Archie Parr was born in December 1859 in Saluria, Calhoun County, Texas. His father, George Parr, served with the Virginia Volunteers in the Mexican-American War (1846–1848). After the war, no doubt seeking adventure, George Parr went to Texas, landing on Matagorda Island, where he met and married Sarah Pamela Givens in 1857. She was the third of eight children

Fig. 17.1 Archie Parr (1859–1942) was a Texas state senator and the first Duke of Duval. Courtesy of The State Preservation Board, Austin, Texas, Legislative Reference Library of Texas, https://lrl.texas.gov

born to Samuel S. Givens and Ann Mary Sutton, prominent citizens in Saluria. Parr was 31, ten years Sarah's senior. The couple had three children, Archie being the middle issue.[2]

To escape the chaos Saluria was undergoing during the Civil War, in 1864 Parr joined his brother-in-law, John S. Givens, at Oakville in Live Oak County. In 1857 Givens had hung his law shingle in Oakville and served as interim Live Oak County Clerk and then district attorney for the Fourteenth Judicial District, which included the future Duval County, then in the care of Nueces County. In 1860 Givens got involved in the judge's election for the Fourteenth Judicial District, supporting Joseph F. McKinney. Givens was among a group of McKinney backers from Goliad who took notice of the lopsided Tejano voting at Agua Poquita in Duval County and attacked it as corrupt. Little did Givens know that his nephew, who was then learning how to crawl, would later use bloc voting as an art form.[3]

In 1864 the Live Oak County Commissioners Court appointed Parr as deputy county clerk, perhaps on Givens's recommendation. In August he ran unopposed for office, winning with thirty-nine votes, and then gained reelection two years later. Givens and Parr appeared poised for a promising future in Live Oak County; however, it all vanished on November 25, 1867, when Parr fell victim to a fatal late-night altercation. An assailant fatally stabbed him with a Bowie knife. The alleged culprit absconded from the area, was not brought to trial for six years, and was ultimately acquitted. A motive for the attack is not discernible from official records, but alcohol may have played a part.[4]

Eight-year-old Archie and his two siblings were fatherless, prompting Givens to abandon his lucrative lifestyle in Live Oak County and return to Calhoun County to care for his sister and her family. While Givens assumed the provider role for Sarah and her children, Sarah worked as a teacher, and her three youngsters attended school.[5]

In 1874 Givens moved his family to Corpus Christi and reestablished his law practice. Givens secured a job for 14-year-old Archie with one of his clients, the Coleman-Fulton Pasture Company, in San Patricio County. Indeed, Uncle John's advice and help with employment opportunities gave young Archie direction during his formative years. Archie Parr grew into manhood at the Coleman-Fulton operation, where he learned the ranching business and the Spanish language from Tejano vaqueros; the experience led him to build a lifelong empathy for both ranching and Tejanos, a relationship he nurtured throughout his life.[6]

Parr's Introduction to Duval County

Givens's law practice extended from Nueces to Duval County. During one of his many trips to Duval County, Givens purchased land near the Sweden Ranch next to Uriah Lott, who had built the railroad through Duval County. In 1882 Givens must have convinced Lott, who was inexperienced in the ranching business, to hire his 22-year-old nephew Archie Parr to oversee the Lott and Nelson Pasture Company. Givens died in Corpus Christi five years later; although he had many friends who valued him, none mourned him more than Archie Parr.[7]

Perhaps in deference to his friendship with Givens, District Judge John Russel named Archie Parr to the Duval County Grand Jury in 1887. A year later the 28-year-old Parr got an up close and personal look at the modus operandi of his future nemeses, the Texas Rangers. Parr was selected to serve on a jury considering the murder of Abrán Reséndez, admittedly killed by Texas Ranger A. Dillard and Rio Grande City River Guard Victor Sebree. Both claimed self-defense before an all-Americano jury, which deliberated for three days without reaching a verdict. One member insisted on the men's innocence. Available information suggests Parr was not the holdout.[8]

Then, in 1896, Parr sought the nomination for the Democratic primary for Benavides County Commissioner and won. Through the years newspapers applied various royal titles to Parr, including "czar," among others, but the one that stuck was "duke." The first mention of Parr as a duke may have been in 1899 when the *Texas Stock and Farm Journal* referred to Archie Parr as the Duke of Benavides. It was a recognition that the 40-year-old native of Saluria had found his niche in the cacti country of South Texas.[9]

Parr's political base in Benavides mainly rested with the Tejano population; all his neighbors were Tejanos, including the Salinas, Ramírez, Cadena, García, and Elizondo families. His experience of living among Tejano vaqueros in San Patricio made him feel welcomed in these Mexican surroundings. On the other hand, Parr had a second residence in San Diego, home to a significant Americano community that had dominated county politics since Duval's inception. Parr had many friends among them, as well. Moreover, when picking a spouse, he married an Americana, Elizabeth Allen, in 1891. Then, all his children's first spouses were English named. While he appeared to have his feet firmly planted with his Tejano political allies, separate from them was an Americano world in which he socialized.[10]

Parr served as county commissioner from Benavides through 1901, then took some time off from elected office to tend to his various business enterprises. Simultaneously, he continued being active in Democratic Party politics. By 1901 he was head of the Duval Democratic Party, and his fellow Democrats regularly picked him as a delegate to party conventions. In 1908 Parr again won the election to the office of commissioner from Benavides. Also that year Parr replaced D. McNeil of Nueces County on the State Democratic Committee, a position he held until he became a state senator in 1915.[11]

Tejanos Increase Their Influence in County Politics

In 1912, the year of the courthouse massacre, C. M. Robinson, brother to Frank Robinson, one of the shooters in the courthouse murders, asserted authority over the chair of the Duval Democratic Party. He declared to have secured an attorney general's opinion confirming that since there were no members on the party's executive committee, Robinson could appoint an executive committee of his choosing; not surprisingly, all but one of his appointments were Americanos.[12]

Parr did not look favorably on this development and pursued a plan to take the Democratic apparatus away from his Americano antagonist. He organized an alternate executive committee composed of his Tejano political allies. Among them were Francisco Salinas, J. A. Treviño, C. T. Hinojosa, and C. Carrillo. On primary day in 1912, Parr informed Robinson that his alternate county executive committee was ready to meet with him, but Robinson contended that a bona fide committee was already in place. Rather than draw their pistols, the two men resolved the matter in court before District Judge W. B. Hopkins. The judge decided in Parr's favor, and his executive committee remained in place through 1914.[13]

Apparently the Democratic candidates swept to victory.[14] While election results are unavailable, some were later discerned from commissioners court minutes showing who held various positions. Thus, the following were the officials who most likely won in 1912: J. F. Clarkson, county judge; J. O. Treviño, county clerk; Alonso López, county treasurer; Amado Garza, sheriff; W. L. Rogers, treasurer; Luciano Hinojosa, commissioner, Precinct One; Archie Parr, commissioner, Precinct Two; E. Carrillo. commissioner, Precinct Three; and M. Garza, commissioner, Precinct Four.[15]

After defeating the Republican ticket and Robinson's Independents, Parr and Tejanos completely dominated Duval County politics. No one "dared to challenge his power."

Table 17.1 Duval County elected officials, 1914–1920

Position	1912	1914	1916	1918	1920
County Judge	J. F. Clarkson	A. W. Tobin[2] / G. A. Parr[3]	G. A. Parr / J. F. Clarkson[4]	J. F. Clarkson	J. F. Clarkson
County Clerk	J. O. Treviño	J. V. Palacios	J. V. Palacios	J. V. Palacios	J. V. Palacios
County Attorney		J. F. Clarkson	J. F. Clarkson / F. Lotto		
County Treasurer	Alonso López	Alonso López	Alonso López	Leónides González	Horacio Sáenz
County Surveyor			R. M. González	R. M. González	R. M. González
Sheriff	Amado Garza	A. de la Peña	A. W. Tobin	J. O. Treviño	Jesús Oliveira
Tax Assessor	W. L. Rogers	W. L. Rogers	T. G. Rogers	T. G. Rogers	T. G. Rogers
Inspector of Hides		M. A. Muñoz[5]	M. A. Muñoz		
Commissioner, Precinct One	Luciano Hinojosa	Luciano Hinojosa	Luciano Hinojosa	Luciano Hinojosa	
Commissioner, Precinct Two	Archie Parr	Archie Parr	O. G. Allen	O. G. Allen	
Commissioner, Precinct Three	Eusebio Carrillo	Eusebio Carrillo	Eusebio Carrillo	Eusebio Carrillo	
Commissioner, Precinct Four	M. Garza	Manuel Garza	Manuel Garza	Manuel Garza	
Justice of the Peace, Precinct One		B. Mirer	B. Mirer	Louis G. Robers / F. Lotto[6]	
Justice of the Peace, Precinct Two			W.A. Tinney	W.A. Tinney	
Justice of the Peace, Precinct Three			Práxedis Sáenz	Práxedis Sáenz	
Justice of the Peace, Precinct Four			Zaragoza López	Cenobio Cantú	
Justice of the Peace, Precinct Five		Domingo Reyes	Domingo Reyes	Domingo Reyes	
Justice of the Peace, Precinct Six			Rafael Arredondo	E.J. Rogers	
Justice of the Peace, Precinct Seven			O.H. Bone	O.H. Bone	

(Continues)

Table 17.1 (Continued)

Position	1912	1914	1916	1918	1920
Justice of the Peace, Precinct Eight			*Teodoro Sendejó*	*Teodoro Sendejó*	*Teodoro Sendejó*
Justice of the Peace, Precinct Nine[7]		*Teodoro Sendejó*			
Constable, Precinct One		*Félix Vera*	*Pedro R. Garza*	*Ventura Sánchez*	
Constable, Precinct Two	*Dolores Lozano*	*Aurelio Alemán*	*Isaac González*	*C. García*	
Constable, Precinct Three		*Dolores Lozano*	*Filomeno Martínez*	*Ismael Chapa*	
Constable, Precinct Four			*Abelardo Pérez*		
Constable, Precinct Five			*Liborio Barrera*	*Casimiro Lozano*	
Constable, Precinct Six				L.L. Coleman	
Constable, Precinct Seven		*Jesús V. Rodríguez*[8]	*Jesús Villarreal*	*Flavio García*	
Constable, Precinct Eight		*Amado Sáenz*	*Mariano Benavides*	*Mariano Benavides*	
Constable, Precinct Nine		*Mariano Benavides*			

Source: Texas Secretary of State, Elections Division: An Inventory of Election Returns (county by county), 1835–1980, TSLAC.

1 Compiled from Commissioners Court Minutes.

2 Italicized names are Tejanos.

3 Appointed March 26, 1915.

4 Parr resigned May 18, 1917, and on the same day, J. F. Clarkson replaced him, and F. Lotto replaced Clarkson as county attorney.

5 Appointed by Governor James E. Ferguson in 1915.

6 Created out of Precinct One in San Diego and appointed April 13, 1915.

7 Rogers resigned, and Lotto replaced him.

8 Felix Escobar failed to give bond for constable, Precinct Seven, and the commissioners court named Jesus V. Rodríguez in his place.

Other Tejano officers serving in November 1912 likely were appointed to the post, such as W. L. Rogers, tax assessor; Juan T. Sáenz, county treasurer; and Dolores Lozano, constable for Precinct Two. The commissioners court minutes indicate Alonso López and Juan T. Sáenz as the new county treasurer. Moreover, the commissioners approved bonds for these individuals in September 1914 because their original bonds were lost in a fire that razed the courthouse.[16]

In December 1914 the Duval County Commissioners Court met—with Archie Parr seated at his county commissioner's post—and declared that Givens A. Parr, Archie Parr's eldest son, could not give bond for the sheriff's office; thus, the court proceeded to name A. de la Peña as sheriff and tax collector. There was no way a Parr could not have been able to make a bond; this move was no doubt orchestrated by Archie Parr to name his son county judge.[17]

Beginning in 1912 every office in Duval County, save that of the county attorney, was held by a Tejano. Moreover, it was Tejanos who provided security bonds for every office. The 1912 murders on the courthouse lawn proved to be the complete undoing of Americano rule in the county. Its repercussions led to what Tejanos had been unable to do for thirty-eight years; from then on Tejanos presided over most elective offices in Duval County. Of course, an Americano named Parr orchestrated who ran for office, but arguably he could only do so with the agreement of Tejanos.

From 1914 to 1934, the only offices Americanos consistently held were those of the county judge and county attorney. The county judge was usually a member of the Parr family, and Americanos served as county attorney because no Tejano attorneys practiced law in Duval. In time, however, even that office became a Tejano domain. Election returns through 1920 indicate only one other Americano held a policy-making office: Parr's brother-in-law O. G. Allen replaced him as county commissioner from Benavides. Allen had close ties to the Tejano community, having been married to a Tejana.[18]

Serving in elective office allowed Tejanos to make significant decisions. Tejanos in the commissioners court used their authority to employ scores of Tejanos, permitting them to make a decent living. These Tejanos were in charge of projects such as constructing or repairing bridges, building and maintaining public roads, repairing the courthouse and jail, maintaining town plazas, providing interpretation services for the district court, conducting general elections, and engaging in other duties.

Parr Seeks More Opportunities for Patronage

Parr also sought to assist Tejano constituents in the county by attempting to create opportunities for more elected officials and public employment jobs. In 1911 the state erected Brooks and Willacy Counties, followed in 1912 by Jim Wells County. Then came Kleberg and Jim Hogg Counties in 1913. Parr surmised that if the state planned to continue organizing new counties, it could split Duval County, thus doubling the number of elected officials and creating more patronage jobs.

As Parr and his Tejano Duval County Commissioners Court friends visualized matters, Benavides and San Diego could be the seats of two counties, doubling patronage opportunities. In 1913 Pat Dunn–representing Duval County in the House—proposed the creation of Lott County out of Duval, and two days later the Senate approved the bill by Senator John Willacy to create the new county but named it Dunn County.[19]

However, events did not unfold as intended. In December 1913, as Tejano Duval County officials were preparing to oversee an election to organize Dunn County, the Fourth Court of Appeals ruled the process to create the new county adopted by the Duval County Commissioners Court was improper. After three hearings on this matter, the court of appeals ruled the Texas Constitution prohibited a new county's boundary to be within twelve miles of the neighboring county seat. The Dunn-Duval northern border was seventy feet short of the twelve-mile requirement; thus, Dunn County's creation was unconstitutional.[20]

That settled the Dunn County matter but not Parr's determination to increase patronage opportunities. The day after the first appellate court in December 1913 ruled against Dunn County, Parr announced his candidacy for the Texas Senate. Upon taking office in 1915, he offered a bill to create the Lanham County out of Duval County. The measure followed the same path as had the previously considered Dunn County legislation. In two weeks the Senate favorably voted for the proposal and sent it to the House, where it faced opposition.[21]

Representative Dunn again sponsored the bill in the House, maintaining that "small landowners," such as Tejanos, "wanted the new county." Dunn pointed out those against it were "certain big landowners," many who did not live in Duval County, and were "tax dodgers." Parr's opponents countered that a "political machine" was behind the legislation and offered a petition signed by five hundred taxpayers, most not citizens of Duval County, opposing the initiative. After the debate the House rejected Dunn's proposal. That ended Parr's obsession to split the county and create additional patronage.[22]

The five hundred Duval County landowners who opposed the Dunn bill, emboldened by Parr's defeat in creating new counties, petitioned the Texas Legislature to dissolve Duval County and attach it to Live Oak County. Many, if not most, of these Americano landowners complained that Parr deprived them of their voting rights. However, most did not live in Duval County and were thus not eligible to vote there. They also declared that the situation in Duval County had become intolerable. Representative Frank Burmeister of McMullen County introduced the legislation to dissolve Duval County. While some Live Oak residents ostensibly supported the idea, their state representative, John William Flournoy, objected. "Live Oak County does not want to wash Duval County's dirty linen," Flournoy declared, adding that Duval should be attached to McMullen County. While proponents of the bill managed to get it approved by a House committee, it did not go any further.[23]

Property Owners Continue to Apply Pressure on Elected Officials

In early 1914 sixty individuals claiming wrongdoing in the county's finances signed a petition asking the district judge to appoint a committee to audit the county's books, which they claimed had not been examined adequately since 1903. To foil the landowners' request, the Duval County Grand Jury, on January 15, asked District Judge W. B. Hopkins to name an audit committee.

Parr was a Grand Jury and County Commissioners Court member involved in a plan to derail the complainants' efforts.[24]

Judge Hopkins promptly appointed M. D. Cohn, P. Hickey, and F. Vaello to an audit committee. However, since the committee was entitled to only $15 by law, the appointees refused their assignment. Ed C. Lasater, a citizen of Brooks County with extensive property in Duval County, offered to provide $3,000 for a proper audit by a professional accountant. The property owners' cabal accepted Lasater's proposal and employed a Houston accountant. However, the auditor resigned within a few days, informing the committee and Judge Hopkins that county officials had denied him access to the county's financial records.[25]

In June, Lasater, R. H. Corbet, and others filed a writ of mandamus against County Clerk J. V. Palacios and the commissioners court, demanding access to the county's books necessary to conduct a proper audit. Hopkins considered the litigation on June 19 and granted the request directing county officials to allow Houston accountant George Kid to examine their records. In response to the judge's ruling, County Judge S. H. Woods, Sheriff Tobin, Treasurer Alonso López, County Clerk J. V. Palacios, and Commissioner Parr resigned. Their mass departure was a ploy to muddle the financial audit and to prevent the district from appointing their replacements.[26]

Six weeks later, at 3:30 a.m. on August 11, the courthouse burned to the ground. The fire started at the county clerk's office, destroying numerous records, although officials were able to save many documents. While newspaper accounts indicate that commissioners had met the previous day, August 10, official minutes for that meeting do not exist. Available records from that period resume on September 14, 1914, and indicate the commissioners directed the county attorney to collect the insurance on the courthouse.[27]

Given the background surrounding the county audit, many people assumed that arson was the cause of the courthouse conflagration. No one could determine the source of the fire, but it did not stop the commissioners court opponents from suspecting county officials. Soon, commissioners resumed the day-to-day business of the county—and so did property owners, who again demanded an audit.

On October 12, 1914, the commissioners court directed County Attorney J. F. Clarkson to secure a list of all Duval County delinquent taxpayers from 1885 to 1913. The following year, on March 9, 1915, commissioners authorized printing 1,500 copies of the delinquent tax records of Duval County, which the court had secured from the Texas comptroller of public accounts. It was unclear why commissioners ordered so many reproductions; perhaps some of their nemeses urging the audit were on the list.[28]

The financial review affair intensified in January 1915 when the grand jury indicted Duval County Commissioner Luciano Hinojosa for extortion in an official capacity. Previously, Sheriff Augustine Peña had arrested County Judge Antonio W. Tobin, County Clerk Palacios, Treasurer Alonzo López, Constable Aurelio Aleman, and ex-Justice of the Peace González on the same charge.

Unlike Duval County elected officials, mostly Tejanos, the twelve-member grand jurors the district judge appointed were mainly Americanos, with a Spaniard, F. Vaello, in its ranks. In a report the grand jury provided to Judge Hopkins, the grand jurors pointed out, "affairs in our county are in most deplorable conditions." Its members said, "most men now conducting the affairs of our county are utterly incompetent . . . and were forced upon the community." The fact that most of Duval County's citizens had elected the officials escaped the grand jury's examination.[29]

Finally, on June 11, 1915, the Texas Supreme Court upheld the lower courts and gave the green light to an official audit. The private auditors, Kidd, Aikman & Company of Houston, did not take long to complete their findings. As critics expected it was not a complimentary review. "In general, it appears from the facts and findings, and from observations generally, that the Commissioners Court have conducted the county's business without regard to statutory provisions relating to the conduct of public business," concluded the auditors. Moreover, they reported discovering overpayments, illegal expenditures, and shortages totaling $59,897.91.[30]

The auditors broke down the sum among the elected officials; since most public officers were Tejanos, the report blamed them for the county's shortages. Commissioner Parr and former County Judge Woods escaped without a blemish. Not surprisingly, County Treasurers Alonso López and

Lino T. García bore responsibility for a combined $37,958.25 of the alleged shortage. Almost all of that amount was "money received on orders of county judge." Auditors accused three sheriffs of mishandling funds, including Tobin for misappropriating $11,096.15, Amado Garza for $259.50, and A. de la Peña for $196.71. Other elected officials, including three Americano county attorneys and citizens, misapplied $10,388.30. This latter group included F. P. Gonzales, a private citizen and the owner of *La Libertad*, who stood accused of inappropriately using county funds for "circulating delinquent tax list," which the Duval County Commissioners Court had requested done. The fact that the publisher was a private citizen who had accepted the county's purchase order in the capacity of a businessman did not enter into the auditor's conclusion.[31]

Once the accountants completed the audit, Parr's opponents moved to prove misconduct by holding a grand jury inquiry. But Parr sought to sidetrack them. On December 15, 1914, the Duval County Commissioners Court had voted that no one could inspect books and records of county offices without the presence of the person in charge of those records. The court further directed that no one could remove the records from the courthouse. A year later, on December 10, 1915, Parr—no longer a county commissioner but serving in the Texas Senate—walked into the grand jury room accompanied by Sheriff Antonio W. Tobin and took the county's records the grand jury was examining. The jury foreman, Milton Dubose, alerted District Judge Voll M. Taylor of the transgression. Judge Taylor appointed Paul McAllister and C. K. Gravis as additional bailiffs to the grand jury and ordered them to arrest anyone who attempted to interfere with the grand jury's work.[32]

The following Monday, December 13, Judge Taylor fined Parr and Tobin $100 each and sentenced them to one hour in jail. He directed Texas Ranger Captain J. J. Sanders to execute his order and not release the accused until the hour had lapsed and they had paid their fine. Next, Parr's opponents, all Americanos led by Charles Hoffman, asked the district court to remove Judge Givens A. Parr and County Commissioners Hinojosa, Allen, Carrillo, and García from office. Among the charges alleged were improper payment of county funds, failure to correctly audit claims paid out of county funds, and refusal to bring suit against county officers and former officers who defaulted on payments due to Duval County. Another charge claimed Senator Parr received a $150 allowance for duties as road supervisor, which was not allowed by law. In all the claimants filed thirty-seven allegations of misconduct with the court.[33]

On January 10, 1916, Judge Taylor removed all four Duval County Commissioners from office but passed on removing 24-year-old County Judge Givens Parr. Once again, the judge aimed at Tejano officials but gave the Americano chief executive a pass. The district judge replaced the deposed commissioners with Manuel Rogers, Precinct One; S. S. Jameson, Precinct Two; A. V. Puig, Precinct Three; and V. Mendoza, Precinct Four. Judge Taylor denied a request from complainants to stop the construction of a new county courthouse, whose estimated cost to build was $60,000 and paid with county securities.[34]

In 1917, 102 individuals from outside the county—all opponents of Tejano elected officials—signed a pamphlet telling the Duval story of the previous three years as they saw it. The breakdown of the group was seventy-four Americanos and twenty-eight Tejanos. They asked in the petition, "Has the Average Citizen of Duval County a White Man's Chance?" suggesting that Americanos were woefully disadvantaged politically in Duval County. If the Americano majority that wrote the tract had posed it as an ethnocentric question—which they did—then perhaps the Americanos did not have a chance. However, the average Americans in Duval County were Tejanos, who appeared by the early twentieth century to finally have an equal opportunity in pursuing the American dream. That reality and Americanos' continued empty victories and other developing matters forced Americanos to hold in abeyance efforts to regain political power.[35]

Plan of San Diego Prompts More Americanos to Leave

In August 1915 fear over the Plan of San Diego prompted many Americanos in Duval County to send their families to Corpus Christi for safety. On August 26, 1915, newspapers reported that only thirteen Americano men remained in San Diego. Their departure from Duval County further limited the Americanos' chances for a political resurgence.[36]

The Plan de San Diego was an irredentist plot signed by nine Mexican expatriates in January 1915. No signer was from Duval County, although a couple had ties there. Locals, moreover, took little interest in it. However, two area Tejanos faced arrest because of the similarity of their names to two of the signers. In February 1915 US Deputy Marshal John McKinney arrested Manuel Flores and Anatolio González, both of San Diego. Authorities cleared both men two weeks later for mistaken identity. While some residents were asking state and national leaders to send Rangers and troops to San Diego, Archie Parr asked Austin and Washington to remove them from San Diego because they were unnecessary. Nothing in his political history suggests that Parr had any use for Rangers, who had an unsavory reputation among his Tejano partners.[37]

A case unrelated to the Plan of San Diego illustrates the judicial system's unfairness. On January 26, 1915, Tejano Hilario Alanis shot and killed Linton Shaw at a Tejano dance in San Diego. This tragic event had no political implications; it was no more than a disagreement in the early morning hours as a dance was winding down. Unlike the Americano shooters at the courthouse who walked away from the trial with their rights intact, a jury found young Alaniz guilty two years later. The judge sentenced him to fifteen years in prison.[38]

It was irregularities like this in the administration of justice and other realms affecting the Tejano working class and poor that Tejano leaders sought to reverse with Parr's help. To his credit, whether his motivations were altruistic or self-serving, Parr favored the county's Tejano population, unlike some of his Americano political predecessors.

Parr Saw Austin as an Opportunity to Effect Meaningful Change

While Parr always won in raw politics at the local level, Austin offered grander opportunities to advance his Tejano constituents' situation. In late 1913 he announced for the seat from the Twenty-Third Senate District, which covered the Trans-Nueces, the area between the Nueces River and the Rio Grande. The incumbent was not seeking reelection, and anti-Parr Americanos urged others to enter the race, which Jim Wells County Judge

W. R. Perkins did. In June 1914 the *Houston Post* declared that Perkins would win the Senate race. A month later, as primary returns began to come in, the *Austin Statesman* reported that Parr was running behind the Jim Wells County judge. However, when all the votes were in, Parr emerged as the Democratic candidate and won the Senate seat in November. The press's antipathy toward Parr persisted for most of his political life.[39]

Parr went to work in Austin, secure in the belief that his Tejano allies on the commissioners court would attend to people's business back in Duval. He quickly introduced several legislative initiatives to help them carry out their duties. One bill increased the authority and responsibilities of the Duval County Commissioners Court and permitted the issuance of bonds to finance road and bridge projects. He also introduced legislation creating the Benavides Independent School District. He added certain lands and territory in Jim Wells County to the San Diego Independent School District for school purposes. Parr also created Common School District Number Twenty-Four of Duval County.[40]

Circumstances occasionally called him to challenge the power structure, such as the Texas Rangers. For example, on September 15, 1918, Rangers arrested and tortured Duval County Constable Jesús Villareal, who they believed was abetting "slackers" (draft dodgers) to avoid military service by smuggling them back to Mexico. On that assumption they smothered and pistol-whipped a fellow lawman.[41]

Duval County and World War I

From the beginning of Duval County, Tejanos sought ways to be part of the community. They tried to observe the new country's laws and embrace their new neighbors' business and social practices, all while they held on to their faith, customs, and language. They tried to meld these elements into a new cultural identity. But as much as they tried, some Americanos resisted and fought them at every turn. These clashes became evident during World War I (1914–1919) when Americanos felt threatened by the fighting across the Atlantic and took it out on their Tejano neighbors. It did not help that Tejanos in the Lower Valley were in a revolt prompted by the Plan of San Diego, drafted in Duval County's seat of government. Not surprisingly, the Texas Rangers were ready to provide the Americanos with support and cover.

It is important to remember that these challenges came as Tejanos, with the help of a new ally, were working to achieve the equality promised by the US Constitution. They and Archie Parr were trying to keep their political balance against an onslaught of legal challenges launched by Americanos. Fortunately, as José de la Luz Sáenz wrote, Tejanos received support in their efforts "for democracy, humanity, and justice." Equally important, they received moral support from their Tejano brothers throughout Texas and Mexican Americans across the United States. Sáenz explained, "Americans expect recognition and fairness in light of this hopeless and pervasive situation. . . . The 'slackers' committed an unfortunate mistake when they failed to answer the call from a nation in crisis and encouraged the public to think the rest of us did not want to make the sacrifice." In Duval County, the "fairness" Sáenz wrote about was in short supply. Hence, a few chose to dodge responsibility.[42]

Still, many others, the vast majority of eligible Duval County Tejano men, registered for the draft, and many joined the armed forces and made every effort to demonstrate their patriotism. Yet some in the county, including Rangers and Americanos, could not accept Tejanos as legitimate citizens, even denying that they harbored loyalty and allegiance to the land they considered their home. Indeed, while the Rangers presumably were trying to curb draft dodging, one Duval County resident, Virginia Yaeger, reported to the governor that "any one of them [Tejanos] would go to war" if it were not "for the brutality" of the Rangers.[43]

In keeping with beliefs of Tejano's disloyalty, in September 1917 the Bureau of Investigations began a probe in Duval County relative to "Mexicans" circumventing the draft. The inquiry quickly became a smear of Archie Parr and his Tejano supporters. At every step in the process, investigators pointed at Parr and his "Mexican" friends as unpatriotic and irresponsible. In October the bureau accused the exemption board of fraud and favoritism, maintaining that various county officials or Parr associates were getting draft exemptions for individuals in exchange for pay.[44]

US Justice Department Agent Erby E. Swift, on October 24, 1917, initiated an investigation in San Diego to determine the extent of wrongful activity. Swift worked under the assumption that anyone making a statement against the Parr faction would result in Parr supporters forcing any snitch to leave the county or "lose his life." The state of Texas, Swift surmised, would not protect anyone speaking against Mexican wrongdoing in Parr's thirty-two county Senate district, covering all of South Texas, because the "Mexican votes count too much."[45]

At the urging of Duval Exemption Board members, County Judge J. F. Clarkson, and Jesús Sáenz, Washington removed the board's third member, Dr. E. E. Wilson. People did not want to get involved in exposing the draft exemption scandal, and Dr. Wilson's dismissal for speaking up on the subject significantly intensified this apprehension. Agent Swift wrote to the District Exemption Board in Houston that Washington should remove Judge Clarkson and Sáenz and reinstate Dr. Wilson. US Attorney John Edward Green concurred, and a recommendation went up the chain of command to the secretary of war with the additional request that authorities initiate prosecutorial action against Clarkson and Sáenz. These suggestions were to no avail. Federal officials, perhaps acting under political pressure from Parr's friends in Austin, kept Dr. Wilson off the board and named a "Mexican," a Parr adherent named Liborio Cadena, in Wilson's place. Agent Swift indicated that the board had "two Mexicans and an American" when, in truth, they were all Americans. As a result, Swift pointed out, when an examination of applicants claiming an exemption for medical reasons was necessary, the board had to call an Alice doctor. There was no reason for the board not to use Dr. Wilson since no one had questioned his medical standing. The investigator also appeared unaware that Dr. José García had been practicing in San Diego since at least 1904. Unlike Dr. Wilson, Dr. García, a resident alien, registered for the draft.[46]

County Judge Clarkson reportedly boasted that Parr's allies could bring back the slackers from Mexico with impunity, and no one would harm them. He bragged that the county had retrieved two hundred draft evaders without being caught. The Texas Rangers, however, had arrested fifteen slackers as deserters and taken them to Camp Travis in San Antonio. Sáenz, in his

World War I diary, noted that Rangers had treated Mexicans in Realitos, the place of his birth, "like criminals and brought many of them in at gunpoint to register for military service, which they did not understand." Saenz, a committed patriot, wrote, "I swear that if I had been there and if they had tried to drag me in the same way, I would have been the first 'slacker.'" Texas Rangers, urged on by local newspapers, were said to have executed as many as one hundred and perhaps as many as three hundred Mexican "bandits."[47]

In October 1917 an agent for the Bureau of Investigation reported to his superiors that Judge Clarkson, aside from being a Parr lackey, was a drunkard and a gambler who spent most of his time in brothels, which were readily available in San Diego. "These facts," wrote the agent, "should be sufficient for his removal" from the Draft Board. Juan F. Sáenz, the other member of the exemption board, was "a young Mexican" of draft age (as were his brother and several friends) who, because of his empathy for slackers, was also a candidate for replacement. On the contrary, the investigator noted that Dr. Wilson was a recent arrival to town and immune to the Parr venom and appeared to be "an honorable gentleman" who had dutifully pointed to the other two members (Clarkson and Sáenz) as participating in granting unearned exemptions to Parr supporters, "Mexicans," and those willing to pay.[48]

The agent accused one Mexican, an American-born citizen, Adolfo Cuéllar, of trying to avoid the draft, even though Cuéllar registered for the draft on June 4, 1917. Investigators alleged that Cuéllar had lied in an affidavit that he was the sole support of his widowed mother when, in fact, his older brother Candelario was not only their mother's caregiver but Adolfo's as well. The case lingered until 1919, and no prosecution ever occurred.[49]

Another case investigated in October 1917 was made known to the governor's staff in Austin by the deposed Dr. Wilson. The doctor said Sáenz advised Tejano registrants to see Juan O. Treviño, a Parr confidant, who would help them with the paperwork. Treviño, the doctor said, would then split the fees he received from the draft dodger with Sáenz. Based on this information, federal investigators pursued their inquiry. While this investigation yielded no known arrests or convictions, it intimidated Tejanos.

Every Tejano investigated had already signed up for the draft, while only one Americano accuser had done the same.

The reality was that Mexicanos, Tejanos, and Americanos engaged in evading registration. Mexicanos and Tejanos, including some from Duval County, crossed to Mexico to avoid the draft during World War I. One newspaper account had twelve draft evaders surrendering to federal authorities at Corpus Christi, eleven of whom were Tejanos from Duval County. In a related story, the press reported that forty-four naturalized Tejanos from Duval County pled guilty in federal district court to violating the draft. On the other hand, one news outlet stated that six hundred registered for the selective service in Duval County and that "no Mexicans from San Diego crossed into Mexico and all enrolled cheerfully, there being not the slightest complaint or disposition to resist."[50]

Nonetheless, the historical record shows Tejanos displaying patriotic loyalty to the nation. Most likely, Americanos, the Rangers, and Dr. Wilson, convinced that Tejanos lacked loyalty and patriotism to the country, did not know of the actions of San Diego resident Felipe García, who, three weeks after President Wilson asked Congress for a declaration of war, telegraphed General John J. Pershing, volunteering to "enlist companies of Spanish-speaking boys." The commander of the American Expeditionary Forces replied to García to "express his appreciation for the offer . . . but at present, there is no requirement to enlist volunteer companies." According to one source, a soldier by the same name received the highest ranking, sergeant major, of all Duval County soldiers.[51]

Other brave men from Duval County, ostensibly unknown to Americanos, the Rangers, and Dr. Wilson, served in the European theater of war, including Pablo Pérez, Pablo López, and Eduardo Barrera. Thanks to the Sáenz diary, their families and the general public fully understand Tejanos' contributions to the Great War. López, for example, signed up for a squad that used 240 mm trench mortars. Young men like López exhibited an outstanding commitment to military life and took much pleasure in their duties, Sáenz wrote. They saw action on many battlefields: at one time, Sáenz, Lopez, and Barrera received news that the enemy had killed Pérez in action. Fortunately, the Germans had merely gassed Pérez at Saint-Mihiel. Patriotic efforts like this went unnoticed by Rangers and some Americanos who could not accept Tejanos as legitimate citizens.[52] Indeed, according to draft board records, 1,531 men from Duval County registered for the draft during World War I. Of these 1,379 were Tejanos and 152 were Americanos.

Among the latter was George B. Parr, Senator Parr's son. There is no evidence that the younger Parr brother served in the military; however, evidence shows him having signed up in Corpus Christi for a cavalry troop of the Texas Guard earlier that year. The Young Parr's older brother, Givens, enlisted in the army on June 3, 1917. On May 31, 1918, he received an honorable discharge to obtain a commission as a second lieutenant. He separated from duty on December 11, 1918.[53]

With a population of 8,251, the 1,531 draftees listed represented 18.6 percent of the county's residents. Factoring in the number of females, children under 18, and those older than 65, 1,531 draftees seem close to the entire male population eligible to be drafted. Draft Board deputies, appointees who oversaw the draft process in the county, did not meet the same standards, with 56 percent being Americanos and only 44 percent Tejanos. Draft registrants represented twenty-nine Duval County communities, including rancherías. The most significant number came from San Diego, with 583, followed by Benavides, 260; Realitos, 133; and Concepción, 105.

Young men from Duval County openly and actively met their civic duties, demonstrating their patriotic commitment to the country. Indeed, the *Houston Post* reported that draft boards across the state had difficulty signing up Americanos and specifically cited Duval County, where out of twenty-three draftees on that particular day, twenty-two were Tejanos and only one an Americano.[54]

One hundred thirty-one Duval men saw active duty during World War I, with 110 of those being Tejanos and 21 Americanos. Of these enrollees, 68 served overseas: 5 fell victim to what may have been the Spanish fever pandemic, although the official cause of death was pneumonia; 8 received wounds; and 6 made the ultimate sacrifice: Guadalupe Garza, Oliver W. Gausch, Daniel R. Herman, Rafael Palacios, Mauricio Pérez, and Estanislado Zapata were killed in action or died from their wounds.[55]

After the war Tejanos demanded "privileges and rights that their fellow comrades in the army were granted as loyal citizens of the United States" for their "service and sacrifice." But they did so with a measure of humility and charity. On December 5, 1917, when San Diego serviceman Porfirio Banda died in a stateside hospital of pneumonia, 1,500 of his fellow citizens attended his funeral. Two-thirds of the mourners paying homage to him had to stand outside the church. In October 1919 the community of San Diego planned to use $1,000 raised in donations to honor men from their town who had served the nation. But Duval war veterans instead asked organizers to redirect the money to the victims of the September 14, 1919, hurricane that devastated Corpus Christi, saying, "We willingly offered our lives for humanity; we are more than willing to give up a day of pleasure for humanity." On this occasion, and in others later, Duval County Tejanos displayed their sensibilities and independence without answering or checking with politicians such as Archie Parr.[56]

Tejanos at the home front also supported the war effort. Private Manuel Vela, a member of the Texas Cavalry, went around the brush country making speeches on behalf of liberty loans and in one week sold $50,000 in bonds in the area that included Duval County. Vela may have inspired Sejita farmer Rafael Flores, who walked into the Corpus Christi National Bank with a sack full of money from his cotton sale and invested all $1,600 in war bonds.[57]

In 1919, after fighting off an extended challenge revolving around the impact the "Mexican vote" had in his Senate victory, Parr asked for time to address his colleagues in the Senate and, through the media present, his fellow Texans. Senator Parr indicated that his opponent had made a great deal about the Tejano vote; it looked like "they didn't want the Mexican vote" counted. Eighty percent of the men who went to war from his district were Tejanos, he stated with conviction, and that number was 95 percent in Duval County. Moreover, Tejanos from Duval County joined the Red Cross and purchased war savings stamps. It was not just, Parr emphasized, to expect Tejanos to be patriots during the war and then deny them the franchise.[58]

The contribution that Duval County young men, most of them Tejanos, made to the country's involvement in World War I shone a spotlight on the freedoms they had yearned for from the earliest times of Duval County's existence. For over half a century since the area became a part of the United States, visions and dreams of equality had been elusive for Tejanos. Under Parr some saw an opportunity for more tangible advancement, even as the politico employed, in the view of some, undemocratic means to establish a world conducive to Tejanos' progress.

War or No War, Americanos Continued Attacks on Parr and His Tejano Allies

After repeatedly failing to overturn the county takeover by Parr and his Tejano allies, Americanos and their backers in the print media renewed, in 1916, their attacks on Parr's electoral tactics. At about the same time, federal authorities had investigated voting in Nueces County and had successfully sent several politicians to prison. National law enforcement officers then made noise about turning their investigation on Duval County. Parr responded with a novel strategy to thwart this effort: he vowed to advise voters not to cast ballots in national elections but to participate in state and local contests. His first test was the Democratic primary in 1916, in which he was a candidate for reelection to the Texas Senate. Parr delivered 803 votes to his candidates for state office in that election, from governor to the Supreme Court. Any candidate opposing Parr's preferred candidate received zero votes. The *Temple Daily Telegram* called it a "freak" election.[59]

Ashley Evans, the editor of the *Bonham News*, explained the outcome this way: "This is not an exceptional occurrence in that section of Texas. The practice of fraud in elections is the rule, not the exception. This has been known for years. Every man, at all informed, has known that thousands of ignorant and irresponsible Mexicans, many of them not even citizens, have been herded like cattle and driven to the polls on election day to do the bidding of the men who had them under control."[60] Evans's views demonstrate the viewpoint of many Americanos. And so it went in newspapers throughout Texas. While there may have been some truth in their criticisms, the broad and harsh brush they used to blame and demean Tejanos only rallied Tejanos behind their political ally and partner, who worked to meet their needs.

The editors' biased approach provided more grist to rant against Parr when Judge D. W. Glasscock from Mission in the Rio Grande Valley announced in June 1918 that he would challenge Parr for his Senate seat, Parr's first serious challenge since he entered the Senate in 1915.[61] After the primary election polls closed at the end of July 1918, newspaper accounts showed that Glasscock had achieved a comfortable win; curiously, Parr defeated Glasscock in the judge's home county of Hidalgo. Word started making the rounds throughout the state that Parr would somehow try to snatch a win from Glasscock. Governor William Hobby's organization vowed to fight such shenanigans.[62]

As rumors spread that Parr was up to no good, Americanos took aim at Tejanos, who could swing a victory for Parr. Americanos maintained that Duval County's Mexicans should not be allowed to vote if they avoided military service, which Tejanos had not. Moreover, Americanos intimated that the federal government should launch an investigation to determine if Americans, meaning those of the white persuasion and not Tejanos, had been denied the vote. At the same time, every report coming in gave Glasscock a comfortable lead.[63]

On August 24, 1918, Democrats met at Corpus Christi for the Twenty-Third Senatorial District Convention. The meeting soon split in two, each group claiming legitimacy. The Glasscock crowd threw out all the Duval County votes for Parr and declared Glasscock the winner. Meanwhile, the Parr convention did not throw out any ballots, asserting that the ballots from Duval County were sufficient to give the senatorial nomination to Parr by a 118-vote margin. Newspapers continued to report that Glasscock was the nominee of the Democratic Party, and the August 1918 state convention in Waco confirmed that line. A month later the secretary of state decided that Glasscock's name would appear on the November ballot.[64]

At the beginning of October, however, a district court declared the convention had erred in disqualifying Parr and ruled that he would appear on the November ballot. As expected, Glasscock and his supporters rejected the ruling and embarked on a write-in campaign on Glasscock's behalf. Although Glasscock's write-in committee included South Texas representatives, not one was from Duval County, nor did it include Tejanos. Joining the anti-Parr cavalcade were his political enemies, including Governor Hobby and women activists whom Parr had shunned by opposing the state referendum granting them the right to vote.[65]

While published returns gave Glasscock a 224-vote margin of victory, Parr announced that he had edged out his opponent by 500. Indeed, Parr won by that margin when election officials tabulated all the votes. The *Corpus Christi Times* ran an editorial proclaiming that Parr's victory had been fair and square. "Parr is elected, and without Duval County, and the war is over," the *Times* concluded. The newspaper opined that Parr's opponents needed to accept reality and move on. The *Times* feared, however, that they would not, and they did not.[66]

Glasscock and his supporters, not the least of whom was Governor Hobby, still had cards to play. The governor ordered the Texas Rangers to investigate every vote in the general election. In the meantime, Glasscock's supporters announced they would take the matter before the Texas Senate, a move with risk since Parr had senatorial privilege and many of his colleagues would likely stand by him. Glasscock supporters felt encouraged because Texas Rangers and Department of Justice investigators had compiled sworn statements showing numerous irregularities.[67]

In mid-January 1919 the Texas Senate convened with a jovial Senator Parr at his seat. Despite a challenge to Parr's presence, the Senate voted that he be "temporarily" sworn in. The first order of business was the Glasscock-Parr hearing before the Committee on Privileges and Elections. Glasscock's attorneys charged that the Parr campaign violated almost every aspect of Texas's election law. But Parr told his colleagues, "I beat him fair and square, and this Senate will say so when it has heard the evidence." Which they did, but much drama remained to unfold.[68]

The Duval boss continued in his offensive. He quickly charged the Texas Rangers with using guns to intimidate voters in six of his strongest counties, adding that every affidavit the Rangers secured was obtained and tainted by the force of revolvers. Indeed, the *rinches* regularly positioned themselves at polling places, often arresting Parr's Tejano supporters. One writer observed they "did not distinguish between . . . innocent or guilty." Company A of the Texas Rangers, stationed in nearby Alice, was "known as one of the most vicious," carrying out their role "by any means necessary."[69]

Glasscock's attorney countered by reading off a lengthy list of charges, accusing Parr of violations such as making liquor available to election workers and the public at voting stations. He also complained that election officials rejected thousands of Glasscock ballots for alleged misspellings. Parr's attorney, meanwhile, said they could not dispute these charges, nor could Glasscock's lawyers prove them, because they were all too general. He specifically named counties where numbers of ballots allegedly had been tampered with by changing them as votes for Glasscock and not Parr as the voter had marked them. "I want a committee appointed to go down on the ground and learn the truth," Parr told the hearing.[70]

In 1918, in a surprisingly low vote, voters cast 288 ballots in the Duval County general election; 207 (72 percent) were Tejanos and 31 (28 percent) Americanos. Since Americanos were only 10 percent of the population, their turnout ratio was 300 percent higher than the number in the county. Moreover, Parr received 226 votes. If every Tejano voted for Parr, 207, this leaves nineteen votes (23 percent) for Parr coming from Americanos in Duval County.

Glasscock's attorneys continued to complain, asserting a "conspiracy" had produced Parr's victory. He listed ten charges to make a case for fraud and corruption; all but one directly used the term *Mexican* in one form or another. He argued that the "Mexican race" constituted a large part of the district, that a significant number of the "Mexican race is illiterate" and wholly "ignorant" of election laws, that most of the "Mexican race" could not read, write, or understand English, that a large part were "aliens," citizens of Mexico, and that a large amount of Mexicans were transients. Turning to Parr, the attorney argued that the senator spoke the "Mexican language" fluently, controlled the "Mexican population," led a political machine that maintained control by illegal voting of "illiterate Mexicans," and that Parr and his cohorts illegally paid poll taxes for those same "illiterate Mexicans." Perhaps Senator William Lucas Hall captured the essence of the investigation when he observed that the Glasscock case relied wholly on "opinion testimony."[71]

Still, Glasscock's attorneys and supporters made no effort to conceal the underlying reason driving their political endeavors—to wit, disfranchising Tejanos, or Mexicans, as they called them. Glasscock attorney Claude Pollard stated openly, "A great movement in that county [Duval] is to try to get the Anglo-Saxon on top." Pollard contended that if left alone, the Duval County Mexicans would take as much interest in politics as Blacks in East Texas, which ostensibly meant near nil. But "white bosses" like Parr refused to leave the Mexicans alone, he elaborated. This last observation underlines the weakness of Glasscock's argument because it failed to recognize and accept that the Tejanos were Parr's willing supporters, indeed partners. Moreover, they had been fighting for the right to vote for over half a century.

On March 10, 1919, three months after the general election, the Texas Senate voted 16–14 to seat Parr. Perhaps Senator Lon A. Smith from Henderson County caught the gist of the fight better than most of his colleagues, observing, "With the Constitution, the evidence, the application of the law on matters of elections and contests before me, I could not, without stultifying my conscience, vote differently on this question." He noted that the evidence indicated both candidates pursued the "Mexican vote," a reality since Tejanos comprised the majority in South Texas. Any honest candidate would need to court them; Glasscock and his ilk lacked the social and political skills or the desire to attract them. They could hardly expect to win them over by demeaning their existence.[72]

Still, after the Senate trial ended in Parr's favor, the legislature approved a law making it illegal to help individuals with their ballot unless they were physically unable or were older than sixty; the bill aimed to disenfranchise Tejanos.[73]

A Period of Calm and Growth in Duval County

After the Glasscock challenge, Archie Parr turned his attention to his Senate job and left his Duval County machine in the hands of Tejanos; of course, he was never far away, if need be, and his sons served as county judge for most of the time. However, Parr's oldest son, Yale-educated Givens A. Parr, left politics to take up banking in nearby Alice. The move opened the door for his younger, 26-year-old brother, George, to assume the mantle as duke in waiting. However, the duke could hardly prioritize son George over his base. The Tejano community was a reliable partner and source of governance.

Indeed, a Tejano occupied the county judge position through most of Duval County's subsequent history.

By 1920 modernity, brought about by new technologies, was changing the world, including that area called Duval County. Automobiles, trucks, and tractors needed petroleum byproducts. It was an incredibly good fortune that Duval County was rich in oil. Not a week passed in 1920 without state newspapers running a story about the growing number of oil wells in Duval County.

This development had several effects on life in Duval County. First, it created jobs in the oil fields and indirectly for wholesale suppliers that served petroleum operators with goods required in their industry. As it turned out, most of the oilfield jobs went to Americanos. The 1940 Census confirmed that 96 percent of the new oil field labor force were Americanos. Nevertheless, the petroleum industry bolstered retail companies, providing the everyday needs of oil field workers and extending business opportunities and jobs for Tejanos. Further, it offered the county a new and exceptional tax revenue source, further employment for Tejanos, and a gold mine for the political boss's coffers.

The oil boom was not the only change in Duval County during the 1920s. Modern technologies require infrastructure. Electricity demanded wiring, poles, and related facilities. The gas industry needed a distribution system such as pipelines. The automobiles and trucks relied on petroleum to power them and depended on paved roads. Infrastructure requirements opened opportunities for new jobs in the county since it was responsible for the new transportation systems. Naturally, these needs from the county yielded options for Boss Parr to line his pockets with road-building company kickbacks and to reward supporters with jobs with suppliers and contractors that did business with the county. Finally, the latest industry provided jobs with the county itself and was a reliable source of tax revenue for the local government.

These new sources of revenue and jobs enhanced the county's fiscal standing. Buttressing it was the continued expansion of the old cotton and livestock economy. In 1920 cotton production rose by 1,500 acres, a 22 percent increase and the most significant yield in the county's history. Livestock values stood at $1.5 million. Officials assessed land at $4 million. Rather than reduce taxes, the Duval County Commissioners Court took advantage of the buoyant economy by setting a $2.40 tax rate on private property.[74]

With new roughnecks coming into the county daily, but with a 1918 amendment prohibiting the "manufacture, sale, or transportation of intoxicating liquors" and a state prohibition amendment reinforcing temperance the following year, liquor smuggling became a viable business in Duval County's brush country. Soon, illegal saloons, gambling casinos, and brothels promoting prostitution became part of the Duval County underground economy. Vice became another revenue source for the Parrs and those who ran the political machine.

The duke always looked for ways to line his pockets, and his Tejano supporters provided tacit consent. For example, in September 1927, 455 citizens petitioned the commissioners court to call an election to approve $575,000 in county bonds, money intended to build, maintain, and operate county roads. Voters approved the measure thirty days later, 453–121. The county was to pay the bonds in annual installments over thirty years. Five months later 738 citizens presented a petition to the commissioners court for $800,000 in bonds for more roads, which not surprisingly received voter approval within the scheduled thirty days. The court also okayed bonds to make improvements at various county school districts.[75]

These projects appeared ripe for graft. Indeed, in 1931 the Refugio newspaper reported that work had begun on a highway leading from Benavides to Archie Parr's ranch. Nine months later a federal grand jury indicted a Houston company for giving kickbacks of $100,000 to Senator Archie Parr and $25,000 to Duval County Judge George B. Parr and several other South Texas politicians. With so much debt accumulated from earlier bond issues, in 1931 the commissioners court approved a tax rate of $3.12 per $100 of valuation. The following year, with property values at $14.7 million, the commissioners were able to lower the tax to $2.73. Yet no grand jury indicted a Tejano elected official from Duval County for receiving a kickback from Parr-initiated projects during this era. Tejanos most likely could squeeze small amounts of cash from county workers or local Tejano businesses, but the Parr family had dibs on primo graft opportunities.[76]

Table 17.2 Duval County elected officials, 1922–1930

	1922	1924	1926	1928	1930
Judge	G. A. Parr	G. A. Parr	G. B. Parr	G. B. Parr	G. B. Parr
Clerk	J. V. Palacios (resigned on September 30, 1922)/Court named J. O. Treviño as his replacement.)	J. O. Treviño	J. O. Treviño	J. O. Treviño	J. O. Treviño
Attorney	J. F. Clarkson	J. F. Clarkson	J. F. Clarkson	J. F. Clarkson	J. F. Clarkson
Treasurer	Horacio Sáenz	Horacio Sáenz	Horacio Sáenz	Horacio Sáenz	Horacio Sáenz
Surveyor		R. M. Gonzalez	R. M. Gonzalez		
Sheriff	Jesús Oliveira	Jesús Oliveira	Jesús Oliveira	Dan Tobin	Dan Tobin
Tax Assessor	Alonso López	Alonzo López		Clemente Garcia	Clemente Garcia
Inspector of Hides					A. J. Wiederkehr**
Tax Collector	Jesús Oliveira	Jesús Oliveira	Jesús Oliveira	Jesús Oliveira	Jesús Oliveira
Commissioner, Precinct One	Luciano Hinojosa	Luciano Hinojosa	Luciano Hinojosa	Luciano Hinojosa	J. A. Tobin
Commissioner, Precinct Two	O. G. Allen	O. G. Allen	O. G. Allen	José Hancock	José Hancock
Commissioner, Precinct Three	Eusebio Carrillo	Eusebio Carrillo	Eusebio Carrillo	D. C. Chapa	D. C. Chapa
Commissioner, Precinct Four	Manuel Garza	Manuel Garza	Manuel Garza	Evaristo Valerio	Evaristo Valerio
Justice of the Peace, Precinct One	F. Lotto (resigned on October 9, 1922)/ Henry P. Rogers appointed.	F. Lotto		O. E. Tobin	O. E. Tobin*/ P. Rogers**

(Continues)

Table 17.2 (Continued)

	1922	1924	1926	1928	1930
Justice of the Peace, Precinct Two	P. H. Reyna	_Juan F. Gonzalez_		_Juan F. Gonzalez_/ J. O. Stockwell	J. O. Stockwell*/ _Domingo García_**
Justice of the Peace, Precinct Three	_Práxedis Sáenz_	_Práxedis Sáenz_		_Práxedis Sáenz_	_Práxedis Sáenz_
Justice of the Peace, Precinct Four					
Justice of the Peace, Precinct Five					
Justice of the Peace, Precinct Six	_R. J. Treviño_	O. Coody		_R. S. Flores_	
Justice of the Peace, Precinct Seven					_Flavio García_* (resigned)/_Hermilio Villarreal_**
Justice of the Peace, Precinct Eight		_Teodoro Sendejó_		_Teodoro Sendejó_	_Teodoro Sendejó_
Justice of the Peace, Precinct Nine**					
Constable, Precinct One	_Emeterio Barrera_	_Emeterio Barrera_			_George Gonzales_
Constable, Precinct Two	_Camilo G. Ramirez_	_Alfredo Hinojosa_		_Herminio Salinas_	
Constable, Precinct Three	_Ismael Chapa_	_Ismael Chapa_		_Ismael Chapa_	
Constable, Precinct Four	_Guillermo Vera_ (appointed May 22, 1922)				
Constable, Precinct Five	W. M. Donahoe			_Desiderio Serna_	
Constable, Precinct Six				_Guillermo Guerra_	
Constable, Precinct Seven					_Santiago Sánchez_

Source: Duval County Commissioners Court Minutes. The italicized names are Tejanos.

*Resigned.

**Appointed by commissioners court.

Gaining the Duval County Commissioners Court approval, the Parrs designated the Texas State Bank of Alice as its depository, facilitating the opportunity for further misconduct. The bank's officers included Senator Archie Parr, former Duval County Judge Givens A. Parr, Atlee Parr (the senator's youngest son), Lillian Parr (his daughter), and Jesús Oliveira. It was one more tool to funnel kickbacks.[77]

Cities Emerge in Duval County

As the county continued to grow to a population of 20,565 in 1940, its budding towns sought authority to manage their development. In 1935 the commissioners court okayed a petition from San Diego citizens to hold an election to determine the town's incorporation. On Valentine's Day 1935, the proposal received the approval of San Diego's residents, 217–4. They also elected C. G. Muil as mayor, Teodoro Sendejo as the town marshal, and Crestonio Martínez, Clemente García, C. G. Palacios, and Guillermo García as aldermen. It came twenty-three years after the first attempt to incorporate the town, which had led to the courthouse massacre.

Then, on October 17, 1935, the commissioners court approved a petition by the Benavides citizens to hold an incorporation election for their town. Benavides voters chose J. M. Momeny as mayor, Orlando Oliveira as the town marshal, and J. M. Salinas, Servando Caballero, Ireneo Canales, Santiago García, and F. Vaello Jr. as aldermen. Despite Tejanos' exceptional electoral progress, they continued to yield to Americanos behind the wheel in both cities.

Finally, in March 1936 citizens in the new Duval County community of Freer also asked permission to incorporate. The commissioners court and the town's voters approved the request and selected W. H. Appell as mayor and B. F. Floyd and R. N. Hudgens as town commissioners. Tejanos had not yet risen to influence in the new community.

This growth meant more streets to pave, water systems to develop, and sewage plants to build—not to mention personnel to hire. For the Parr machine, incorporation allowed the patronage wheels to be kept well-oiled. He may not have been able to split the county in two, but he achieved similar ends by increasing the number of governing units in the county.[78]

In July 1933 the county established the Duval County Board of Welfare and Employment Committee, led by Senator Parr, Jesús Oliveira, C. G. Palacios, Dan Tobin Jr. (the former sheriff's son), and Juan O. Treviño. The following November the commissioners court created an agency designed to help those in need and as a vehicle for distributing political favors. H. P. Rogers served as the agency's "relief committee administrator."[79]

Senator Archie Parr, praised and disparaged by many, passed away at age 82 on Sunday, October 19, 1942, at the home of his daughter in Corpus Christi. The burial took place the following day at his ranch near Benavides. Many political leaders throughout Texas, none of them Tejanos, served as honorary pallbearers. Four of the eight actual pallbearers were Tejanos, three of whom were José Ángel Heras, Juan O. Treviño, and Jesús Oliveira, all from Duval County. His wife, five children, and five grandchildren survived the longtime senator. The flags at the state capitol flew at half-mast in his honor.[80]

Despite the spiteful opinions that many of his fellow Americanos harbored against the Duval politico, Parr earned accolades throughout his career. On May 24, 1916, the *San Antonio Express* noted, "Senator Archie Parr of Duval County shows no effects of the stormy petrel career that he has lived. . . . He is still the same old loyal, consistent Archie Parr that he has always been, and still owns and possesses the best smile . . . south of the cap rock of Texas." The *Austin Statesman and Tribune* penned on December 14, 1915, that Senator Parr "presents one of the most unique figures in Texas politics today, simply because he has gone through so much political war, strife, and bitterness, and has held his self-possession and poise so well at all times."[81]

C. L. Turner wrote in the *Alice News* in August 1931, "In Texas, there is no man who has been cussed and discussed during the past fifteen or twenty years more than has Senator Archie Parr, alleged Czar of Duval County, but when it comes to courage, you simply gotta hand it to him. In the Senate, his power is almost unlimited, and it is said that politicians tremble in their boots when he nods his head. Into the Capitol, politicians come and go, but sooner or later, they all fall under the spell of this quiet, courageous man who knows what he wants and gets it." And when Parr visited Schulenburg (Fayette County) the following year, the local newspaper editor wrote, "Senator Archie Parr, one of the greatest fighters for the common people Texas ever produced."[82]

However, what the senator created in Duval County did not die with him. His son George B. Parr inherited his title as duke of Duval and preserved a community that both oddly allowed for corruption and graft and facilitated Tejanos' advancement.[83]

Chapter 18

Tejanos and the End of the Parr Era

George B. Parr came of age in his mid-20s. Still, it took him time to move away from the shadows of his father, Archie Parr, who, although of average build, was a giant in South Texas, not just in Duval County. In truth, George B. Parr never approached his father's accomplishments or public service. If one judges him on his political skills, he may have been as effective as his father, but he fell short as a public servant. Archie Parr was a state senator for twenty years, during which time he did much to move South Texas forward in the twentieth century. George B. Parr did not have such an expansive public career. He spent the last half of his life in and out of courtrooms trying to stay out of jail.

Although George reached state and national fame, or infamy, his penchant for playing outside the boundaries of acceptable political behavior tainted his accomplishments. While he skirted many of his legal troubles, he served time in federal prison as a young man, and when faced with further imprisonment in his twilight years, he chose to take his life. He lived experiences that few knew or will know; he was always center stage, but it is difficult to judge whether his time on earth was a political drama or a personal tragedy. Even though his Tejano political partners gave him respect, it sometimes seemed strained or required and not always genuine and sincere.

Fig. 18.1 George Parr (1901–1975) was the second duke of Duval. Dudley Lynch, *The Duke of Duval: The Life and Times of George B. Parr, a Biography* (Waco, TX: Texian Press, 1976).

Nevertheless, he had an influential impact on Duval County and its people. Some loved Choche, as his Tejano friends called him; others loathed him. Many were his loyal supporters; others stood quietly on the sidelines for many years but, in the end, got in the game and exposed Parr as a self-centered, angry, power-hungry man. Beginning in the 1950s, his legion of Tejano friends realized they could get by without him and all the attendant legal anguish and gradually started to pull away. Unfortunately, some had to pay with the shame of being accused of corruption, and others with jail time.

George B. Parr's Early Years

On March 1, 1901, in a rented house off the main plaza in San Diego, Elizabeth Allen Parr gave birth to a son, and she and her husband, Archie, named him after his paternal grandfather, George B. Parr. Why the infant was born in San Diego and not at the family's ranch south of Benavides is unknown, but the county seat became George's home, from where he manipulated power for nearly half a century.[1]

Historians know little of Parr's early childhood other than he spent time between his father's ranch (some five miles south of Benavides off State Highway 339) and Corpus Christi, with an occasional stop in San Diego to visit his friend W. W. Meek Jr. At the ranch he could have spent time with about five neighborhood boys his age: Ignacio Garza, a recent immigrant from Mexico; Guevalido Martínez; Evaristo País; Alfonso Adame, also a recent immigrant; and Macario Vela. But none of these boys appear in his later life, perhaps because George attended San Antonio and Corpus Christi schools instead of Benavides or San Diego or because the Tejano youth worked in fields or the range and never crossed paths with the patron's son.[2]

In 1915 one of the first things Archie Parr did upon being sworn in as senator was arrange for George to be named a Senate page. Some senators objected, but the attorney general's office decided it would not violate nepotism rules. It was among many occasions when Senator Parr played favorite to his son George. At the peak of World War I, in 1918, George was one of the youngest recruits to the Texas Guard. While he reported to the military draft board shortly after enlisting in the guard, some may have speculated the move to join the Texas Guard was perhaps hatched by his father to keep the young man from being sent to the front.[3]

During the war George was enrolled at the West Texas Military Academy in San Antonio; in 1920 he returned to South Texas and graduated high school at age 20 in Corpus Christi. He then enrolled at Texas A&M College, where his father again came to his aide. The young Mr. Parr complained that upperclassmen at the school were paddling freshmen as a form of hazing, much like what George and his schoolmates did to first-year students at West Texas Military School. Still, acting on Senator Parr's initiative, the Senate investigated the practice.[4]

After graduating from high school, he attended the University of Texas and Southwestern University in Georgetown but did not complete his studies. After three years at the University of Texas Law School, he passed the state bar without graduating. In 1926, at the age of 26, when his brother Givens Parr had enough of Duval County politics, their father—by then the unquestioned ruler of Duval County—tapped 25-year-old George as the new county judge.[5]

Archie Parr spoiled the young Mr. Parr. Not only did he indulge his son, but he also set an example of how to conduct himself as a Parr. Unfortunately, the young man failed to emulate his father in many respects. But his father was not his only role model; Archie's Tejano political associates, who, after all, had daily contact with him, also contributed to his shaping as a politician and a man.

The Parrs's Tejano Collaborators

Throughout the 1920s Duval County continued the pattern of political office holding established after the 1912 massacre at the courthouse. The only offices consistently held by Americanos were the county judge, invariably a Parr family member, and the county attorney. Tejanos dominated the majority of the commissioners court for the entire 1920s and claimed all county commissioners posts in the final four years of the decade. They filled every justice of the peace position except for one term; constables were all Tejanos during this time. Of course, Archie Parr oversaw the county's business, even though he was often absent tending to his Senate duties and constituents throughout the thirty-two-county Senate district. He issued his directives through his sons and key Tejano lieutenants.[6]

George B. Parr in time proved to be a natural politician; his Ivy League–educated older brother, Givens, not so much. Perhaps that is why Archie Parr's brother-in-law, O. G. Allen, replaced Archie in the commissioners court in 1915 when Archie assumed his seat in the Texas Senate: to provide Givens—who took over as county judge—with experienced counsel. Allen had been at Archie's side for some time, mainly in Democratic Party circles. During the 1912 courthouse shooting, while Archie had his hands full assisting his Tejano allies, Allen ran the party apparatus as county chairman. Allen told a Senate committee in 1919 that his role on the political front was as Democratic Party Chairman and election judge during voting. Once George replaced Givens in 1926, Allen stopped serving as county commissioner but retained his party duties.[7]

Table 18.1 Duval County elected officials, 1920–1928

Position	1930	1932	1934	1936	1938
Judge	G. B. Parr	G. B. Parr	G. B. Parr (resigned June 5, 1936) / Dan Tobin	Dan Tobin	Dan Tobin
County Clerk	J. O. Trevino	J. O. Trevino	J. O. Trevino	J. O. Trevino	J. O. Trevino
District Clerk	Liborio Cadena	L. Cadena			H. P. Rogers
Attorney	J. F. Clarkson (died in office Oct. 1932) / F. Lotto	R. F. Luna	R. F. Luna	R. F. Luna	R. F. Luna
Treasurer	Horacio Saenz	Horacio Saenz	Horacio Saenz	Horacio Saenz	Horacio Saenz
Surveyor	R. M. Gonzalez	R. M. Gonzalez	L. M. Brumfield	L. M. Brumfield	L. M. Brumfield
Sheriff	Dan Tobin	Dan Tobin (resigned June 5, 1936) / Daniel U. Garcia	Daniel U. Garcia	Daniel U. Garcia	Daniel U. Garcia
Tax Assessor	Clemente Garcia	Jesus Oliveira	Jesus Oliveira	Clemente Garcia	Clemente Garcia
County Superintendent			R. L. Adame	R. L. Adame	R. L. Adame
Inspector of Hides		Jim Barton (appointed)			

Table 18.1 (Continued)

Position	1930	1932	1934	1936	1938
Tax Collector	Jesus Oliveira	Jesus Oliveira	Jesus Oliveira	Clemente Garcia	Clemente Garcia
Commissioner, Precinct One	J. A. Tobin	Joe A. Tobin	J. A. Tobin (resigned June 5, 1936) / Clemente Garcia	J. A. Tobin	J. A. Tobin
Commissioner, Precinct Two	Jose Hancock	Jose Hancock	Jose Hancock	Jose Hancock	Jose Hancock
Commissioner, Precinct Three	D. C. Chapa	D. C. Chapa	J. C. Turnham	J. C. Turnham	J. C. Turnham
Commissioner, Precinct Four	Evaristo Valerio	Evaristo Valerio	Evaristo Valerio	Felipe Valerio Jr.	Felipe Valerio Jr.
Justice of the Peace, Precinct One	H. P. Rogers	Daniel U. Tobin	Daniel U. Garcia / J. C. Martinez	J. C. Martinez	J. C. Martinez
Justice of the Peace, Precinct Two	W. C. Barton	W. C. Barton	W. C. Barton	W. C. Barton	W. C. Barton
Justice of the Peace, Precinct Three	Prajedis Saenz	Prajedis Saenz	Prajedis Saenz	Prajedis Saenz	Prajedis Saenz
Justice of the Peace, Precinct Four				R. S. Davidson	R. S. Davidson

(Continues)

Table 18.1 (Continued)

Position	1930	1932	1934	1936	1938
Justice of the Peace, Precinct Five	Fidencio Cantu	W. P. Lacy	L. W. Lacy		
Justice of the Peace, Precinct Six	R. A. Flores	Valdemar P. Flores	Baldemar P. Flores	R. S. Flores	R. S. Flores
Justice of the Peace, Precinct Seven	Elirario Villarreal	Elirario Villarreal	Abel Lozano	Fidencio Garcia	Alberto Ayzergoita
Justice of the Peace, Precinct Eight	F. Benavides		F. Benavides		
Justice of the Peace, Precinct Nine		Teodoro Sendejo (resigned)/Manuel Sanchez	Manuel Sanchez (resigned)/Eduardo Perez		
Constable, Precinct One	Teodoro Sendejo			Ed Perez Jr.	Ed Perez Jr.
Constable, Precinct Two	Camilo Ramirez	Camilo Ramirez	Camilo G. Ramirez	Leonardo Chapa Jr.	Leonardo Chapa Jr.
Constable, Precinct Three	George Gonzales	Victor C. Gonzales	Victor C. Gonzales	Felix Vera	Felix Vera
Constable, Precinct Four	A. S. Roach		A. S. Roach	N. C. Pugh	N. C. Pugh

(Continues)

Table 18.1 (Continued)

Position	1930	1932	1934	1936	1938
Constable, Precinct Five	*Desiderio Serna*			*Guadalupe Lopez*	*Guadalupe Lopez*
Constable, Precinct Six	*Fernando Galvan*			*Andres Garcia*	*R. S. Flores*
Constable, Precinct Seven	*Santiago Sanchez*	*J. N. Olivarez*	*Santiago Sanchez*	*Juan N. Olivarez*	*Juan N. Olivarez*
Constable, Precinct Eight					
Constable, Precinct Nine					

Source: Duval County Commissioners Court Minutes and Election Returns, Duval County Clerk. Italicized names indicate Tejanos.

Besides his family, others close to Archie Parr included Eusebio Carrillo, Antonio W. Tobin, Juan O. Treviño, José Angel Heras, and Jesús Oliveira, all becoming part of Archie's inner circle in 1912. These Tejanos' progeny also served Archie and George but were more connected with the younger duke. These men were tested in political combat in the second decade of the twentieth century when Americanos constantly challenged the Parr-Tejano political apparatus in the courts.

Eusebio Carrillo was born in Roma, Texas, on March 5, 1867. He received his education in Texas and was fluent in English. His entry into Duval County politics began in 1890 as a deputy under Sheriff John Buckley; he subsequently worked with Sheriffs Charles K. Gravis and Antonio W. Tobin. In the year of the courthouse massacre, Carrillo was elected county commissioner and served until 1928. When Carrillo resigned in 1928, his son D. C. Chapa replaced him, holding that post through 1934. Following his public career, Carrillo entered the ranching trade and passed away on March 22, 1947. His son, D. C. Chapa, and his grandsons—Oscar, Ramiro, and Olivero—continued his political legacy through the end of the Parr political machine in the mid-1970s.[8]

Antonio W. Tobin was two years older than Archie Parr. As young boys they both experienced the brutal killing of their fathers. Tobin's father, Daniel Tobin, came to Texas from South Carolina and married Josefa Navarro of San Antonio. The 1860 Census lists Daniel Tobin as a Ranger, and by 1872 other sources show him in the position of county clerk in Atascosa County. There, an unknown assailant murdered him in 1872. Having their fathers slain when they were very young may have formed a special kinship between Tobin and Parr. After his father's death, the young Tobin moved to Zapata County, where in 1880 he received his first experience as a law officer, serving as a deputy sheriff. Nine years later he married Gerónima Canales at Benavides and began farming there. At that time he likely became acquainted with Parr, who had also only recently moved to the same part of the country.[9]

Tobin entered politics in 1908 when, a week after Democrats nominated him as "the Parr Ticket" candidate for sheriff, the commissioners court appointed him to replace Charles K. Gravis. That same year, the Duval County Democratic Executive Committee unanimously elected Tobin as

Fig. 18.2 Sheriff Antonio Tobin (1858–1919), patriarch of the Tobin family, was prominent in Duval County through 1975. Courtesy of Ricky Tobin.

their chairman. Then, in December, Duval County elected officials joined Sheriff Tobin in a letter admonishing Lieutenant Governor A. B. Davidson for serving as a defense attorney for the man accused of murdering John Cleary. There was no doubt, including to Archie Parr, that the new sheriff meant to look after the citizens of Duval County in more ways than law enforcement. Tobin's willingness to stand up for his Tejano friends and neighbors was on display seven years later, in August 1915. As the Plan of San Diego gained momentum, Sheriff Tobin dispatched a letter to the editor of the *San Antonio Light* complaining that their Corpus Christi correspondent had erroneously reported that "conditions are becoming serious in San Diego,

Duval County, and that Mexican citizens are arming themselves." Tobin said there was "not a grain of truth in the assertion" and that San Diego had some of the best people in the country except for "the grand liars in this grand state of ours." Undoubtedly, the sheriff aimed his "grand liars" comment at those citizens who challenged, at every opportunity, elected officials who represented the powerless.[10]

Tobin was a leader of his fellow Tejanos. On that fateful day on May 18, 1912, he arrested the three shooters responsible for the spilling of Tejano blood on the courthouse grounds. Later that year the commissioners court named him county judge. These years were a dramatic and tense time for the people of Duval County, especially its Tejano public officials like Sheriff Tobin, because Tejanos expected their officials to lead and protect their hard-earned rights. On the other hand, Americanos saw Tobin and his fellow Tejano officials as usurpers and a threat to Americano supremacy.[11]

At the opening of 1914, on January 20, Duval County taxpayers, including those residing in Duval County and others who merely owned land but lived elsewhere in the area, filed a lawsuit asking the court to restrain county officials from collecting "certain taxes levied for the year 1913." All the twenty-seven named plaintiffs were Americanos. As the tax collector, Antonio W. Tobin was the lead defendant.[12]

The court granted the taxpayers' claim and ordered Tobin not to collect a twenty cent per one hundred dollar valuation tax approved by the commissioners court to build a new courthouse and jail to replace the one that had burned down. Emboldened by their court victory, the property owners called on the court to get Tobin to desist from collecting certain road taxes. Moreover, the court ordered all county officials to make their records available for a financial audit. Parr, Tobin, and other officials resigned in response to the ruling; in this way the remaining commissioners would appoint replacements rather than the district judge.[13]

By the end of 1915, Archie Parr had won a seat in the Texas Senate, and Tobin had returned to his old office when the voters elected him as sheriff. Parr, Tobin, and the Duval voters, overwhelmingly Tejanos, had no fear of the Americano complainants. But Parr saw who his Tejano right-hand was, and Tobin seemed more than ready to represent his *compañeros politicos* (political companions).[14]

Duval County's frequent political storms seemed to have calmed down for the next few years. In 1919, however, the Texas Senate called many Duval County Tejano citizens to Austin to testify in a Senate hearing to determine the winner of the Senate district Parr represented. The issue was how the county managed the poll tax. Tobin told the Senate committee that as tax collector, he oversaw the administration of the poll tax in Duval County. Tobin informed the committee that many poll taxes, probably four or five hundred annually, were paid by written authorization from the voters. In the past, the commissioners court had given road overseers the authority to collect consent from county employees. The road overseers subsequently distributed the poll taxes to the road workers. Occasionally, the post office returned mail from nonexistent addresses that road overseers had assigned to voters. Under cross-examination Tobin acknowledged that it was also customary for merchants and bankers to register voters who lived in remote ranches. A good many people independently paid their poll taxes, Tobin added. He emphasized that this method of issuing poll tax authorizations had been in place since before he became sheriff.[15]

Less than a month after giving his testimony, on March 4, 1919, Tobin died. He fell victim to arteriosclerosis, an affliction contributing to a stroke. He was 61. Two Tejano professionals, Dr. Andrés Tamez and mortician Librado González, attended to him and the widow, Gerónima. Tobin's offspring served as crucial players in Duval County politics through 1975.[16]

A later advisor to Archie Parr, José Ángel Heras, was born in Benavides in 1893; by age 19 he was in partnership with his two older brothers, Valentín and Florencio, in a general merchandise/grocery store in Benavides where their father, Gerónimo, also owned a barber shop. In 1917 José Ángel registered for the draft, with records indicating he was married, had a child, and worked for the Texas Mexican Railroad. Heras had not yet crossed paths with Parr, already a state senator. But the following year, Heras served as the election clerk for Precinct Two and testified in the Senate hearing on the question of Parr's reelection. He told the committee that Parr carried Precinct Two, receiving almost all of the 377 votes cast, half of them being women who presumably had no qualms over Parr's objection to granting women the right to vote.[17]

In 1920 Heras owned a general merchandise store in Benavides, but he eventually moved to the farming and ranching sector, where he worked the land for the remainder of his life. At the outbreak of World War II, the 50-year-old Heras signed up for the Old Man's Draft and, a few months later, in October, served as a pallbearer for Archie Parr, to whom he had been a friend and advisor in Duval political functions outside the public eye. In 1953 Heras also served as a pallbearer for Parr's brother-in-law, O. G. Allen.[18]

There is no record of Heras serving in elected office. His friendship with Archie Parr perhaps emanated from the ranching and farming enterprises they both engaged in. But in 1954 he served as a jury commissioner, whose duties were to name grand and petit jurors. Newly appointed District Judge J. S. Broadfoot removed Heras, J. A. Tobin from San Diego, and Tyson Summy from Freer as jurors because, according to him, they had not used "due care and diligence in selecting fair and impartial grand and petit jurors." Heras died on July 17, 1980.[19]

Juan O. Treviño was born in 1888, and in 1900 he was enrolled in school and spoke and wrote in English. At the age of 24, Treviño made his political debut in 1912 during the tumult of the courthouse massacre. He was a member of the Democratic Party Executive Committee headed by Parr's brother-in-law, O. G. Allen. The young Treviño soon gained the appreciation of Archie Parr and was on his way to an interesting political career.[20]

In October 1917 the governor's office received a complaint that accused, among other things, Treviño of helping young men evade the draft. Nothing came out of the investigation, and on November 18, 1919, the Duval County Commissioners Court appointed Treviño to finish the term of Sheriff J. F. Sáenz, who had passed away suddenly. The new sheriff soon faced questions as to his role in the 1918 reelection of his friend Archie Parr. Sheriff Treviño confessed before the Texas Senate committee investigating the 1919 Parr-Glasscock race that he had received the election results and that he and County Judge Clarkson had destroyed them after ninety days, even though both knew an election contest was looming. They had done so because the county needed the election boxes for the next election.[21]

The young sheriff was still in for more grief during his tenure. In 1919 Texas Rangers alleged that Sheriff Treviño was involved in an illicit liquor smuggling operation. In a separate report, Ranger J. J. Edds wrote that a confidential source had revealed that Sheriff Treviño and the Duval County attorney controlled the illegal liquor business in San Diego. "They have two or three men constantly making trips to the border and bring mescal, aguardiente to San Diego in wagon loads," Edds reported. No charges ever ensued regarding these accusations. Notwithstanding his entanglements, Juan O. Treviño's participation in Duval County politics continued on September 30, 1922, when County Clerk J. V. Palacios resigned, and the commissioners court named Treviño as Palacios's replacement. Treviño's tenure as county clerk and association with the Parr family political operation continued through 1950. On January 3, 1953, Treviño passed away in his San Diego home.[22]

Another Parr devotee, Jesús Oliveira, followed a path parallel to Treviño's. Oliveira grew up on a farm in the Benavides area, but his place of birth is nebulous. He consistently indicated to census takers that he was born in Texas and spoke and wrote in English, but his draft registration showed his birthplace as Paras, Nuevo León. Perhaps he felt being foreign-born would minimize his chances of being drafted, although he conceded to being a "naturalized citizen." Oliveira reportedly helped his cousin, Leopoldo Romano, once a Duval County deputy, to escape military service when Romano deserted the army at Fort Funston in Kansas on July 21, 1918. According to Bureau of Investigation officers, Oliveira facilitated Romano's getaway from San Antonio to Laredo, where the defector crossed into Mexico.[23]

Like Tobin, Heras, and Treviño, Oliveira testified before the Senate committee investigating the 1918 senate election. He told the committee that he served as the election judge for Precinct Ten, where people cast 270 votes: all the votes went to Parr and the senator's preferred candidates in other races. Oliveira revealed he knew as much because he filled out all the ballots as the only one at that precinct with a mastery of English. According to the report of the *Houston Post*, Oliveira explained to the committee that "the voters told him they wanted to vote for Mr. Parr and for all the men Mr. Parr wanted to be elected; they did not know all the men running, but they knew there was a Parr ticket, and that was what they wanted; he too knew who

Mr. Parr wanted . . . whenever Mr. Parr wanted anything then the people of his box wanted him to have it."[24]

The following year, in 1920, Oliveira entered the political arena, following in the footsteps of his father, Crescencio. The elder Oliveira served as Precinct Two constable from 1894 to 1910. In 1920 Jesús won the Duval County sheriff's seat and held the post through 1926. He next won an appointment to the office of tax collector, which he held until 1932, when Texas adopted a constitutional amendment combining the office of assessor and collector. From 1934 to 1936, Oliveira served in the combined office of county tax assessor and collector.[25]

Gradually, however, Oliveira distanced himself from elective office but continued a close relationship with Archie Parr. In 1931 he joined the Parr family as the lone Tejano director of the Texas State Bank of Alice, which served as Duval County's depository. Oliveira also joined Senator Parr as a Duval County Board of Welfare and Employment Committee member. Finally, in 1942, he, Heras, and Treviño paid their final homage to Archie Parr, serving as pallbearers at his funeral ceremonies.[26]

Although having been in the private sector for some time, Oliveira did not escape the political controversies that dogged George B. Parr. In the 1950s and through the mid-1960s, Oliveira came under the scrutiny of state and federal investigations launched against George B. Parr and his associates. For Oliveira it started in 1954 following his reentrance into politics. He had won back his old office of tax assessor-collector but immediately faced indictments of theft as director at the Texas State Bank of Alice. To avoid prosecution Oliveira resigned from the post minutes after being sworn in as tax assessor-collector under the Parr ticket. The commissioners court quickly chose his son Luis to fill the empty seat.

As to the Oliveira patriarch, following several appeals, the US Supreme Court dismissed the charges against him. He died on January 10, 1964, and his long association with the Parr machine ended. His sons continued the family's involvement in politics with mixed results. Luis Oliveira lost the tax assessor-collector seat to a Parr adversary in 1956. Jesús Oliveira Jr., however, continued his father's legacy by running as a Parr candidate in 1960 and prevailed over two opponents. He held the office of tax assessor-collector until

1974, when he died of a heart attack at 55. His widow, Luz, assumed the post, but two years later, in 1976, she faced a tax delinquent lawsuit, and her political career ended abruptly. The Oliveira-Parr political link came to an end.[27]

Tobin, Carrillo, Treviño, Heras, Oliveira, and others who served as friends and political soldiers for Archie Parr continued to be part of Duval County politics under George B. Parr. After the Parr reign ended, these families remained rightfully proud of their ancestral legacy but, at the same time, may have sought to distance themselves from the politics of the past and to move forward to create historical memories for their children and grandchildren, one of political independence from the Parr era but not from their ancestors, to whom they owed much. They have continued to stand on their accomplishments as public servants, lawyers, doctors, educators, ranchers, farmers, and other public service fields.

George's First Run-In with the Feds

While the young Parr's initial years as county judge were one of learning and adjustment to the job, in March 1932 the Internal Revenue Service handed him a wake-up call. The government obtained an indictment against him for failing to report a $25,000 fee he received from a contractor working in the Rio Grande Valley. Parr made a $5,000 bond and was released. Despite the troubling episode, in July 1932 Duval County Democrats again renominated George B. Parr for county judge and every incumbent, all Tejanos, for reelection.[28]

After two years of delay, Judge Parr went before the law. The IRS investigator informed the court that the $25,000 Parr failed to report came from a check Parr had signed and had the money returned to him in "small bills." The agent added that Parr had been accepting money from "gambling concessions" and failed to report it as income. Moreover, the revenue agent testified that from 1928 to 1932, Parr had received $25,000 annually from illegal gambling houses. Finally, the agent told the judge that when he had gone to Parr's office to review his records, Parr had told him, "I don't give a damn about the government's time or money." Parr defended his reaction to the agent's "brusque" manner.[29]

"We have here a county judge taking cash in a little black bag directly from a road estimate check and receiving gambling money. He is not being tried for that, but it at least shows a motive for failure to file an income tax on it," the prosecuting attorney told the court. Parr pled guilty to income tax evasion and received a $5,000 fine and a two-year probated sentence.[30]

As a convicted felon, George B. Parr had to relinquish his county judge's seat and could not vote. But he could help his father run their political operation. However, Parr soon found himself facing legal problems. His deer-hunting habit drew him into difficulty with area game wardens. Parr and his hunting party trespassed on the fifty-five-thousand-acre Dobie Ranch northwest of Freer, extending to LaSalle and Webb Counties. After being found guilty in county court and the verdict confirmed by the district court, he had to pay a fine of $91.95. It was the second of many negative encounters with the law.[31]

Unlike his father, who reportedly had a mild-mannered approach to life, George B. Parr began to reveal a cocky, vulgar, and do-not-care attitude. Perhaps it revealed a spoiled upbringing or intoxication with power or both. It was a behavior that he exhibited for the rest of his life. His feeling of invincibility in Duval County and his temper would get him in frequent trouble. His reaction to the IRS investigators was only the beginning of his public displays of anger. He acted similarly with the game wardens when he appeared in court, and later, in 1936, he flared up at former State Representative J. T. Canales and slapped him "mightily" in the Duval County Courthouse.[32]

The federal prosecutor used these incidents and others—such as failing to report to his probation officer, engaging in the "illegal liquor business," and taking money from gamblers—against him to revoke his probation in 1936 and send him to serve time behind bars. An appeal for executive clemency delayed his transfer to federal prison in Oklahoma only temporarily. His father's hand was undoubtedly behind a last-minute initiative to gain his son's freedom. The appeal failed, and in July 1936 a federal marshal transported him from the Bexar County jail to El Reno federal prison in Oklahoma. Shortly after arriving there, prison authorities certified Parr as a teacher, and he led classes for "illiterate partners" in reading, writing, and arithmetic.[33]

Less than a year later, however, the federal parole board released Parr, and he returned home to San Diego, where he resumed his life outside as before, except for not being able to serve in public office. By then Archie Parr's time as duke was winding down. It was a bittersweet time for Archie, who loved George but had to continuously reach out to his friends in high places to help his son. At home Archie still had his Tejano supporters who comforted him during a father's trying time. Among them were Heras, Treviño, and Oliveira, and two of Antonio Tobin's sons who were now active in the county/family business.

Daniel Tobin became county judge upon resigning from his sheriff's post in 1936 when federal authorities hauled George B. Parr off to prison; with the addition of a Tejano County attorney, R. F. Luna, every countywide office and all but one commissioner after the mid-1930s were Tejanos. Most of them held the same office through the early 1950s. Tobin kept the post until he died in 1949. Judge Tobin's brother, J. A. Tobin, served as county commissioner for San Diego for all the decade of the 1930s. While this record of Tejanos' incumbency sounds impressive, it also mirrored Parr's method of leadership, to keep company, preferably, with family and a few people he trusted.

Tejanos Flourished in Favorable *Convenio Político* (Political Pact)

However, politics was not the only area where Tejanos prominently contributed to Duval County's history and progress during this time. While they had always been part of the commercial establishment, Tejano businesses multiplied during the Parr era from 1912 to 1975. Successful enterprises in San Diego included: *La Libertad* (Francisco F. P. Gonzales, editor), Cuéllar Motor Company, the Chevrolet dealership (C. and A. B. Cuéllar, proprietors), Bruno Rios Drug Company, Martínez Gin (C. and R. Martínez, owners), O. G. García & Company, R. S. González Dry Goods, F. G. García & Son Garage, Jim's Café (Santiago Castañón, proprietor), Southwest

Texas Distributing Company (J. C. Pérez, manager), Manuel Olivares & Company General Merchandise, R. G. Solis (painter and sign maker), M. Pruneda Barber Shop, Ladislao Fresnillo (chocolate maker), Cirino Cárdenas Grocery, C. H. Hinojosa & Company, José L. García Barber Shop, *La Voz, Seminario Independiente de Información* (Carlos Peña, publisher, and Servando Cárdenas, editor), Teatro Río (Abel C. Ramírez, operator), Royal Cleaners (Santos Ibañes, proprietor), José O. Martínez (merchant), Juan G. García (realtor), F. G. García & Son Texaco Products, the Duck's Quack (J. R. López, proprietor), San Diego Bakery, Garza Barber Shop, Dr. Eulogio Garza (dentist), Ramírez Art Printing, Cash System Store (Jesús Garza, manager), San Diego Clinical and X-Ray Laboratory (Arnoldo García, director), Morales Funeral Home, Franklin & Schwarz Appliances Company (Pedro Ramírez, agent), San Diego Hospital (Dr. A. Duran, Dr. R. Rocha Garfias, and Dr. George G. Wyche), Gongora's Flower Shop, Regis Drug Company (David Hinojosa, pharmacist), Modern Cleaners (Chema Treviño, proprietor), Peña Barber Shop (E. Peña, owner), and F. G. García & Son Ford Dealership (Dan U. García, president). Tejanos not only operated mom-and-pop stores in the barrios but also managed dealerships for some of the most prominent corporate brands in the country, such as Chevrolet, Ford, and Texaco.[34]

In Benavides, similarly, several Tejanos owned and operated commercial enterprises, including De Leon Household Appliances, Empress Theater (Andrés Farías, owner), the Benavides Drug Store (J. R. De León and R. García, owners), Piggly Wiggly Grocery (F. Vaello, proprietor), Texas Café (Mr. and Mrs. Joe Trujillo), and Faust Café (M. Ramírez, vendor).[35]

Even though Freer had a newspaper, extant copies are unavailable to researchers. The 1940 Census provided some information. Although Freer had a thriving commercial community, the census reflects only two Tejano business owners. They were Antonio Canales, who operated a grocery store, and Jesús Rodriguez, who owned a butcher shop.

As indicated in the 1940 census, many Tejanos held professional positions, including 4 doctors, 3 pharmacists, 5 school administrators, and a lawyer. Comprising the trade category were 42 barbers, 21 mechanics, 20 butchers, 8 bakers, and 2 printers. Government workers in the county numbered 105, with 94 percent being Tejanos. The one occupation where Tejanos did not do well was the new and expanding oil-field economy, where only 36, or 4 percent, of the 924 oilfield-related workers were Tejanos.

The business and professional sectors were not the only areas where Tejanos enjoyed success and strengthened Duval County institutions. During the Parr era, they made their mark in education. In 1932, for example, every San Diego school board member was a Tejano, as was the librarian. The teaching staff included 24 teachers, the majority being Tejanos. At the time of the 1940 Census enumeration, the county had 112 teachers, with 62 being Tejanos and Tejanas—55 percent. In March 1932 the San Diego school board selected Maria García as superintendent. From that point forward, except for a brief period in the mid-1960s, every San Diego school district superintendent was a Tejano or Tejana. By comparison, no area school district employed a Tejano superintendent until the last quarter of the century.

Compared to other South Texas counties, where Tejanos were belittled, denigrated, and suppressed at every turn, *la gente* (the people) in Duval County lived under circumstances that allowed them to create and maintain social systems that encouraged the community's growth, reinforced their cultural identity, and encouraged success. Derisive attitudes toward Tejanos prevailed in surrounding counties in the Coastal Bend, and Americanos practiced open and hostile discrimination in schools and public places. Those in authority relegated Tejanos to the most menial and low-paying jobs. In contrast, the Parr political machine, in which Tejanos were involved partners, provided an advantageous environment where they could confidently aim for their rightful role in the American dream.

Tejano Civil Rights leader Alonso S. Perales perceived the constructive roles Tejanos played in Duval County. In 1937 he presciently observed, "As Mexican Americans from San Antonio and other places, we rejoice and feel pride upon seeing our fellow Mexican American citizens from Duval, Webb, Zapata, and Starr guide their communities towards the future."[36] He added that Mexican Americans over "the entire world, feel at home" in those counties that are totally "devoid of racial prejudice and symbolize the ideal circumstance that no doubt existed in the minds, souls, and hearts of Antonio Navarro and Francisco Ruiz, signers of the Texas Declaration of

Independence." Little did he know that Navarro's great-grandson, Daniel Tobin, was then county judge of Duval County. Perales pointed to these counties and communities as models of governance, public spirit, and progress. They were managed as effectively by Tejanos as were counties governed by Americanos.[37]

George B. Parr Returns from Prison and Finds the Nation and Tejanos Preparing for War

In January 1938, after his two-year sentence expired, George B. Parr was free to return to the political scene. However, he could not hold office as a convicted felon, even under his father Archie's influence. Nevertheless, George B. Parr longed to flex his political muscle. He arranged to appear as a private citizen before the Duval County Commissioners Court to propose that the court call an election to gain voter approval for $1.6 million in road bonds. A delegation of oil company representatives pointed out that they would be responsible for paying back 75 percent of the bonds. They asked commissioners to include more specificity regarding how many miles of roads the county would overlay and which routes the highways would take. Parr pressed the commissioners to pay no attention to the oil company officials and approve his request, which they did without hesitation. The court scheduled an election for the following month, asking voters for authorization. Predictably, the proposition passed.[38]

Parr's endeavor at a political comeback was hastened in 1940 when President Franklin D. Roosevelt's reelection campaign named him its finance chairman for Duval County. Other committee members, mostly Tejanos, included J. R. de León, chairman, F. Vaello Puig from Benavides, County Judge Tobin, Daniel U. García from San Diego, and Frank Williams from Freer. Then, in a somewhat ironic twist, Governor Coke Stevenson named Parr to the Duval County Parole Board. It was strange because Parr's duties included watching over men released on probation—which applied to himself—and helping them rebuild their lives. A second irony was that Governor Stevenson would, eight years later, become possibly the most vigorous Parr hater after the duke deprived him of a seat in the US Senate.[39]

While George B. Parr was rebuilding his political dossier, other, more critical issues beckoned people's attention. The war in Europe, which started spreading across the continent in 1939, grew and expanded every month in 1940. It quickly impacted the United States, calling men to the armed services. Duval County Tejano communities and rancherías wasted no time standing up for the country. In 1940 Tejano leaders at the courthouse set the example, urging their fellow Tejanos to register for the draft. Among the 32 early registrants were 24 Tejanos and 8 Americanos, including County Attorney Reynaldo Luna (43 years old), County Commissioners Juan Antonio Tobin and Felipe Valerio, Sheriff Daniel U. García, and several deputy sheriffs and clerks. As the conflict became real for Americans after the Pearl Harbor attack of December 7, 1941, some 904 Duval County residents signed up for military service. Of these, 644 were Tejanos and 260 Americanos, primarily newcomers to the county, brought in by the oil fields around Freer and Benavides.[40]

Of the nearly 1,000 men who joined the war campaign, 24 died in combat. Those making the ultimate sacrifice included Otilio C. Benavides, Raymundo Bustos, Ireneo Canales Jr., Victoriano Casas, and John F. Champion Jr. Also left on the battlefields of Europe were Rodolfo M. Dávila, Richard Donahue, Eladio E. García, Librado García, Gilberto Guerra, Joe B. Guerra, and J. R. Harrison. Others killed in action were Santos Ibáñez Jr., Marcos C. Martínez, Rodolfo Mireles, Severo Morin, Manuel D. Ramos, and Agapito V. Sánchez. Finally, Regino B. Sánchez, Israel Soliz, Olegario C. Soliz, José M. Treviño Jr., Robert L. Treviño, and Carl E. Woodward also sacrificed their lives.[41]

Thirteen other Duval County men in uniform perished during the war but not on the killing fields. Three, Ruben Chapa, José A. Garza, and Ramiro Garza, passed away later from wounds suffered on the battlefield. Others who died outside combat areas (including training and maneuver deaths) included Val T. Albritten, Francisco Flores, Néstor M. Garza, James J. Higgins, John D. Ray, Blas C. Soto Jr., and Reynaldo Trejo. Finally, the army declared three Duval County missing service members as "presumed dead"; this determination allowed their families to receive survivor benefits. The three Duval County soldiers categorized as missing were Fidel Flores, Natividad R. Rangel, and A. D. Robert Jr. The final tally of Duval County soldiers declared dead as a result of their participation was thirty-seven.[42]

While not a Duval County resident then, Archer Parr, George's nephew, registered for the draft in Goliad, where his mother, Mrs. R. A. Thompson, lived during the war. He served in the Marine Corps and earned the Bronze Star Medal. Archer went on to serve as Duval County judge on several occasions. Also, George's older brother, Givens, registered for the draft in Jim Wells County at age 50, as did George's younger brother Atlee, 38, who signed up for the draft at Benavides. Eleven of Atlee's Tejano ranch employees also registered for the draft.[43]

Unlike World War I, there was no question about Duval County Tejanos' patriotism, as their predecessors experienced during the first war. They were ready to serve and defend. The same patriotism existed with soldiers' families back home.

George B. Parr did not volunteer to wear the uniform. But he did begin engaging in his community's World War II effort. In April 1942 Texas Attorney General Gerald C. Mann named Parr head of the Navy Relief Society Citizens Committee in Duval County. The following month, Parr assumed the position of chair of the defense bond effort, tasked with raising $8,400.[44]

Investigations, Indictments, and Convictions Started to Mount in 1950

On February 20, 1946, President Harry Truman restored George B. Parr's civil rights with the pardon he sought. After Parr underwent social and political rehabilitation, he left no doubts that he was ready to assume the mantle of the duke of Duval; however, it was unlikely that the mild-mannered Archie Parr could have imagined where his son would take the Parr legacy. During George B. Parr's rule in Duval County from 1942 to 1975, there was one controversy after another. The press bemoaned his tactics, but they could count on Parr to sell newspapers.[45]

While his father, as a state senator, influenced most South Texas politics, many counties in his district, especially those on the border with Mexico—such as Webb, Zapata, Starr, Hidalgo, and Cameron—operated under political bosses. These men were friends and political associates of the senator, but they ruled their counties, not Parr. George mistakenly believed that he had inherited control over this area but soon realized the nature of the bosses' relationship was not that of subservience to Parr but as equals.[46]

While well entrenched in Duval as political boss after Archie Parr's death, George also had a hand in neighboring Jim Wells County affairs, where he had been active since 1941. George B. Parr earned notoriety from his involvement in the 1948 US Senate election. Without belaboring the facts of that incident, which are well-known to most readers, Parr maneuvered election results in Jim Wells County to swing the statewide race from Governor Coke Stevenson to Lyndon B. Johnson. That enraged the state Democratic pols in Austin for years, and they took every opportunity to clip Parr's political wings.

Beginning in 1954 Austin power brokers used all the influence at their disposal to do just that. On February 3, 1954, before the Federated Women's Club in San Antonio, Governor Allan Shivers declared that Texas had no room "for political thieves and ballot gangsters." He added that he was committed to "cleaning up the mess in Duval County." Governor Shivers requested the Texas attorney general, the Texas Education Agency, the Department of Public Safety, and the Bureau of the Internal Revenue Service to coordinate an investigation of Duval County entities' expenditures of public funds.[47]

Meanwhile, Attorney General John Ben Shepherd partnered with Governor Shivers to bring Parr down and aggressively pursued an investigation of Duval County. Shivers was also willing to use all state and federal assets to "stamp out" the political mess in Duval County and believed they could do it before the end of 1954. The governor added the state had been working on the problem for a long time.[48]

Attorney General Shepherd also noted that the US Postal Service and the state auditor were part of the investigative effort. State, school, welfare, and highway funds had already been under careful examination for a year. Investigators found that 105 vouchers totaling $57,464 were paid to fictitious individuals, and another 24 checks went to persons who had not worked for the payments. The governor said his focus was to end the political corruption in a place where "the light of freedom has almost been snuffed out."[49]

On February 3, 1954, the Duval County Grand Jury began investigating the use of public-school funds in Benavides. One of the first witnesses was

Diego Heras, who had served as the acting secretary of the Benavides Independent School District until nine months before his grand jury appearance.
Since Parr's political ally, District Judge Woodrow Laughlin, named the grand
jury, the Texas attorney general feared it would "whitewash" those involved.
"Evidence now in our hands is conclusive. It has been common knowledge
in your county for several months that violations of our criminal laws have
occurred and that we have evidence of them," Attorney General Shepherd
wrote to the grand jury.[50]

The *Corpus Christi Caller* reported that, with federal and state
investigators creeping all over the county, George B. Parr "had become
a bitter, if not fearful man." Parr was not taking kindly to investigators
poking their noses into his business. And yet, there they were, at the
schools, the courthouse, the post offices, and the banks. Indeed, reporter
James Rowe observed that Parr's usually cheerful and welcoming smile
was fading. Perhaps the boss saw things beginning to crumble from within.
For example, Heras, who served as secretary of the Benavides School
Board from 1940 to 1951 and as its tax collector for six months before
the board fired him, was cooperating with investigators. When the school
dismissed him, Heras took some financial records with him, which impli-
cated Parr in wrongdoing.[51]

Meanwhile, at the beginning of February 1954, the governor and attorney
general continued to fling uncomplimentary remarks about Duval County's
residents, most of whom did not take the disparagement well. A reporter
for the *San Antonio Light* pointed out that Duval County Tejanos wanted to
make it known that "there are honest folks in Duval County just as there are
elsewhere." These people expressed the same views that Parr had hurled at
Governor Shivers two years earlier when he said, "Even as Governor Shivers
resents the encroachment of federal power on states' rights, so do we rebel
against the state trying to run the affairs of the county without regard to the
will of the majority."[52]

State and county investigators received clarity about who should
control the Duval County inquiry when Administrative Judge W. R. Blalock
appointed Harlingen District Judge Arthur Klein to lead the investigation.
Attorney General Shepherd asked Judge Klein to grant immunity to Heras,

Alvaro Guevara, and Eusebio Carrillo Jr., which he did and had armed guards escort the men to meetings with investigators and the grand jury. The three were to testify about the "misappropriation, mishandling, and misuse" of Benavides school money.[53]

In light of the ongoing scrutiny, local Benavides leaders, who had been supporters of Parr, now joined the movement for change. Joe and Jimmy Vaello, with the Mercantile Exchange Bank in Benavides, and Dr. J. C. González demanded from Parr that he remove School Tax Collector D. C. Chapa and his son, Board President Oscar Carrillo, immediately. The investigation that had been working underground for more than a year had become public, and people took notice, calling for a break from the past. The first week of February 1954, the Benavides School Board and Tax Collector Carrillo resigned en masse. Joe Vaello was named school board president and promptly pointed out that school officials were not Parr's "henchmen" and were not against him unless he was found guilty.[54]

Meanwhile, Shepherd continued to battle the Duval County Grand Jury, which appeared determined to conduct its investigation independently. Undeterred by local resistance, state and local investigators pressed forward, looking into the use of public funds, while the IRS examined Parr's tax returns. On February 10, 1954, State Auditor C. A. Caveness had seven investigators, assisted by two detectives from the comptroller's office, reviewing financial records at the county and the San Diego and Benavides School Districts. Over the February 5–8 weekend, eight hundred checks disappeared from the county courthouse, prompting Judge Klein to order county and school officials to stop destroying public records. The attorney general informed the judge that since the state launched its investigation, "various books, records, accounts, canceled checks and receipts and invoices" from the county and schools had disappeared. The probe, however, cast a wide net, and many, some perhaps innocent, were being dragged in.[55]

Despite disagreements from constituents, Parr remained in good standing with much of the Duval County Tejano population. "*Es de muy buen corazón*" (He has a very good heart), Deputy Manuel Amaya told a reporter with the *San Antonio Express and News*. Amaya added, "The people like him. There is no secret why we support him politically—it is because we appreciate him." Parr indicated that whatever power he had came from the people.[56]

"They say I am a dictator and that I control votes," Parr continued. "The truth is that I don't control a single vote. I couldn't even control my wife's vote when I was married." Moreover, the don claimed it was not his organization but that of his constituents. Parr declared he had always helped people and would continue to meet families' needs, financial or otherwise.[57]

"If he liked the people so much, he would give them a better opportunity to prosper and progress," Donato Serna, a World War II veteran, told the reporter. "We want to move ahead; we want our children to have opportunities that were denied to us." Serna was a Purple Heart and Bronze Star recipient from the war in the Pacific. The *Express* reporter described him as "a slightly built, meek-looking man whose appearance, talk, and manner belies his courage." The war veteran said, "I hold no bitterness for George B. Parr. I don't hate him personally. I hate and will fight his system. Stealing is bad, but a system of stealing is terrible."[58]

Freedom Party and Other Fissures in Parr Machine

As Parr faced assorted legal troubles during the 1950s, challenges to his power began to appear. The most significant test of Parr's *Partido Viejo* (Old Party), as locals called George B. Parr's party in Spanish, came from a group of Tejano World War II veterans who formed the Freedom Party with the intent to challenge the longstanding power of the duke of Duval. The veterans, who had been overseas fighting for the American way of life, freedom, liberty, civil and human rights, and economic autonomy, believed it was time for Duval County to partake in the American dream. They had returned home with vivid reminders of the price they had paid for freedom. Some had battle wounds, and all had experienced the horrors of war. Back in Duval they could see more clearly than ever that their war experience would have been for nothing unless they took the battle cry of freedom to their backyard.

In an interview with Jesenia Guerra, who in 2005 was working on a master's thesis at Texas A&M University–Kingsville, Donato Serna recalled the party's inception. In early 1952 Serna informed Guerra that Carlos Barrera, a Duval County deputy sheriff, awoke Serna at 11:00 p.m. with a message from Barrera's boss, Sheriff Daniel U. García. The sheriff wanted Serna to meet him at Arnulfo Farias's grocery store in San Diego. Upon his arrival at the location, Serna found several of his fellow veterans with Sheriff García, a longtime Parr confidante. To their amazement García confided to the group that he had decided to challenge Parr for county judge in the next election. From this meeting emerged the idea of a Freedom Party, those present taking an oath "that if harm befell any of them, the others would 'get' George Parr." The seven would-be founders were undoubtedly encouraged by this plan to launch a new organization.[59]

On March 26, 1952, the group formally organized the Freedom Party in Benavides. New Freedom Party Secretary Manuel D. García announced that the membership would put up a complete ticket for the upcoming Democratic Party Primary on July 26. García accused the Duval County administration under County Judge George B. Parr as having its "prime objective" practices "so ably displayed by the dictators of our time and others before them."[60] "The time has come to change the old ways of our grandparents and follow the example of other modern countries, and if we can't be better than them, at least be their equal," Manuel Sánchez, president, Duval County Freedom Party, told Spanish-language Corpus Christi newspaper *La Libertad* in 1952.[61]

Freedom Party President Sanchez explained the challengers' frustration in a July 18, 1952, interview with a Corpus Christi radio station. Duval County needed new industries and jobs, he said. It required progress that could bring about change to their oppressive conditions. The veterans expected "justice and equality for all." To accomplish this mission, they first had to end political corruption, moral decadence, and the conditions that had impoverished their families, friends, and neighbors.[62]

In a conversation with a friendly *Laredo Times* reporter, Jack Yeaman, Parr tried to counter the veterans' assertions. Parr went back one hundred years, speaking of the setbacks Tejanos suffered under Americanos' rule. He explained what Tejanos experienced under "Anglo Americans with little understanding of the problems or customs" of their Tejano neighbors and who were out to get what they could. He talked about the carpetbaggers who came after the Civil War "to reap the harvest of their victory," despoiling

Tejanos. Furthermore, the railroad drew to Duval County "more of the northern strangers" who knew the English language and the law, exercised "complete political control," and had their way with the local inhabitants. For his part, Parr stressed, he had, since assuming the leadership mantle, followed his father's guiding principle: "They run their own show, their own way." George B. Parr elaborated that he only played the "adviser and mediator" if misunderstandings arose.[63]

In 1952 George B. Parr was hardly an advisor and mediator amid the Freedom Party's challenge. Instead, he proclaimed to the *Laredo Times* reporter, "On the border, we fry our own chickens, and we kill our own snakes," which the admiring journalist interpreted to mean that the people "preferred to celebrate their own victories and settle their own problems without outside interference." After speaking with rich and poor Americano and Tejano, the *Times* reporter concluded that Duval County had one of the best road networks in South Texas and schools rated as good or better as any other in the region. Parr financed many local young men's education and business ventures, including veterans.[64]

The Freedom Party's leader, Sánchez, denounced the Parr machine for forgetting the people. Parr and his assistants, nearly all Tejanos, had little interest in the county's rural schools, which were no better than "shacks," dangerous for the children who walked miles on muddy roads to attend classes—hardly the account the Laredo reporter had made. Meanwhile, the elite who served under Parr sent their children to schools in Alice, Corpus Christi, and San Antonio.[65]

Ten years later, Dr. E. E. Dunlap echoed Sánchez's condemnation when recreating a conversation with George B. Parr in the early 1940s. After Dr. Dunlap explained his views on education, Parr replied, "Doctor, if you educate a Mexican, he is as smart as you are, and then you can't control him. If we had good schools, the oil field workers will settle down and put their children in school here in Duval County; we can't control that type of people. If our schools are bad, the Anglos will live in Alice and elsewhere, putting their children in better schools and driving to work, but they won't vote here." In agreement with Sánchez, the doctor disclosed, "The most condemning fact concerning our schools is the fact that now and, in the past, all the members of the school board of trustees, that could afford to do so, have sent their children away to private or boarding schools."[66]

Meanwhile, the parents of the children in the Duval County schools, out of necessity, traveled out of the county to find decent-paying jobs. With reasonable work unavailable in Duval County except for the supporters of Parr's political machine, they put themselves in danger on the highways, running the risk of having an accident just to provide for their families.

News of the rise of the Freedom Party and attacks on his regime did not escape Parr's attention. When Sheriff García resigned, Parr took preemptive action. He stepped down as county judge to fill the sheriff position, and Dan Tobin Jr. took his place as county judge. Meanwhile, the Freedom Party announced its slate of candidates, including Carlos McDermott as their candidate for sheriff to take on Parr. McDermott was a Bataan Death March survivor.

In preparation for the election, the Freedom Party began holding political rallies throughout Duval County. On June 7, 1952, a caravan of seventy-seven cars, escorted by two Texas Rangers, paraded throughout the county promoting the Freedom Party platform, concluding their excursion in Freer in front of the American Legion Hall, where District Judge Sam Reams declared his "one thousand percent support" for the Freedom Party. The judge added that Parr was running scared. On July 6, 1952, an estimated 1,000 people checked out a Freedom Party rally in Ramirez, and the following weekend, on July 13, 1,200 came to hear the Freedom Party's candidates at the Dan Foster Ranch near Freer. Of the 30 Freedom Party candidates, all but 2 were Tejanos.[67]

Table 18.2 Freedom Party candidates, primary election, July 26, 1952

Candidate	Office
Donato Serna	County Judge
Carlos T. McDermott	County Sheriff
Lawrence H. Warburton Jr.	County Attorney
Ponciano Ruiz	County Tax Assessor & Collector
Eligio A. Saenz	County Clerk
Gilberto A. Hinojosa	County Treasurer

(Continues)

Table 18.2 (Continued)

Candidate	Office
Robert Leo	County School Superintendent
Pedro R. Sendejo	District Clerk
Matias D. Garcia	Chairman, County Committee
Mateo Valadez	County Commissioner, Precinct One
Raymundo Garcia	County Commissioner, Precinct Two
Dan R. Foster	County Commissioner, Precinct Three
Enrique Lichtenberger	County Commissioner, Precinct Four
Louis Rogers	Chairman, Voting Precinct One
Ismael Chapa	Chairman, Voting Precinct Three
Adan Rodriguez	Chairman, Voting Precinct Seven
Leonides Gonzalez	Chairman, Voting Precinct Eight
Amando Cantu	Chairman, Voting Precinct Fourteen
Serafin Guevara	Chairman, Voting Precinct Two
Mrs. Clarice Long Wilkins	Chairman, Voting Precinct Twelve
Jose D. Ramos	Chairman, Voting Precinct Five
Raul Ramirez	Justice of the Peace, Precinct One
Eduardo Pena	Justice of the Peace, Precinct Seven
Amando L. Garcia	Constable, Precinct One
Enrique Chapa	Constable, Precinct Three
Antonio Recio	Constable, Precinct Seven
Pablo F. Flores	Constable, Precinct Fourteen
Juan G. Alaniz	Constable, Precinct Six
Dan Adami Jr.	Constable, Precinct Eight
Juan E. Valerio	Constable, Precinct Five

Source: TSLAC.

Despite the enthusiasm of Freedom Party supporters, Parr's Old Party swept the election. The patron outpolled his opponent for sheriff, war hero McDermott, by a margin of 2,952 to 961.[68]

Parr, meanwhile, resigned from the sheriff's position on October 1, before the general election, and the commissioners court named Archer Parr, the Duke's nephew, as his replacement. Archer Parr was a decorated World

War II veteran, making his political debut like his Freedom Party counterparts. He easily held off three write-in candidates in the general election that
November 1952.[69]

Responding to complaints from constituents, Governor Shivers
directed Homer Garrison, head of the Texas Department of Public Safety,
to look into protests that Parr's followers were harassing Freedom Party
members. According to some complainants, one particular criticism was
that Parr's deputy sheriffs, mostly Tejanos, drove by Freedom Party
members' homes and used floodlights to expose their living quarters in
the middle of the night.[70]

Freedom Party members Donato Serna, J. L. McDonald, Manuel
Sánchez, Cristóbal Ybáñez, and Manuel Marroquín complained to a federal
panel in Houston that they were targets of Parr's angry tendencies. The
complainants said they believed that their lives and those of their families
stood in danger, as Duval County deputies were prone to do anything that
Parr dictated. Moreover, they contended that Parr's political success rested
on the sustained "use of threats, violence, and economic pressure to control
the electorate of Duval County to the extent that his candidates received
99 percent of all votes cast in all primary and general elections." Serna
alleged that Parr had not only interfered with his business and intimidated
his customers, but on one occasion, the duke had "pistol whipped" him.
After Parr had him arrested, Serna claimed that Parr struck him in the head
with a flashlight.[71]

Similar harassment visited McDonald, Sánchez, Marroquín, and
Ybáñez. McDonald, who had a special Texas Ranger commission, said that
Parr, on two occasions, had him arrested and menaced him. Parr and his
lieutenants spread the word around Sánchez's neighborhood not to shop at
his small grocery store; the boycott practically killed his business. Further,
Sheriff Archer Parr had raided the Sánchez home and threatened his wife
when Sánchez was not present. Marroquin, who operated a tortilla factory,
complained that George B. Parr and Juan "Canante" Barrera had vowed
to kill him and everyone present at his business establishment during a
Freedom Party political meeting. Ybáñez stated that while talking with
friends on San Diego's main street, George B. Parr confronted him with a

Winchester rifle. Ybáñez's crime was that he had laughed at Parr. The politico then tried to get even for the insult with the Winchester, but Ybáñez managed to deflect the blow with his arm. Despite numerous attempts by Ybáñez to get County Attorney R. F. Luna to file charges against Parr, nothing happened.[72]

In 1954 the Freedom Party again had its hopes of electoral success raised. McDonald announced he was running for sheriff on the Freedom Party ticket. However, McDonald, a former Texas Ranger, created a rift within the party's nine-member executive committee, as four members voted against his candidacy. Those who opposed him viewed McDonald as a contentious "cloak and dagger" figure.[73]

Indeed, not everyone in Duval County was catching the Freedom Party fever. In June 1954 a group of women in the county formed an organization to support the Old Party. "George B. Parr is one of the leaders of the Old Party, and therefore . . . we support him," Mrs. F. H. Canales told a women's meeting in Alice. "The majority of voters here are supporters of the Old Party." Others at the meeting denounced "outside interference" in local elections. The list of members of the Old Party League of Women Voters, the OPLWV, was a veritable who's who of Duval County society. Among them were Lela Alaniz, Barbara González, Emma Barton, Odilia García Wright, Beatrice Sáenz Ramírez, Inez Heras Sáenz, Mrs. Reyes Ramos, Mrs. Watson, Mrs. E. S. García, Mrs. Amando García Jr., Mrs. Edmundo B. García, Mrs. Emede García, Mrs. Pedro Treviño, Mrs. Gabriel Chapa, Mrs. Charles Stansell, Bernarda Jaime, Mrs. Armando Barrera, Mrs. J. Richards, Mrs. Nago Alaniz, Mrs. Manuel Amaya, Pajita García, Mrs. Antonio Tobin Sr., Mrs. Ricardo Tobin, Juanita Pérez, and Mamie Corrigan.[74]

The Freedom Party had its own women's support group, the United Mothers and Wives of Duval County. The members intended "to protect" their children "from any effort to instill in them a fear of individuals, shield them from becoming servants of the machine or system, and to guard them against fear to speak, think, or vote according to their conscience." The United Mothers and Wives included 422 concerned citizens, led by Mrs. Hugo Ibáñez, Mrs. J. J. Treviño from Benavides, and Freer resident Mrs. J. H. Rutledge. In February 1954 the group wrote to Governor Allan Shivers, asking him to preserve "the physical security and Constitutional rights of all citizens." The women emphasized to the governor that "for years, the citizens of Duval County have suffered physical violence and economic reprisal as the penalty for opposing the Parr regime." They explained to the governor that they wanted their "children to grow up with the same privileges and . . . appreciation of democratic principles enjoyed by other Texas children." Moreover, they wanted to ensure school officials used education funds for their intended purposes.[75]

They further explained their concerns to the governor: "We do not want our children to grow up with an ingrained idea of servitude to a boss. We want our children to think of deputy sheriffs as protectors, not as instruments of oppression to be hated and feared. We want our husbands and sons to come home safe at night. We are tired of locking our doors." In an April 12, 1954, letter to Homer Garrison, the Freedom Party women leaders asked for a Texas Ranger to be assigned permanently in Duval County because they feared "unbridled retaliation" should the Old Party men realize that "all is lost." They pointed out they did not necessarily like having the Rangers in Duval County but were "grateful for their presence." Finally, the mothers pledged to work with school administrators and teachers; study citizenship rights and obligations; encourage public attendance at school, city, and county meetings; pay their poll tax and vote; and work with public officials to promote honest governance.[76]

On March 20, 1954, three OPLWV members went to the state capitol to express their concerns to the governor about the harm the state's constant investigations were having on Duval County, especially children. Those making the trip to Austin included Mrs. Mary Jo Mattson, a second-grade teacher in the Freer schools and the daughter of newly appointed County Commissioner O. D. Barrington; Miss Bernarda Jaime, a public-school librarian in San Diego; and Mrs. F. H. Canales from Benavides. They took a petition with 1,274 signatures endorsing their cause. Mrs. Mattson, who served as the voice of the delegation, told the governor that his impressions about Duval County were wrong. Not only were the petitioners very satisfied with the county's administration but so were most Duval County residents. After sitting quietly and listening to Mattson's presentation, the governor tried to set her straight. He told them they were misinformed about the facts, which indicated that public records were missing or burned, that checks were made to fictitious persons, and that "thousands of dollars have been misappropriated."[77]

"If there is nothing wrong in Duval County, then why do you have to keep a private army?" the governor asked the OPLWV representatives. He, for one, could not comprehend the need for three hundred special deputies. After the sit-down with the governor, Mrs. Mattson told the reporter with the *San Antonio Express* she did not believe a word the governor had said. "I was bored," she said, "we did not come here for a lecture." Governor Shivers was misinformed about the feelings of the majority of citizens of Duval County, Mrs. Mattson informed the *Express* correspondent. "The overwhelming majority are good, hardworking, peaceable people who love their homes and families and believe in the government of the people, by the people, and for the people." She said the women had gotten involved in this matter after the San Antonio Livestock Show participants booed students wearing Duval County jackets.[78]

The contests between the Old Party and the Freedom Party continued throughout the 1950s, with the Old Party winning most elections at the county, city, and school levels. While Parr and the Old Party continued to score victories at the polls, the boss faced losses in his battle against the ongoing local, state, and federal investigations. The Texas Supreme Court removed Parr's district judge, Woodrow Laughlin, and named the boss's archenemy, Donato Serna, the new county auditor. The courts then upheld the appointment of a new grand jury dominated by Freedom Party supporters. The panel swiftly indicted Parr for the attempted murder of Cristóbal Ybáñez, and District Judge Maxwell Welch barred Parr-supported District Attorney Raeburn Norris from prosecuting the case. Moreover, the grand jury capped Parr's public relations nightmare with a second indictment for corruption regarding funds at the Benavides School District.[79]

Cracks in the Parr machine finally appeared after the 1955 Democratic Primary when Dan Tobin Jr., the elected county judge on the Parr ticket, openly split with Parr. In December 1955 Tobin met with the Freedom Party to discuss a possible alliance. These talks, however, did not prove beneficial.

Tobin had disagreements with the candidates selected to run for particular offices. He maintained that rumors that he sought to form or lead his own Party—the so-called Tobin Party—was a figment. Tobin urged all citizens to vote for the candidate that best suited their interests. It was hardly a notion with which the Freedom Party could argue.[80]

The Freedom Party proceeded with its aspirations. On February 22, 1956, it held a meeting in Benavides to prepare a slate for the upcoming 1956 election. But in the end Parr candidates swept all openings except one city council seat, which went to Amado García of the Tobin Party, the faction that Tobin had denied existed. Freedom Party candidates came in a distant third in all races. In Benavides the Parr candidate for mayor, Octavio Sáenz, outdistanced Freedom Party candidate Regulo Benavides, 602–374. Old Party candidates Leopoldo Chapa and Reyes Ramon turned back Edelmiro Chapa and Máximo Vera.[81]

Despite their best efforts, the Freedom Party could not dent the Parr machine. In the 1956 Democratic Primary, George B. Parr, relying on absentee ballots, recaptured the sheriff's seat he had abandoned in 1952. Parr outdistanced three opponents, including J. P. Stockwell of the Freedom Party, 2,708–2,568. Parr, however, could not take his seat because the commissioners court, which did not include any Old Party members, refused to certify his or Amando García Jr.'s election as county clerk. The court's majority consisted of three Tobin Party members, County Judge Dan Tobin Jr., Commissioners Tomás Molina and Juan Leal, and Freedom Party Commissioners Dennis McBride and José D. Ramos.[82]

In the next biennial election for county offices in 1958, three complete slates were on the ballot: Parr's Old Party, the Tobin Party, and the Freedom Party. When the smoke cleared on election day, the Parr candidates received 44 percent of the vote, suggesting that most Tejanos were ready to move on from Parr. To the surprise of incumbent County Judge Dan Tobin Jr., his slate was nudged out of the runoff by Freedom Party candidates who received 31 percent of the vote. With a combined vote of 56 percent, the outsiders, particularly the Freedom Party, appeared poised to knock off Parr and his cronies. But it was not to be. A week after the vote, Tobin announced he had negotiated accommodation with George B. Parr to return to the fold. He was back in the machine, and the Freedom Party had to continue its battle alone. An upset Freedom Party candidate for County Judge, H. R. "Lacho" Canales, lashed out. "Dan Tobin has always been a Parr man in disguise," Canales told the *Alice Daily Echo*. "The party is disgusted with political leaders who move from party to party with the flick of a switch."[83]

The Freedom Party appeared to have made a successful comeback on May 10, 1960, when the County Democratic Committee refused to certify absentee ballots that had thrown the election to the Parr forces. As a result, George B. Parr lost the Democratic Party's chairmanship to Freedom Party candidate Santiago Cantú. In an ironic turn of events, the Freedom Party candidate for county judge, Canales, received the most votes; however, he died before voters cast their ballots. The apparent good fortunes for the Freedom Party were short-lived. On June 9, 1960, Parr's friend District Judge Woodrow Laughlin reversed the Democratic Party Executive Committee's May 10 decision to throw out absentee ballots that favored the Old Party. But it was not a complete reversal. Freedom Party candidates Walter Purcell and A. M. Sáenz won the county attorney and school superintendent positions. E. B. García of the Tobin Party was the voters' choice for county tax collector. The Parr candidates for these offices, O. P. Carrillo, Emede García, and Jesús Oliveira, did not roll over but ran as write-in candidates in the general election and won. The Freedom Party did not win another election again.[84]

While the Freedom Party did not achieve its ultimate goal, it was one of the leading forces that eventually ended Parr's rule. Given Tejanos' population numbers, Freedom Party members fully grasped their forefathers' dream of achieving parity in governing and other fields. The Parrs provided corruption, far removed from the promise that the 1912 courthouse massacre birthed. Freedom Party members disagreed with the type of cogovernance Parr offered. Instead of being ruled by 10 percent of the county's population—which was bad enough—they were now under the thumb of a single man. As Greatest Generation members, they embraced personal responsibility, humility, work ethic, commitment, integrity, and self-sacrifice, not found under the Parr regime. In its wake the Freedom Party's momentum to see Tejanos reach *un fin que ellos tenían en mente* (the outcome they had in mind) persisted, and the leaders who inherited the political mess left by the Parrs in 1975 took them up.[85]

Revolt From within Partido Viejo

In July 1961 remnants of the Freedom Party morphed into the Progressive Club. The organizers prepared to make political war against a proposed $36 million road bond issue that the Duval County Commissioners Court, led by Archer Parr, had put to a vote of the people. Dan U. García Jr., whose father was the first to challenge George B. Parr, led the Progressive Club; others in the group's leadership included John Campos, Sam Burris, and Donato Serna. The Progressive Club asserted the road bond proposal would cost too much; each resident in Duval County, young or old, would pay $462. Moreover, Serna explained that each Duval County resident, young or old, would pay $800 when the county sold the bonds.[86]

George B. Parr did not play a public role in the Progressive Club's challenge; his recent legal problems had become a financial nightmare, and he was busy finding ways to rebuild his financial house. Still, as had been the practice since the early days of the Parr machine under his father, Boss George B. Parr directed who held which position. In other words, George remained the boss, and he picked his nephew Archer for the county judge post and his brother Atlee Parr as commissioner from Benavides. The other commissioners were three Tejanos: Dan Tobin Jr., Juan Leal, and Juanita Valerio. Parr's attorney, O. P. Carrillo, also served as county attorney.[87]

There is no record that the Progressive Club ever put up candidates for elective office. Still, in 1962 Republicans headed by Clarence Schroeder surfaced to organize an all-out offensive against the status quo. They put up a slate for the April primary election. Without Dr. E. E. Dunlap's permission, they drafted the well-liked physician as a write-in candidate for the county judge. Other GOP candidates in the primary election included Serafín Rivera, county clerk; Roberto Hinojosa for treasurer; Delfino Loredo, district clerk; Ponciano Ruiz, animal inspector; Manuel Sáenz, commissioner of Precinct Two; and Emilio Reyna for Precinct Four commissioner.[88]

On July 28, 1962, Republican Chairman Schroeder moved forward with a planned rally in San Diego for Jack Cox, the GOP candidate for governor. Caravans of supporters arrived for the mass gathering from various points of Texas, including the Rio Grande Valley. The committee coordinating the candidate's visit included Mrs. H. M. González, S. O. Campos, Nap Chandler, Cato Pérez, and Roberto Hinojosa. County Judge Archer Parr welcomed some seven hundred people to town while Homero Barrera served as master of ceremonies. Although they could hold an impressive rally with out-of-town guests, winning an election against the Parr machine was different. On November 7, 1962, the *Alice Daily Echo* reported that County Judge Archer Parr and the rest of the Democratic slate had won every contested seat by a margin better than three to one.[89]

In February 1964 Republicans once again fielded a ticket for county offices. Their candidates included Salvador Campos, sheriff; Heriberto M. González, tax assessor-collector; James M. Baker, school superintendent; John S. Dunne, commissioner for Precinct One; and Dillard Weid, commissioner for Precinct Three. They sought to oust Sheriff Vidal García, Tax-Assessor Collector Jesús Oliveira, School Superintendent Emede García, Commissioner for Precinct One Daniel Tobin Jr., and Atlee Parr, commissioner for Precinct Three. Only County Attorney O. P. Carrillo did not get an opponent. Unfortunately for the Republicans, Duval County was not ready for them, and all candidates lost by a margin of better than ten to one. That ended the Republican experiment in Duval County for another fifty years.[90] In 1966 the party's standard-bearer, John Tower, got less than two hundred votes in Duval County while he captured the US Senate seat from Texas.[91]

George Parr's next challenge was more severe, as it derived from within his inner circle. The Old Party fissures had begun in 1952 when Sheriff Dan U. García had considered breaking with the Old Party and joining the Freedom Party. However, George B. Parr got word of the sheriff's plans and forced García to resign from the post he had held for twenty years. Then, several years later, in 1955, Daniel Tobin Jr. revealed his effort to part company with Parr, but following failed negotiations with the Freedom Party, he returned to

the Parr tent. More than a decade later, the Carrillo family from Benavides began
to make noises about leaving the Parr family. These Tejano defectors descended
from Archie Parr's trusted collaborators.

The Parr-Carrillo feud surfaced in December 1973 after the IRS once
again slapped the Duval *patrones* George and Archer Parr with charges
of failure to file income tax reports. When the *San Antonio Light* asked
County Commissioner Ramiro Carrillo who would take over once his family
removed the Parrs, the commissioner responded, "The Carrillos." The
Carrillo clan included former State Representative Oscar Carrillo, District
Judge O. P. Carrillo, County Commissioner Ramiro Carrillo, and their father,
D. C. Chapa, who had served in numerous posts. "We have the power.
We have the votes, and that's where the power is," he declared. Expounding
upon a scenario when the Parrs would be defeated, Ramiro Carrillo asserted,
"We provide lots of services; we take care of the people." In a forceful tone,
he said he was his own man. "I don't just do what George or Judge Parr
says. Sometimes, we discuss things even argue. Sometimes I win, sometimes
I lose," Ramiro Carrillo continued.[92]

Then, in a repetition of what had occurred in 1915, absentee landowners
decided to take on George B. Parr's power. In 1973 the Duval County
Commissioners Court published a budget (the first one in twelve years) that
prompted the organization of the Duval County Taxpayers League. County
Commissioner Ramiro Carrillo sharply observed that the league's membership was mostly nonresident property owners. "The people who live here
are happy," he said. The Parrs maintained that the malcontents consisted of
longstanding political adversaries with "no voting power in the county."[93]

The *San Antonio Light* did a line-by-line budget comparison with
neighboring Webb County. Although Webb County had four times the
population of Duval County, the Parr province had twice as large a budget,
with expenditures of $233.33 per resident. In contrast, the larger Webb
County provided only $31.25. Of course, most of Webb County's population
resided in the city of Laredo, which had a budget that the newspaper did
not consider. In fairness, the newspaper did not count allocations from
Duval County's three organized cities that served most of the county's
population.[94]

Table 18.3 Budget expenditures, Duval and Webb Counties, 1973

Budget Item	Webb County	Duval County
Population	80,000	18,000
Square Miles	3,293	1,814
Total Budget	$2,500,000.00	$4,200,000.00
Expenditure per Resident	$ 31.25	$ 233.33
County Shop Expenses	$ 39,727.52	$ 225,781.40
County Commissioners	$ 0.00	$ 316,945.52
Janitors	$ 34,838.00	$ 49,201.20
Welfare Budget	$ 1,400.00	$ 9,600.00
Clothing for Poor	$ 500.00	$ 7,800.00
Food for Poor	$ 2,000.00	$ 24,000.00
Hospital, Medical Fees	$ 30,000.00	$ 21,200.00
Drugs (Medicine)	$ 8,000.00	$ 19,400.00
Equipment Repair	$ 0.00	$ 24,000.00
Attorney's Fees	$ 8,000.00	$ 24,000.00
Game Wardens	$ 0.00	$ 16,288.00

Source: *San Antonio Light*, December 12, 1973.

The following month, on January 29, 1974, Ramiro Carrillo's brother Oscar, who had previously served on the Texas House of Representatives for three terms with George B. Parr's blessing, declared that he would challenge incumbent Senator John Traeger, who had Parr's support. Oscar Carrillo acknowledged that he was running for political office without Parr's consent. The rift widened in April 1974 when the commissioners court took actions designed to cut off Commissioner Ramiro Carrillo's authority over Precinct Two. Oscar Carrillo quickly came to Ramiro's aid by obtaining a temporary restraining order against the commissioners court. The order prevented commissioners from firing Commissioner Carrillo's employees. The seriousness of the Carrillo challenge came into focus on April 11, when the Carrillos won a Benavides council seat and tied for the mayor's position. Incumbent Benavides Mayor Octavio Sáenz, the Carrillo-backed candidate, finished in a 350-vote tie with the George B. Parr candidate Armando L. Garza.[95] Carrillo-supported nominee Barbara S. González prevailed over Ruben Chapa, the Parr candidate, in the only contested council race.[96]

The Benavides city election in the Carrillos' backyard seemed inconsequential when considered against the political backdrop in which it occurred, most notably the conviction of George B. Parr on income tax fraud a month before. On March 20 a Corpus Christi jury found the 73-year-old political patriarch guilty of income tax evasion and perjury. He was facing a possible thirty-two years in prison. Two months later, on May 10, a San Antonio jury convicted George's nephew Archer Parr on six counts of perjury. On May 21 the court sentenced Archer to ten years in federal prison and assessed a fine of $63,810.82, which oilman Clinton Manges immediately paid.[97]

Matters began to get intense a year later when, on March 21, 1975, District Judge O. P Carrillo removed four Parristas from the Benavides school board and replaced them with four individuals allied with the Carrillo group. The judge ejected board President M. K. Bercaw, a Freer resident, Luis Elizondo from Benavides, Concepción representative Enrique García, and Joe García. The replacements, all Carrillo supporters, were Freer residents Morris Ashby, Pete Hunter, Leonel Garza, and Bill Hand. Ashby and Nichols worked at the Duval County Ranch, which Clinton Manges owned. Four days later Judge Carrillo expelled the convicted Archer Parr from the county judge position for "incompetence and official misconduct" and named Dan Tobin Jr. to the county judge post. The splinter between the Carrillos, including the family patriarch, D. C. Chapa, and the Parrs was now a reality. Further weakening the Parrs, the US Fourth Court of Appeals denied George B. Parr's income tax evasion appeal.[98]

The Carrillo family's sudden rise to power, however, was short-lived. On April 11, 1975, newspaper headlines proclaimed that a federal grand jury had indicted District Judge Carrillo and his brother Ramiro (the Duval County commissioner) for income tax evasion. As if this was not enough to mar the Carrillos' political fortunes, six weeks later the Texas House of Representatives began hearings for the impeachment of District Judge Carrillo. Before the House Impeachment Committee, witnesses testified that Judge Carrillo had used county employees, equipment, and supplies on several building projects at his ranch. Others disclosed that he utilized heavy equipment at his farm, such as a backhoe belonging to the Duval County Water & Conservation District, where the judge's father, D. C. Chapa, served as board president. Judge Carrillo allegedly used workers paid from his brother's, Commissioner Ramiro Carrillo, county payroll. One witness told the committee that the judge owned and ran a farm and ranch store, the Benavides Implement and Hardware Company, where he sold to the county materials the county had already paid for.[99]

On July 23, 1975, the House Impeachment Committee approved eleven articles against Judge O. P. Carrillo and forwarded them to the Texas Senate, which received the House Articles of Impeachment on September 3, 1975. Throughout the fall of 1975, the Judicial Qualifications Commission thoroughly reviewed the articles of impeachment, and the Senate certified Article VII on January 23, 1976, removing Judge Carrillo from the bench and prohibiting him from "holding any office of honor, trust or profit under the State." Article VII read as follows: "While holding office as district judge for the 229th Judicial District of Texas, O. P. Carrillo conspired with others to use for his personal benefit materials and supplies owned by Duval County and other governmental entities, which he was not entitled to receive. This conduct included but was not limited to . . . fuel owned by Duval County in his personal vehicles."[100]

The following year Oscar Carrillo, who had thus far escaped the state and federal investigators, became immersed in a scandal akin to one that had befallen his brothers. In September 1976 Carrillo went on trial at a Jourdanton courtroom for illegally appropriating a Benavides School District postage meter to send out political material in his 1972 campaign for the Texas Senate. On September 22 the jury found the former state representative guilty and handed him a seven-year probated sentence, which Carrillo indicated he would appeal. By the fall of 1976, all three Carrillo brothers and both Parrs were effectively out of the political picture in Duval County, but apparently that was not enough for prosecutors. A week after Oscar Carrillo was found guilty, a trial got underway in San Antonio for the 80-year-old patriarch of the Carrillo family, D. C. Chapa. Authorities charged the elderly defendant with misappropriating $400 from the Benavides School District while he served on the school's board.[101]

Meanwhile, Dan Tobin Jr. and eighty-four other Duval County officials and citizens were under indictment for various public crimes. By the end of 1976, no one of political consequence was free of accusation to run for public office. Duval County appeared postured to begin a new era in its political life.[102]

The End of the Parr Era

In late March 1975, the Fifth US Circuit Court of Appeals confirmed Parr's guilt of income tax evasion and perjury, a sentence that threatened him with five years in prison. He had just turned 74 and was no longer of age to serve the time. His nephew had been the county judge for fifteen years but was in a similar fix, facing prison time.

To add to Parr's troubles, on March 31 US District Judge Owen Cox expressed the belief that Parr "may pose a danger" and ordered him to report to his courtroom that afternoon and tell the judge why he should not be considered a menace to his community. The US attorney informed the judge that Parr had threatened several people with a concealed weapon. The following morning, after Parr failed to comply with his order, Judge Cox directed his arrest. Law enforcement from several jurisdictions launched a search for Parr. At 11:15 a.m. a Department of Public Safety helicopter spotted Parr's car in a remote area of Los Horcones Ranch. Upon landing the investigators found Parr's lifeless body behind the steering wheel. Suicide was the definite conclusion as the cause of death. Justice of the Peace Luis Elizondo concurred with the investigation of the Texas Rangers and FBI and issued a ruling that Parr "shot self in the right side of the head while sitting in the automobile with the bullet exiting on the left side of the head and out the car window."[103]

George B. Parr had met his fate at Los Horcones Ranch, his father's estate. Perhaps he had gone there hoping to get inspiration on what his father would do or apologize for what he was about to do. Who would care for his wife and young daughter, he must have thought? These, and perhaps other concerns, may have been going through Parr's mind on that fateful week.[104]

The Parr family was Episcopalian, but a Catholic priest celebrated his funeral services, perhaps in deference to his many Tejano friends. Mourners attended a rosary at the Parr home on Wednesday, and the next day more than two thousand people paid their last respects at the funeral service conducted by Father Antonio Arguelles. A Parr relative had anticipated that the funeral would be small, with only family and a few personal friends attending. She said, "George was a public figure, but a funeral is a private thing." But she misjudged Parr's popularity in Duval County, for many people loved him. San Diego pharmacist Chris S. Hinojosa Jr. said he owed his career to Parr. Hinojosa relayed to a reporter that when he needed $500 for a pharmacist license during the Great Depression, Parr gave him the money. When a Tejana's car broke down, Parr bought her a new one. Stories like this were legendary. "If you were his friend," Hinojosa said, "he'd go to hell for you. He'd do all kinds of favors." Of course, his adversaries would point out that it was easy to do favors with other people's money. Local lore, family recollections, and archival records tell that Parr could do much good for his supporters and considerable harm to his enemies.[105]

Nevertheless, some four hundred cars lined up for the procession from the Los Horcones to the cemetery in Benavides; cars were bumper to bumper on the five miles from the ranch house to the graveyard. "The atmosphere was heavy with emotion," a UPI reporter wrote. Tejanos greeted each other with abrazos, and tears flowed down the cheeks of both men and women. Pallbearers included State Representative Terry Canales, Norman Ransleben, Vitalio Briones, Vidal García, Walter Meek Jr., A. E. García, Rene Martínez, Raúl Tijerina Sr., and Harris Fender.[106]

The Carrillos had planned to fill the vacuum created by George's death and Archer's federal conviction, but they, too, were thwarted by legal problems and could not assume the Parr mantle. The Parr era passed into the annals of history on that emotional day when El Patron's friends said their final goodbyes at the Benavides campo santo.

Officials had to make replacements for several officers who were in legal trouble. On October 31, 1975, Brownsville District Judge Darrel Hester named Gilberto Uresti as county judge to replace Dan Tobin Jr., who had resigned from the post after being indicted for theft and preferred to spend his time defending himself against the charges.

Uresti had no political affiliation or experience but came to the office with an impressive résumé of involvement with professional and civic groups. He was chairman of the Texas Pharmaceutical Association and had been pharmacist of the year in 1975. Uresti was the past president of the Benavides Rotary Club, a former officer of the Knights of Columbus at Santa Rosa de Lima Catholic Church, an enthusiastic supporter of the Benavides Little League, and Benavides school PTA president. He was also active in the Booster Club and Boys Scouts. Judge Uresti soon showed his operating method by inviting the public to the first meeting of the commissioners court, which had financial matters on its agenda.[107]

Uresti, of course, did not restore Duval County by himself. Many others came forward during his administration, and those that followed undertook the needed change. The reformers were not always in agreement, but that is the nature of a democracy. They differed in approach and came from distinct political backgrounds. Some had ties to the Parrs, Carrillos, or the Freedom Party, others to none. They came from different upbringings and all corners of the county: San Diego, Benavides, Freer, Concepción, Realitos, and other rancherías. But what coalesced them was the common goal of putting distance between the future of Duval and the past. The post-Parr world would be one wherein people could strive unfettered to realize their full potential and attain the ultimate promise of the American dream.

Epilogue

"Soy de Duval"

Since circa 1805, when Spain began to settle in the area known as Duval County, Tejanos residing there have possessed a sense of confidence and self-worth. It is an attribute passed down through tradition from generation to generation. The initial settlers could not count on *la patria* (state or nation) for their well-being; instead, loyalty and political identity were to what historian David J. Weber calls allegiance to "one's *patria chica*" (their local community). In the uncharted frontier that became Duval County, pobladores fended for themselves with little to no support from their national leaders in Spain and Mexico. They first looked to their immediate family, then their extended family, next to the ranch owner (the patron), and finally to their *patria chica* for support against the perils of the hinterland. For most settlers in Duval County, *la patria chica* meant the Villas del Norte communities of Mier and Camargo across the Rio Grande from Rio Grande City and Roma.[1]

After the United States acquired sovereignty over the region in 1848, the locals saw no change in national attention extended to them. They continued to rely on *la patria chica*; they still had to provide for themselves, but now they relied on Nueces County instead of Mier and Camargo. They had no idea where the cities of Austin or Washington, DC, were and assumed leaders in those places did not know or care who Duval Tejanos were. As English-speaking strangers arrived during the 1850s to direct their community, they knew little about the resident Tejanos, who now had to adjust to the new reality. There was a novel language, a different government structure and laws, and unfamiliar customs. What had not changed was the certainty that they still depended on themselves, their family, and their God.

The emerging circumstances initially did not transform their identity but sharpened Tejanos' survival instincts in this antagonistic environment. Tejanos gradually acquired English, even if they sometimes applied their twists to the language. It was no different for Americanos, who were also undergoing adaptation; Americanos also had to adjust to Spanish Mexican surroundings and adopt variations in their English linguistic terminology. The two people had to live together and try to make a better life for themselves and their children.

But therein was the challenge for Tejanos. They needed to acquire the education required to communicate in the language of their new government if they were to fully comprehend its legal, political, and civic requirements and benefits. But even acquiring these skills still meant submission to the minority Americanos. Succumbing to Americanos seemed an anomaly to the Tejanos, for the very essence of being an Americano was "that all men are created equal, that they are endowed, by their Creator, with certain unalienable rights, that among these are life, liberty, and the pursuit of happiness."[2]

The reality was that Americanos had the upper hand over Tejanos. The Americanos understood the language and the legal system. But Tejanos adjusted to change and to the demands of American culture. Over time the Tejano character traits of independence, self-reliance, self-worth, self-esteem, and the "*Si se puede*" attitude their ancestors passed on to them became helpful in their adaptation to American life.

Tejanos made this adjustment, bolstered by their conviction and self-assuredness, feelings and thoughts of being in control, and the "swagger" in "Soy de Duval." The *consejos* (advice) passed down to them by their forefathers played an instrumental role in their ability to work with new local governments under Americano domination. The pages of this book abundantly demonstrate this dynamic.

Moreover, *Duval County Tejanos* counters depictions of recently published works that stigmatize Duval County, and, by extension, its residents as corrupt and sleazy. These tomes depict Duval County during most of the twentieth century under George B. Parr as an arena where the worst kind of political despotism thrived. They describe the years from the early twentieth century until the middle of the 1970s as permeated with graft, embezzlement, extortion, electoral fraud, personal misuse of law enforcement, mistreatment of people experiencing poverty, and political assassinations. These studies and others portray Duval County Tejanos as ignorant, helpless, and willing collaborators in their political abuse. Unfortunately, that reputation of infamy—fostered by the available scholarship—persists.

Indeed, much wrongdoing existed during the George B. Parr era, but there is more to Duval County's past. It comprises Tejanos seeking parity with the majority population and striving for cogovernance, constitutional rights, economic independence, social prominence, and the privilege of practicing the Tejano way. Tejanos' efforts to achieve these ends were not without obstacles. In the way of their aspirations were Americano bigotry, political ambition, stereotyping, greed, distrust and suspicion, land grabbing, *los rinches*, accusations of disloyalty, and more. Imbued with the confidence they learned from venerable ancestors, Tejanos took on all obstacles.

Moreover, Tejanos possessed foundational pluses that bolstered their efforts to ward off obstacles to achieving their goals, including population dominance, which malleated discrimination and segregation, and broad space to carry on a Tejano identity. Such circumstances allowed Tejanos to employ personal instincts to negotiate an accommodation—an *arreglo político* (political arrangement) with the Parrs, to use entrepreneurial acumen to dominate the local economy and to form an ethnic community loyal and ready to contribute to American life.

Writers have tossed by the wayside Tejano's constructive contributions. *Duval County Tejanos* corrects this lingering caricature Americanos initiated in the nineteenth century, and scholars have perpetuated and embellished in the twentieth century and beyond. *Duval County Tejanos* is testimony to everyday people living as law-abiding citizens and contributing to their community and society. Like people everywhere in the world and throughout generations, Tejanos were people of faith who built churches and followed the call to help their neighbors, honored their ancestors, cherished their families, and worked daily to ensure a hopeful future for their children. And like others who have faced prejudice and degradation, their past is one of a people with an indomitable spirit willing to confront life's ups and downs.

Duval County's historical record does not conform to traditional history as it is currently told, especially for the twentieth century. The refrain of existing publications on Duval County persists with the claim that in counties controlled by Americano farmers, Tejanos were stripped of political influence, denied economic options, and subjected to bigotry and discrimination. While this was true in some South Texas counties, such an order did not take root in Duval County. Why?

For one, Tejanos profited from their nineteenth-century experience as active members, forming everyday decisions affecting Duval County. Through the years they performed a constructive role in their local government and proactively participated in the commercial and industrial sectors of the economy. The cultural seeds planted and harvested in the nineteenth century allowed political progress to blossom in the twentieth century. Early on Americanos in Duval County realized that the Tejano majority was ready and willing to work with them but on an equal plane. Second, Tejanos considered themselves community builders and, as a people, able to ward off threatening forces. Finally, commercial farming did not decimate elements of the diverse Duval County economy in the twentieth century as it did in other Trans-Nueces communities.

Moreover, existing population numbers relegated Americanos to an unenviable position. These several factors softened bigotry and removed blatant discrimination as a concern. The most important result of these circumstances was an enduring can-do ethic that inspired Tejano society.

As the title of this book indicates, Duval County served as a place where Tejanos pursued a path toward dignity and independence. To paraphrase popular lyrics of the Mexican ballad, *El Rey*, "*supieron llegar*," they knew how to get where they wanted to go. Over one hundred years, they struggled to win, protect, and preserve Tejanos' rights at the voting booth, the tax office, the battlefield, and many other settings. The state of mind that took shape due to these experiences affirms that Tejanos were and are American and all that entails. After all, Duval is in America, and its sons and daughters continue to live by the mantra: "Soy de Duval."

Endnotes

Notes for the Preface

1. Adam Goodman, "The Promise of New Approaches and Persistence of Old Paradigms in Mexican American History," *Journal of American Ethnic History* 32, no. 3 (Spring 2013): 83, https://doi.org/10.5406/jamerethnhist.32.3.0083.

2. James West Davidson, "The New Narrative History: How New? How Narrative?," *Reviews in American History* 12, no. 3 (September 1984): 333.

3. Omar S. Valerio-Jiménez, *River of Hope: Forging Identity and Nation in the Rio Grande Borderlands* (Durham, NC: Duke University Press, 2013); and Miguel Ángel González-Quiroga's *War and Peace on the Rio Grande Frontier: 1830–1880*, New Directions in Tejano History 1 (Norman: Oklahoma University Press, 2020).

4. Armando C. Alonzo, *Tejano Legacy, Rancheros and Settlers in South Texas, 1734–1900* (Albuquerque: University of New Mexico,1998); Arnoldo De León, *The Tejano Community, 1836–1900* (Dallas: Southern Methodist University Press, 1997); Andrés Tijerina, *Tejano Empire: Life on the South Texas Ranchos*, 1st ed., Clayton Wheat Williams Texas Life Series, no. 7 (College Station: Texas A&M University Press, 1998).

5. Arnoldo De León, *They Called Them Greasers: Anglo Attitudes toward Mexicans in Texas, 1821–1900* (Austin: University of Texas Press, 2010); David Montejano, *Anglos and Mexicans in the Making of Texas, 1836–1986* (Austin: University of Texas Press, 2009).

6. Elena Bilbao and María Antonia Gallart, *Los Chicanos: segregación y educación* (Mexico DF: Editorial Nueva Imagen, 1981); Andrés Sáenz, *Early Tejano Ranching: Daily Life at Ranchos San José and El Fresnillo*, edited and with an introduction by Andrés Tijerina (College Station: Texas A&M Press, 2001); and Ana Carolina Castillo Crimm and Sara R. Massey, *Turn-of-the-Century Photographs from San Diego, Texas* (Austin: University of Texas Press, 2003).

7. Sister Mary Xavier, IWBS, *Father Jaillet: Saddlebag Priest of the Nueces*, 2nd ed. (Corpus Christi, TX: Duval County Historical Commission, 1996); Dorothy Abbott McCoy's, *Oil, Mud & Guts: Birth of a Texas Town* (Brownsville, TX: Springman-Hill Lithograph, 1977); Coleman McCampbell's *Texas Seaport: The Story of the Growth of Corpus Christi and the Coastal Bend Area* (New York: Exposition Press, 1952); Agnes G. Grimm, *Llanos Mesteñas: Mustang Plains* (Waco, TX: Texian Press, 1968); and Val W. Lehmann and José Cisneros, *Forgotten Legions: Sheep in the Rio Grande Plain of Texas* (El Paso: Texas Western Press, 1969).

8. Dudley Lynch, *The Duke of Duval: The Life and Times of George B. Parr, a Biography* (Waco, TX: Texian Press, 1976); John E. Clark, *The Fall of the Duke of Duval: A Prosecutor's Journal, 1st ed.* (Austin: Eakin Press, 1995); Sheila Allee, *Texas Mutiny: Bullets, Ballots and Boss Rule* (Austin: SAC Press, 1995); Anthony R. Carrozza, *The Dukes of Duval County: The Parr Family and Texas Politics* (Norman: University of Oklahoma Press, 2017).
9. Daniel Arreola, *Tejano South Texas: A Mexican American Cultural Province* (Austin: University of Texas Press, 2002), 7.

Notes for Chapter 1

1. Robin Varnum, *Álvar Núñez Cabeza de Vaca: American Trailblazer* (Norman: University of Oklahoma Press, 2014), 129–42.
2. John G. Johnson, "Narváez, Pánfilo de," *Handbook of Texas Online*, accessed February 27, 2023, https://www.tshaonline.org/handbook/entries/narvaez-panfilo-de.
3. Bethel Coopwood, "The Route of Cabeza de Vaca: Part I," *Quarterly of the Texas State Historical Association* 3, no. 2 (1899): 121–29; Varnum, *Álvar Núñez Cabeza de Vaca*, 123; Andrés Reséndez, *A Land So Strange: The Epic Journey of Cabeza de Vaca: The Extraordinary Tale of a Shipwrecked Spaniard Who Walked across America in the Sixteenth Century* (New York: Basic Books, 2007), 180; Donald E. Chipman, "In Search of Cabeza de Vaca's Route across Texas: An Historiographical Survey," *Southwestern Historical Quarterly* 91, no. 2 (1987): 143, 145; Donald W. Olson et al., "Piñon Pines and the Route of Cabeza de Vaca," *Southwestern Historical Quarterly* 101, no. 2 (1997): 181.
4. Jerry D. Thompson, *A Wild and Vivid Land: An Illustrated History of the South Texas Border* (Austin: Texas State Historical Association, 2012), 19; Robert S. Weddle, "Nuevo Santander," *Handbook of Texas Online*, accessed December 7, 2023, https://www.tshaonline.org/handbook/entries/nuevo-santander.
5. Thompson, *Wild and Vivid Land*, 22; Homero Vera, "El Camino Real de Duval County," *El Mesteño* 5, no. 1 (2002): 13; "San Diego de Arriba y Abajo," San Patricio 1st 000423, Flores, Julian, and Flores, Ventura, Archives and Records Division, Texas General Land Office, (ARD GLO), accessed May 11, 2019, http://www.glo.texas.gov/ncu/SCANDOCS/archives_webfiles/arcmaps/webfiles/landgrants/PDFs/5/4/1/541154.pdf (hereafter cited as "San Diego de Arriba y Abajo").
6. Jerry D. Thompson, *Sabers on the Rio Grande*, 1st ed. (Austin: Presidial Press, 1974), 13.
7. Thompson, *Sabers on the Rio Grande*, 13.
8. Thompson, *Sabers on the Rio Grande*, 13.
9. I. J. Cox, "The Southwest Boundary of Texas," *Quarterly of the Texas State Historical Association* 6, no. 2 (1902): 91.

10. Herbert Eugene Bolton, "Tienda de Cuervo's Inspección of Laredo, 1757," *Quarterly of the Texas State Historical Association* 6, no. 3 (January 1903): 203; Víctor M. Sáenz Ramírez, *Los Protocolos de La Villa de Nuestra Señora Santa Anna de Camargo, 1762–1809* (Parroquia de Camargo, Tamps., Mexico: Palibrio, 2011), 6–9.

11. Ramírez, *Los Protocolos*, 21.

12. Ramírez, *Los Protocolos*, 13, 370–71.

13. All Spanish grants will be discussed in greater detail in a subsequent chapter. Information for these grants was extracted from files in the Spanish Collection at the Texas General Land Office Archives.

14. Juan Fidel Zorrilla, Maribel Miró Flaquer, and Octavio Herrera Pérez, eds., *Tamaulipas: Textos de Su Historia, 1810–1921*, 1st. ed. (San Juan, Mixcoac, Mexico, DF: Gobierno del Estado de Tamaulipas; Instituto de Investigaciones Dr. José María Luis Mora, 1990), 19–21; Omar S. Valerio-Jiménez, "Neglected Citizens and Willing Traders: The Villas Del Norte (Tamaulipas) in Mexico's Northern Borderlands, 1749–1846," *Mexican Studies* 18, no. 2 (August 2002): 254.

15. Zorrilla, Flaquer, and Pérez, *Tamaulipas*, 19–21.

16. Leroy P. Graf, "Colonizing Projects in Texas South of the Nueces, 1820–1845," *Southwestern Historical Quarterly* 50, no. 4 (1947): 435.

17. Jesús F. de la Teja, "Coahuila and Texas," *Handbook of Texas Online*, accessed June 26, 2020, http://www.tshaonline.org/handbook/online/articles/usc01; Martha Menchaca, *Naturalizing Mexican Immigrants: A Texas History*, 1st ed. (Austin: University of Texas Press, 2011), 24; Christopher Long, "McMullen-McGloin Colony," *Handbook of Texas Online*, accessed June 20, 2019, https://tshaonline.org/handbook/online/articles/uem01.

18. Manuel de Mier y Terán, *Texas by Terán: The Diary Kept by General Manuel de Mier y Terán on His 1828 Inspection of Texas*, ed. Jack Jackson, trans. John Wheat, with botanical notes by Scooter Cheatham and Lynn Marshall, 1st ed., Jack and Doris Smothers Series in Texas History, Life, and Culture 2 (Austin: University of Texas Press, 2000), 156–57; Terry G. Jordan-Bychkov, *North American Cattle-Ranching Frontiers: Origins, Diffusion, and Differentiation*, 1st ed., Histories of the American Frontier (Albuquerque: University of New Mexico Press, 1993), 134.

19. Lehmann and Cisneros, *Forgotten Legions*, 22.

20. Thompson, *Sabers on the Rio Grande*, 67.

21. "The Treaty of Velasco (Private), May 14, 1836," Texas State Library and Archives Commission (hereafter cited as TSLAC), accessed December 30, 2019, https://www.tsl.texas.gov/treasures/republic/velasco-private-1.html; "Treaty," *Merriam-Webster*, accessed December 30, 2019, https://www.merriam-webster.com/dictionary/treaty.

22. Roseann Bacha-Garza, Christopher L. Miller, and Russell K. Skowronek, eds., *The Civil War on the Rio Grande, 1846–1876*, 1st ed., Elma Dill Russell Spencer Series in the West and Southwest 46 (College Station: Texas A&M University Press, 2019), 18.

23. Juan Mora-Torres, *The Making of the Mexican Border: The State, Capitalism, and Society in Nuevo León, 1848–1910*, 1st ed. (Austin: University of Texas Press, 2001), para. 217, Kindle.

24. Joseph Milton Nance, *After San Jacinto: The Texas-Mexican Frontier, 1836–1841* (Austin: University of Texas Press, 2011), 46–47, 65–66.

25. Nance, *After San Jacinto*, 8–9, 47.

26. David Vigness, "Republic of the Rio Grande," *Handbook of Texas Online*, accessed February 20, 2023, https://www.tshaonline.org/handbook/entries/republic-of-the-rio-grande.

27. Josefina Zoraida Vázquez, "La Supuesta República Del Rio Grande," *Historia Mexicana* 36, no. 1 (1986): 73; Beatriz Eugenia de la Garza, *From the Republic of the Rio Grande: A Personal History of the Place and the People*, 1st ed., Jack and Doris Smothers Series in Texas History, Life, and Culture 35 (Austin: University of Texas Press, 2013), 21–22; Henderson K. Yoakum, *History of Texas: From Its First Settlement in 1685 to Its Annexation to the United States In 1846* (Provo, UT: Repressed Publishing, 2013), 288–89; González-Quiroga, *War and Peace on the Rio Grande Frontier*, 76.

28. Lipantitlán was located seventeen miles north of present-day Agua Dulce off FM 70, north of the Nueces River in the Republic of Texas.

29. Vázquez, "La Supuesta República Del Rio Grande," 72–73.

30. Thompson, *Sabers on the Rio Grande*, 91–92; Leslie A. Jones Wagner, "Disputed Territory: Rio Grande/ Rio Bravo Borderlands, 1838–1840" (master's thesis, University of Texas at Arlington, 1998), 59.

31. Vigness, "Republic of the Rio Grande"; González-Quiroga, *War and Peace on the Rio Grande Frontier*, 123.

32. C. T. Neu, "Annexation," *Handbook of Texas Online*, accessed December 20, 2019, https://tshaonline.org/handbook/online/articles/mga02.

33. Center of Military History, "The Mexican War and After," in *American Military History*, Army Historical Series (Washington DC: Office of the Chief of Military History, United States Army, 1989), 163.

34. Center of Military History, "Mexican War and After," 163; Thompson, *Wild and Vivid Land*, 39; Republic Ranger Quartermaster Records, Ranger Records, Texas Adjutant General's Department, Archives and Information Services Division, TSLAC (hereafter cited as Ranger Records); González-Quiroga, *War and Peace on the Rio Grande Frontier*, 81–82.

35. K. Jack Bauer, "Mexican War," *Handbook of Texas Online*, accessed December 8, 2023, https://www.tshaonline.org/handbook/entries/republic-of-the-rio-grande.

36. "Rancho de Carricitos," *Palo Alto Battlefield, National Historical Park, Texas, National Park Service*, accessed October 27, 2022, https://www.nps.gov/paal/learn/historyculture/ranchodecarricitos.htm.

37. Center of Military History, "Mexican War and After," 164–66.

Notes for Chapter 2

1. González-Quiroga, *War and Peace on the Rio Grande Frontier*, 9.

2. David J. Weber, *The Mexican Frontier, 1821–1846: The American Southwest under Mexico*, 1st ed., Histories of the American Frontier (Albuquerque: University of New Mexico Press, 1982), 240.

3. González-Quiroga, *War and Peace on the Rio Grande Frontier*, 276.

4. Mora-Torres, *Making of the Mexican Border*, para. 215; González-Quiroga, *War and Peace on the Rio Grande Frontier*, 56–63.

5. Mora-Torres, *Making of the Mexican Border*, 1–7, 30.

6. Keith Guthrie, "San Patricio County," *Handbook of Texas Online*, accessed February 20, 2023, https://www.tshaonline.org/handbook/entries/san-patricio-county; Christopher Long, "Nueces County," *Handbook of Texas Online*, accessed February 20, 2023, https://www.tshaonline.org/handbook/entries/nueces-county; John Leffler and Christopher Long, "Webb County," *Handbook of Texas Online*, accessed February 20, 2023, https://www.tshaonline.org/handbook/entries/webb-county.

7. *American Flag* (Matamoros, Tamaulipas, Mexico), August 28, 1847, p. 2, Portal to Texas History (hereafter cited as Portal), https://texashistory.unt.edu/ark:/67531/metapth478848/m1/2/zoom/.

8. "San Andrés," San Patricio 1st 000531, García, Andrés (Heirs of), ARD GLO, accessed June 28, 2019, http://www.glo.texas.gov/ncu/SCANDOCS/archives_webfiles/arcmaps/webfiles/landgrants/PDFs/5/4/1/541421.pdf; Wagner, "Disputed Territory," 59; Nueces County Commissioners Court Minutes, 24, Nueces County Clerk, n.d.

9. *Corpus Christi Star*, November 21, 1848, Texas Newspaper Collection (hereafter cited as TX News. Coll.), Dolph Briscoe Center for American History (hereafter cited as DBCAH).

10. "Eagle Pass Road," *Nueces Valley*, July 13, 1850, p. 2, Portal, https://texashistory.unt.edu/ark:/67531/metapth179329/m1/2/zoom/.

11. "Transportation Line," *Corpus Christi Star*, December 23, 1848, p. 1, Portal, https://texashistory.unt.edu/ark:/67531/metapth80209/m1/1/zoom/.

12. "Our City," *Corpus Christi Star*, November 21, 1848, p. 2, Portal, https://texashistory.unt.edu/ark:/67531/metapth80205/m1/2/zoom/.

13. "A Los Mexicanos," *Corpus Christi Star*, September 19, 1848, p. 3, Portal, https://texashistory.unt.edu/ark:/67531/metapth80197/m1/3/zoom/.

14. "The Mexicans," *Corpus Christi Star*, September 19, 1848, p. 1, Portal, https://texashistory.unt.edu/ark:/67531/metapth80197/m1/1/zoom/; "Peones," *Corpus*

Christi Star, September 26, 1848, p. 1, Portal, https://texashistory.unt.edu/ark:/67531/metapth80196/m1/1/zoom/.

15. *Corpus Christi Star*, November 7, 1848, TX News. Coll.; *Nueces Valley*, July 17, 1858, TX News. Coll.; *Corpus Christi Star*, October 10, 1848, TX News. Coll.

16. *Corpus Christi Star*, September 26, 1848, TX News. Coll.

17. "Protection to the Frontier," *Corpus Christi Star*, June 2, 1849, p. 2, Portal, https://texashistory.unt.edu/ark:/67531/metapth80229/m1/2/zoom/.

18. "Protection to the Frontier," *Corpus Christi Star*, June 2, 1849, p. 2; Homero Vera, "Lomas Blanca," *El Mesteño*, February 10, 2020.

19. John Salmon Ford, *Rip Ford's Texas*, ed. Stephen B. Oates (Austin: University of Texas Press, 1963), 189; Thompson, *Sabers on the Rio Grande*, 169–70.

20. Ford, *Rip Ford's Texas*, 188; Dorman H. Winfrey and James M. Day, eds., *The Indian Papers of Texas and the Southwest, 1825–1916*, 5 vols. (Austin: Texas State Historical Association, 1995), 5:169–171, accessed February 25, 2020, Portal, https://texashistory.unt.edu/ark:/67531/metapth786486/.

21. Nance, *After San Jacinto*, 106.

22. *Corpus Christi Gazette*, January 18, 1846.

23. Alexander Mendoza, "'For Our Own Best Interests': Nineteenth-Century Laredo Tejanos, Military Service, and the Development of American Nationalism," *Southwestern Historical Quarterly* 115, no. 2 (2011): 135.

Notes for Chapter 3

1. Galen D. Greaser and Jesús F. de la Teja, "Quieting Title to Spanish and Mexican Land Grants in the Trans-Nueces: The Bourland and Miller Commission, 1850–1852," *Southwestern Historical Quarterly* 95, no. 4 (April 1992): 446–47, http://www.jstor.org/stable/30242000.

2. Armando C. Alonzo, "Mexican-American Land Grant Adjudication," *Handbook of Texas Online*, accessed December 9, 2023, https://www.tshaonline.org/handbook/entries/mexican-american-land-grant-adjudication.

3. "Texas Annexation Questions and Answers," *Texas State Library and Archives*, April 5, 2011, https://www.tsl.texas.gov/exhibits/annexation/part5/question8.html.

4. De León, *Tejano Community*, 17.

5. Greaser and de la Teja, "Quieting Title," 45q, 454.

6. "Transcript of Treaty of Guadalupe Hidalgo (1848)," www.OurDocuments.gov, accessed November 29, 2019, https://www.ourdocuments.gov/print_friendly.php?flash=false&page=transcript&doc=26&title=Transcript+of+Treaty+of+Guadalupe+Hidalgo+(1848).

7. "Transcript of Treaty of Guadalupe Hidalgo (1848)"; Jesse S. Reeves, "The Treaty of Guadalupe-Hidalgo," *American Historical Review* 10, no. 2 (1905): 309–24, https://doi.org/10.2307/1834723.

8. "Transcript of Treaty of Guadalupe Hidalgo (1848)"; Reeves, "Treaty of Guadalupe-Hidalgo," 323–24.

9. *McKinney v. Saviego*, 59 U.S. 235 (US Supreme Court 1856).

10. "An Act to Provide for the Investigation of Land Titles in Certain Counties Therein Mentioned" (1850), https://texashistory.unt.edu/ark:/67531/metapth6728/m1/586/zoom/?resolution=1&lat=2498.4609374999995&lon=660.8281249999994.

11. Todd Lowry, "Bourland, William H.," *Handbook of Texas Online*, accessed October 27, 2022, https://www.tshaonline.org/handbook/entries/bourland-william-h; "Miller, James B.," *Handbook of Texas Online*, accessed October 27, 2022, https://www.tshaonline.org/handbook/entries/miller-james-b.

12. Hans Peter Mareus Neilsen Gammel, *The Laws of Texas, 1822–1897*, 11 vols. (Austin: Gammel Book Company, 1898) 3:582–587.

13. Gammel, *Laws of Texas*, 3:798.

14. Greaser and de la Teja, "Quieting Title," 457.

15. Greaser and de la Teja, "Quieting Title," 457.

16. Alonzo, *Tejano Legacy*, 152–53; Greaser and de la Teja, "Quieting Title," 454–57; Gammel, *Laws of Texas*, 3:798.

17. Gammel, *Laws of Texas*, 3:941.

18. The enabling legislation creating Starr County in 1848 did not spell out its boundaries. Instead, it delineated them as "that territory within the present county of Nueces fronting the Rio Grande, and not included in the counties of Webb, Cameron, and Nueces" would constitute Starr County. Gammel, *Laws of Texas*, 3:24.

19. Gammel, *Laws of Texas*, 3:24.

20. W. H. Bourland and James Miller, "Report of W. H. Bourland and James R. Miller Commissioner to Investigate Titles West of the Nueces" (Austin: Texas General Land Office, 1852), para. Starr #13, Historical Volumes, GLO Archives, https://s3.glo.texas.gov/glo/history/archives/map-store/index.cfm#item/94259 (hereafter cited as Bourland and Miller, "Report"); "San Francisco," San Patricio 1st 000537, Falcón, Juan José M. de la Garza, ARD GLO, accessed May 15, 2019, http://www.glo.texas.gov/ncu/SCANDOCS/archives_webfiles/arcmaps/webfiles/landgrants/PDFs/5/4/1/541434.pdf; Brian Stauffer email to author re: patent files, April 3, 2020; patents are kept in bound volumes in a special vault at the General Land Office.

21. "Palo Blanquito," San Patricio 1st 000306, Cuellar, Jose Antonio, ARD GLO, accessed April 3, 2020, https://s3.glo.texas.gov/ncu/SCANDOCS/archives_webfiles/arcmaps/webfiles/landgrants/PDFs/5/4/0/540655.pdf (hereafter cited as "Palo Blanquito").

22. Tijerina, *Tejano Empire*, 6; De León, *Tejano Community*, 114–16.

23. Tijerina, *Tejano Empire*, 6; De León, *Tejano Community*, 114–16.

24. Bourland and Miller, "Report," para. Starr #5; "Palo Blanquito."

25. Bourland and Miller, "Report," para. Starr #24; "Palo Blanco," San Patricio 1st 000440, Hinojosa Marcelo, ARD GLO, accessed April 13, 2020, https://s3.glo. texas.gov/ncu/SCANDOCS/archives_webfiles/arcmaps/webfiles/landgrants/ PDFs/5/4/1/541211.pdf; "Santos Flores, Agostadero de Agua Poquita," *El Mesteño* 1, no. 10 (1997): 8.

26. San Patricio 1st 000439, García, Santos, ARD GLO, accessed August 18, 2021, https://s3.glo.texas.gov/ncu/SCANDOCS/archives_webfiles/arcmaps/ webfiles/landgrants/PDFs/5/4/1/541208.pdf (hereafter cited as SP439, García, Santos); San Patricio 1st 000441, Hinojosa, Diego, ARD GLO, accessed August 18, 2021, https://s3.glo.texas.gov/ncu/SCANDOCS/archives_webfiles/ arcmaps/webfiles/landgrants/PDFs/5/4/1/541214.pdf.

27. Bourland and Miller, "Report," para. Starr #24; "El Charco de Palo Blanco," ARD GLO; SP 439 García, Santos; "Santos García, 'Agostadero El Charco de Palo Blanco,'" *El Mesteño* 2, no. 18 (1998): 8.

28. Bourland and Miller, "Report," para. Starr #24; "San Rafael de Los Encinos," San Patricio 1st 000441, Hinojosa, Marcelo, ARD GLO, accessed April 13, 2020, https://s3.glo.texas.gov/ncu/SCANDOCS/archives_webfiles/arcmaps/webfiles/ landgrants/PDFs/5/4/1/541214.pdf.

29. Bourland and Miller, "Report," para. Starr #10; "Santa Rosalía," San Patricio 1st 000451, Ramírez, Rafael, ARD GLO, accessed April 3, 2020, https://s3.glo. texas.gov/ncu/SCANDOCS/archives_webfiles/arcmaps/webfiles/landgrants/ PDFs/5/4/1/541246.pdf; "San Pedro Del Charco Redondo," San Patricio 1st 000450 Ramirez, Rafael, ARD GLO, accessed April 3, 2020, https://s3.glo. texas.gov/ncu/SCANDOCS/archives_webfiles/arcmaps/webfiles/landgrants/ PDFs/5/4/1/541243.pdf; "Rafael Ramírez Yzaguirre, Agostadero La Rosalía," *El Mesteño* 3, no. 24 (1999): 8.

30. Records for this grant include a detailed description of the process in certifying a grant. It is included here to provide the reader the meticulous nature involved.

31. "Santa Cruz de Concepción," San Patricio 1st 000311, Cordente, Francisco, ARD GLO, accessed May 11, 2019, http://www.glo.texas.gov/ncu/SCANDOCS/ archives_webfiles/arcmaps/webfiles/landgrants/PDFs/5/4/0/540685.pdf. (hereafter cited as "Santa Cruz de Concepción").

32. "Santa Cruz de Concepción."

33. "Santa Cruz de Concepción."

34. "Santa Cruz de Concepción."

35. "Santa Cruz de Concepción."

36. "Santa Cruz de Concepción."

37. "Santa Cruz de Concepción"; "Francisco Cordente, 'Mexico Deaths, 1680–1940,'" *Family Search*, accessed April 15, 2020, https://www.familysearch.org/ ark:/61903/1:1:N8FV-BHT; "Francisco Cordente Agostadero La Santa Cruz de La Concepción," *El Mesteño*, 1998, 8; "Original Survey of the Agostadero La Santa Cruz de La Concepción," *El Mesteño*, 1998, 17.

38. "Santa Cruz de Concepción."
39. Bourland and Miller, "Report," para. Starr #109; "Santa Cruz de Concepción."
40. "Las Anacuas," San Patricio 1st 000416, Ynojosa, Vicente, ARD GLO, accessed June 28, 2019, http://www.glo.texas.gov/ncu/SCANDOCS/archives_webfiles/arcmaps/webfiles/landgrants/PDFs/5/4/1/541130.pdf; Bourland and Miller, "Report," para. Nueces #6.
41. "Las Anacuas."
42. Gammel, *Laws of Texas*, 4:1471.
43. George Washington Paschal, *A Digest of the Laws of Texas* (Houston: W. H. & O. H. Morrison, 1873), 1447–50.
44. Gammel, *Laws of Texas*, 4:1470–73.
45. "San Diego de Arriba y Abajo"; José Noe Martinez, *St. Francis de Paula Catholic Church: The Story of Its Founding and Early History*, ed. Sonia C. Barrera (San Diego, TX: Duval County Historical Commission, 2008), 1.
46. *Trinidad Flores y Perez v. State of Texas*, n.d., file 423, GLO.
47. "San Diego de Arriba y Abajo."
48. "San Diego de Arriba y Abajo."
49. "San Diego de Arriba y Abajo"; "San Diego de Arriba and San Diego de Abajo," *El Mesteño* 1, no. 3 (1997): 8; "Paraje San Diego," *El Mesteño* 4, no. 37 (n.d.): 6.
50. "Agostadero de La Huerta" San Patricio 1st 000539, Gonzales, José Antonio, ARD GLO, accessed June 20, 2019, http://www.glo.texas.gov/ncu/SCANDOCS/archives_webfiles/arcmaps/webfiles/landgrants/PDFs/5/4/0/540685.pdf. (hereafter cited as "Agostadero de La Huerta").
51. *Ignacio Gonzales et. al. v. Gertrudes Chartier*, 63 Texas Reports 35 (Texas Supreme Court, January 16, 1885).
52. *State v. Palacios*, 150 S.W. 229, CourtListener.Com, accessed March 21, 2020, https://books.google.com/books?id=jHk7AAAAIAAJ&q=Palacios#v=snippet&q=Palacios&f=false.
53. "Agostadero de La Huerta."
54. "Agostadero de La Huerta."
55. Gammel, *Laws of Texas*, 5:568.
56. "El Señor de La Carrera," San Patricio 1st 000542, Elizondo, Dionisio, ARD GLO, accessed April 3, 2020, https://s3.glo.texas.gov/ncu/SCANDOCS/archives_webfiles/arcmaps/webfiles/landgrants/PDFs/5/4/1/541444.pdf.
57. File 579, 1810, Deed Records, Nueces County District Clerk, Corpus Christi, TX; "San Leandro," San Patricio 1st 000424, Salinas, José Rafael García, ARD GLO, accessed May 11, 2019, http://www.glo.texas.gov/ncu/SCANDOCS/archives_webfiles/arcmaps/webfiles/landgrants/PDFs/5/4/1/541159.pdf (hereafter cited as "San Leandro").
58. "San Leandro."
59. "San Leandro."

60. "San Leandro."

61. "Agua Poquita," San Patricio 1st 000446, Flores, Santos, ARD GLO, accessed June 28, 2019, http://www.glo.texas.gov/ncu/SCANDOCS/archives_webfiles/ arcmaps/webfiles/landgrants/PDFs/5/4/1/541230.pdf (hereafter cited as "Agua Poquita").

62. "Agua Poquita."

63. "Santa María de Los Ángeles de Abajo," San Patricio 1st 000640, Vela, Trinidad, ARD GLO, accessed May 11, 2019, http://www.glo.texas.gov/ ncu/SCANDOCS/archives_webfiles/arcmaps/webfiles/landgrants/PDFs/ 5/4/1/541563.pdf (hereafter cited as "Santa María de Los Ángeles de Abajo").

64. "Santa María de Los Ángeles de Abajo."

65. "Santa María de Los Ángeles de Abajo."

66. "Santa María de Los Ángeles de Abajo."

67. "San Andres," San Patricio 1st 000531, Garcia, Andres (Heirs of), ARD GLO, accessed June 28, 2019, http://www.glo.texas.gov/ncu/SCANDOCS/archives_ webfiles/arcmaps/webfiles/landgrants/PDFs/5/4/1/541421.pdf (hereafter cited as "San Andres").

68. "San Andres."

69. "San Andres"; "Andrés García, 'Agostadero San Andrés,'" *El Mesteño* 1, no. 9 (1997): 8.

70. Ty Cashion, "What's the Matter with Texas? The Great Enigma of the Lone Star State in the American West," *Montana: The Magazine of Western History* 55, no. 4 (Winter 2005): 13, http://www.jstor.org/stable/4520740.

71. "Preliminary Thoughts on Region and Period," *Center for Great Plains Studies*, accessed August 23, 2021, https://www.unl.edu/plains/about/thoughts. shtml; Michael Kuby, John Harner, and Patricia Gober, *Human Geography in Action* (Hoboken, NJ: John Wiley & Sons, 2013), 60; Cashion, "What's the Matter with Texas?," 13.

Notes for Chapter 4

1. John Martin Davis, *Texas Land Grants, 1750–1900: A Documentary History* (Jefferson, NC: McFarland, 2016), 27; "Categories of Land Grants in Texas," GLO, March 13, 2021 https://www.glo.texas.gov/history/archives/forms/files/ categories-of-land-grants.pdf.

2. "Categories of Land Grants in Texas"; "Land Districts," *Handbook of Texas Online*, accessed April 15, 2021, https://www.tshaonline.org/handbook/entries/ land-districts.

3. "Categories of Land Grants in Texas."

4. "Categories of Land Grants in Texas."

5. "Categories of Land Grants in Texas."

6. "Categories of Land Grants in Texas."

7. "Categories of Land Grants in Texas."

8. Mark K. Leaverton, "The Genesis of Title: Land Grants, Patents & State-Owned Minerals," (2nd Texas Mineral Title Examination Course, Houston, Texas, 2015), 9; Margaret S. Henson, "McKinney, Thomas Freeman," *Handbook of Texas Online*, accessed March 20, 2021, https://www.tshaonline.org/handbook/entries/mckinney-thomas-freeman; Joe B. Frantz, "The Mercantile House of McKinney & Williams, Underwriters of the Texas Revolution," *Bulletin of the Business Historical Society* 26, no. 1 (1952): 1–18, https://doi.org/10.2307/3111339.

9. "Categories of Land Grants in Texas."

10. Susan Dorsey, email message to author, March 22, 2021.

11. Dorsey, email message to author, March 22, 2021.

12. Dorsey, email message to author, March 22, 2021.

13. Dorsey, email message to author, March 22, 2021.

14. Dorsey, email message to author, March 22, 2021.

15. Dorsey, email message to author, March 22, 2021.

16. Dorsey, email message to author, March 22, 2021.

Notes for Chapter 5

1. De León, *Tejano Community*, 81.

2. Jordan-Bychkov, *North American Cattle-Ranching Frontiers*, 152–53; Jesús F. De La Teja, Paula Mitchell Marks, and Ronnie C. Tyler, *Texas: Crossroads of North America* (Boston: Houghton Mifflin, 2004), 79, 306.

3. Valerio-Jiménez, "Neglected Citizens and Willing Traders," 254–55, 264.

4. "Santa María de Los Ángeles de Abajo"; "San Leandro."

5. Alonzo, *Tejano Legacy*, 88–89.

6. Jack Jackson, *Los Mesteños: Spanish Ranching in Texas, 1721–1821*, 1st ed., Centennial Series of the Association of Former Students, Texas A&M University, 18 (College Station: Texas A&M University Press, 1986), 608–9, 615, 617.

7. "Nueces County, Its Location, Population, Productions, Water, Stock-Raising, Geology, Roads, Prospects, Etc.," *Ranchero* (Corpus Christi), May 12, 1860, p. 2, Portal, https://texashistory.unt.edu/ark:/67531/metapth852478/m1/2/zoom/.

8. "Texas, County Tax Rolls, 1837–1910," 1850, accessed November 6, 2022, https://www.familysearch.org/ark:/61903/3:1:939J-4R3K-M?wc=M63N-HP8%3A161812001%2C161400001&cc=1827575.

9. "1860 United States Federal Census," *HeritageQuest*, accessed November 6, 2022, https://www.ancestryheritagequest.com/search/collections/7667/.

10. "Texas, County Tax Rolls, 1837–1910."

11. "1870 United States Federal Census," *Ancestry*, accessed November 6, 2022, https://www.ancestryheritagequest.com/search/collections/7163/; "Texas, County Tax Rolls, 1837–1910."

12. "1870 United States Federal Census." Note: Search criteria, Duval County, Precinct 4, Concepción and Nueces County, Precinct 3, San Diego.

13. Charles Julian Bishko, "The Peninsular Background of Latin American Cattle Ranching," *Hispanic American Historical Review* 32, no. 4 (1952): 507, 510, https://doi.org/10.2307/2508949.

14. Henry A. Maltby, "Fac Similes of Brands," *Ranchero* (Corpus Christi), January 19, 1861, Portal, https://texashistory.unt.edu/ark:/67531/metapth852514/m1/1/zoom/.

15. Jordan-Bychkov, *North American Cattle-Ranching Frontiers*, 8; Andrés Tijerina and Ricardo M. Beasley, *Beasley's Vaqueros: In the Memoirs, Art, and Poems of Ricardo M. Beasley* (Austin: Texas State Historical Association, 2022), 35.

16. Jordan-Bychkov, *North American Cattle-Ranching Frontiers*, 8.

17. Alonzo, *Tejano Legacy*, 198.

18. Arnoldo De León, "Vamos Pa' Kiansis: Tejanos in the Nineteenth-Century Cattle Drives," *Journal of South Texas* 27, no. 2 (Fall 2014): 6.

19. Bishko, "Peninsular Background of Latin American Cattle Ranching," 506; "The Cattle Folk Timeline," *Texas State History Museum*, accessed January 27, 2021, https://www.thestoryoftexas.com/discover/campfire-stories/cattle-folk.

20. J. Frank Dobie and John Duncan Young, *A Vaquero of the Brush Country* (Austin: University of Texas Press, 1998), 60; Alonzo, *Tejano Legacy*, 197–204; Bishko, "Peninsular Background of Latin American Cattle Ranching," 501.

Notes for Chapter 6

1. Alonzo, *Tejano Legacy*, 191, 196–97; González-Quiroga, *War and Peace on the Rio Grande Frontier*, 278.

2. Alonzo, *Tejano Legacy*, 207, 209; McCampbell, *Texas Seaport*, 18.

3. McCampbell, *Texas Seaport*, 18.

4. Gary Kraisinger (coauthor of *The Western: The Greatest Texas Cattle Trail, 1874–1886* [2004]), in discussion with the author, December 31, 2020; Bishko, "Peninsular Background of Latin American Cattle Ranching," 498–99, 509.

5. "Cattle Folk Timeline."

6. "Duval County Tax Rolls, 1877–1910," 1880, *FamilySearch*, accessed January 7, 2021, https://www.familysearch.org/search/image/index?owc=M638-NZ4%3A161469401%3Fcc%3D1827575.

7. Vicki Ruiz, *From out of the Shadows: Mexican Women in Twentieth-Century America*, 10th anniversary ed. (Oxford: Oxford University Press, 2008), xi, 4.

8. *Trinidad Flores y Perez v. State of Texas*, No. 590 (14th District of Texas, December 11, 1860); Power of Attorney, Antonio Garcia Flores, Juan D. Garza, María Flores Gonzalez, G. Flores, Santos Flores (Mark), Rafael Garcia Flores, Pablo Perez (Mark), Trinidad Flores de Perez, José María G. Flores, Eduardo G. Flores, E. Garcia Perez, 1869, Duval County Clerk.

9. David Dary, "Cattle Brands," *Handbook of Texas Online*, accessed January 19, 2021, https://www.tshaonline.org/handbook/entries/cattle-brands; Homero Vera, "Ranchos in Duval County," *El Mesteño* 1, no. 5 (February 1998): 16.

10. Most ranchos with Americano names evolved in the last quarter of the nineteenth century.

11. Vera, "Ranchos in Duval County," 1–24.

12. Reference to Benavides, which did not exist at this time, is provided here as a geographic tool for the reader. The community of Benavides did not come into existence until 1880, while most of these ranchos existed before that time.

13. Vera, "Ranchos in Duval County," 1–24.

14. Vera, "Ranchos in Duval County," 1–24.

15. Vera, "Ranchos in Duval County," 1–24.

16. "1880 United States Federal Census," AncestryHeritageQuest.com, accessed September 9, 2018, https://www.ancestryheritagequest.com/interactive/6742/4244720-00598?backurl=https%3a%2f%2fsearch.ancestryheritagequest.com%2fsearch%2fdb.aspx%3fdbid%3d6742%26path%3d&ssrc=&backlabel=ReturnBrowsing#?imageId=4244720-00634.

17. "1880 United States Federal Census."

18. "Texas, County Tax Rolls, 1837–1910."

19. "Texas, County Tax Rolls, 1837–1910," Duval County.

20. E. Levan, "Some West Texas Ranches," *Corpus Christi Caller*, December 9, 1883.

21. "Twelve Thousand Cattle Stampeded by a Storm–Heavy Shipments to Wichita Falls," *Fort Worth Daily Gazette*, April 23, 1884, p. 5, Portal, https://texashistory.unt.edu/ark:/67531/metapth89234/m1/5/zoom/; "San Diego Pencilings," *Corpus Christi Caller*, September 12, 1884.

22. "San Diego Notes," *Corpus Christi Caller*, June 14, 1885; Wayne Gard, *Rawhide Texas* (Norman: University of Oklahoma Press, 2015), 14.

23. "Miscellaneous Mention," *Corpus Christi Caller*, May 31, 1885; "San Diego Notes," *Corpus Christi Caller*, June 14, 1885.

24. "San Diego Siftings," *Corpus Christi Caller*, November 21, 1886; "Miscellaneous Mention," *Corpus Christi Caller*, December 3, 1887; "San Diego Siftings," *Corpus Christi Caller*, February 22, 1885; "San Diego Siftings," *Corpus Christi Caller*, April 30, 1887; "Realitos Weekly Record," *Corpus Christi Caller*, June 25, 1887; Jeffreys, "From Duval's Capital," *Corpus Christi Caller*, September 17, 1887.

25. McCampbell, *Texas Seaport*, 18, 65.

26. "Texas, County Tax Rolls, 1837–1910," Duval County.

27. "1900 United States Federal Census," Ancestry.com, accessed November 13, 2022, https://www.ancestryheritagequest.com/imageviewer/collections/7602/images/4118457_00600?ssrc=&backlabel=Return.

28. "Weather and Crops," *Galveston Daily News*, May 20, 1894, p. 5, Portal, https://texashistory.unt.edu/ark:/67531/metapth467991/m1/5/zoom/?q=Duval&resolution=1&lat=1061.2954469748693&lon=4561.212690899652; "Seven-Year Drouth, Condition of the Ranch Owners in Southwestern Texas–Can't Pay Their Taxes, Appeal to Texas for Aid," *Galveston Daily News*, May 20, 1894, p. 3, Portal, https://texashistory.unt.edu/ark:/67531/metapth467991/m1/3/zoom/.

29. "Laredo Notes," *Galveston Daily News*, April 29, 1894, Portal, https://texashistory.unt.edu/ark:/67531/metapth465415/m1/9/zoom/?q=%22Duval%20County%22%20date:1890-1899&resolution=1.5&lat=720.3636093139648&lon=4348.954345703125.

30. "Duval County Drouth, A Car of Corn Distributed Among the Sufferers–A Good Rain," *Galveston Daily News*, May 16, 1894, Portal, https://texashistory.unt.edu/ark:/67531/metapth466078/m1/5/zoom/?q=%22Duval%20County%22%20date:1890-1899&resolution=1.5&lat=6159.247682372103&lon=1732.4809737827532.

31. "Duval County Drouth," *Galveston Daily News*, May 16, 1894.

32. "Duval County Drouth," *Galveston Daily News*, May 16, 1894.

33. Alonzo, *Tejano Legacy*, 206–7.

34. Alice Evans Downie, *Terrell County, Texas, Its Past, Its People: A Compilation, Pictures of and Writings by or about People Places, and Events in Terrell County* (Sanderson, TX: Terrell County Heritage Commission, 1978), 240–41.

35. "From Benavides," *Corpus Christi Caller*, January 12, 1900.

36. González-Quiroga, *War and Peace on the Rio Grande Frontier*, 12.

Notes for Chapter 7

1. Jerry D. Thompson, *Vaqueros in Blue & Gray* (Austin: State House Press, 2000), 7; Charles David Grear, *Why Texans Fought in the Civil War* (College Station: Texas A & M University Press, 2012), 152; James Marten, *Texas Divided Loyalty and Dissent in the Lone Star State, 1856–1874* (Lexington: University Press of Kentucky, 2015), 30, 106.

2. Teresa Palomo Acosta and Ruthe Winegarten, *Las Tejanas: 300 Years of History*, 1st ed, Jack and Doris Smothers Series in Texas History, Life, and Culture 10 (Austin: University of Texas Press, 2003), 57.

3. "The Laredo Vote," *Ranchero* (Corpus Christi), September 3, 1863, p. 2, Portal, https://texashistory.unt.edu/ark:/67531/metapth852627/m1/2/zoom/; Marten, *Texas Divided Loyalty*, 29–30, 106; Grear, *Why Texans Fought in the Civil*

War, 9, 158; Marten, "Patriots and Dissidents: The Role of Ethnicity in Civil War Texas," *Heritage of the Great Plains* 22, no. 3 (1989): 18–19.

4. Santiago Escobedo, "Iron Men And Wooden Carts: Mexican American Freighters During the Civil War," *Journal of South Texas* 17, no. 2 (Fall 2004): 51–52; Miguel Ángel González-Quiroga, "Mexicanos in Texas during the Civil War," in *Mexican Americans in Texas History, Selected Essays*, ed. Emiliano Zamora, Cynthia Orozco, and Rodolfo Rocha (Austin: Texas State Historical Association, 2000), 61–62.

5. "Texas Items," *Weekly Telegraph* (Houston), November 20, 1860, 2, Portal, https://texashistory.unt.edu/ark:/67531/metapth236120/m1/2/zoom/; Mendoza, "For Our Own Best Interests," 136–39; Jerry D. Thompson and Lawrence T. Jones, *Civil War and Revolution on the Rio Grande Frontier: A Narrative and Photographic History* (Austin: Texas State Historical Association, 2004), 69; DeLeon, *They Called Them Greasers*, 55, 59; Marten "Patriots and Dissidents," 18; Marten, *Texas Divided Loyalty*, 123, 126.

6. Nueces County Commissioners Court Minutes, 1860, Book B, 1858–1863, p. 162, Nueces County District Clerk; Marten, *Texas Divided Loyalty*, 96, 126.

7. This was likely Captain James Ware, stationed in Corpus Christi, who undertook various responsibilities for the rebel cause.

8. Judy Ware, "Cavalry and Cotton," chap. 8 in *Ware Family Genealogy*, accessed October 28, 2022, http://www.waregenealogy.com/ForSouthlandLoved-Chapter08.html; Menchaca, *Naturalizing Mexican Immigrants*, 42; Grear, *Why Texans Fought in the Civil War*, 135; Thompson, *Vaqueros in Blue & Gray*, 56–57; Nueces County Commissioners Court Minutes, 1876, p. 162; Ford, *Rip Ford's Texas*, 350.

9. Jerry D. Thompson, *Mexican Texans in the Union Army*, 1st ed., Southwestern Studies 78 (El Paso: Texas Western Press, 1986), 17.

10. Robert N. Scott, *The War of the Rebellion: A Compilation of the Official Records of the Union and Confederate Armies*, 128 vols. (Harrisburg, PA: National Historical Society; distributed by Broadfoot, Historical Times, Morningside House, 1985), 26:898; Nueces County Commissioners Court Minutes, Book C, n.d., Nueces County District Clerk; "1860 United States Federal Census."

11. Cortina's operations during the Civil War were mostly on the Mexican side of the Rio Grande.

12. Thompson, *Mexican Texans in the Union Army*, 38; Marten, *Texas Divided Loyalty*, 123; "USS Harriet Lane (1861–1863)," *Naval History and Heritage Command*, accessed June 26, 2022, https://www.history.navy.mil/our-collections/photography/us-navy-ships/alphabetical-listing/h/uss-harriet-lane--1861-1863-0.html.

13. Thompson, *Wild and Vivid Land*, 111.

14. Ford, *Rip Ford's Texas*, 359; Scott, *War of the Rebellion*, 26:1033, 1106, 1312.

15. Thompson, *Vaqueros in Blue & Gray*, 102.

16. Thompson, *Vaqueros in Blue & Gray*, 102; Ford, *Rip Ford's Texas*, 347–48.

17. Thompson, *Vaqueros in Blue & Gray*, 103.

18. Ford, *Rip Ford's Texas*, 353–54; Thompson, *Wild and Vivid Land*, 111.

19. Thompson, *Vaqueros in Blue & Gray*, 28, 56–57, 102–3, 130–32; Grear, *Why Texans Fought in the Civil War*, 96; Thompson, *Wild and Vivid Land*, 111; Scott, *War of the Rebellion*, 34:1, 11, 1106, 48:1, 1312; Thompson, *Mexican Texans in the Union Army*, 22, 26, 36; Marten, *Texas Divided Loyalty*, 123; Menchaca, *Naturalizing Mexican Immigrants*, 42; Thompson, *Sabers on the Rio Grande*, 208, 210; Ford, *Rip Ford's Texas*, 347–48, 350, 353–54, 359, 636–39.

20. Thompson, *Mexican Texans in the Union Army*, 36; González-Quiroga, *War and Peace on the Rio Grande Frontier*, 157.

21. González-Quiroga, *War and Peace on the Rio Grande Frontier*, 284.

22. "Corpus Christi," *Ranchero*, May 12, 1860, p. 2, Portal, https://texashistory.unt.edu/ark:/67531/metapth852478/m1/2/zoom/; Thompson, *Sabers on the Rio Grande*, 170; Ford, *Rip Ford's Texas*, 167.

23. *Ranchero*, November 3, 1860, p. 2, Portal, https://texashistory.unt.edu/ark:/67531/metapth852564/m1/2/zoom/.

24. "1870 United States Federal Census."

25. Norman C. Delaney, *The Maltby Brothers' Civil War* (College Station: Texas A & M University Press, 2013), 107; Ford, *Rip Ford's Texas*, 347–48; Thompson and Jones, *Civil War and Revolution on the Rio Grande Frontier*, 69; Thompson, *Mexican Texans in the Union Army*, 22; De León, *They Called Them Greasers*, 72; Dobie and Young, *Vaquero of the Brush Country*, 60; Nueces County Commissioners Court Minutes, book C, n.d.; *Corpus Christi Gazette*, April 12, 1873.

26. Nueces County Commissioners Court Minutes, book B, n.d.; Election Returns from Nueces County, October 8, 1860, Nueces County District Clerk, Executive Department, TSLAC; *Ranchero*, August 25, 1860.

27. Randolph B. Campbell, *Grass-Roots Reconstruction in Texas, 1865–1880* (Baton Rouge: Louisiana State University Press, 1997), 195; Election Returns from Nueces County, October 8, 1860.

28. Election Returns from Nueces County, October 8, 1860.

29. Election Returns from Nueces County, October 8, 1860; Mike Kingston, Sam Attlesey, and Mary G. Crawford, *The Texas Almanac's Political History of Texas* (Austin: Eakin Press, 1992), 60, 74.

30. Randolph B. Campbell, "Reconstruction in Nueces County, 1865–76," *Houston Review* 16, no. 1 (January 1994): 16–18; Ford, *Rip Ford's Texas*, 263–64.

31. Delaney, *Maltby Brothers' Civil War*, 55; Campbell, *Grass-Roots Reconstruction in Texas*, 196–97, 217–18.

32. Nueces County Commissioners Court Minutes, book C, n.d.

33. Campbell, *Grass-Roots Reconstruction in Texas*, 202.

34. Randolph B. Campbell, "Grass Roots Reconstruction: The Personnel of County Government in Texas, 1865–1876," *Journal of Southern History* 58, no. 1 (1992): 101, https://doi.org/10.2307/2210476; Delaney, *Maltby Brothers' Civil War*, 56.

35. Campbell, *Grass-Roots Reconstruction in Texas*, 204.

36. Campbell, *Grass-Roots Reconstruction in Texas*, 206–7.

37. Nueces County Commissioners Court Minutes, book C, n.d.

38. Nueces County Commissioners Court Minutes, book A, n.d.; Campbell, *Grass-Roots Reconstruction*, 202–4, 206–7.

39. Nueces County Commissioners Court Minutes, October 23, 1865, February 24, 1868, January 19, 1869, July 5, 1870, January 31, 1871, March 28, 1871, September 25, 1871, January 29, 1872, July 27, 1873, January 29, 1874, April 20, 1874, July 28, 1874, November 30, 1874, March 1875, July 28, 1875, and December 4, 1875.

40. Nueces County Commissioners Court Minutes, November 30, 1870, February 1872; Campbell, *Grass-Roots Reconstruction in Texas*, 206–7.

41. "County Election, Republican ticket elected," *Nueces Valley* (Corpus Christi), October 22, 1870; Menchaca, *Naturalizing Mexican Immigrants*, 61; Campbell, *Grass-Roots Reconstruction in Texas*, 209; John Henry Brown, *Indian Wars and Pioneers of Texas* (Greenville, SC: Southern Historical Press, 1978), 504.

42. Campbell, *Grass-Roots Reconstruction in Texas*, 213–14.

43. County Election Results, Nueces County, 1873, Texas Secretary of State, TSLAC.

44. Campbell, "Grass Roots Reconstruction," 101; Menchaca, *Naturalizing Mexican Immigrants*, 58; Nueces County Commissioners Court Minutes, n.d.

Notes for Chapter 8

1. Other Duval County communities were developed as a direct response to the arrival of the railroad and will be discussed in a later chapter.

2. La Vaca grant was in the southeast side of the creek in what became Jim Wells County.

3. Duval County Deed Records, 120–21; Duval County Deed Records, vol. 1, 83–85.

4. J. W. Moses, "History of San Diego: Origins and Growth of the City in the Woods," September 1887, Archival Record, San Diego, TSLAC.

5. The location of the store, whether on the north or south side of the river, is not known.

6. Moses, "History of San Diego."

7. Duval County Deed Records, vol. 1, 122–28; *John Levy vs. The State of Texas* (Nueces County District Clerk, January 9, 1862), Records Office, Nueces County District Clerk; Duval County Deed Records, 150–53.

8. Moses, "History of San Diego"; Duval County Deed Records, vol. A, 162–64.

9. *Corpus Christi Gazette*, November 6, 1875.

10. Xavier, *Father Jaillet*, 91.

11. Acosta and Winegarten, *Las Tejanas*, 10, 28.

12. *Alonzo, Tejano Legacy*, 122.

13. "Catholic Church," *Handbook of Texas Online*, accessed January 24, 2022, https://www.tshaonline.org/handbook/entries/catholic-church; Ruiz, *From out of the Shadows*, 4.

14. Gregory Hernández, Gloria Hernández, and Raúl J Guerra, *Capilla de La Misión de Roma Marriage Book, Roma, Texas* (San Antonio: Los Béxareños Genealogical Society, 2012), 40.

15. Hernández, Hernández, and Guerra, *Capilla de La Misión de Roma Marriage Book*, 78–80.

16. Hernández, Hernández, and Guerra, *Capilla de La Misión de Roma Marriage Book*, 78–80.

17. Claude Jaillet, "Historical Sketch" (Corpus Christi, TX, n.d.), 2; Jaillet and Francis X. Reuss, "Sketches of Catholicity in Texas," *Records of the American Catholic Historical Society of Philadelphia*, no. 2 (1886): 152; Xavier, *Father Jaillet*, 18.

18. "Some Texas Parishes, San Diego," *Southern Messenger* (San Antonio), June 7, 1900, p. 1, Portal, https://texashistory.unt.edu/ark:/67531/metapth1266521/m1/1/zoom/; Xavier, *Father Jaillet*, 20; Martinez, *St. Francis de Paula Catholic Church*.

19. Agnes G. Grimm, "Bard, John Peter," *Handbook of Texas Online*, accessed March 10, 2023, https://www.tshaonline.org/handbook/entries/bard-john-peter., https://www.tshaonline.org/handbook/entries/bard-john-peter; "San Diego Siftings," *Corpus Christi Caller*, July 2, 1887.

20. "From San Diego," *Laredo Daily Times*, December 29, 1888; "West Texas Conference M. E. Church, South, Appointment of Preachers, 1880–81," *Galveston Daily News*, October 21, 1880, p. 4, Portal, https://texashistory.unt.edu/ark:/67531/metapth464889/m1/4/zoom/.

21. ATHOS, "San Diego Siftings," *Corpus Christi Caller*, October 5, 1884.

22. "San Diego Siftings," *Corpus Christi Caller*, April 26, 1888.

23. Lewis E. Daniell, *Personnel of the Texas State Government: With Sketches of Representative Men of Texas* (San Antonio: Maverick Print. House, 1892), 512–13.

24. "1870 United States Federal Census."

25. "1870 United States Federal Census."

26. John J. Germann and Myron R. Jansen, *Texas Post Offices* (Houston, J. J. Germann, 1989); Alfredo E. Cárdenas, "Newspaper Correspondent Jeffreys Identified as Dr. William C. Jefferies," *Soy de Duval* (blog), January 21, 2018 https://soydeduval.blogspot.com/2018/01/newspaper-correspondent-jeffreys.html; Lehmann and Cisneros, *Forgotten Legions*, 26.

27. Valerio-Jiménez, *River of Hope*, 16.

28. "Direct Communication with Rockport and Corpus Christi," *Galveston Daily News*, August 22, 1875, p. 4, Portal, https://texashistory.unt.edu/ark:/67531/metapth461054/m1/4/zoom/.

29. Menchaca, *Naturalizing Mexican Immigrants*, 15, 33, 48, 57–56, 71. Note: While Tejanos had gained citizenship of the Republic of Texas in 1836, American citizenship occurred in 1848 when the United States accepted Texas as a state and defeated Mexico in the Mexican American War.

30. Walter Meek, "History of San Diego," n.d., unpublished manuscript, in author's possession; Duval County Deed Records, vol. A, n.d., 541; "1880 United States Federal Census."

31. "Texas News Briefs," *Galveston Daily News*, August 27, 1880, Portal, https://texashistory.unt.edu/ark:/67531/metapth461956/m1/3/zoom/?q=center%20of%20mail%20routes&resolution=2&lat=7805.699350920227&lon=3718.4463025678815.

32. "The Second Biennial Report of the State Board of Education, for the Scholastic Years Ending August 31, 1879–1880" (Galveston, TX: Department of Education of the State of Texas, n.d.), 39, TSLAC.

33. "Second Biennial Report of the State Board of Education"; 1880 Census of the United States.

34. Francisco Gonzales and F. de P. González may be the same person.

35. Ellis Arthur Davis and Edwin H. Grobe, eds., *The Encyclopedia of Texas*, 2 vols. (Dallas: Texas Development Bureau, 1922), 1:171, Portal, https://texashistory.unt.edu/ark:/67531/metapth41244/m1/153/zoom/; "The History of Duval County Part II: Early Settlements," *Duval County Picture* (San Diego, TX), January 21, 1987, p. 3, Portal, https://texashistory.unt.edu/ark:/67531/metapth1009713/m1/3/zoom/; "Texas News Items: Duval County," *Galveston Daily News*, June 10, 1880, Portal, https://texashistory.unt.edu/ark:/67531/metapth461479/m1/3/zoom/?q=%22San%20Diego%20Tribune%22&resolution=3&lat=2495.575527321823&lon=3124.012587886969; Lynch, *Duke of Duval*, 10; "Kenedy Collection, fol. 0053," South Texas Archives, Texas A&M University–Kingsville, accessed November 28, 2020, https://archives.tamuk.edu/; Elliott Young, "Remembering Catarino Garza's 1891 Revolution: An Aborted Border Insurrection," *Mexican Studies / Estudios Mexicanos* 12, no. 2 (1996): 262, https://doi.org/10.2307/1051845.

36. J. Williamson Moses and Murphy D. Givens, *Texas in Other Days* (Corpus Christi: Friends of Corpus Christi Public Libraries, 2005); Alfredo E. Cárdenas,

"The Early Stirrings of the 'Town' of San Diego," *Soy de Duval* (blog), August 15, 2013, https://soydeduval.blogspot.com/2013/08/the-early-stirrings-of-of-san-diego.html; Cárdenas, "Newspaper Correspondent Jeffreys."

37. *Corpus Christi Caller*, March 25, 1883.
38. Jeffreys, "San Diego Siftings," *Corpus Christi Caller*, December 10, 1887.
39. "Knights of Honor," *Wikipedia*, accessed August 30, 2022, https://en.wikipedia.org/w/index.php?title=Knights_of_Honor&oldid=1107545808; "History," *Knights of Pythias*, accessed March 15, 2023, https://www.pythias.org/supreme/history; "History of Woodmen of the World," USGenNet.org, accessed March 15, 2023, http://www.usgennet.org/usa/ar/county/greene/historywood.htm; "From Duval County," *Corpus Christi Caller*, September 22, 1899.
40. E. T. M., "Rock for Aransas Pass," *Corpus Christi Caller*, March 25, 1883; "San Diego execution Refugio Gomez pays the death penalty for the murder of Estevan Dimas," *Corpus Christi Caller*, June 8, 1884.
41. "A Visit to San Diego," *Corpus Christi Caller*, May 14, 1887; "San Diego Gossip," *Corpus Christi Caller*, June 11, 1887.
42. "San Diego Siftings," July 18, 1886; GENERAL, "Another County Heard From," *Corpus Christi Caller*, March 31, 1888; GENERAL, "San Diego News," *Corpus Christi Caller*, April 14, 1888.
43. Jeffreys, "From Duval's Capital," *Corpus Christi Caller*, August 6, 1887; Jeffreys, "From Duval's Capital," *Corpus Christi Caller*, September 17, 1887; "From Duval's Capital," *Corpus Christi Caller*, October 1, 1887.
44. Jeffreys, "From Duval's Capital," *Corpus Christi Caller*, September 29, 1887.
45. "From Duval's Capital," *Corpus Christi Caller*, October 1, 1887.
46. "San Diego Siftings," *Corpus Christi Caller*, April 26, 1888; "From San Diego," *Laredo Daily Times*, April 23, 1889; "Baseball in the County," *Corpus Christi Caller*, May 5, 1888.
47. "From San Diego," *Laredo Daily Times*, July 24, 1888; "From San Diego," *Laredo Daily Times*, May 29, 1889.
48. "Sport," *Corpus Christi Caller*, May 11, 1884.
49. Sesom, "Rock for Aransas Pass," *Corpus Christi Caller*, April 4, 1883; "Monterey orchestra . . . ," *Corpus Christi Caller*, November 2, 1884.
50. "Miscellaneous Mention," *Corpus Christi Caller*, May 13, 1883.
51. "H. Maas Killed," *Corpus Christi Caller*, July 7, 1883.
52. "San Diego Doings," *Corpus Christi Caller*, July 5, 1885.
53. "A Grand Calico Ball," *Corpus Christi Caller*, February 28, 1886.
54. "San Diego Siftings," *Corpus Christi Caller*, July 18, 1886; "Letter from Jonis," *Corpus Christi Caller*, September 19, 1886.
55. "From Duval's Capital," *Corpus Christi Caller*, July 9, 1887.
56. "Another County Heard From," *Corpus Christi Caller*, March 31, 1888; "San Diego Siftings," *Corpus Christi Caller*, April 26, 1888; "San Diego Siftings," *Corpus Christi Caller*, May 15, 1888.

57. "San Diego Siftings," *Corpus Christi Caller*, May 15, 1888.
58. "Cinco de Mayo in Benavides," *Corpus Christi Caller*, May 5, 1888.
59. "San Diego Siftings," May 15, 1888.
60. "San Diego Siftings," *Corpus Christi Caller*, January 3, 1889.
61. "From San Diego," *Laredo Daily Times*, July 23, 1889.
62. "From San Diego," *Corpus Christi Caller*, August 6, 1889; Mary J. Straw Cook, *Doña Tules: Santa Fe's Courtesan and Gambler*, illustrated ed. (Albuquerque: University of New Mexico Press, 2007), 28.
63. "From Realitos," *Corpus Christi Caller*, June 30, 1899.
64. "From San Diego," *Corpus Christi Caller*, July 7, 1899.
65. "From Duval County," *Corpus Christi Caller*, September 22, 1899.

Notes for Chapter 9

1. *Corpus Christi Gazette*, May 31, 1873.
2. "Two Men Killed - Murder and Justifiable Homicide-An Englishman and a Mexican the Victims," *Corpus Christi Gazette*, September 26, 1874.
3. "Two Men Killed."
4. "Two Men Killed"; "Captured at Last," *Corpus Christi Caller*, June 15, 1884.
5. "Texas News Items," *Galveston News*, October 24, 1879, p. 4, Portal https://texashistory.unt.edu/ark:/67531/metapth460930/m1/4/zoom/?q=%22Rafael%20Salinas%22%20Duval%20County%22%201879&resolution=2&lat=7052.788198470267&lon=2616.4532695471053; "Texas State Items: Nueces," *Galveston Daily News*, October 28, 1879, p. 4, Portal, https://texashistory.unt.edu/ark:/67531/metapth462927/m1/4/zoom/.
6. "State News: Duval," *Galveston Daily News*, November 8, 1879, p. 4, Portal, https://texashistory.unt.edu/ark:/67531/metapth463925/m1/4/zoom/; "Texas Inside," *Norton's Union Intelligencer* (Dallas), November 22, 1879, Portal, https://texashistory.unt.edu/ark:/67531/metapth444697/m1/1/zoom/; "State News Items: Duval," *Galveston Daily News*, November 23, 1879, p. 1.
7. Wagner, "Disputed Territory," 59.
8. *Corpus Christi Gazette*, January 18, 1846, TX News. Coll.; Nance, *After San Jacinto*, 424.
9. *Nueces Valley* (Corpus Christi), October 8, 1870, TX News. Coll.; Sykes, *Corpus Christi Weekly Gazette*, October 4, 1873, Local History Archives, La Retama Central Library, Corpus Christi, TX (hereafter cited as Local History Archives, La Retama); *Corpus Christi Weekly Gazette*, December 2, 1873, Local History Archives, La Retama.
10. *Floresville Chronicle*, March 28, 1952; *Corpus Christi Gazette*, December 2, 1873; *Corpus Christi Weekly Gazette*, October 24, 1874, TX News. Coll.
11. "The Mexican and Indian Raid of '78," *Quarterly of the Texas State Historical Association* 5, no. 3 (January 1902): 216.

12. "Mexican and Indian Raid of '78," 232–35.

13. "Mexican and Indian Raid of '78," 219.

14. "Mexican and Indian Raid of '78."

15. "Mexican and Indian Raid of '78," 241.

16. "Mexican and Indian Raid of '78," 239–40, 242.

17. "Mexican and Indian Raid of '78," 216–21, 233–41, 245.

18. Hämäläinen, Pekka, "Conclusion: The Shape of Power," in *The Comanche Empire* (New Haven, CT: Yale University Press, 2008), 361, http://www.jstor.org/stable/j.ctt1njn13.13.

19. "From San Diego," *Corpus Christi Gazette*, April 5, 1873.

20. "Piedras Pintas," *Corpus Christi Gazette*, April 12, 1873.

21. *Corpus Christi Gazette*, April 26, 1873.

22. Dobie and Young, *Vaquero of the Brush Country*, 60.

23. "The Impudent Brave," *Corpus Christi Gazette*, May 3, 1873.

24. *Corpus Christi Gazette*, May 31, 1873.

25. "A Remedy Needed," *Corpus Christi Gazette*, June 7, 1873; "Cattle Thieves Again," *Corpus Christi Gazette*, August 30, 1873.

26. *Corpus Christi Gazette*, September 6, 1873; *Corpus Christi Gazette*, September 20, 1873.

27. "A Bold Robbery," *Corpus Christi Gazette*, November 16, 1873.

28. *Corpus Christi Gazette*, November 20, 1873.

29. "Texas Items, Duval County," *Galveston Daily News*, January 14, 1875, p. 2, Portal, https://texashistory.unt.edu/ark:/67531/metapth462073/m1/2/zoom/.

30. Dobie and Young, *Vaquero of the Brush Country*, 59.

31. Dobie and Young, *Vaquero of the Brush Country*, 59, 68; George Durham and Clyde Wantland, *Taming the Nueces Strip: The Story of McNelly's Rangers* (Austin: University of Texas Press, 2006), 72.

32. *Corpus Christi Weekly Gazette*, September 19, 1874, TX News. Coll.

33. "Gov. Coke's Usurpations," *Daily Express* (San Antonio), August 18, 1874, p. 2, Portal, https://texashistory.unt.edu/ark:/67531/metapth441033/m1/2/zoom/.

34. "Gov. Coke's Usurpations," 2.

35. "Gov. Coke's Usurpations," 2.

36. John W. Clark, Jr., "Santos Coy, Manuel de Los," *Handbook of Texas Online*, accessed December 31, 2023, https://www.tshaonline.org/handbook/entries/santos-coy-manuel-de-los; Robert H. Thonhoff, "Coy, Trinidad," *Handbook of Texas Online*, accessed December 31, 2023, https://www.tshaonline.org/handbook/entries/coy-trinidad.

37. "Horse Thieves," *Corpus Christi Caller*, February 11, 1883.

38. "Killed While Resisting Arrest," *Corpus Christi Caller*, December 9, 1883.

39. "Coy Gets Another Man," *Corpus Christi Caller*, January 6, 1884.

40. "Collins Letter," *Corpus Christi Caller*, April 18, 1886.

41. "Two Murdered While in Custody in Collins," *Corpus Christi Caller*, April 26, 1886.

42. "Two Murdered While in Custody in Collins."

43. Collins was the predecessor of modern-day Alice. It was located three miles east of Alice and was relocated in 1885 to be on the path of the San Antonio and Aransas Pass Railway.

44. "From Corpus Christi," *San Antonio Express*, April 28, 1886, p. 4.

45. "Good Coy, One Mexican Who Is on the Side of the Law Most Emphatically," *Fort Worth Daily Gazette*, April 29, 1886, p. 4, Portal, https://texashistory.unt.edu/ark:/67531/metapth86801/m1/4/zoom/?q=hORSE%20THIEVES&resolution=1.5&lat=5458.072912503522&lon=1492.275208094829.

46. "Good Coy."

47. *San Antonio Express*, May 2, 1886.

48. "A Slur on Corpus Christi," *Corpus Christi Caller*, May 9, 1886; "Personal Mention," *Corpus Christi Caller*, May 16, 1886.

49. "Officials on Alert," *Corpus Christi Caller*, September 5, 1886.

50. "Frontier Ranger Battalion, Company C Monthly Returns," Ranger Records, TSLAC

51. Catarino Garza, *La Era de Tuxtepec en Mexico, o sea, Rusia en América* (San José, Costa Rica: Imprenta Comercial, 1894), 32.

52. "Gracias," *El Regidor* (San Antonio), May 10, 1890.

53. "San Diego Siftings," *Corpus Christi Caller*, May 15, 1888.

54. "San Diego Siftings."

55. "Noticias Varias," *El Regidor*, June 21, 1890; "El Baluarte," *El Regidor*, July 4, 1891.

56. Young, "Remembering Catarino Garza's 1891 Revolution," 262.

57. "Special to the *Statesman*: From the Border, One Whole Prisoner Captured by Federal Troops, A Slight and Unimportant Engagement with the Revolutionists–Very Little Damage Being Done on Either Side," *Austin Weekly Statesman*, December 7, 1891.

58. "The Garza Affair, His Movements Creating Some Interest, But Still the Affair Is Believed to Be a Huge Hoax," *Fort Worth Daily Gazette*, September 19, 1891, p. 3, Portal, https://texashistory.unt.edu/ark:/67531/metapth89809/m1/1/zoom/?q=%22September%2019,%201891%22%20%22Fort%20Worth%20Gazette%22%20%22Garza&resolution=1.5&lat=5979.125356549806&lon=2756.5411448105833; "A Few Nights Ago a Couple of Mexicans rode into Realitos . . . ," *Temple Weekly Times*, September 25, 1891, p. 3, Portal, https://texashistory.unt.edu/ark:/67531/metapth585178/.

59. "A Few Nights Ago a Couple of Mexicans rode into Realitos."

60. Francisco J. Montemayor, "Sabinas Hidalgo, En La Tradición, Leyenda, Historia" (Sabinas Hidalgo, Nuevo León, Mexico, September 29, 1949), in author's possession; "A Typical Revolutionist," *Aransas Harbor*, October 22, 1891, p. 1, Portal, https://texashistory.unt.edu/ark:/67531/metapth882081/m1/1/zoom/?q=Nunez&resolution=2&lat=9474.620573212933&lon=4982.980395784073.

61. "Still No Sign of Garza, He Is Believed to Be in the Brush," *Galveston Daily News*, January 13, 1892, p. 2, Portal, https://texashistory.unt.edu/ark:/67531/metapth468942/m1/2/zoom/?q=%22Captain%20George%20F.%20Chase%22%20%22San%20Diego%22&resolution=1.5&lat=5813.552943703137&lon=2819.4305725972617.

62. "The State Press, What the Newspapers Throughout Texas Are Talking About," *Galveston Daily News*, January 13, 1892, p. 4, Portal, https://texashistory.unt.edu/ark:/67531/metapth468942/m1/4/zoom/?q=%22better%20class%20of%20people%22%20%22Laredo%20News%22&resolution=1.5&lat=6146.883022478215&lon=3197.4075244685223.

63. "Killed by Garza's Men, A Scouting Party Fired on at Soledad Wells, Rufus Glover Killed, and a Horse Shot, the People Angry and Crying Vengeance," *Galveston Daily News*, February 2, 1892, p. 2, Portal, https://texashistory.unt.edu/ark:/67531/metapth466574/m1/2/zoom/; "The Dead Bandit, More About the Killing of Eusebio Martinez," *Daily Herald* (Brownsville, TX), February 25, 1893; "Bail Fixed at $12,000," *Galveston Daily News*, February 28, 1893, p. 4.

64. "Will Go for Two Prisoners," *Fort Worth Gazette*, February 4, 1892, p. 6, Portal, https://texashistory.unt.edu/ark:/67531/metapth89889/m1/6/zoom/.

65. Robert J. Brown, "With the Rangers," *Fort Worth Gazette*, February 4, 1892, p. 6, Portal, https://texashistory.unt.edu/ark:/67531/metapth89889/m1/6/zoom/.

66. Robert J. Brown, "Two Garza Followers," *Fort Worth Gazette*, February 7, 1892, p. 8, Portal, https://texashistory.unt.edu/ark:/67531/metapth89892/m1/8/zoom/.

67. "Ranger Killed," *Daily Hesperian* (Gainesville, TX), March 25, 1892, p. 1, Portal, https://texashistory.unt.edu/ark:/67531/metapth503916/m1/1/zoom/; "A Border Fight," *San Saba News*, April 1, 1892, p. 2, Portal, https://texashistory.unt.edu/ark:/67531/metapth111182/m1/2/zoom/; "Notes From San Diego," *Corpus Christi Caller*, June 4, 1887; "Tardy Justice," *Bastrop Advertiser*, July 17, 1886, p. 2, Portal, https://texashistory.unt.edu/ark:/67531/metapth204953/m1/2/zoom/?q=Robert%20Doughty&resolution=1.5&lat=3319.4835922408647&lon=3332.725433761533.

68. "Alleged Garzaites Released," *Galveston Daily News*, March 12, 1892, p. 5, Portal, https://texashistory.unt.edu/ark:/67531/metapth468851/m1/3/zoom/; "Garzaites in Count," *Austin Weekly Statesman*, May 19, 1892, p. 5, Portal, https://texashistory.unt.edu/ark:/67531/metapth278594/m1/5/zoom/.

69. Elliott Young, *Catarino Garza's Revolution on the Texas-Mexico Border*, American Encounters / Global Interactions (Durham, NC: Duke University Press, 2004), 107–8.

70. There is no evidence that Luby was involved with the White Men's Party. No such involvement is suggested here.

71. Acosta and Winegarten, *Las Tejanas*, 60; Young, *Catarino Garza's Revolution on the Texas-Mexico Border*, 183.

72. "Needed Ballot Reform," *Velasco Daily Times*, March 5, 1892, p. 2, Portal, https://texashistory.unt.edu/ark:/67531/metapth185220/m1/2/zoom/;"The State Press, What the Newspapers throughout Texas Are Talking About," *Galveston Daily News*, February 28, 1892, p. 8, Portal, https://texashistory.unt.edu/ark:/67531/metapth468846/m1/8/zoom/.

73. "Needed Ballot Reform," 2.

74. Young, *Catarino Garza's Revolution on the Texas-Mexico Border*, 108.

75. Young, *Catarino Garza's Revolution on the Texas-Mexico Border*, 234.

76. Young, *Catarino Garza's Revolution on the Texas-Mexico Border*, 259.

77. "Garza Wants to Surrender, His Father-In-Law Tried to Make Terms for Him But Failed," *Galveston Daily News*, March 3, 1892, p. 5, Portal, https://texashistory.unt.edu/ark:/67531/metapth468068/m1/5/zoom/; "Garza's Brother, the Chief Confidant of the Revolutionist in Town, Arrested in Key West," *Galveston Daily News*, October 16, 1892, p. 6, Portal, https://texashistory.unt.edu/ark:/67531/metapth467421/m1/5/zoom/.

78. "The State Press, What the Papers throughout the State Are Talking About," *Galveston Daily News*, November 5, 1892, p. 4, Portal, https://texashistory.unt.edu/ark:/67531/metapth469182/m1/4/zoom/?q=%22Duval%20County%22%20date:1890-1899&resolution=1&lat=2344.7895243028197&lon=1286.119203891631.

79. Alfredo E Cárdenas, "Mexican Americans Fared Well under Parr's Duval County Machine" (Master's thesis, Texas State University, 2018), 59.

Notes for Chapter 10

1. Yoakum, *History of Texas*, 83–85; Lehmann and Cisneros, *Forgotten Legions*, 26; Terry G. Jordan-Bychkov, *North American Cattle-Ranching Frontiers*, 134–36.

2. L. G. Connor, "Brief History of the Sheep Industry in the United States," *Agricultural History Society Papers* 1 (1921): 136–40, https://www.jstor.org/stable/44216164.

3. "1880 United States Federal Census."

4. "1880 United States Federal Census."

5. Records of Bonds and Mortgages, June 15, 1869, Book A, Folio S, Nueces County District Clerk; "Direct Communication with Rockport and Corpus Christi, to the Merchants of Galveston," *Galveston Daily News*, August 22, 1875, p. 4, Portal, https://texashistory.unt.edu/ark:/67531/metapth461054/m1/4/zoom/?q=San%20Diego&resolution=3&lat=7453.67132292797&lon=3094.881726535297.

6. "Nueces County, Its Location, Population, Productions, Water, Stock-Raising, Geology, Roads, Prospects, Etc.," *Ranchero*, May 12, 1860, pp. 18, 52–53; McCampbell, *Texas Seaport*, 18, 57–58.

7. *Corpus Christi Weekly Gazette*, September 19, 1874, TX News. Coll.; "State News, Nueces County," *Galveston Daily News*, May 7, 1876, p. 2, Portal, https://texashistory.unt.edu/ark:/67531/metapth465008/m1/2/zoom/.

8. *Corpus Christi Weekly Gazette*, October 24, 1874, TX News. Coll.

9. "The Largest Purchase of Wool," *Galveston Daily News*, July 21, 1876, p. 2, Portal, https://texashistory.unt.edu/ark:/67531/metapth460940/m1/2/zoom/; "State News, Nueces County," *Galveston Daily News*, April 5, 1876, p. 2, Portal, https://texashistory.unt.edu/ark:/67531/metapth462392/m1/2/zoom/.

10. Texas, County Tax Rolls, 1837–1910, Duval County, 1877, 1–36. Note: This, and subsequent figures, complied by author from data in this source.

11. Texas, County Tax Rolls, 1837–1910, Duval County, 1877, 1–36.

12. Lehmann and Cisneros, *Forgotten Legions*, 28–29, 31.

13. "Sheep and Wool," *Galveston Daily News*, September 21, 1880, p. 3, Portal, https://texashistory.unt.edu/ark:/67531/metapth462439/m1/3/zoom/; Texas, County Tax Rolls, 1837–1910, Duval County, 1877.

14. Lehmann and Cisneros, *Forgotten Legions*, 28; Lynch, *Duke of Duval*, 10; J. L. Allhands, *Uriah Lott* (San Antonio: Naylor, 1949), 25; Alfredo E. Cardenas, "Givens, John Slye," *Handbook of Texas Online*, accessed March 02, 2023, https://www.tshaonline.org/handbook/entries/givens-john-slye.

15. ATHOS, "San Diego Pencilings," *Corpus Christi Caller*, August 31, 1884, TX News. Coll.; Texas, County Tax Rolls, 1837–1910, Duval County, 1877.

16. "Nopal as Sheep Food," *Corpus Christi Caller*, March 18, 1883, TX News. Coll.

17. *Corpus Christi Caller*, December 9, 1883, TX News. Coll.

18. "Mr. Gueydan and Nopal," *Corpus Christi Caller*, February 4, 1884, TX News. Coll.

19. "San Diego Letter," *Corpus Christi Caller*, February 25, 1883, TX News. Coll.; "Sheep Shearing Has Commenced," *Corpus Christi Caller*, April 4, 1883, TX News. Coll.; "San Diego Letter," *Corpus Christi Caller*, May 20, 1883, TX News. Coll.

20. "Duval County, Business Revived, the Railroad Repaired, Ranch Talk, Cattle, Sheep and Horses," *Fort Worth Daily Gazette*, September 23, 1883, p. 6, Portal, https://texashistory.unt.edu/ark:/67531/metapth114546/m1/6/zoom/.

21. Texas, County Tax Rolls, 1837–1910, Duval County, 1877–1884; ATHOS, "San Diego Pencilings," *Corpus Christi Caller*, September 14, 1884, TX News. Coll.; ATHOS, "San Diego Pencilings," *Corpus Christi Caller*, October 5, 1884, TX News. Coll.

22. "San Diego Pencilings," *Corpus Christi Caller*, February 22, 1885, TX News. Coll.; E. T. M., "San Diego Notes," *Corpus Christi Caller*, June 14, 1885, TX News. Coll.; Texas, County Tax Rolls, 1837–1910, Duval County, 1877–1885.

23. E. T. M., "San Diego Wool Notes," *Corpus Christi Caller*, October 25, 1885, TX News. Coll.; E. T. M., "Encouraging News," *Corpus Christi Caller*, October 10, 1885, TX News. Coll.; Texas, County Tax Rolls, 1837–1910, Duval County, 1886.

24. "Sheep vs. Cattle," *Corpus Christi Caller*, October 17, 1885, TX News. Coll.

25. "A Visit to San Diego," *Corpus Christi Caller*, May 14, 1887, TX News. Coll.

26. "Visit to San Diego"; "A Trip to the Country," *Corpus Christi Caller*, April 21, 1888, TX News. Coll.; Texas, County Tax Rolls, 1837–1910, Duval County, 1888.

27. Texas, County Tax Rolls, 1837–1910, Duval County, 1877–1900.

28. Tex McCord, "San Diego Has Romantic Past, Bright Future," *San Antonio Express*, October 18, 1954.

29. McCord, "San Diego Has Romantic Past."

30. B. W. Johnson, *Bell Punch* (San Diego, TX), November 6, 1882.

31. Wichter Zach, "America's Tariff Men: Connecting McKinley to Trump," *New York Times*, December 6, 2018, sec. Business, https://www.nytimes.com/2018/12/06/business/william-mckinley-trump-tariffs.html.

32. "Laredo Daily Times Recommend Capt. E. N. Gray of Duval County for Candidate of Democratic Party for State Representative," *Corpus Christi Caller*, July 17, 1888, TX News. Coll.

33. "From Alice," *Corpus Christi Caller*, February 17, 1899, Local History Archives, La Retama; "From San Diego," *Corpus Christi Caller*, June 14, 1901, Local History Archives, La Retama.

Notes for Chapter 11

1. Milton P. August Norton, Milton P. Norton Papers, 1842–1860, TSLAC (hereafter cited as M. P. Norton Papers).

2. Alfredo E. Cardenas, "Duval County Style Politics Predated, Fashioned the Parr Machne," *Journal of South Texas* 25, no. 1 (Spring 2012): 43; *John F. McKinney v. Joseph O'Connor*, 26 Texas 5 (Texas Supreme Court, 1861).

3. *McKinney v. Saviego*, 59 US 235 (US Supreme Court, 1856); *Journal of the House of Representatives, Eighth Legislature of Texas* (Austin, TX.: John Marshall & Company, State Printers, 1860), 186, https://lrl.texas.gov/scanned/Housejournals/8/H_8_0.pdf#page=733; *Journal of the Senate of Texas, Eighth Legislature* (Austin, TX.: John Marshall & Company, State Printers, 1860), 149, https://lrl.texas.gov/scanned/Senatejournals/8/S_8_0.pdf#page=615.

4. "Letter from Austin," *Ranchero*, February 18, 1860, p. 2, Portal, https://texashistory.unt.edu/ark:/67531/metapth852490/m1/2/zoom/.

5. "Charles Lovenskiold," n.d., Vertical Files, DBCAH; Hortense Warner Ward, "Blücher, Anton Felix Hans Hellmuth Von," *Handbook of Texas Online*, accessed December 5, 2017, http://www.tshaonline.org/handbook/online/articles/fbl64.

6. "1860 United States Federal Census."

7. Nueces County Commissioners Court Minutes, 1860, Book B, 1858–1863, Nueces County Clerk; "Announcements," *Ranchero*, July 21, 1860, 2, Portal, https://texashistory.unt.edu/ark:/67531/metapth852570/m1/2/zoom/.

8. Nueces County Commissioners Court Minutes, n.d., Nueces County District Clerk; M. P. Norton Papers.

9. Hobart Huson, *District Judges of Refugio County* (Refugio, TX: Refugio Timely Remarks, 1941), 80; S. C. Easley, *Memorial and Genealogical Record of Southwest Texas: Containing Biographical Histories and Genealogical Records of Many Leading Men and Prominent Families* (Signal Mountain, TN: Southern Historical Press, 1978), 280; Letters Received by the Adjutant General, 1822–1860, Page 1, *Folder 3*, accessed May 21, 2020, https://www.fold3.com/?xid=2044&slid=&pgrid=5617008421&ptaid=kwd-45770711341&s_kwcid=fold3&gad_source=1&gclid=Cj0KCQjw5ea1BhC6ARIsAEOG5pwW6t3H-tvaFmNim0foK8OTh_ley-48BqY0g9kGmnIulU-f9rn3srsYaAsqUEALw_wcB&pcrid=160191094318&pkw=fold3&mkwid=s_dc&pmt=e.

10. "The Election," *Ranchero*, August 25, 1860, p. 2, Portal, https://texashistory.unt.edu/ark:/67531/metapth852573/m1/2/zoom/.

11. Rafael Salinas, "Election Results Nueces County Precinct Number Nine," August 6, 1860, TSLAC.

12. County Election Results, n.d., Texas Secretary of State, TSLAC; Elections Book, 1860, Nueces County District Clerk.

13. Record Group 307–3, n.d., Series 84, Nueces County, TSLAC.

14. Election Returns from Nueces County, October 8, 1860, Nueces County District Clerk, Executive Department, TSLAC; Charles Lovenskiold to William G. Hale, September 5, 1860, William G. Hale Papers, 1819–1931, DBCAH (hereafter cited as W. G. Hale Papers); Samuel R Miller et al. to the governor, secretary of state, and attorney general, September 6, 1860, Governor's Papers: Samuel Houston, TSLAC (hereafter cited as Houston Papers).

15. Miller et al. to the governor, secretary of state, and attorney general, September 6, 1860, Houston Papers.

16. Miller et al. to the governor, secretary of state, and attorney general, September 6, 1860, Houston Papers.

17. Lovenskiold to Governor Sam Houston, September 16, 1860, Houston Papers; Edward B. Mosely, Deposition of H. W. Berry, August 25, 1860, Houston Papers.

18. Sam Houston, *Speech of Hon. Sam Houston, of Texas, Exposing the Malfeasance and Corruption of John Charles Watrous, Judge of the Federal*

Court in Texas [. . .] (London: Forgotten Books, 2018); Lovenskiold to Hale, September 5, 1860, W. G. Hale Papers; John F. McKinney to Governor Sam Houston, September 23, 1860, Houston Papers.

19. Miller et al. to the governor, secretary of state, and attorney general, September 6, 1860, Houston Papers; RG 307–3, Nueces County, Series 84, TSLAC.

20. Miller et al. to the governor, secretary of state, and attorney general, September 6, 1860.

21. "From the State," *State Gazette*, October 13, 1860, p. 2, Portal, https://texashistory.unt.edu/ark:/67531/metapth81455/m1/2/zoom/.

22. "A Dangerous Precedent," *Ranchero*, October 27, 1860, p. 2, Portal, https://texashistory.unt.edu/ark:/67531/metapth852500/m1/2/zoom/.

23. *Ranchero*, October 27, 1860, p. 2, Portal, https://texashistory.unt.edu/ark:/67531/metapth852500/m1/2/zoom/; "Contested Election," *Ranchero*, October 27, 1860, p. 2, Portal, https://texashistory.unt.edu/ark:/67531/metapth852500/m1/2/zoom/.

24. Answers by William L. Rogers to Interrogatories, Spring 1861, Office of the District Clerk, Victoria County District Court.

25. *Joseph O'Connor vs. John F. McKinney*, No. 597 (District Court of Victoria County March 1, 1861).

26. "Affidavit of Rodrigo Ynojosa," September 8, 1860, TSLAC.

27. "Affidavit of Rodrigo Ynojosa," September 8, 1860, TSLAC; "1860 United States Federal Census."

28. "Affidavit of Chipito Sandoval," September 29, 1860, TSLAC; "1860 United States Federal Census."

29. "Affidavit of George W. Foster," September 29, 1860, TSLAC; "1860 United States Federal Census."

30. Fielding Jones, *Joseph O'Connor v. John F. McKinney*, Victoria County District Clerk (Texas 14th Judicial District 1861).

31. Rafael Salinas, "Poll Book," August 6, 1860, County of Nueces, TSLAC; "1860 United States Federal Census."

32. "A Registry Law," *Ranchero*, October 6, 1860, p. 2, Portal, https://texashistory.unt.edu/ark:/67531/metapth852530/m1/2/zoom/.

33. "Registry Law," 2; *Joseph O'Connor v. John F. McKinney*.

34. *John F. McKinney v. Joseph O'Connor*, 26 Texas 5 (Texas Supreme Court 1861).

35. *John F. McKinney v. Joseph O'Connor*, 26 Texas 5 (Texas Supreme Court 1861).

36. Henson, "McKinney, Thomas Freeman."

Notes for Chapter 12

1. Minutes, Nueces County Commissioners Court, 1876, p. 3, Nueces County District Clerk.
2. Minutes, Nueces County Commissioners Court, 11–12.
3. Minutes, Nueces County Commissioners Court, 45.
4. Minutes, Nueces County Commissioners Court, 3.
5. Gammel, *Laws of Texas*, 4:92, https://texashistory.unt.edu/ark:/67531/metapth6730/m1/963/?q=%22rep-tex%22.
6. Duval County Commissioners Court Minutes, 1878, bk. A, Duval County Clerk.
7. Duval County Commissioners Court Minutes, 1878, bk. A.
8. Duval County Commissioners Court Minutes, 1878, bk. A.
9. Duval County Commissioners Court Minutes, 1878, bk. A.
10. Duval County Commissioners Court Minutes, 1878, bk. A.
11. Duval County Commissioners Court Minutes, 1879, pp. 66–68, Duval County Clerk.
12. Duval County Commissioners Court Minutes, 1879, pp. 66–68.
13. Duval County Commissioners Court Minutes, 1879, pp. 66–68.
14. Duval County Commissioners Court Minutes, 1878, 71–75.
15. Homer S. Thrall, *The People's Illustrated Almanac, Texas Hand-Book and Immigrants' Guide, for 1880* [. . .] (St. Louis, MO: N. D. Thompson & Company, 1880), 272; "Norman G. Collins," Legislative Reference Library of Texas, Legislators and Leaders Member Profile, accessed October 21, 2020, https://lrl.texas.gov/legeleaders/members/memberdisplay.cfm?memberID=4025.
16. *Advertiser* (Bastrop, TX), June 14, 1879, p. 1, Portal, https://texashistory.unt.edu/ark:/67531/metapth204683/m1/1/zoom/.
17. "From Duval's Capital," *Corpus Christi Caller*, July 3, 1887; "District Court in San Diego," *Corpus Christi Caller*, January 14, 1888; "San Diego Locals," *Corpus Christi Caller*, July 14, 1888.

Notes for Chapter 13

1. Allhands, *Uriah Lott*, 15, 25; Grimm, *Llanos Mesteñas*, 128; "Personal," *Galveston Daily News*, March 1, 1881, p. 4, Portal, https://texashistory.unt.edu/ark:/67531/metapth461027/m1/4/zoom/.
2. Allhands, *Uriah Lott*, 12.
3. Allhands, *Uriah Lott*, 12; *Corpus Christi Weekly Gazette*, September 19, 1874.
4. Gammel, "Laws of Texas," vol. 8; Allhands, *Uriah Lott*, 14.
5. Allhands, *Uriah Lott*, 12.
6. Allhands, *Uriah Lott*, 14.
7. "Personal," *Galveston Daily News*, March 1, 1881, p. 2, Portal, https://texashistory.unt.edu/ark:/67531/metapth461027/m1/4/zoom/; "Railroad News," *Galveston*

Daily News, July 3, 1877, p. 1, Portal, https://texashistory.unt.edu/ark:/67531/metapth461860/m1/1/zoom/.

8. Allhands, *Uriah Lott*, 15–16.

9. "Duval," *Galveston Daily News*, September 22, 1880, p. 4, Portal, https://texashistory.unt.edu/ark:/67531/metapth464147/m1/4/zoom/.

10. Sesom, "Duval," *Galveston Daily News*, October 4, 1879, p. 4, Portal, https://texashistory.unt.edu/ark:/67531/metapth460951/m1/4/zoom/.

11. "1880 United States Federal Census."

12. "State Specials," *Dallas Times Herald*, July 1, 1881, p. 1, Portal, https://texashistory.unt.edu/ark:/67531/metapth286516/m1/1/zoom/.

13. "Work In Aransas Pass," *Corpus Christi Caller*, March 4, 1883; E. T. M., *Corpus Christi Caller*, March 25, 1883; *Corpus Christi Caller*, April 22, 1883.

14. "San Diego Siftings," *Corpus Christi Caller*, August 23, 1883.

15. "San Diego Siftings," *Corpus Christi Caller*, August 23, 1883; "Local Traffic," *Corpus Christi Caller*, August 24, 1884; GENERAL, "Duval County Notes," *Corpus Christi Caller*, August 18, 1888.

16. "New Advertisements," *Galveston Daily News*, November 11, 1879, p. 4, Portal, https://texashistory.unt.edu/ark:/67531/metapth465055/m1/2/zoom/; "Railroad News," *The Galveston Daily News*, December 5, 1880, p. 2, Portal, https://texashistory.unt.edu/ark:/67531/metapth461291/m1/2/zoom/.

17. Arnoldo De León, *Benavides: The Town and Its Founder, 1881* (Benavides, TX: Benavides City Council / Benavides Centennial Committee, 1980).

18. Allhands, *Uriah Lott*, 20.

19. "From San Diego," *Laredo Daily Times*, December 20, 1888; Jonis, "Weekly Gossip from Jonis," *Corpus Christi Caller*, November 21, 1886; *Corpus Christi Caller*, July 2, 1887.

20. William Neale and J. C. Rayburn, *Century of Conflict, 1821–1913* (New York: Arno, 1976), 58.

21. Allhands, *Uriah Lott*, 20; Germann, *Texas Post Offices*.

22. Jonis, "Weekly Gossip from Jonis," *Corpus Christi Caller*, November 21, 1886; Jonis, "Realitos Locals," *Corpus Christi Caller*, February 26, 1887.

23. Jonis, "Notes From Realitos," *Corpus Christi Caller*, January 29, 1887; Jonis, "Realitos Locals," February 26, 1887; Jonis, "Realitos Local Dots," *Corpus Christi Caller*, April 13, 1887; Jonis, "Realitos Weekly Record," *Corpus Christi Caller*, June 25, 1887.

24. Jonis, "Realitos Local Dots," *Corpus Christi Caller*, April 30, 1887; "From Realitos," *Corpus Christi Caller*, June 30, 1899.

25. Lehmann and Cisneros, *Forgotten Legions*, 171.

26. Jonis, "Realitos Local Dots," *Corpus Christi Caller*, April 23, 1887; Jonis, "Realitos Locals," *Corpus Christi Caller*, December 1887.

27. Agnes Grimm, "Peña Station," *Handbook of Texas Online*, accessed October 27, 2020, https://www.tshaonline.org/handbook/entries/pena-station.

28. Alicia A. Garza, "Hebbronville, TX," *Handbook of Texas Online*, accessed October 27, 2020, https://www.tshaonline.org/handbook/entries/hebbronville-tx.

Notes for Chapter 14

1. "List of Recessions in the United States," *Wikipedia*, December 7, 2020, https://en.wikipedia.org/w/index.php?title=List_of_recessions_in_the_United_States&oldid=992913215; Alwyn Barr, "Late Nineteenth-Century Texas," *Handbook of Texas Online*, accessed December 17, 2020, https://www.tshaonline.org/handbook/entries/late-nineteenth-century-texas.

2. de la Teja, Marks, and Tyler, *Texas*, 305.

3. "Gray Family, El Rancho La Gloria Receives Official Texas Historical Marker," *Duval County Historical Museum*, accessed December 16, 2020, https://duval-countymuseum.weebly.com/historical-markers.html.

4. "Gray Family, El Rancho La Gloria Receives Official Texas Historical Marker"; Dallas Lith. Company, S. M. Smith, "Plat of La Gloria Ranch in Duval County, Texas.," Map, (Fort Worth: Land Title Block, 1892), Portal, https://texashistory.unt.edu/ark:/67531/metapth190425/m1/2/zoom/.

5. "Wheat," *Ranchero*, May 18, 1861, p. 2, Portal, https://texashistory.unt.edu/ark:/67531/metapth852487/m1/2/zoom/; E. N. Gray, "La Gloria Rancho, Duval County, Texas," *Corpus Christi Caller*, December 24, 1883.

6. Gray, "La Gloria Rancho, Duval County, Texas"; "State Press, What the Interior Papers Say," *Galveston Daily News*, October 31, 1885, p. 4, Portal, https://texashistory.unt.edu/ark:/67531/metapth461327/m1/4/zoom/.

7. Vigilanti, "San Diego Siftings," *San Antonio Express*, March 25, 1889; Vigilanti, "From San Diego," *Laredo Daily Times*, July 24, 1889.

8. McCampbell, *Texas Seaport*, 17, 45; Alonzo, *Tejano Legacy*, 90–91.

9. "Farming in Duval County," *Corpus Christi Caller*, March 21, 1886; "San Diego: Duval Cotton Gins Her First Bale of Cotton–In Need of Rain," *Fort Worth Daily Gazette*, February 9, 1887, p. 6, Portal, https://texashistory.unt.edu/ark:/67531/metapth85346/m1/6/zoom/.

10. "Fabian Fabela, 'Texas, Voter Records, 1867–1918,'" FamilySearch.org; "Fabela - Land Grant Results," ARD GLO; Germann, *Texas Post Offices*.

11. Texas, County Tax Rolls, 1837–1910.

12. "Going to Raise Cotton," *Corpus Christi Caller*, January 17, 1886; "San Diego: Copious Rains to Gladden the Hearts of the Farmers–Duval County Notes," *Galveston Daily News*, March 8, 1886, p. 7, Portal, https://texashistory.unt.edu/ark:/67531/metapth86749/m1/7/zoom/.

13. "Farming in Duval County," *Corpus Christi Caller*, March 21, 1886; Texas, County Tax Rolls, 1837–1910, Duval County, 1877.

14. Jeffreys, "From Duval's Capital," *Corpus Christi Caller*, July 9, 1887; Jeffreys, "San Diego Locals," *Corpus Christi Caller*, July 28, 1888.

15. "San Diego: Agreements Made for the Cultivation of Cotton in Duval County," *Fort Worth Daily Gazette*, August 17, 1886, p. 7, Portal, https://texashistory. unt.edu/ark:/67531/metapth89431/m1/7/zoom/.

16. "San Diego: Duval County Gins Her Frist Bale of Cotton–In Need of Rain"; "From Duval's Capital," *Corpus Christi Caller*, October 15, 1887; "A Trip to the Country," *Corpus Christi Caller*, April 21, 1888.

17. Jeffreys, "From Duval's Capital"; "San Diego Locals"; GENERAL, "Duval County Notes," *Corpus Christi Caller*, August 18, 1888; "Men of Progress," *Corpus Christi Caller*, August 25, 1888; Vigilanti, "From San Diego," *Laredo Daily Times*, October 2, 1888; Vigilanti, "From San Diego," *Laredo Daily Times*, October 17, 1888.

18. Alonzo, *Tejano Legacy*, 178; De La Teja, Marks, and Tyler, *Texas*, 302–303; Duval County Tax Rolls, 1877–1910.

19. Vigilanti, "From San Diego," *Laredo Daily Times*, September 18, 1888; "From Duval County," *Corpus Christi Caller*, September 13, 1901.

20. De León, *Tejano Community*, 65–66; Manuel Andrés Soto, *Life in a South Texas Colonia* (Corpus Christi, TX: MCM Books, 2017), 4.

21. Carol Coffee Reposa, "Ginning the Years: A Memoir," *Valley Voices: A Literary Review* 20, no. 2 (Fall 2020): 69–71.

22. "Cotton to Be Tried in Duval County, Work of County Commissioners," *Fort Worth Daily Gazette*, February 18, 1886, Portal, https://texashistory.unt.edu/ ark:/67531/metapth86732/m1/2/zoom/.

23. Roberto Tino Martinez, "E. Martinez Gin Owner," email to author, January 7, 2021.

24. A. H. Belo & Company, *Texas Almanac and State Industrial Guide for 1904* (Galveston, TX: Clark & Courts, 1904), Portal, https://texashistory.unt.edu/ ark:/67531/metapth123779/m1/266/.

25. "San Diego Siftings," *Corpus Christi Caller*, January 3, 1889; Vigilanti, "From San Diego," *Laredo Daily Times*, July 24, 1889; "The First Bale," *Evening Tribune* (Galveston), July 25, 1889, p. 4, Portal, https://texashistory.unt.edu/ ark:/67531/metapth1234903/m1/4/zoom/.

26. "Five covered wagons . . . .," *Brenham Daily Banner*, November 21, 1889, p. 4, Portal, https://texashistory.unt.edu/ark:/67531/metapth483861/m1/3/zoom/.

27. "San Diego: Magnificent Crop Reports–False Reports Cause Investigation–Railroad Items," *Galveston Daily News*, March 20, 1890, p. 1, Portal, https:// texashistory.unt.edu/ark:/67531/metapth467658/m1/1/zoom/; "Duval County in this state . . .," *El Paso International Daily Times*, March 22, 1890, p. 4, Portal, https://texashistory.unt.edu/ark:/67531/metapth460330/m1/4/zoom/.

28. "Texas Journalism," *Fort Worth Gazette*, April 27, 1891, p. 5, Portal, https:// texashistory.unt.edu/ark:/67531/metapth109543/m1/5/zoom/; "The Stockman Land Farmer speaks of a in Duval County . . .," *Brenham Weekly Banner* (TX), March 26, 1891, Portal, https://texashistory.unt.edu/ark:/67531/ metapth115656/m1/3/zoom/.

29. "Had a Big Time Over It, Corpus Christi Paints a Little Over That Duval First Bale," *Fort Worth Gazette*, July 7, 1891, p. 4, Portal, https://texashistory.unt.edu/ark:/67531/metapth89735/m1/4/zoom/.

30. "State Press: The *San Diego Sun* Says," *Galveston Daily News*, July 17, 1891, p. 4, Portal, https://texashistory.unt.edu/ark:/67531/metapth467224/m1/4/zoom/.

31. "Government Rain-Makers, Flooded Out on the Texas Coast, They Retire to Duval County to Try Their Science There," *Fort Worth Gazette*, October 1, 1891, p. 4, Portal, https://texashistory.unt.edu/ark:/67531/metapth89821/m1/4/zoom/.

32. Edward Powers, *War and the Weather: Or, the Artificial Production of Rain* (Chicago: S. C. Griggs & Company, 1871), 9, 41, 65, *Internet Archive*, accessed December 23, 2020, http://archive.org/details/warweather00powe; Committee on Commerce, Science, and Transportation, *Weather Modification: Programs, Problems, Policy, and Potential* (Washington DC: Government Printing Office, 1878), 17, 30, *University of Florida Digital Collections*, accessed December 23, 2020, https://ufdc.ufl.edu/AA00025909/00001.

33. John C. Rayburn, "The Rainmakers in Duval," *Southwestern Historical Quarterly* 61, no. 1 (1957): 103–4.

34. Rayburn, "Rainmakers in Duval," 105–6.

35. Rayburn, "Rainmakers in Duval," 106–9.

36. Rayburn, "Rainmakers in Duval," 109.

37. Rayburn, "Rainmakers in Duval," 105, 111–12.

38. Rayburn, "Rainmakers in Duval," 110–15.

39. "The First Bale," *Taylor County News* (Abilene, TX), July 7, 1893, p. 1, Portal, https://texashistory.unt.edu/ark:/67531/metapth314416/m1/1/zoom/; "State News," *Brenham Weekly Banner*, July 10, 1890, p. 1, Portal, https://texashistory.unt.edu/ark:/67531/metapth115629/m1/1/zoom/; "The First Bale, Duval County Again Gets There—Houston Gets the Bale," *Austin Weekly Statesman*, July 14, 1892, p. 3, Portal, https://texashistory.unt.edu/ark:/67531/metapth278602/m1/3/zoom/.

40. *La Grange Journal*, July 19, 1894, p. 2, Portal, https://texashistory.unt.edu/ark:/67531/metapth997133/m1/2/zoom/; "State News," *Southern Mercury* (Dallas), June 28, 1894, p. 16, Portal, https://texashistory.unt.edu/ark:/67531/metapth185567/m1/16/zoom/; "Texas Cotton Crop, Duval County," *Fort Worth Gazette*, June 7, 1894, p. 7, Portal, https://texashistory.unt.edu/ark:/67531/metapth109856/m1/7/zoom/.

41. "The First Bale, San Diego Beats the South, As Usual," *Daily Herald*, July 13, 1895, p. 2, Portal, https://texashistory.unt.edu/ark:/67531/metapth84722/m1/2/zoom/.

42. "What's the matter with . . .," *Hallettsville Herald*, July 18, 1895, p. 4, Portal, https://texashistory.unt.edu/ark:/67531/metapth1000593/m1/4/zoom/.

43. "In Response to the *Herald's* query . . .," *Hallettsville Herald*, July 25, 1895, p. 4, Portal, https://texashistory.unt.edu/ark:/67531/ metapth1000598/m1/4/zoom/?q=Duval%20County&resolution= 2&lat=3536.500000000001&lon=2260.5.

44. "First Bale From Duval, A Telegram Announcing Its Shipment Was Received Here Yesterday, No Change in Spots," *Galveston Daily News*, July 3, 1896, p. 9, Portal, https://texashistory.unt.edu/ark:/67531/metapth465231/m1/9/zoom/.

45. "The Brownsville papers are ever alert . . .," *Daily Herald*, February 11, 1896, 2, Portal, https://texashistory.unt.edu/ark:/67531/metapth61902/m1/2/ zoom/; "Duval County," *Galveston Daily News*, September 8, 1896, p. 9, Portal, https://texashistory.unt.edu/ark:/67531/metapth465787/m1/9/zoom/.

46. "Weather and Crops, Duval County Cotton Acreage to Be Increased," *Houston Post*, March 23, 1897, 3, Portal, | https://texashistory.unt.edu/ark:/67531/ metapth90459/m1/3/zoom/; "The Cotton Acreage of Texas, Duval County," *Houston Daily Post*, April 30, 1897, p. 9, Portal, https://texashistory.unt.edu/ ark:/67531/metapth84166/m1/9/zoom/; "Texas Newspaper Comment, Standard Advocate (Hearne)," *Galveston Daily News*, June 22, 1897, p. 6, Portal, https:// texashistory.unt.edu/ark:/67531/metapth441733/m1/6/zoom/; "The 'first bale' has been sent . . .," *Daily Herald*, June 24, 1897, p. 2, Portal, https://texashis-tory.unt.edu/ark:/67531/metapth115983/m1/2/zoom/.

47. "From Benavides," *Corpus Christi Caller*, February 24, 1899; "Rain All Over Texas," *Houston Daily Post*, April 7, 1899, p. 4, Portal, https://texashistory.unt.edu/ark:/ 67531/metapth82988/m1/4/zoom/; "Weather and Crops," *Houston Daily Post*, July 29, 1899, p. 5, Portal, accessed December 23, 2012, https://texashistory.unt.edu/ ark:/67531/metapth83099/m1/5/zoom/?q=Houston%20Daily%20Post %20July%20291%201899&resolution=3&lat=3353.5570853628683&lon= 3002.5753403555814; "From Duval County," *Corpus Christi Caller*, September 22, 1899.

Notes for Chapter 15

1. Duval County Commissioners Court Minutes, 1878, Duval County Clerk.

2. Election Returns, Duval County, 1880, Box 2-12/591, Texas Secretary of State, TSLAC.

3. Dermot H. Hardy and Ingham S. Roberts, *Historical Review of South-East Texas: And the Founders, Leaders, and Representative Men of Its Commerce, Industry, and Civic Affairs* (Chicago: Lewis Publishing, 1910), 992; "Election in Duval County," *Corpus Christi Caller*, November 9, 1884.

4. Brown, *Indian Wars and Pioneers of Texas*, 507.

5. "Democratic Convention in Duval County Broke Up and Some Bolted to Have Their Own Confab: Meeting of Bolters at School House," *Corpus Christi Caller*, July 4, 1886.

6. "Democratic Convention in Duval County Broke Up."

7. "Democratic Convention in Duval County Broke Up."
8. "Democratic Convention in Duval County Broke Up."
9. "Democratic Convention in Duval County Broke Up."
10. "Democratic Convention in Duval County Broke Up."
11. "Democratic Convention in Duval County Broke Up."
12. "Democratic Convention in Duval County Broke Up."
13. "Democratic Convention in Duval County Broke Up."
14. "Democratic Convention in Duval County Broke Up."
15. The newspaper referred to them as the Guarache Party, but the correct Spanish spelling is Huarache. While Luby had not been a part of the Democratic split, since he was a Republican and apparently did not attend Democratic meetings, they still referred to the bolters as the Luby Party. Many of Luby's closest supporters, such as Collins and Hoffman, were part of the delegates that left the courthouse convention.
16. "Weekly Gossip from Jonis," *Corpus Christi Caller*, October 24, 1886.
17. Seb S. Wilcox, "The Laredo City Election and Riot of April 1886," *Southwestern Historical Quarterly* 45, no. 1 (1941): 6; Emilio Zamora, Cynthia Orozco, and Rodolfo Rocha, eds., *Mexican Americans in Texas History: Selected Essays* (Austin: Texas State Historical Association, 2000), 71.
18. Joe Robert Baulch, "James B. Wells: South Texas Economic and Political Leader" (PhD diss., Texas Tech University, 1974), 32.
19. Vigilanti, "From San Diego," *Laredo Daily Times*, October 2, 1888.
20. Thomas Woods, "Laredo Election Riot (1886)," *Handbook of Texas History Online*, accessed February 8, 2021, https://www.tshaonline.org/handbook/entries/laredo-election-riot-1886.
21. "Weekly Gossip from Jonis," *Corpus Christi Caller*, October 24, 1886; "Frontier Ranger Battalion, Company C Monthly Reports," n.d., TSLAC.
22. "Weekly Gossip from Jonis," *Corpus Christi Caller*, November 7, 1886; "San Diego Siftings," *Corpus Christi Caller*, November 7, 1886.
23. "The Count Goes On, Duval County," *Fort Worth Daily Gazette*, November 7, 1886, Portal, https://texashistory.unt.edu/ark:/67531/metapth86838/m1/1/zoom/.
24. "Duval County Democrats," *Corpus Christi Caller*, May 26, 1888.
25. "From San Diego," *Corpus Christi Caller*, June 16, 1888.
26. "From San Diego," *Corpus Christi Caller*, July 7, 1888.
27. "Mexicans Organizing," *Corpus Christi Caller*, July 21, 1888.
28. "Mexicans Organizing."
29. Vigilanti, "From San Diego," *Laredo Daily Times*, August 14, 1888.
30. Vigilanti, "From San Diego," August 14, 1888
31. GENERAL, "Duval County Notes," *Corpus Christi Caller*, August 18, 1888.
32. Vigilanti, "From San Diego," August 14, 1888
33. In the South Texas political vernacular, a *maromero* is someone who flips or changes sides for his or her convenience.

34. Vigilanti, "From San Diego," *Laredo Daily Times*, September 18, 1888.
35. Vigilanti, "From San Diego," *Laredo Daily Times*, October 22, 1888.
36. Vigilanti, "From San Diego," October 22, 1888.
37. "Tragedy at San Diego," *Galveston Daily News*, October 22, 1888, Portal, https://texashistory.unt.edu/ark:/67531/metapth469369/m1/1/zoom/.
38. "Tragedy at San Diego."
39. "Tragedy at San Diego"; "1880 United States Federal Census."
40. *Laredo Daily Times*, November 10, 1888.
41. Duval County Commissioners Court Minutes, November 12, 1888, Book A, 405–6, Duval County District Clerk.
42. "Duval County Politics, Over 400 Votes Thrown Out, A Technicality, Changing the Results," *Laredo Daily Times*, November 15, 1888.
43. "What Is the Remedy?," *Laredo Daily Times*, November 16, 1888.
44. Charles L. Coyner to James Stephen Hogg, December 4, 1888, James Stephen Hogg Papers, DBCAH (hereafter cited as Hogg Papers); Charles F. Stillman to Hogg," December 1, 1888, Hogg Papers; R. H. Hannison to Stillman, December 10, 1888, Hogg Papers.
45. "Duval County Court Meets," *Dallas Morning News*, July 10, 1889.
46. "Duval County Court Notes," *Dallas Morning News*, January 10, 1889; "Duval County District Court," *San Antonio Express*, January 13, 1889; *L. L. Wright v. The State of Texas, ex rel Jno. Buckley* (Supreme Court of Texas, June 27, 1890); "Ex Rel," *Law.com Legal Dictionary*, accessed August 19, 2018, https://dictionary.law.com/Default.aspx?selected=705.
47. Vigilanti, "San Diego Doings, Proving His Citizenship," *San Antonio Express*, January 18, 1889.
48. *L. L. Wright v. The State of Texas*, No. 7607 (Texas Supreme Court June 28, 1890).
49. *L. L. Wright v. The State of Texas*, No. 7607 (Texas Supreme Court June 28, 1890).
50. *L. L. Wright v. The State of Texas*, No. 7607 (Texas Supreme Court June 28, 1890).
51. Duval County Commissioners Court Minutes, July 30, 1890, 445–48, Duval County District Clerk.
52. Evan Anders, *Boss Rule in South Texas: The Progressive Era*, 1st ed. (Austin: University of Texas Press, 1982), 4–5.
53. "Duval County Democratic Convention," *Galveston Daily News*, May 8, 1892, p. 2, Portal, https://texashistory.unt.edu/ark:/67531/metapth468392/m1/2/zoom/?q=%22Duval%20County%22%20date:1890-1899&resolution=1.5&lat=2789.7058823529414&lon= 1410.5.
54. "Duval County," *Galveston Daily News*, May 25, 1892, p. 2, Portal, https://texashistory.unt.edu/ark:/67531/metapth468452/m1/2/zoom/?q=%22Duval%20County%22%20date:1890-1899&resolution =1&lat=1391.5&lon=2674.

55. "In the Southwest," *The Galveston Daily News*, November 5, 1892, p. 1, Portal, https://texashistory.unt.edu/ark:/67531/metapth469182/m1/1/zoom/.

56. Frank Wagner, "Moses, John Williamson," *Handbook of Texas Online*, updated June 1, 2016, https://www.tshaonline.org/handbook/entries/moses-john-williamson; Election Returns, Duval County, 1892, Box2-12/646, Texas Secretary of State, TSLAC.

57. Duval County Commissioners Court Minutes, December 7, 1892, 550–51, Duval County District Clerk.

58. Wagner, "Moses, John Williamson"; Duval County Commissioners Court Minutes, June 27, 1893, Duval County District Clerk.

59. "State Press, A Dark Horse Trotted Out," *Galveston Daily News*, June 8, 1894, p. 4, Portal, https://texashistory.unt.edu/ark:/67531/metapth466612/m1/4/zoom/?q=dark%20horse&resolution=1&lat=2162.5&lon=1681.4999999999993.

60. "Duval County Politics," *Galveston Daily News*, August 24, 1894, p. 6, Portal, https://texashistory.unt.edu/ark:/67531/metapth466210/m1/6/zoom/?q=%22Duval%20County%20Politics%22%20%22The%20Galveston%20Daily%20News%22%20%22August%2024,%201894%22&resolution=1.5&lat=5919.776191697216&lon=1814.7184845787438; "Duval County Politics," *Galveston Daily News*, September 5, 1894, p. 6, Portal, https://texashistory.unt.edu/ark:/67531/metapth468456/m1/6/zoom/?q=%22Duval%20County%20Politics%22%20%22The%20Galveston%20Daily%20News%22%20%22September%205,%201894%22&resolution=4&lat=3402.5&lon=2451.5.

61. "The State Campaign . . . Crain at San Diego," *Galveston Daily News*, October 31, 1894, p. 6, Portal, https://texashistory.unt.edu/ark:/67531/metapth466507/m1/3/zoom/?q=%22Crain%20at%20San%20Diego%22&resolution=3&lat=4464.999999999999&lon=2097.4999999999995; Election Returns, Duval County, 1894, Box 2-12/655, Texas Secretary of State, TSLAC.

62. Election Returns, Duval County, 1894.

63. Duval County Commissioners Court Minutes, December 10, 1894, 612, Duval County District Clerk.

64. Duval County Commissioners Court Minutes, April 21, 1895, Duval County District Clerk.

65. Duval County Commissioners Court Minutes, May 13, 1895, Duval County District Clerk.

66. "Duval County Republicans," *Galveston Daily News*, February 17, 1896, p. 4, Portal, https://texashistory.unt.edu/ark:/67531/metapth465797/m1/4/zoom/?q=Duval%20County%20Republicans%20The%20Galveston%20Daily%20News%20February%2017,%201896&resolution=2&lat=4936.4811699522215&lon=3343.268662442025.

67. "Republican Club Organized," *Galveston Daily News*, March 2, 1896, p. 4, Portal, https://texashistory.unt.edu/ark:/67531/metapth465429/m1/4/zoom/?q=

Republican%20Club%20Organized&resolution=2&lat= 1437.4275230659896&lon=1583.6221803381823.

68. "Duval County Democrats," *Galveston Daily News*, June 17, 1896, p. 4, Portal, https://texashistory.unt.edu/ark:/67531/metapth465743/m1/6/zoom/?q= Duval%20County%20Democrats&resolution=4&lat=3400&lon=2576.5.

69. "Duval County Democrats."

70. "Duval County Democrats."

71. "Duval County Democrats."

72. "Eleventh District," *Galveston Daily Herald*, November 6, 1896, p. 3, Portal, https://texashistory.unt.edu/ark:/67531/metapth465254/m1/3/zoom/?q= Duval&resolution=2&lat=5805.820681326796 &lon=1980.49859732451.

73. Duval County Commissioners Court Minutes, November 8, 1896, 35–36, Duval County District Clerk; Alvin Felzenberg, "How William F. Buckley, Jr., Changed His Mind on Civil Rights," *POLITICO Magazine*, accessed February 4, 2022,https://www.politico.com/magazine/story/2017/05/13/ william-f-buckley-civil-rights-215129.

74. Duval County Commissioners Court Minutes, November 8, 1896, 34–35, Duval County District Clerk.

75. Duval County Commissioners Court Minutes, November 8, 1896, 34–35.

76. Duval County Commissioners Court Minutes, November 8, 1896, 34–35.

77. "Same Old Trick To Be Tried," *Houston Daily Post,* November 3, 1898, p. 7, Portal, https://texashistory.unt.edu/ark:/67531/metapth114556/m1/7/zoom/?q= Duval%20County&resolution=2&lat=5897&lon= 2714.499999999999.

78. Duval County Commissioners Court Minutes, December 8, 1898, 100, Duval County District Clerk.

79. Duval County Commissioners Court Minutes, December 8, 1898, 100.

80. Duval County Commissioners Court Minutes, December 8, 1898, 100.

81. Duval County Commissioners Court Minutes, December 8, 1898, 100.

82. "Duval County Conventions, Instructions for Sayers, Bailey and Kleberg," *Houston Daily Post*, April 4, 1900, p. 4, Portal, https://texas-history.unt.edu/ark:/67531/metapth83245/m1/4/zoom/?q=Duval%20 County&resolution=4&lat=3785.4603174603176&lon=2523.5.

83. Election Returns, Duval County, 1900, Texas Secretary of State, TSLAC.

84. Duval County Commissioners Court Minutes, November 12, 1900, 164–65, Duval County District Clerk.

Notes for Chapter 16

1. "The State Lost Again," *Bastrop Advertiser*, March 3, 1906, p. 1; "Old Land Case Up," *Houston Post*, June 6, 1912, p. 14.

2. "Texas, County Tax Rolls, 1837–1910," 63; F. R. Crichton et. al, "Has the Average Citizen of Duval County a White Man's Chance?" (Austin, TX, 1917), 1–2, TSLAC.

3. "26,000 Acre Ranch Sold," *San Antonio Daily Express*, November 4, 1906, p. 4.

4. Montejano, *Anglos and Mexicans in the Making of Texas*, 108; "26,000-Acre Ranch Sold," *Brownsville Daily Herald*, November 6, 1906.

5. "Duval County Oil Well," *Corpus Christi Caller*, May 24, 1901.

6. These figures represent Duval County residents appearing in the 1900 census; others engaged in farming and cattle raising may have been absentee operators residing in neighboring counties; "Texas, County Tax Rolls, 1837–1910," 63.

7. "From Duval County: Fine Crop Outlook - The Oil Wells at Piedras Pintos, Cattle Shipments, Etc.," *Corpus Christi Caller*, May 4, 1900; "From San Diego: Boring for Oil – the Shooting at Hebbronville – Dry Weather Affecting the Wells," *Corpus Christi Caller*, May 17, 1901; "From San Diego: Oil Excitement in Duval County - Lands Selling at High Prices," *Corpus Christi Caller*, June 14, 1901.

8. *Fort Worth Record and Register*, March 8, 1906, p. 8; "Prices Sag under Heavy Offerings—Hogs Decline Another Nickel," *Fort Worth Record and Register*, May 3, 1907, p. 9; "Cattle Trade Is Lively," *San Antonio Express*, May 24, 1912, p. 14.

9. "Three Arrests For Cattle Stealing at San Diego Occurred, Officers Allege 17 Head of Cattle Were Stolen and Shipped," *Corpus Christi Caller*, February 25, 1915.

10. "From the Land of Cactus," *Democrat*, March 7, 1901, 6; "From Duval County: Rain - Horse Buyers - Twisted Casing - School, Etc.," *Corpus Christi Caller*, September 13, 1901; "Texas, County Tax Rolls, 1837–1910," 63.

11. "From Benavides: Considerable Cotton to Be Planted, Also Plenty of Feed Stuff - District Court," *Corpus Christi Caller*, January 12, 1900; "From Benavides: Purchase of a Note Ranch, Cotton Sales, Well News," *Corpus Christi Caller*, September 14, 1900; "Field, Ranch, Garden," *Meridian Tribune*, October 19, 1900, p. 2.

12. "Duval Cotton," *Corpus Christi Caller*, October 6, 1905; "New and Old Counties Producing More and More Wealth or the Farmers," *San Antonio Express*, May 14, 1913, p. 6S; John R. Peavey, *Echoes from the Rio Grande* (Brownsville, TX: Springman-King, 1963), 62.

13. Alfredo E. Cardenas, "Piedras Pintas Fights Cattle Thieves," *Duval County Picture*, February 25, 1987, p. 2, Portal, https://texashistory.unt.edu/ark:/67531/metapth1009606/m1/2/zoom/;"Reports Indicate . . . ," *Alice Echo*, July 27, 1905, p. 8.

14. "Water That Burns," *Corpus Christi Caller*, July 26, 1885.

15. Vigilanti, "From San Diego," *Laredo Daily Times*, August 14, 1888; L. B. Shook, *Abilene Reporter*, March 30, 1900, p. 8; "Texas Items," *Brenham Daily Banner*, March 31, 1900, p. 2; "From Benavides: Oil Prospectors Visit Duval County – Cotton Acreage – Mescal Joints," *Corpus Christi Caller*, February 15, 1901.

16. "From San Diego," *Corpus Christi Caller*, May 10, 1901; "From San Diego: Miss Buckley Won the Watch – a Good Crop Outlook – Big Leases – W. D. Strickland Dead, Etc.," *Corpus Christi Caller*, April 29, 1901; "From San Diego: Boring for Oil – the Shooting at Hebbronville – Dry Weather Affecting the Wells," *Corpus Christi Caller*, May 17, 1901; "From San Diego: Oil Boring and Land Booming Two Sunstrokes Reported," *Corpus Christi Caller*, August 9, 1901; "Duval County Oil Well," *Corpus Christi Caller*, May 24, 1901.

17. "News Notes," *Daily Tribune* (Bay City, TX), April 11, 1907, p. 1.

18. "Benavides Oil Field Interest Production Has Reached Car Shipment Stage, Using It in Corpus For Fuel-Oil Experts Believe That an Extensive Pool Will Be Found," *Corpus Christi Caller*, January 10, 1908; "Gusher in Duval County," *Austin Statesman*, March 23, 1907, p. 1.

19. "Oil Men Flocking to Duval County Since Oil Reported Found," *Corpus Christi Caller*, November 30, 1919, p. 6; "Duval County Expects to Find Oil from Some of Test Wells," *Corpus Christi Caller*, January 9, 1920, p. 3.

20. McCoy, *Oil, Mud & Guts*, 2; Bilbao and Gallart, *Los Chicanos*, 102.

21. "No Clue to Assassin of Cleary," *Corpus Christi Weekly Caller*, January 3, 1908, p. 1.

22. "No Clue to Assassin of Cleary."

23. "No Clue to Assassin of Cleary"; Garcia v. Cleary, 50 Tex. Civ. App. 465 (Court of Civil Appeals 1908); J. D. Dunnaway to Gen. J. O. Newton, December 21, 1907, Adjutant General, General Correspondence, Box 401–506, Folder 506–21, TSLAC; "Noticias Varias," *El Regidor*, December 20, 1906, p. 1. Note: Historians have hinted that Archie Parr may have been involved in Cleary's murder but the record seems to contradict this theory. First, through the years Parr and Cleary had a working relationship in local Democratic confabs. Second, Parr on more than one occasion provided Cleary's bond for offices to which he had won election. Third, Parr announced a $4,300 reward for information leading to the arrest and conviction of Cleary's killers; *Daily Express*, February 29, 1908, p. 2.

24. Dunnaway to Newton, December 21, 1907; "The Lawsons Released," *Corpus Christi Caller*, April 24, 1908; "Saenz Was Denied Bail," *Corpus Christi Weekly Caller*, May 11, 1908.

25. F. de P. González, *La Libertad* (San Diego, TX), Saturday, May 25, 1912, Portal, https://texashistory.unt.edu/ark:/67531/metapth1009578/m1/1/.

26. Lynch, *Duke of Duval*, 3, 13–14; "Duval County Officers," *Daily Express*, November 12, 1906, p. 9.

27. Walter Wilson Meek, "Election Day 1912," (San Diego, Texas, March 2, 1973), 1–2, Walter W. Meek Jr. Papers (A1981-040), Texas A&M University–Kingsville.

28. Meek, "Election Day 1912."

29. Meek, "Election Day 1912"; Cárdenas, "Mexican Americans Fared Well under Parr's Duval County Machine," 79–80. Note: Most, if not all, newspaper

accounts were seriously lacking journalism integrity, suggested that the Tejanos shot first but did so wildly, so the Americanos responded with the skill of sharp-shooters. The fact is that Anguiano and Sáenz were longtime peace officers and must have known how to handle firearms. Indeed, most people in those frontier times knew how to handle weapons, perhaps including an Americano physician.

30. F. de P. González, "Luctuoso Dia," *La Libertad*, May 25, 1912, p. 1, Portal, https://texashistory.unt.edu/ark:/67531/metapth1009578/m1/1/.

31. A couple of histories covering the Parrs suggest that Parr had a falling out with Cleary and was suspected in his killing. Neither of those accounts provide historical evidence for their conclusions.

32. "Grand Jury Indicts Three at San Diego," *San Antonio Light*, June 13, 1912, p. 1; "Transferred to Richmond," *Corpus Christi Caller & Daily Herald*, October 3, 1912; Lynch, *Duke of Duval*, 14; Carrozza, *Dukes of Duval County*, 10. Note: The 1910 Census for Fort Bend County is estimated at 1,373. A perusal of individuals yields a very small number of residents born in Mexico.

33. Carrozza, *Dukes of Duval County*, 9–10.

34. "In Memoriam," *La Libertad*, October 12, 1912, p. 1.

Notes for Chapter 17

1. Lehmann and Cisneros, *Forgotten Legions*, 172.

2. Sarah G. Parr, "Widow's Brief," October 25, 1887, WC 6762 Mexican War, National Archives and Records Administration; Louise Lyle Givens Williams, "The Givens Family," typescript, May 15, 1969, Givens-Hopkins Family Papers, Dupré Library, University of Louisiana at Lafayette; Alfredo E. Cardenas, "Parr, George Berham [1829–1867]," *Handbook of Texas Online*, July 27, 2009, https://www.tshaonline.org/handbook/entries/parr-george-berham-1829-1867. Note: While some historical accounts say that Archie Parr was born on December 25, 1860, according to the United States Census of 1860, taken in Calhoun County on July 17, 1860, Parr was seven months old. This places his birth in December 1859. For a more comprehensive history of Parr's early life, see Alfredo E. Cárdenas, "The Rearing of Duval County Political Kingpin Archie Parr," *Journal of South Texas* 22, no. 2 (Fall 2009): 134–44.

3. Ervin L. Sparkman and Mary Sparkman Roberts, *The People's History of Live Oak County, Texas* (Mesquite, TX: Ide House, 1981), 59; Samuel R. Miller et al. to the governor, secretary of state, and attorney general, September 6, 1860, Houston Papers; Election Record Book, vol. 1, n.d., Live Oak County District Clerk.

4. "Commissioners Court Minutes," n.d., 136, Live Oak County Clerk; Election Record Book, vol. 1; File 96, n.d., Live Oak County District Clerk;

Frank Cormier, "Money, Ballots and Blood: The Corrupt Lives and Violent Times of Archie and George Berham Parr," unpublished manuscript, (Kingsville, TX, 1990), 7, Special Collections, South Texas Archives, Texas A&M University–Kingsville.

5. "For Dist. Attorney 16th Judicial District," *Indianola Bulletin*, September 4, 1872, p. 2; "1870 United States Federal Census."

6. Payroll Records, Coleman Fulton Pasture Company, June 30, 1878, Coleman-Fulton Pasture Company Records, DBCAH (hereafter cited as CFPC Records); Cash Book, Coleman Fulton Pasture Company, August 13, 1881, CFPC Records.

7. Files 004427, 004428, 004429, March 20, 1882, ARD GLO; Lynch, *Duke of Duval*, 11; *Dallas Weekly Herald*, August 21, 1884; *Corpus Christi Caller*, August 3, 1884.

8. Jeffreys, "From Duval's Capital," *Corpus Christi Caller*, July 23, 1887; "Interesting Letter from Duval," *Corpus Christi Caller*, July 21, 1888; "San Diego Locals," *Corpus Christi Caller*, July 28, 1888.

9. "The Opinions of Two Prominent Cattlemen," *Henderson Times*, March 16, 1899, p. 1; Texas Secretary of State, Election Returns, Duval County, 1896, Austin, Box 2-12/665, TSLAC.

10. Evan Anders, "Parr, Archer," *Handbook of Texas Online*, April 25, 2019, https://www.tshaonline.org/handbook/entries/parr-archer.

11. "Components of New Executive Committee," *Daily Express*, August 12, 1908, p. 2; "Duval County Conventions, Instructions for Sayers, Bailey and Kleberg," *Houston Daily Post*, April 4, 1900, 4.

12. "Denied C. M. Robinson Application to Dissolve Duval Company Injunction," *Corpus Christi Caller & Daily Herald*, October 27, 1912.

13. "Parr Supporters Won in Court," *Houston Post*, October 27, 1912, p. 3.

14. Courthouse records from this period were lost in a fire that destroyed the county courthouse in 1914.

15. Texas Secretary of State, Election Returns, Duval County, 1912, Austin, Box 2-12/725, TSLAC; Anders, *Boss Rule in South Texas*, 179; note: 1912 officials were extracted from various commissioners court minutes from 1914, which listed various officials holding office, which would have been elected in 1912 and sworn into office in January 1913 and would not have been replaced until January 1915.

16. Duval County Commissioners Court Minutes, September 14, 1914, Minute Books, Duval County Clerk.

17. Duval County Commissioners Court Minutes, December 1, 1914, Minute Books, Duval County Clerk.

18. "1920 United States Federal Census," AncestryHeritageQuest.com, accessed December 13, 2023, https://www.ancestryheritagequest.com/

discoveryui-content/view/22383391:6061?_phsrc=Ajz4&_phstart=suc-
cessSource&gsln=Allen&ml_rpos=1&queryId=58a971f87739faca282d-
f8ed9884a2a0.

19. "House Bills," *Austin Statesman*, August 14, 1913, p. 2; "New Measures Up at
Austin," *El Paso Herald*, August 18, 1913, p. 2; "County Named for Dunn,"
San Antonio Express, August 19, 1913, p. 3; "'Residence' Defined as Applied
to Voting," *Brenham Daily Banner-Press*, July 25, 1924, p. 1; "Dunn County-
Creating Same," S.B. 4, 33rd Leg. (1913), chapt. 35, p. 86.

20. "Court Postpones Election Tuesday in Dunn County," *San Antonio Express*,
December 18, 1913, p. 3; "Creation of Dunn County Void Says Appellate
Court," *San Antonio Express*, April 9, 1914, p. 7.

21. Archie Parr, SB 12, 34th R.S. (Texas Senate, January 13, 1915), Legislative
Reference Library of Texas, https://lrl.texas.gov/legis/billsearch/text.cfm?leg-
Session=34-0&billtypeDetail=SB&billNumberDetail=12&billSuffixDetail=;
"Lanham County Hearing Set," *San Antonio Express*, February 1, 1915, p. 3,
Portal, https://texashistory.unt.edu/ark:/67531/metapth431904/m1/3/zoom/.

22. Lloyd P. Lochridge, "House Decides Not to Create Lanham County," *Austin
Statesman*, February 11, 1915, p. 4.

23. "Live Oak County Officials Urge Merging with Duval," *Austin American*,
March 10, 1915, p. 3; "Burmeister Urges Relief for People of Duval County,
Asks Legislature to Place Duval County in McMullen or Live Oak, Citizens
Now Disenfranchised," *Corpus Christi Caller and Daily Herald*, March 6,
1915, p. 1.

24. "Petition Duval County Property Owners for Audit County Books to Be Heard
before Judge Hopkins," *Corpus Christi Caller*, June 14, 1914, p. 2.

25. "Petition Duval County Property Owners for Audit County Books to Be Heard
before Judge Hopkins."

26. "Duval Cases Will Be Heard Before Hopkins Monday," *Corpus Christi
Caller*, June 10, 1914; "People Win Fight; Duval Officers Quit Under Fire,"
San Antonio Express, July 17, 1914, p. 2; "Five County Officials Resigned,
Successors Were Named," *Houston Post*, July 17, 1914, p. 2.

27. Duval County Commissioners Court Minutes, October 12, 1914, Minute
Books, Duval County Clerk; "The Duval County Courthouse Burned,"
Falfurrias Facts, August 20, 1914, p. 1.

28. Duval County Commissioners Court Minutes, October 12, 1914.

29. "Sixth Official Duval County Was Arrested," *Corpus Christi Caller*, January
29, 1915; "Duval Audit to Proceed," *San Antonio Express*, June 14, 1915, p. 4;
Otto Brandt et al., "Grand Jury Report, Senator Parr's Home County Grand
Jury Expresses Official Opinion to District Judge," Duval County Grand Jury
Report, January 29, 1915, TSLAC.

30. Kidd, Aikman & Company, Public Accountants, Duval County 1915 Financial
Audit, August 26, 1915, 17–23, TSLAC.

31. Kidd, Aikman & Company, Duval County 1915 Financial Audit, 17–18.

32. Duval County Commissioners Court Minutes, December 15, 1914, Minute Books, Duval County Clerk; "Duval County Books Removed from Grand Jury Room by Parr," *Austin American*, December 11, 1915, p. 3.

33. "Senator Parr Jailed and Fined $100 for Contempt of Court," *Austin American*, December 14, 1915, p. 3. Note: Ranger Sanders was relieved from Ranger service on March 4, 1919, as a result of the 1919 Ranger Investigation; "Hearing to Remove Officers of Duval County Started," *Austin American*, December 29, 1915, p. 3.

34. "New Commissioners for Duval County," *Austin Statesman and Tribune*, January 11, 1916, p. 2.

35. F. R. Crichton et. al, "Has the Average Citizen of Duval County a White Man's Chance?" (Austin: 1917), TSLAC.

36. "Americans Flee from Border City," *Upshur County Echo* (Gilmer, TX), August 26, 1915, p. 1.; "Americans Flee from Border City," *Upshur County Echo*, August 26, 1915, p. 1.

37. Alfredo E. Cardenas, "Plan of San Diego Narrative," *Soy de Duval* (blog), August 20, 2023, https://soydeduval.blogspot.com/2023/08/plan-of-san-diego-narrative.html; "Manuel Flores Was Arrested by Deputy Marshall Yesterday, San Diego Man Charged with Conspiracy against Government," *Corpus Christi Caller*, February 15, 1915; "Charge of Sedition Against San Diego Citizen Is Made, U.S. Marshall Yesterday Noon Arrested Anatolio Gonzalez," *Corpus Christi Caller*, February 16, 1915; "Flores and Gonzalez Released by U. S. Commissioner Southgate," *Corpus Christi Caller*, February 28, 1915; Charles H. Harris and Louis R. Sadler, *The Texas Rangers and the Mexican Revolution: The Bloodiest Decade, 1910–1920* (Albuquerque: University of New Mexico Press, 2004), 276.

38. "Linton Shaw Killed at San Diego, Two Others Wounded," *Corpus Christi Caller*, January 31, 1915; "Non-Toxicants Under Tax Law, Court Decides," *San Antonio Express*, December 6, 1917.

39. "South Texas Race Now Neck and Neck," *Houston Post*, July 21, 1914, p. 3; "Ferguson Develops Surprising Strength in the Counties of North and East Texas," *Austin Statesman*, July 26, 1914, p. 1.

40. "Norman George Collins," *Legislative Reference Library of Texas*, accessed October 21, 2020, https://lrl.texas.gov/legeleaders/members/memberdisplay. cfm?memberID=4025; "Advanced Search Results for Archer Parr," *Legislative Reference Library of Texas*, accessed August 18, 2023, https:// lrl.texas.gov/legis/billsearch/searchresults.cfm?authors=Parr_Archer%20 %22Archie%22:AU.

41. Harris and Sadler, *Texas Rangers and the Mexican Revolution*, 437–38.

42. Jose A. Ramirez, *To the Line of Fire: Mexican Americans and World War I* (College Station: Texas A & M University Press, 2009), 34.

43. Ramirez, *To the Line of Fire*, 34.

44. "In Re Duval County Exemption Board," *Fold3,* November 7, 1917, 40, http://www.fold3.com/image/862064.

45. "Duval County Exemption Board."

46. "Duval County Exemption Board"; "Lista de Contribuyentes," *El Regidor,* May 26, 1904, p. 5.

47. "In Re Duval County Exemption Board"; José de la Luz Sáenz, Emilio Zamora, and Ben Maya, *The World War I Diary of José de La Luz Sáenz,* C. A. Brannen Series 13 (College Station: Texas A&M University Press, 2014), 100, ebook; Thompson, *Wild and Vivid Land,* 140–41.

48. "In Re Local Exemption Board of Duval County, Texas, Alleged Irregularities" (National Archives, October 9, 1917), 41, Fold 3, https://www.fold3.com/image/862190.

49. "In re Duval County Exemption Board," Fold3, November 6, 1917, 38, http://www.fold3.com/image/860000?terms=county,board,   investigation, exemption,duval.

50. "12 Mexican Slackers Surrender at Corpus," *Gainesville Daily Register and Messenger,* March 21, 1919, p. 1; "Kleberg County Shows 657 Registrations and Duval County About 600," *Corpus Christi Caller and Daily Herald,* June 7, 1917, p. 1; "Forty-Six Draft Evaders Sentenced in Corpus Christi," *Houston Post,* May 28, 1919, p. 1.

51. Sáenz, Zamora, and Maya, *World War I Diary of José de La Luz Sáenz,* 31–32.

52. Sáenz, Zamora, and Maya, *World War I Diary of José de La Luz Sáenz,* 86, 113, 206, 234.

53. "Givens A. Parr, 85713803," RG-64, *FamilySearch,* accessed November 8, 2023, https://www.familysearch.org/ark:/61903/3:1:3QHV-N3Z8-D1QD?view=index&personArk=%2Fark%3A%2F61903%2F1%3A1%3A6DQW-SKZ1&action=view; "US, WWI, Draft Registration Cards, 1917–1918," June 30, 1916, National Archives, Fold3, accessed August 22, 2023, https://www.fold3.com/publication/959/us-wwi-draft-registration-cards-1917-1918; "Man of Forty; Boy of Eighteen Sign to Serve in New Texas Cavalry," *San Antonio Express,* May 4, 1918, p. 3.

54. "District Board Is Finishing Up Work," *Houston Post,* September 17, 1917, p. 5.

55. The San Diego VFW Post lists eleven men in its monument of WWI dead. They all died while in service during WWI, but one died at sea when the ship he was in sank and five died stateside from illness, mainly pneumonia.

56. Jeffrey T. Lambert, "Decade of Change: Origins of a Mexican American Identity in Texas, 1910–1920" (diss., Texas State University, 2009), 6; "Many Attend Soldier's Funeral," *San Antonio Express,* December 5, 1917, p. 5; "Duval County Lads Forego Celebration to Assist Sufferers, San Diego Lads Forego Celebration to Assist Sufferers," *Corpus Christi Caller,* October 4, 1919, p. 6.

57. Ramirez, *To the Line of Fire,* 62, 68.

58. "In the Senate of Texas, D. W. Glasscock vs. A. Parr Contestee Procedures," Texas Senate, February 14, 1919, 37201–2, DBCAH.

59. "Freak of Election Is the Vote Recorded in the County of Duval," *Temple Daily Telegram*, July 26, 1916, p. 2.

60. "The Danger at Home," *Bonham News*, August 8, 1916, p. 2.

61. "Announcements," *Mercedes Tribune*, June 14, 1918, p. 4.

62. "Glasscock Wins Race for Senate in 23d District," *San Antonio Express*, August 2, 1918, p. 4; "Hobby Organization to See That Glasscock Is Given a Square Deal, *Weekly Corpus Christi Caller*, August 2, 1918, p. 1.

63. "Duval Election Is Subject to Gossip," *Corpus Christi Caller*, August 3, 1918, p. 4.

64. "Glasscock and Parr Nominated," *Houston Post*, August 25, 1918, p. 7; "The Parr Resolution," *Houston Post*, September 5, 1918, p. 2.

65. "Court Rules in Favor of Archie Parr," *Brownsville Herald*, October 7, 1918, p. 4; "Men of Rio Grande Valley Trying to Ouster Parr," *Austin American*, October 21, 1918, p. 2; "Hobby Throws Influence for D. W. Glasscock," *Austin Statesman*, October 25, 1918, p. 8; "Women Throwing Their Influence to Glasscock," *San Antonio Express*, October 27, 1918, p. 9.

66. "The Kaiser and His Gang Surrenders; Glasscock and the Big 'K' Machine Defeated; 'The World Will Be Free," *Matagorda County Tribune* (Bay City, TX), November 15, 1918, p. 4.

67. "Parr's Election to Senate Questioned," *San Antonio Express*, December 7, 1918, p. 7.

68. "Sen. Strickland to Wield Gavel in Upper House," *San Antonio Express*, January 15, 1919, p. 5; "Glasscock-Parr Election Case With Committee," *Corpus Christi Caller*, January 17, 1919, p. 1.

69. Lambert, "Decade of Change," 34, 38, 40.

70. "Parr-Glasscock Contest Promises Stirring Feature," *San Antonio Express*, January 17, 1919, p. 4.

71. "In the Senate of Texas," February 14, 1919, DBCAH.

72. Montejano, *Anglos and Mexicans in the Making of Texas*, 146; "Seat in Senate Awarded to Parr by 16–14 Vote," *Houston Post*, March 14, 1919, pp. 1–2.

73. Carey Smith, "Matagorda County Tribune," *Matagorda County Tribune*, March 7, 1919, p. 8; J. A. Fernandez, "Election Law Is Amended by the Legislature in Record Time," *Austin Statesman*, March 11, 1919, p. 2.

74. "Wealth Above and below Duval County Assured," *San Antonio Express*, January 30, 1920, p. 90; "Duval County Prosperous, San Antonio Express," *San Antonio Express*, September 21, 1920, p. 7; Duval County Commissioners Court Minutes, April 11, 1927, Minute Books, 357, Duval County Clerk.

75. Duval County Commissioners Court Minutes, September 27, 1927, October 31, 1927, February 8, 1928, and March 16, 1928, Minute Books, Duval County Clerk.

76. "Tivoli Tidings," *Refugio Timely Remarks*, July 31, 1931, p. 4; "Alleged Payments Listed," *Lampasas Daily Leader*, March 9, 1932, p. 1.
77. Duval County Commissioners Court Minutes, January 3, 1931, August 31, 1931, and September 12, 1932, Minute Books, Duval County Clerk.
78. Duval County Commissioners Court Minutes, January 14, 1935, February 15, 1935, October 14–15, 1935, March 9, 1936, Minute Books, Duval County Clerk.
79. Duval County Commissioners Court Minutes, July 24, 1933, and November 13, 1933, Minute Books, Duval County Clerk.
80. "Ex Senator Archie Parr Passed Away Sunday in Corpus Christi After a Long and Colorful Career," *Benavides Facts*, October 23, 1942, pp. 1, 4; "State Capitol's Flag Half-Staffed Honoring Parr," *Corpus Christi Times*, October 20, 1942, p. 7.
81. "Convention Sidelights," *San Antonio Express*, May 24, 1916, p. 3; "Parr An Odd Figure," *Austin Statesman and Tribune*, December 14, 1915, p. 4.
82. "Tanner Admirer of Nerve," *Hebbronville News*, September 2, 1931, p. 2; "Schulenburg to Be Host to Governor Sterling Rally at 2 p.m. Tuesday, July 12th," *Schulenburg Sticker*, July 8, 1932, p. 1.
83. "In Memoriam," *La Libertad*, October 12, 1912, p. 1.

Notes for Chapter 18

1. Lynch, *Duke of Duval*, 7.
2. "1910 United States Federal Census, Duval County, Texas," May 9, 1910, https://www.ancestryheritagequest.com/imageviewer/collections/6061/images/4391971_00644?ssrc=&backlabel=Return.
3. "Party Platform Demands," *Daily Tribune*, January 26, 1915, p. 1; "Man of Forty; Boy of Eighteen Sign to Serve in New Texas Cavalry," *San Antonio Express*, May 4, 1918, p. 3.
4. "Heights Eleven Takes Brilliant Game From Corpus Christi, 7–6," *Houston Post*, December 26, 1920, pp. 1–2; "Dr. Vinson Invited," *San Antonio Express*, December 26, 1920, p. 16; "Paddling Favorite Method of Hazing At A & M College," *Austin Statesman*, February 17, 1921, pp. 1, 3; Evan Anders, "Parr, George Berham [1901–1975]," *Handbook of Texas Online*, accessed September 3, 2023, https://www.tshaonline.org/handbook/entries/parr-george-berham-1901-1975.
5. "State Society," *San Antonio Express*, June 8, 1926, p. 64.
6. Duval County Election Returns, 1934, p. 43, Duval County Clerk.
7. "Duval County Case for Dissolution of Injunction Today," *Corpus Christi Caller & Daily Herald*, October 26, 1912; "Hearing in Election Contest," *Denton Record-Chronicle*, February 7, 1919, p. 2.
8. Chapa's middle initial stood for Carrillo. His brother Eusebio Carrillo Jr. once said that his brother began using Chapa, his mother's surname, as his last name

in 1910. Eusebio, however, did not provide a reason for the change. "1880 United States Federal Census"; "Cuatro Generaciones Presentada Por Una Familia Popular de Benavides," *El Demócrata* (San Diego, TX), February 23, 1945, p. 4; "Injunction Prevents Officials of Duval Quitting Their Jobs," *Austin American*, September 4, 1915, p. 3; "Eusebio Carrillo Indicted in Duval County," *Alice Daily Echo*, August 22, 1954, pp. 1, 6.

9. David R. McDonald, *José Antonio Navarro: In Search of the American Dream in Nineteenth-Century Texas*, Watson Caufield and Mary Maxwell Arnold Republic of Texas Series (Denton: Texas State Historical Association, 2010), 246; "1870 United States Federal Census"; "DANIEL TOBIN - *Pleasanton Express*," Pleasanton Express, November 25, 2015, https://www.pleasantonexpress. com/articles/daniel-tobin/; "1860 United States Federal Census"; "Antonio W Tobin, Texas, County Marriage Index, 1837–1977," *FamilySearch*, accessed October 30, 2023, https://www.familysearch.org/ark:/61903/1:1:XL8V-PQ9.

10. "Duval County Democratic Ticket," *Daily Express*, June 20, 1908, p. 3; "Is Appointed Sheriff in Duval County," *Daily Express*, June 28, 1908;. "Democrats of Duval County for Williams," *Daily Express*, July 9, 1908, p. 2.; "To the Democratic Voters of Texas," *Daily Express*, July 22, 1908, p. 5; Duval County Commissioners Court Minutes, December 1, 1914, 3, Minute Books, Duval County Clerk; "1860, 1870, 1880, and 1900 United States Federal Census"; "DANIEL TOBIN - Pleasanton Express"; "Letters to the Light," *San Antonio Light*, August 30, 1915, p. 4.

11. "Rangers Make Arrest," *Houston Post*, May 21, 1912, p, 1.

12. At time the sheriff also served as tax collector. "Taxpayers Ask Court to Enjoin Tax Collections," *San Antonio Express*, January 30, 1914, p. 1.

13. "Court Grants Injunction," *San Antonio Express*, January 31, 1914, p. 1; "Mandamus Is Granted," *Galveston Tribune*, June 19, 1914, p. 7.

14. "Archie Parr and Sheriff of Duval Are Sent to Jail," *Austin Statesman and Tribune*, December 13, 1915, p. 1.

15. "Witnesses Show Parr Dominance in Duval County," *Houston Post*, February 7, 1919, p. 5.

16. "Antonio W. Tobin," *FamilySearch*, accessed April 5, 2023, https://familysearch.org/ark:/61903/3:1:33SQ-GY14-V3B?cc=1983324&wc=9T4K-7MS%3A263835801%2C265707101%2C265739101.

17. "Jose Angel Heras," *FamilySearch*, December 5, 2014, https://familysearch.org/ark:/61903/1:1:JVDQ-MZJ; "Jose A. Heras," AncestryHeritageQuest.com, accessed October 23, 2023, https://www.ancestryheritagequest.com/discoveryui-content/view/144235354:7884?_phsrc=WjY36&_phstart=successSource&gsfn=Jose+Angel&gsln=Heras&ml_rpos=1&queryId=698866c37637489d25c40fbe17928876; "Jose Angel Heras, 1917–1918," *FamilySearch*, December 29, 2021, https://www.familysearch.org/ark:/61903/1:1:KZX7-2Q7; "Many Details of Election Bared in Parr Contest," *San Antonio Express*, February 7, 1919, p. 4.

18. "Jose Angel Heras, Census, United States Census, 1930," AncestryHeritageQuest. com, accessed October 5, 2023, https://www.ancestryheritagequest.com/ discoveryui-content/view/64291712:6224?_phsrc=WjY34&_phstart= successSource&gsfn=Jose+Angel&gsln=HeraS&ml_rpos=1&queryId= 21cc5abb1620aa03990762ad78f3b3a7; "Jose Angel Heras, Census, United States Census, 1940," *FamilySearch*, accessed October 3, 2023, https://www.familysearch. org/ark:/61903/1:1:KWJ1-N78; "Heras, Jose Angel (1893), World War II, US, WWII 'Old Man's Draft' Registration Cards, 1942," *Fold3*, accessed October 12, 2023, https://www.fold3.com/image/592945954?terms=jose,angel,heras; "Jose Angel Heras, Census, United States Census, 1950," AncestryHeritageQuest. com, accessed October 18, 2023, https://www.ancestryheritagequest.com/ discoveryui-content/view/190213967:62308?_phsrc=WjY30&_phstart= successSource&gsfn=Jose+Angel&gsln=Heras&ml_rpos=1&queryId= bb6ceeec3dd17d92133f04b64b9c52c7.

19. "Duval Grand Jury May Report Today," *Corpus Christi Times*, April 1, 1954, p. 6; "Jose Angel Heras Death, Texas Death Index, 1964–1998," *FamilySearch*, December 5, 2014, https://familysearch.org/ark:/61903/1:1:JVDQ-MZJ.

20. "Juan Trevino," AncestryHeritageQuest.com, accessed October 14, 2023, https://www.ancestryheritagequest.com/discoveryui-content/view/70578493: 7602?_phsrc=jiQ3&_phstart=successSource&gsfn=Juan+O.&gsln=Trevino& ml_rpos=1&queryId=77d7ba6074fea2e645e6915afa3a5b70; "Duval County Case for Dissolution of Injunction Today," *Corpus Christi Caller & Daily Herald*, October 26, 1912.

21. "FBI Case Files," *Fold3*, accessed April 16, 2019, http://www.fold3.com:9292/ image/5332301; "Many Details of Election Bared in Parr Contest," *San Antonio Express*, February 7, 1919, p. 4.

22. "In Re Juan Trevino, Sheriff and County Attey, Duval Company, US, FBI Case Files 1908–1922," Fold3, accessed April 16, 2019, http://www.fold3.com:9292/ image/5332301; Duval County Election Returns, n.d., Duval County Clerk; "Juan O. Trevino, Death, Texas Death Index, 1890–1976," *FamilySearch*, January 23, 1953, https://www.familysearch.org/ark:/61903/1:1:K37N-JRR.

23. "Leopoldo Romano, Deserter, Case Number: 282319," *Fold3*, 1–3, accessed October 12, 2023, https://www.fold3.com/image/5044093; "Leopoldo Romano, WWI Registration Card," *Fold3*, "Leopoldo Romano, Deserter, Case Number: 282319," Fold3, 1–3, accessed October 12, 2023, https://www. fold3.com/image/5044093; "Leopoldo Romano, WWI Registration Card," Fold3, accessed October 12, 2023, https://www.fold3.com/image/553419329/ romano-leopoldo-page-1-us-wwi-draft-registration-cards-1917-1918; "Jesus Oliveira," AncestryHeritageQuest.com, accessed October 14, 2023, https://www.ancestryheritagequest.com/discoveryui-content/view/27925080: 7884?_phsrc=WjY10&_phstart=successSource&gsln=Oliveira&ml_rpos= 19&queryId=12e21b637d630c5f49a691da2f302c8f.

24. "Anything Parr Wanted," *Houston Post*, February 6, 1919, p. 5.

25. Under the Texas Constitution of 1836, the sheriff acted as tax collector, while the governing body of the county employed a separate assessor. Subsequent changes modified the structure of the office and counties could separate the collector from the sheriff and have it as a standalone office or combine it with the assessor's functions. Under these provisions Duval County created a separate office in 1926 for the tax collector until it was combined with the assessor's office by a state constitutional amendment in 1932.

26. Duval County Election Returns, n.d., Duval County Clerk; "Tax Assessor-Collector," countyprogress.com, accessed January 1, 2019, https://countyprogress.com/tax-assessor-collector/.

27. "Two Duval Officials in Duval Co, Resign; Garcia Holds Job," *Brownwood Bulletin*, January 4, 1955, p. 1; "Jesus Oliveira Charged With Multiple Theft," *Alice Daily Echo*, July 27, 1954, p. 8; "Conviction of Parr Reversed," *Brenham Banner-Press*, June 13, 1960, p. 13; Duval County Election Returns, n.d., Duval County Clerk; "Jesus M. Oliveira," *FamilySearch*, accessed October 12, 2023, https://www.familysearch.org/ark:/61903/1:1:K3SG-C93; "Duval's Elites Now Facing Tax Suits," *San Antonio Express*, August 25, 1975, p. 3; "San Diego Tax Man Dies at 55," *Corpus Christi Times*, May 23, 1974, p. 60.

28. "Five Valley Men Face Income Case," *Fort Worth Press*, March 17, 1932, p. 3; "Duval Nominates Office Encumbents," *Laredo Times*, July 31, 1932, p. 1.

29. "Received 25 Thousand Dollars of Graft in Nice Black Satchel for Road Contract," *Tribune* (Hallettsville, TX), May 25, 1934, p. 1.

30. "Received 25 Thousand Dollars of Graft in Nice Black Satchel for Road Contract."

31. "Austin Polo Team Blanks Corpus Christi," *Kingsville Record*, December 12, 1934, 1; "Hi-Jacker Pleads Guilty and Gets Fifteen Years," *Cotulla Record*, September 28, 1934, p. 1.

32. Lynch, *Duke of Duval*, 44–45.

33. "Parr's Suspended Term Considered," *Brownsville Herald*, May 18, 1936, p. 1; "Parr May Receive Executive Clemency; Removal Is Delayed," *Alice Echo*, July 2, 1936, p. 1; "Parole Is Granted To Judge Geo. Parr," *Brownsville Herald*, April 12, 1937, p. 1; "Prison Teacher, Former Judge Parr Instructor," *San Antonio Light*, December 30, 1936, p. 13.

34. Taken from issues of: *La Voz* (San Diego TX), December 24, 1935–August 14, 1936, and *El Democrata*, April 21, 1939–February 23, 1945. This list covers businesses only through 1945, many others sprang up between 1945 and 1975.

35. Taken from issues of *Benavides Facts*, June 16, 1939, and December 25, 1942.

36. The comparisons drawn here are to counties removed from the border such as Jim Wells, Brooks, Jim Hogg, Kleberg, Nueces, San Patricio, Live Oak, McMullen, and others in the Trans-Nueces. It is important to note that the counties Perales mentions, save Duval County, are border counties. Duval is one layer away from the border and has a different population makeup.

37. Alonso S. Perales and Emilio Zamora, *In Defense of My People* (Houston: Arte Público Press, 2022), 224–25.

38. "George Parr Back in Duval Politics," *San Antonio Light*, January 13, 1938, p. 3.

39. "Texas Democrats Launch Drive to Return Peresident," *Benavides Facts*, October 18, 1940, p. 1; "Duval Parole Board Chairman Is Appointed," *Benavides Facts*, January 9, 1942, p. 1.

40. "US, WWII Draft Registration Cards, 1940," *Fold3*, accessed November 2, 2023, https://www.fold3.com/search?docQuery=(filters:!((type:place,values:!((label: United+States+of+America,value:rel.148838))),(type:general.title.content. collection,values:!((label:%27World+War+II+-+(United+States)%27,value: world-war-ii-united-states))),(type:general.title.id,values:!((label:%27US, +WWII+Draft+Registration+Cards,+1940%27,value: %27816%27)))),keywords: %27Texas,Duval+County%27);"US, WWII Army Enlistment Records, 1938–1946," Fold3, accessed November 2, 2023, https://www.fold3.com/ search?docQuery=(filters:!((type:place,values:!((label:United+States+ of+America,value:rel.148838))),(type:general.title.content.collection,values:! ((label:%27World+War+II+-+(United+States)%27,value:world-war-ii-united-states))),(type:general.title.id,values:!((label:%27US,+WWII+Army+ Enlistment+Records,+1938-1946%27,value:%27831%27)))),keywords: %27Texa,Duval+County%27,offset:20).

41. "US, WWII Army Enlistment Records, 1938–1946."

42. "US, WWII Army Enlistment Records, 1938–1946."

43. "Archer Parr, US, WWII Draft Registration Cards, 1940," *Fold3*, accessed November 6, 2023, http://www.fold3.com/image/627869700?terms=ii,war,parr,archer,united,america,texas,states,world; "Page 1 US, WWII 'Old Man's Draft' Registration Cards, 1942," *Fold3*, accessed November 6, 2023, http://www.fold3.com/image/592257083?terms=ii,war,parr,archer,united,america,texas,states,world; "Atlee Parr, US, WWII Draft Registration Cards, 1940," *Fold3*, accessed November 6, 2023, http://www.fold3.com/ image/627869714?terms=parr,atlee,war,world,united,america,texas,states,ii.

44. "Many Attend Red Cross Benefit at Parr Home," *Benavides Facts*, April 3, 1942, p. 1; "George B. Parr Heads Navy Relief in Duval County," *Benavides Facts*, April 10, 1942, p. 1; "Geo. B. Parr County Defense Bond Chairman," *Benavides Facts*, May 8, 1942, p. 1.

45. Carrozza, *Dukes of Duval County*, 46.

46. J. Gilberto Quezada, *Border Boss: Manuel B. Bravo and Zapata County* (College Station: Texas A & M University Press, 1999), 65.

47. "Shivers Vows Clean-Up of Duval County 'Mess,'" *Corpus Christi Times*, February 3, 1954, pp. 1, 14.

48. "Attorney General Predicts Downfall of Parr In 1954," *Corpus Christi Times*, January 22, 1954, p. 5.

49. "Shiver to Order Troops If Needed For Duval County," *San Antonio Express*, February 4, 1954, pp. 1–2; "Duval School Fund Studied by Jury," *San Antonio Express*, February 4, 1954, p. 1.

50. "Duval School Fund Studied by Jury"; "Duval Grand Jurors Blast Shepherd," *San Antonio Express*, February 6, 1954, p. 1.

51. "George Parr Under Cross-Fire, Appears a Scared and Angry Man," *Corpus Christi Caller Times*, February 7, 1954, p. 1; "Investigation of Duval Finances, Months in Building Up Steam," *Corpus Christi Caller Times*, February 7, 1954, p. 16.

52. "Duval Action May Backfire," *San Antonio Light*, February 9, 1954, p. 30.

53. "Allee Is Quoted on Death Threat," *San Antonio Express*, February 10, 1954, p. 1; "Substitute Judge Named for Duval County," *Brenham Banner-Press*, February 10, 1954, pp. 1, 6.

54. "Substitute Judge Named for Duval County."

55. "Duval Jury to Resume Inquiry," *Gainesville Daily Register and Messenger*, February 12, 1954, p. 1; "U.S. Agent Says 800 Checks Lost," *Corpus Christi Times*, February 10, 1954, pp. 1, 16.

56. "Parr Supporter Calls Him Leader 'With a Big Heart,'" *San Antonio Express And News*, February 14, 1954, pp. 1, 9.

57. "Parr Supporter Calls Him Leader 'With a Big Heart.'"

58. "Parr Supporter Calls Him Leader 'With a Big Heart'"; "Parr Opposition Leader Hopeful," *San Antonio Express*, n.d., p. 1.

59. Jesenia Guerra, "The Fight for Democracy: An Oral History of the Freedom Party" (master's thesis, Texas A&M–Kingsville, 2005), 22–23; Hill, "Parr Power Ebbs in Texas Politics," *New York Times*, February 7, 1954, TSLAC. Note: For reasons that are not clear on the historical record, García was not a candidate in the Freedom Party slate.

60. "Anti-Parr Party Formed in Duval County," *Corpus Christi Times*, March 28, 1952, p. 5.

61. "Mas Sobre La Politica En Duval," *La Libertad*, July 18, 1952.

62. "Mas Sobre La Politica En Duval."

63. Jack Yeaman, "George Parr Is Symbol of Unity for All Border Area," *Laredo Times*, May 4, 1952, p. 6.

64. Yeaman, "George Parr Is Symbol of Unity."

65. "A Los Votantes del Condado Duval," *La Verdad* (Corpus Christi), July 4, 1952.

66. E. E. Dunlap, "Resume of General Election, Duval Company Nov. 6, 1962," n.d., Impoundment of Election Materials, TSLAC.

67. "Duval Party Caravan Set," *San Antonio Express*, June 4, 1952, p. 16; "Level Campaigning, Going Big-Time And Expensive," *San Antonio Express*, April 6, 1952, p. 48; "El Freedom Party de Duval Toma Fuerza," *La Libertad*, June 26, 1952; "Triunfal Junta Política: Aproximadamente 1000 Personas asistieron a la verificada el Dom. en Ramírez, Por el Freedom Party," La Libertad, July 11,

1952; "Freedom Party Rally In Freer Draws 1,200," *Corpus Christi Caller Times*, July 13, 1952, p. 5.

68. "Reams Loses To Parr-Baked Judge In Battle That Only Dented Czar," *Breckenridge American*, July 28, 1952, p. 1.

69. "Duval County Group Asks for Help," *San Antonio Express*, April 10, 1952, p. 3; "Duval Candidate Death March Survivor," *Corpus Christi Times*, April 30, 1952, p. 9; Duval County Election Returns, 1952, Duval County Clerk; "Forces for Parr Sweep Duval," *San Antonio Express*, July 29, 1952, p. 2; "Parr Resigns Sheriff Post," *Corpus Christi Times*, October 1, 1952, p. 1.

70. "Rangers Fail to Call on Parr on Visit to Duval," *Breckenridge American*, May 6, 1952, p. 1; "FBI Reportedly Probes Violations of Civil Right," *Breckenridge American*, January 25, 1953, p. 5. Note: Most of these investigators, as were the contingent from the press, worked mostly out of Alice.

71. "Freedom Party Enters Parr-Ranger Court War," *Corpus Christi Times*, February 19, 1954, pp. 1, 16.

72. "Freedom Party Enters Parr-Ranger Court War."

73. "Freedom Party Hoping For 'Success at Polls' in Duval County Election," *Orange Leader*, January 1, 1954, p. 6; "Parr Opposition Leader Hopeful," *San Antonio Express*, February 15, 1954, pp. 1–2.

74. "Duval County (Continued from Page 1)," *Orange Leader*, March 5, 1954, p. 2; Info from Caro Brown, Alice, Re: Member of O.P.L.W.V., June 25, 1954, TSLAC.

75. Mrs. J. J. Trevino and Mrs. J. H. Rutledge, "United Mothers and Wives of Duval County," April 12, 1954, TSLAC; John Ben Shepherd, "Duval U.S.A," June 25, 1954, Freedom Party Court Cases, TSLAC; "Ranger Aide Is Assured Duval Wives," *Corpus Christi Caller-Times*, February 21, 1954, pp. 1, 12.

76. "Ranger Aide Is Assured Duval Wives," 1; "Two New Anti-Parr Groups Are Formed," *Corpus Christi Times*, March 2, 1954, p. 1.

77. "Pro-Parr Women Rap 'Publicity,'" *San Antonio Express*, March 20, 1954, p. 1.

78. "Pro-Parr Women Rap 'Publicity.'"

79. "Auditor Appointed in Duval County," *Breckenridge American*, May 26, 1954, p. 1; "Judge Dismisses Injunction Plea," *Daily News-Telegram* (Sulphur Springs, TX), June 27, 1954, p. 4; "Prosecutor Sought By San Diego Court," *Orange Leader*, June 23, 1954, p. 1; "Anti Parr Party Holds Rally," *Sweetwater Reporter*, July 19, 1954, p. 8.

80. "Political Factions Merge For United Opposition To Parr," *Sweetwater Reporter*, December 18, 1955, p. 19; "El Juez Tobin Se Rehúsa A Encabezar Partido Político," *New Duval* (San Diego, TX), February 24, 1956, p. 1; "Parr Is Winner in South Texas Laredo in Probe," *Breckenridge American*, April 4, 1956, p. 1.

81. "Comienza A Accionar El Freedom Party," *New Duval*, February 24, 1956, p. 1; "Power of Parr Is Under Test Today," *Breckenridge American*, April 3, 1956, p. 4; "Parr Is Winner in South Texas Laredo in Probe," 1.

82. "Parr Apparently Wins As Sheriff," *Daily News-Telegram*, July 31, 1956, p. 5; "Two Sheriffs and County Clerks for Duval County," *Duval County Maverick* (San Diego, TX), October 18, 1958, p. 1.

83. "August Run-off Will Decide," *Duval County Maverick*, August 1, 1958, p. 1; "Tobin Reverses Stand," *Duval County Maverick*, August 8, 1958, p. 1.

84. "Duval Absentee Votes Rejected," *Daily News-Telegram*, May 11, 1960, p. 1; "Parr and 'Old Party' Suffer Severe Loss," *Taylor Daily Press*, May 11, 1960, p. 1; "Duke of Duval Keeps Strength," *Daily News-Telegram*, June 9, 1960, p. 4; "Our Side," *Bellaire Texan*, April 29, 1964, p. 14.

85. "The Greatest Generation: Birth Years, Characteristics, and History," *FamilySearch*, June 13, 2020, https://www.familysearch.org/en/blog/greatest-generation-years-characteristics.

86. "New Anti-Parr Faction Springs Up in San Diego," *Laredo Times*, July 2, 1961, p. 1.

87. "Anti-Parr Forces Will Fight Bonds," *Laredo Times*, February 26, 1961, p. 9.

88. "Duval GOP Takes Aim at Parr," *San Antonio Express*, April 28, 1962, p. 2; "Court Order Schroeder Freed," *Corpus Christi Times*, June 8, 1962, pp. 1, 12.

89. "Steps or No, GOP To Have Platform At Duval Gathering," *Corpus Christi Times*, June 22, 1962; "Texas Republicanism and Duval County Demos Clash Head-On," *Brenham Banner-Press*, July 30, 1962, pp. 8, 24; "Dr. Dunlap Charges Vote Buying in Duval," *Alice Daily Echo*, October 31, 1962, pp. 1, 8; "At Freer Polls," *Alice Daily Echo*, November 7, 1962, p. 6; "Duval Demos Win Over GOP In Big Turnout," *Alice Daily Echo*, November 7, 1962; "Duval Balloting Irregularities Are Object of Probe," *Alice Daily Echo*, November 11, 1962, p. 1.

90. In the second decade of the twenty-first century, the Republican Party once again organized to challenge local candidates. In the 2020 presidential election, Republican President Donald H. Trump received 2,443 votes, or 48 percent of the Duval County vote.

91. "Republicans File In Duval County," *San Antonio Express-News*, February 5, 1964, p. 36; "All Demos Sweep to Easy Victories in Duval County," *San Antonio Express-News*, November 5, 1964, p. 36.

92. "Carrillos to Succeed Parrs on Mesquite Curtain Throne?," *San Antonio Light*, December 13, 1973, p. 29.

93. "Carrillos to Succeed Parrs on Mesquite Curtain Throne?"

94. "Duval County: The Budget, Parr Dynasty Threatened," *San Antonio Light*, December 12, 1973, p. 3.

95. Millionaire Clinton Manges had recently moved to Duval County and was meddling in the county's politics. At this time he was on Parr's side, but later Parr accused Manges of supporting the Carrillos.

96. "Ex-Legislator Tells Candidacy," *Corpus Christi Times*, January 29, 1974, 2, Newspaper Archivesp. 2; "Carrillo-Parr Family 'Feud' Continues,"

San Antonio Express-News, April 28, 1974, 24, Newspaper Archivesp. 24; "Next Step Following Tie Vote Awaited," *Corpus Christi Times*, April 9, 1974, 14, Newspaper Archivesp. 14.

97. "Duke of Duval' Convicted," *San Antonio Light*, March 20, 1974, p. 5; "Duval Judge Convicted On Six Counts of Lying," *Alice Daily Echo*, May 10, 1974, p. 1; "Archer Parr Sentenced to 10 Years In Prison," *Corpus Christi Times*, May 21, 1974, pp. 1, 14.

98. "Carrillo Ousts Duval County Judge Archer Parr," *Corpus Christi Times*, May 21, 1975, pp. 1, 10; "Duke of Duval's Dynasty Appears to Be Crumbling," *Brownsville Herald*, March 25, 1975, p. 14; "Parr Income Tax Conviction Upheld," *Brownsville Herald*, March 25, 1975, p. 14.

99. "Carrillo Indictments Make Duval Situation Fuzzier," *Brownsville Herald*, April 11, 1975, p. 1; "Witnesses' Testimony Berates Judge Carrillo," *Alice Daily Echo*, May 22, 1975, p. 1.

100. "Documents Related to the Impeachment of O.P. Carrillo," *Legislative Reference Library of Texas*, accessed November 24, 2023, https://lrl.texas.gov/collections/impeachment.cfm.

101. "Trial for Carrillo Underway," *Brownsville Herald*, September 14, 1976, p. 12; "Oscar Carrillo 'Guilty,'" *Alice Daily Echo*, September 23, 1976, p. 2; "D. C. Chapa Gets Delay in Trial," *Corpus Christi Times*, September 27, 1976, p. 4.

102. "85 Felony Indictments Gained in Duval County Clean Up," *Taylor Daily Press*, March 25, 1976, p. 4.

103. "Parr a Danger? Hearing Ordered," *Corpus Christi Times*, March 31, 1975, p. 1; "Duval Kingpin Arrest Ordered," *San Antonio Express*, April 1, 1975, p. 1; Alfredo E. Cardenas, "Investigation Confirmed Parr Died by Suicide," *Soy de Duval* (blog), March 24, 2018, https://soydeduval.blogspot.com/2018/05/investigation-confirmed-parr-died-by.html.

104. "Courts Deal Upsets to Parrs," *San Antonio Express*, April 28, 1974, p. 1; "George Parr Dead; Apparent Suicide," *Corpus Christi Times*, April 1, 1975, p. 1.

105. "Friends Paying Final Respects To George Parr," *Brownsville Herald*, April 3, 1975, p. 1.

106. "1,000 Mourn Parr at Graveside Rites," *Brownsville Herald*, April 3, 1975, p. 1; "Parr Funeral, Services in Benavides," *Alice Daily Echo*, April 3, 1975, p. 13.

107. "Hester Appoints Uresti As Judge," *Brownsville Herald*, November 4, 1975, p. 12; "Gilberto Uresti Seeks Election as Duval Judge," *Alice Daily Echo*, January 18, 1976, p. 1.

Notes for Epilogue

1. Valerio-Jiménez, "Neglected Citizens and Willing Traders," 259.

2. Declaration of Independence (US 1776), § 2.

Bibliography

Archives

Béxar Archives
Dolph Briscoe Center for American History, University of Texas Austin
    Coleman-Fulton Pasture Company Records
    James B. Wells Papers, 1837–1926
    James Stephen Hogg Papers, 1836–1969
    Texas Newspaper Collection
    William G. Hale Papers, 1819–1931
Dupré Library, University of Louisiana at Lafayette
    Givens-Hopkins Family Papers
Duval County Clerk, San Diego, TX
    County Commissioners Court Minutes
    Duval County Deed Records
    Election Books
La Retama Central Library, Corpus Christi, TX
Legislative Reference Library of Texas
National Archives and Records Administration
Nueces County District Clerk, Corpus Christi, TX
    County Commissioners Court
    Deed Records
    District Court Records
    Election Books
    Records of Bonds and Mortgages
San Diego Independent School District
    Minute Books
The Texas General Land Office Archives
    Archives and Records Division
    Spanish Collection
    Texas County Maps Volume
    Texas General Land Office Publications
Texas State Library and Archives Commission
    County Election Results
    Department of Education
    Freedom Party Court Cases
    Governor's Papers: Samuel Houston
    Milton P. Norton Papers, 1842–1860
    Ranger Records
    Secretary of State

South Texas Archives, Texas A&M University–Kingsville
  Agnes G. Grimm Collection
  Kenedy Collection
  Newspaper Collection
  Special Collections
  Walter W. Meek Jr. Papers
Special Collections and University Archives, Texas A&M University–Corpus Christi
  South Texas Museum Collection of San Diego, Texas Historic Photographs

Secondary Sources

Acosta, Teresa Palomo, and Ruthe Winegarten. *Las Tejanas: 300 Years of History.* 1st ed. Jack and Doris Smothers Series in Texas History, Life, and Culture 10. Austin: University of Texas Press, 2003.

Allee, Sheila. *Texas Mutiny: Bullets, Ballots, and Boss Rule.* Austin: SAC Press, 1995.

Allhands, J. L. *Uriah Lott.* San Antonio: Naylor, 1949.

Alonzo, Armando C. "Mexican-American Land Grant Adjudication." *Handbook of Texas Online,* accessed December 9, 2023. https://www.tshaonline.org/handbook/entries/mexican-american-land-grant-adjudication.

Alonzo, Armando C. *Tejano Legacy: Rancheros and Settlers in South Texas, 1734–1900.* Albuquerque: University of New Mexico, 1998.

Anders, Evan. *Boss Rule in South Texas: The Progressive Era.* 1st ed. Austin: University of Texas Press, 1982.

Anders, Evan. "Parr, Archer." *Handbook of Texas Online,* April 25, 2019. https://www.tshaonline.org/handbook/entries/parr-archer.

Anders, Evan. "Parr, George Berham [1901–1975]." *Handbook of Texas Online.* Accessed September 3, 2023. https://www.tshaonline.org/handbook/entries/parr-george-berham-1901-1975.

"Andrés García, 'Agostadero San Andres.'" *El Mesteño* 1, no. 9 (1997): 8.

Arreola, Daniel. *Tejano South Texas: A Mexican American Cultural Province.* Austin: University of Texas Press, 2002.

Bacha-Garza, Roseann, Christopher L. Miller, and Russell K. Skowronek, eds. *The Civil War on the Rio Grande, 1846–1876.* 1st ed. Elma Dill Russell Spencer Series in the West and Southwest 46. College Station: Texas A&M University Press, 2019.

Barr, Alwyn. "Late Nineteenth-Century Texas." *Handbook of Texas Online.* Accessed December 17, 2020. https://www.tshaonline.org/handbook/entries/late-nineteenth-century-texas.

Bauer, K. Jack "Mexican War." *Handbook of Texas Online.* Accessed December 8, 2023. https://www.tshaonline.org/handbook/entries/republic-of-the-rio-grande.

Baulch, Joe Robert. "James B. Wells: South Texas Economic and Political Leader." PhD diss., Texas Tech University, 1974.

Belo, A. H., and Company *Texas Almanac and State Industrial Guide for 1904.* Galveston, TX: Clark & Courts, 1904.

Bilbao, Elena, and María Antonia Gallart. *Los Chicanos: segregación y educación.* Mexico DF: Editorial Nueva Imagen, 1981.

Bishko, Charles Julian. "The Peninsular Background of Latin American Cattle Ranching." *Hispanic American Historical Review* 32, no. 4 (1952): 491–515. https://doi.org/10.2307/2508949.

Blanton, Carlos Kevin. *The Strange Career of Bilingual Education in Texas, 1836– 1981.* Texas AM University Press, 2007.

Bolton, Herbert Eugene. "Tienda de Cuervo's Inspección of Laredo, 1757." *Quarterly of the Texas State Historical Association* 6, no. 3 (January 1903): 187–203.

Bourland, W. H., and Miller, James. "Report of W. H. Bourland and James R. Miller Commissioner to Investigate Titles West of the Nueces." Historical Volumes. Austin: Texas General Land Office, 1852.

Brown, John Henry. *Indian Wars and Pioneers of Texas.* Greenville, SC: Southern Historical Press, 1978.

Campbell, Randolph B. "Grass Roots Reconstruction: The Personnel of County Government in Texas, 1865–1876." *Journal of Southern History* 58, no. 1 (1992): 99–116. https://doi.org/10.2307/2210476.

Campbell, Randolph B. *Grass-Roots Reconstruction in Texas, 1865–1880.* Baton Rouge: Louisiana State University Press, 1997.

Campbell, Randolph B. "Reconstruction in Nueces County, 1865–76." *Houston Review* 16, no. 1 (January 1994): 16–18.

Cardenas, Alfredo E. "A Brief History of Duval County." Unpublished paper, Corpus Christi, TX, 1984.

Cárdenas, Alfredo E. "The Early Stirrings of the 'Town' of San Diego." *Soy de Duval* (blog), August 15, 2013.

Cardenas, Alfredo E. "Givens, John Slye." *Handbook of Texas Online.* Accessed March 02, 2023. https://www.tshaonline.org/handbook/entries/givens-john-slye.

Cardenas, Alfredo E. "Indian Raid Prompts Request for Soldier." *Soy de Duval* (blog), April 2, 2015.

Cardenas, Alfredo E. "Investigation Confirmed Parr Died by Suicide." *Soy de Duval* (blog), March 24, 2018. https://soydeduval.blogspot.com/2018/05/investigation-confirmed-parr-died-by.html.

Cardenas, Alfredo E. "Man, Who Raised Archie Parr." *Soy de Duval* (blog), November 22, 2015.

Cardenas, Alfredo E. "Mexican Americans Fared Well under Parr's Duval County Machine." Master's thesis, Texas State University, 2018.

Cardenas, Alfredo E. "Name a Duval County Rancho." *Soy de Duval* (blog), April 6, 2020.

Cárdenas, Alfredo E. "Newspaper Correspondent Jeffreys Identified as Dr. William C. Jefferies." *Soy de Duval* (blog), January 21, 2018.

Cardenas, Alfredo E. "Parr, George Berham [1829–1867]." *Handbook of Texas Online*, July 27, 2009. https://www.tshaonline.org/handbook/entries/parr-george-berham-1829-1867.

Cardenas, Alfredo E. "Plan of San Diego Narrative." *Soy de Duval* (blog), August 20, 2023. https://soydeduval.blogspot.com/2023/08/plan-of-san-diego-narrative.html.

Cardenas, Alfredo E. "The Rearing of Duval County Political Kingpin Archie Parr." *Journal of South Texas* 22, no. 2 (Fall 2009): 134–44.

Caro, Robert A. *The Path to Power*. 1st Vintage Books ed. The Years of Lyndon Johnson 1. New York: Vintage Books, 1983.

Carrozza, Anthony R. *The Dukes of Duval County: The Parr Family and Texas Politics*. Norman: University of Oklahoma Press, 2017.

Cashion, Ty. "What's the Matter with Texas? The Great Enigma of the Lone Star State in the American West." *Montana: The Magazine of Western History* 55, no. 4 (Winter 2005): 2–15. http://www.jstor.org/stable/4520740.

Center of Military History. "The Mexican War and After." In *American Military History*, 163–83. Army Historical Series. Washington DC: Office of the Chief of Military History, United States Army, 1989.

Chipman, Donald E. "In Search of Cabeza de Vaca's Route across Texas: An Historiographical Survey." *Southwestern Historical Quarterly* 91, no. 2 (1987): 127–48.

Chipman, Donald E. "Rubí, Marqués De." *Handbook of Texas Online*.

Clark, John E. *The Fall of the Duke of Duval: A Prosecutor's Journal*. 1st ed. Austin: Eakin Press, 1995.

Clark, John W., Jr. "Santos Coy, Manuel de Los." *Handbook of Texas Online*. Accessed December 31, 2023. https://www.tshaonline.org/handbook/entries/santos-coy-manuel-de-los.

Committee on Commerce, Science, and Transportation. *Weather Modification: Programs, Problems, Policy, and Potential*. Washington DC: Government Printing Office, 1878.

Connor, L. G. "Brief History of the Sheep Industry in the United States." *Agricultural History Society Papers* 1 (1921): 89–165, 167–97. https://www.jstor.org/stable/44216164.

Cook, Mary J. Straw. *Doña Tules: Santa Fe's Courtesan and Gambler*. Illustrated ed. Albuquerque: University of New Mexico Press, 2007.

Coopwood, Bethel. "The Route of Cabeza de Vaca: Part I." *Quarterly of the Texas State Historical Association* 3, no. 2 (1899): 121–29.

Cox, I. J. "The Southwest Boundary of Texas." *Quarterly of the Texas State Historical Association* 6, no. 2 (1902): 81–102.

Crimm, Ana Carolina Castillo, and Sara R. Massey. *Turn-of-the-Century Photographs from San Diego, Texas*. Austin: University of Texas Press, 2003.

Daniell, Lewis E. *Personnel of the Texas State Government: With Sketches of Representative Men of Texas*. San Antonio: Maverick Printing House, 1892.

Dary, David. "Cattle Brands." *Handbook of Texas Online*. Accessed January 19, 2021. https://www.tshaonline.org/handbook/entries/cattle-brands.

Davidson, James West. "The New Narrative History: How New? How Narrative?" *Reviews in American History* 12, no. 3 (September 1984): 322–34.

Davis, Ellis Arthur, and Edwin H. Grobe, eds. *The Encyclopedia of Texas*. 2 vols. Dallas: Texas Development Bureau, 1922.

Davis, John Martin. *Texas Land Grants, 1750–1900: A Documentary History*. Jefferson, NC: McFarland, 2016.

de la Garza, Beatriz Eugenia. *From the Republic of the Rio Grande: A Personal History of the Place and the People*. 1st ed. Jack and Doris Smothers Series in Texas History, Life, and Culture 35. Austin: University of Texas Press, 2013.

de la Teja, Jesús F. "Coahuila and Texas." *Handbook of Texas*. Accessed June 26, 2020. http://www.tshaonline.org/handbook/online/articles/usc01.

de la Teja, Jesús F., Paula Mitchell Marks, and Ronnie C. Tyler. *Texas: Crossroads of North America*. Boston: Houghton Mifflin, 2004.

De León, Arnoldo. *Benavides: The Town and Its Founder, 1881*. Benavides, TX: Benavides City Council / Benavides Centennial Committee, 1980.

De León, Arnoldo. *The Tejano Community, 1836–1900*. Dallas: Southern Methodist University Press, 1997.

De León, Arnoldo. *They Called Them Greasers: Anglo Attitudes toward Mexicans in Texas, 1821–1900*. Austin: University of Texas Press, 2010.

De León, Arnoldo. "Vamos Pa' Kiansis: Tejanos in the Nineteenth-Century Cattle Drives." *Journal of South Texas* 27, no. 2 (Fall 2014): 6.

Delaney, Norman C. *The Maltby Brothers' Civil War*. College Station: Texas A & M University Press, 2013.

Dobie, J. Frank. *The Mustangs*. Edison, NJ: Castle Books.

Dobie, J. Frank, and John Duncan Young. *A Vaquero of the Brush Country*. Austin: University of Texas Press, 1998.

Downie, Alice Evans. *Terrell County, Texas, Its Past, Its People: A Compilation, Pictures of and Writings by or about People Places, and Events in Terrell County*. Sanderson, TX: Terrell County Heritage Commission, 1978.

Durham, George, and Clyde Wantland. *Taming the Nueces Strip: The Story of McNelly's Rangers*. University of Texas Press, 2006.

Easley, S. C. *Memorial and Genealogical Record of Southwest Texas: Containing Biographical Histories and Genealogical Records of Many Leading Men and Prominent Families*. Signal Mountain, TN: Southern Historical Press, 1978.

Escobedo, Santiago. "Iron Men And Wooden Carts: Tejano Freighters During The Civil War." *Journal of South Texas* 17, no. 2 (Fall 2004): 51–60.

Felzenberg, Alvin. "How William F. Buckley, Jr., Changed His Mind on Civil Rights." *POLITICO Magazine*. Accessed February 4, 2022. https://www.politico.com/magazine/story/2017/05/13/william-f-buckley-civil-rights-215129

Ford, John Salmon. *Rip Ford's Texas*. Edited by Stephen B. Oates. Austin: University of Texas Press, 1963.

"Francisco Cordente Agostadero La Santa Cruz de La Concepción." *El Mesteño*, 1998, 8.

Frantz, Joe B. "The Mercantile House of McKinney & Williams, Underwriters of the Texas Revolution." *Bulletin of the Business Historical Society* 26, no. 1 (1952): 1–18. https://doi.org/10.2307/3111339.

Gammel, Hans Peter Mareus Neilsen. *The Laws of Texas, 1822–1897*. 11 vols. Austin: Gammel Book Company, 1898.

Gard, Wayne. *Rawhide Texas*. Norman: University of Oklahoma Press, 2015.

Garza, Alicia A. "Hebbronville, TX." *Handbook of Texas Online*. Accessed October 27, 2020. https://www.tshaonline.org/handbook/entries/hebbronville-tx.

Garza, Catarino. *La Era De Tuxtepec en México, o sea, Rusia en América*. San José, Costa Rica: Imprenta Comercial, 1894.

Garza Sáenz, Ernesto. Segundas crónicas de Camargo. Edited by Marco Luis Asociados. Ciudad Victoria, Tamaulipas: Instituto de Investigaciones Históricas, 1994.

Germann, John J., and Myron R. Jansen. *Texas Post Offices*. Houston: J. J. Germann, 1989.

González-Quiroga, Miguel Ángel. "Mexicanos in Texas during the Civil War." In *Mexican Americans in Texas History, Selected Essays*, edited by Zamora, Emiliano, Orozco, Cynthia, and Rocha, Rodolfo, 51–62. Austin: Texas State Historical Association, 2000.

González-Quiroga, Miguel Ángel. *War and Peace on the Rio Grande Frontier, 1830–1880*. New Directions in Tejano History 1. Norman: University of Oklahoma Press, 2020.

Goodman, Adam. "The Promise of New Approaches and Persistence of Old Paradigms in Mexican American History." *Journal of American Ethnic History* 32, no. 3 (Spring 2013): 83–89. https://doi.org/10.5406/jamerethnhist.32.3.0083.

Graf, Leroy P. "Colonizing Projects in Texas South of the Nueces, 1820–1845." *Southwestern Historical Quarterly* 50, no. 4 (1947): 431–48.

Grear, Charles David. *Why Texans Fought in the Civil War*. College Station: Texas A & M University Press, 2012.

Greaser, Galen D., and Jesús F. de la Teja. "Quieting Title to Spanish and Mexican Land Grants in the Trans-Nueces: The Bourland and Miller Commission, 1850–1852." *Southwestern Historical Quarterly* 95, no. 4 (April 1992): 445–64. http://www.jstor.org/stable/30242000.

Grimm, Agnes. "Bard, John Peter." *Handbook of Texas Online*.

Grimm, Agnes. *Llanos Mesteñas: Mustang Plains*. Waco, TX: Texian Press, 1968.

Grimm, Agnes. "Peña Station." *Handbook of Texas Online*. Accessed October 27, 2020. https://www.tshaonline.org/handbook/entries/pena-station.

Guerra, Jesenia. "The Fight for Democracy: An Oral History of the Freedom Party." Master's thesis, Texas A&M–Kingsville, 2005.

Guthrie, Keith, "San Patricio County." *Handbook of Texas Online*. Accessed February 20, 2023. https://www.tshaonline.org/handbook/entries/san-patricio-county.

Hämäläinen, Pekka. "Conclusion: The Shape of Power." In *The Comanche Empire*, 342–62. New Haven, CT: Yale University Press, 2008. http://www.jstor.org/stable/j.ctt1njn13.13.

Hardy, Dermot H., and Ingham S. Roberts. *Historical Review of South-East Texas: And the Founders, Leaders, and Representative Men of Its Commerce, Industry, and Civic Affairs*. Chicago: Lewis Publishing, 1910.

Harris, Charles H., and Louis R. Sadler. *The Texas Rangers and the Mexican Revolution: The Bloodiest Decade, 1910-1920*. Albuquerque: University of New Mexico Press, 2004.

Henson, Margaret S. "McKinney, Thomas Freeman." *Handbook of Texas Online*, accessed March 20, 2021. https://www.tshaonline.org/handbook/entries/mckinney-thomas-freeman.

Hernández, Gregory, Gloria Hernández, and Raúl J Guerra. *Capilla de La Misión de Roma Marriage Book, Roma, Texas*. San Antonio: Los Béxareños Genealogical Society, 2012.

Houston, Sam. *Speech of Hon. Sam Houston, of Texas, exposing the malfeasance and corruption of John Charles Watrous, judge of the federal court in Texas, and of his confederates: delivered in the Senate of the United States, Feb. 3, 1859*. London: Forgotten Books, 2018.

Huson, Hobart. *District Judges of Refugio County*. Refugio, TX: Refugio Timely Remarks, 1941.

Jackson, Jack. *Los Mesteños: Spanish Ranching in Texas, 1721–1821*. 1st ed. Centennial Series of the Association of Former Students, Texas A&M University, 18. College Station: Texas A&M University Press, 1986.

Jaillet, Claude. "Historical Sketch." Corpus Christi, TX, n.d.

Jaillet, Claude, and Francis X. Reuss. "Sketches of Catholicity in Texas." *Records of the American Catholic Historical Society of Philadelphia*, no. 2 (1886): 143–53.

Johnson, John G. "Narváez, Pánfilo De." *Handbook of Texas Online*. Accessed February 27, 2023. https://www.tshaonline.org/handbook/entries/narvaez-panfilo-de.

Jordan-Bychkov, Terry G. *North American Cattle-Ranching Frontiers: Origins, Diffusion, and Differentiation*. 1st ed. Histories of the American Frontier. Albuquerque: University of New Mexico Press, 1993.

"José Rafael Garcia Salinas, 'Agostadero San Leandro.'" *El Mesteño* 2, no. 22 (1998): 8.

Journal of the House of Representatives. Eighth Legislature of Texas. Austin: John Marshall & Company, State Printers.

Kingston, Mike, Sam Attlesey, and Mary G. Crawford. *The Texas Almanac's Political History of Texas*. Austin: Eakin Press, 1992.

Kuby, Michael, John Harner, and Patricia Gober. *Human Geography in Action*. Hoboken, NJ: John Wiley & Sons, 2013.

Lambert, Jeffrey T. "Decade of Change: Origins of a Mexican American Identity in Texas, 1910–1920." Diss., Texas State University, 2009.

"Land Districts." *Handbook of Texas Online*, accessed April 15, 2021. https://www.tshaonline.org/handbook/entries/land-districts

Lasater, Dale. *Falfurrias: Ed C. Lasater and the Development of South Texas*. Texas A&M University Press, 1998.

Leaverton, Mark K. "The Genesis of Title: Land Grants, Patents & State-Owned Minerals." 2nd Texas Mineral Title Examination Course, Houston, Texas, 2015.

Leffler, John, and Christopher Long. "Webb County." *Handbook of Texas Online*. Accessed February 20, 2023. https://www.tshaonline.org/handbook/entries/webb-county.

Lehmann, Val W., and José Cisneros. *Forgotten Legions: Sheep in the Rio Grande Plain of Texas*. El Paso: Texas Western Press, 1969.

Long, Christopher. "McMullen-McGloin Colony." *Handbook of Texas Online*. Accessed June 20, 2019. https://tshaonline.org/handbook/online/articles/uem01.

Long, Christopher. "Nueces County." *Handbook of Texas Online*. Accessed February 20, 2023. https://www.tshaonline.org/handbook/entries/nueces-county.

Lowry, Todd, "Bourland, William H." *Handbook of Texas Online*, accessed October 27, 2022. https://www.tshaonline.org/handbook/entries/bourland-william-h.

Lynch, Dudley M. *The Duke of Duval: The Life and Times of George B. Parr, a Biography*. Waco, TX: Texian Press, 1976.

Marten, James. "Patriots and Dissidents: The Role of Ethnicity in Civil War Texas." *Heritage of the Great Plains* 22, no. 3 (1989): 14–23.

Marten, James. *Texas Divided Loyalty and Dissent in the Lone Star State, 1856–1874*. Lexington: University Press of Kentucky, 2015.

Martinez, José Noe. *St. Francis de Paula Catholic Church: The Story of Its Founding and Early History*. Edited by Sonia C. Barrera. San Diego, TX: Duval County Historical Commission, 2008.

McCampbell, Coleman. *Texas Seaport: The Story of the Growth of Corpus Christi and the Coastal Bend Area*. New York: Exposition Press, 1952.

McCoy, Dorothy Abbott. *Oil, Mud & Guts: Birth of a Texas Town*. Brownsville, TX: Springman-Hill Lithograph, 1977.

McDonald, David R. *José Antonio Navarro: In Search of the American Dream in Nineteenth-Century Texas*. Watson Caufield and Mary Maxwell Arnold Republic of Texas Series. Denton: Texas State Historical Association, 2010.

Menchaca, Martha. *Naturalizing Mexican Immigrants: A Texas History*. 1st ed. Austin: University of Texas Press, 2011.

Mendoza, Alexander. "'For Our Own Best Interests': Nineteenth-Century Laredo Tejanos, Military Service, and the Development of American Nationalism." *Southwestern Historical Quarterly* 115, no. 2 (2011): 125–52.

"The Mexican and Indian Raid of '78." *Quarterly of the Texas State Historical Association* 5, no. 3 (January 1902): 212–51.

Mier y Terán, Manuel de. *Texas by Terán: The Diary Kept by General Manuel de Mier y Terán on His 1828 Inspection of Texas*. Edited by Jack Jackson.

Translated by John Wheat. With botanical notes by Scooter Cheatham and Lynn Marshall. 1st ed. Jack and Doris Smothers Series in Texas History, Life, and Culture 2. Austin: University of Texas Press, 2000.

"Miller, James B." *Handbook of Texas Online*, accessed October 27, 2022. https://www.tshaonline.org/handbook/entries/miller-james-b.

Monday, Jane Clements and Frances Brannen Vick. *Petra's Legacy: The South Texas Ranching Empire of Petra Vela and Mifflin Kenedy*. 1st ed. Perspectives on South Texas. College Station: Texas A&M University Press, 2007.

Montejano, David. *Anglos and Mexicans in the Making of Texas, 1836–1986*. Austin: University of Texas Press, 2009.

Mora-Torres, Juan. *The Making of the Mexican Border: The State, Capitalism, and Society in Nuevo León, 1848–1910*. 1st ed. Austin: University of Texas Press, 2001. Kindle.

Moses, J. Williamson, and Murphy D. Givens. *Texas in Other Days*. Corpus Christi: Friends of Corpus Christi Public Libraries, 2005.

Nance, Joseph Milton. *After San Jacinto: The Texas-Mexican Frontier, 1836–1841*. Austin: University of Texas Press, 2011.

Neale, William, and J. C. Rayburn. *Century of Conflict, 1821–1913*. New York: Arno, 1976.

Neu, C. T. "Annexation." *Handbook of Texas Online*. Accessed December 20, 2019. https://tshaonline.org/handbook/online/articles/mga02.

Olson, Donald W., Marilynn S. Olson, Russell L. Doescher, Lance L. Lambert, David E. Lemke, Angela M. Carl, Ross Johnson, Sandra D. Smith, and Kent H. Trede. "Piñon Pines and the Route of Cabeza de Vaca." *Southwestern Historical Quarterly* 101, no. 2 (1997): 174–86.

"Original Survey of the Agostadero La Santa Cruz de La Concepción." *El Mesteño*, 1998, 17.

"Paraje San Diego." *El Mesteño* 4, no. 37 (n.d.): 6.

Paschal, George Washington. *A Digest of the Laws of Texas*. Houston: W. H. & O. H. Morrison, 1873.

Peavey, John R. *Echoes from the Rio Grande*. Brownsville, TX: Springman-King, 1963.

Perales, Alonso S., and Emilio Zamora. *In Defense of My People*. Houston: Arte Público Press, 2022.

Perales, Monica. *Smeltertown: Making and Remembering a Southwest Border Community*. Chapel Hill: University of North Carolina Press, 2010.

Powers, Edward. *War and the Weather*. Chicago: S. C. Griggs & Company, 1871.

Poyo, Gerald E., Editor. *Tejano Journey, 1770-1850*. Austin: University of Texas Press, 1996.

Quezada, J. Gilberto. *Border Boss: Manuel B. Bravo and Zapata County*. College Station: Texas A & M University Press, 1999.

Quiroz, Anthony. *Claiming Citizenship: Mexican Americans in Victoria, Texas*, eBook, English, Edition:1st ed, Texas A & M University Press, College Station, 2005.

"Rafael Ramires Yzaguirre, Agostadero La Rosalia." *El Mesteño* 3, no. 24 (1999): 8.

Ramirez, Jose A. *To the Line of Fire: Mexican Americans and World War I.* College Station: Texas A & M University Press, 2009.

Ramírez, Víctor M. Sáenz. *Los Protocolos De La Villa De Nuestra Señora Santa Anna De Camargo. 1762-1809.* Parroquia de Camargo, Tamps., Mexico: Palibrio, 2011.

Rayburn, John C. "The Rainmakers in Duval." *Southwestern Historical Quarterly* 61, no. 1 (1957): 101–15.

Reeves, Jesse S. "The Treaty of Guadalupe-Hidalgo." *American Historical Review* 10, no. 2 (1905): 309–24. https://doi.org/10.2307/1834723.

Reposa, Carol Coffee. "Ginning the Years: A Memoir." *Valley Voices: A Literary Review* 20, no. 2 (Fall 2020): 69–72.

Reséndez, Andrés. *A Land So Strange: The Epic Journey of Cabeza de Vaca: The Extraordinary Tale of a Shipwrecked Spaniard Who Walked across America in the Sixteenth Century.* New York: Basic Books, 2007.

Richardson, Chad. *Batos, Bolillos, Pochos, & Pelados: Class and Culture on the South Texas Border.* 1st ed. Austin: University of Texas Press, 1999.

Robertson, Brian. *Wild Horse Desert: The Heritage of South Texas.* Edinburg, Tex.: Published for Hidalgo County Historical Museum by New Santander Press, 1985.

Rubel, Arthur J. *Across the Tracks, Mexican-Americans in a Texas City.* Third Printing. Austin, Tex: University of Texas Press, 1970.

Ruiz, Vicki. *From out of the Shadows: Mexican Women in Twentieth-Century America.* 10th anniversary ed. Oxford: Oxford University Press, 2008.

Sáenz, Andrés. *Early Tejano Ranching: Daily Life at Ranchos San José and El Fresnillo.* Edited and with an introduction by Andrés Tijerina. College Station: Texas A&M Press, 2001.

Sáenz, José de la Luz, Emilio Zamora, and Ben Maya. *The World War I Diary of José de La Luz Sáenz.* C. A. Brannen Series 13. College Station: Texas A&M University Press, 2014. Ebook.

"San Diego de Arriba and San Diego de Abajo." *El Mesteño* 1, no. 3 (1997).

"Santos Flores, Agostadero de Agua Poquita." *El Mesteño* 1, no. 10 (1997): 8.

"Santos García, 'Agostadero El Charco de Palo Blanco.'" *El Mesteño* 2, no. 18 (1998): 8.

Scott, Robert N., *The War of the Rebellion: A Compilation of the Official Records of the Union and Confederate Armies.* 128 vols. Harrisburg, PA: National Historical Society; distributed by Broadfoot, Historical Times, Morningside House, 1985.

Soto, Manuel Andres. *Life in a South Texas Colonia.* Corpus Christi, TX: MCM Books, 2017.

"The Mexican and Indian Raid of "78." *The Quarterly of the Texas State Historical Association* 5, no. 3 (1902): 212–51.

Thompson, Jerry. *Cortina: Defending the Mexican Name in Texas.* 1st ed. Fronteras Series, no. 6. College Station: Texas A & M University Press, 2007.

Thompson, Jerry. *Mexican Texans in the Union Army.* 1st ed. Southwestern Studies 78. El Paso: Texas Western Press, 1986.

Thompson, Jerry. *Sabers on the Rio Grande*. 1st ed. Austin: Presidial Press, 1974.

Thompson, Jerry. *Vaqueros in Blue & Gray*. Austin: State House Press, 2000.

Thompson, Jerry. *A Wild and Vivid Land: An Illustrated History of the South Texas Border*. Austin: Texas State Historical Association, 2012.

Thompson, Jerry D., and Lawrence T. Jones. *Civil War and Revolution on the Rio Grande Frontier: A Narrative and Photographic History*. Austin: Texas State Historical Association, 2004.

Thonhoff, Robert H. "Coy, Trinidad." *Handbook of Texas Online*. Accessed December 31, 2023. https://www.tshaonline.org/handbook/entries/coy-trinidad.

Thrall, Homer S. *The People's Illustrated Almanac, Texas Hand-Book and Immigrants' Guide, for 1880: Being an index to Texas, her people, laws, state and local governments, schools, churches, railroads, and other improvements and institutions*. St. Louis, MO: N. D. Thompson & Company, 1880.

Tijerina, Andrés. *Tejano Empire: Life on the South Texas Ranchos*. 1st ed. Clayton Wheat Williams Texas Life Series 7. College Station: Texas A&M University Press, 1998.

Tijerina, Andrés, and Ricardo M. Beasley. *Beasley's Vaqueros: In the Memoirs, Art, and Poems of Ricardo M. Beasley*. Austin: Texas State Historical Association, 2022.

Valerio-Jiménez, Omar S. "Neglected Citizens and Willing Traders: The Villas Del Norte (Tamaulipas) in Mexico's Northern Borderlands, 1749–1846." *Mexican Studies* 18, no. 2 (August 2002): 251–96.

Valerio-Jiménez, Omar S. *River of Hope: Forging Identity and Nation in the Rio Grande Borderlands*. Durham, NC: Duke University Press, 2013.

Varnum, Robin. Álvar Núñez Cabeza de Vaca: American Trailblazer. Norman: University of Oklahoma Press, 2014.

Vázquez, Josefina Zoraida. "La Supuesta República Del Rio Grande," Historia Mexicana 36, no. 1 (1986): 49–80.

Vera, Homero. "El Camino Real de Duval County." *El Mesteño* 5, no. 1 (2002): 13.

Vera, Homero. "Ranchos in Duval County." *El Mesteño* 1, no. 5 (February 1998): 1–24.

Vera, Homero. "Lomas Blanca." *El Mesteño*, February 10, 2020.

Vigness, David. "Republic of the Rio Grande." *Handbook of Texas Online*. Accessed February 20, 2023. https://www.tshaonline.org/handbook/entries/republic-of-the-rio-grande.

Wagner, Frank. "Moses, John Williamson." *Handbook of Texas Online*. Updated June 1, 2016. https://www.tshaonline.org/handbook/entries/moses-john-williamson.

Wagner, Leslie A. Jones. "Disputed Territory: Rio Grande/Rio Bravo Borderlands, 1838–1840." Master's thesis, University of Texas at Arlington, 1998.

Ward, Hortense Warner. "Blücher, Anton Felix Hans Hellmuth Von." *Handbook of Texas Online*. Accessed December 5, 2017. http://www.tshaonline.org/handbook/online/articles/fbl64.

Warner Ward, Hortense. "Blucher, Anton Felix Hans Hellmuth Von." *Handbook of Texas Online*.

Weber, David J. *The Mexican Frontier, 1821–1846: The American Southwest under Mexico.* 1st ed. Histories of the American Frontier. Albuquerque: University of New Mexico Press, 1982.

Weddle, Robert S. "Álvarez de Pineda, Alonso." *Handbook of Texas Online.*

Weddle, Robert S. "La Salle Expedition." *Handbook of Texas Online.*

Weddle, Robert S. "Nuevo Santander." *Handbook of Texas.* Accessed December 7, 2023. https://www.tshaonline.org/handbook/entries/nuevo-santander.

Wilcox, Seb S. "The Laredo City Election and Riot of April 1886." *Southwestern Historical Quarterly* 45, no. 1 (1941): 1–23.

Winfrey, Dorman H., and James M. Day, eds. *The Indian Papers of Texas and the Southwest, 1825–1916.* 5 vols. Austin: Texas State Historical Association, 1995.

Woods, Thomas. "Laredo Election Riot (1886)." *Handbook of Texas History Online* Accessed February 8, 2021. https://www.tshaonline.org/handbook/entries/laredo-election-riot-1886.

Wright, Robert E., O.M.I., "Catholic Church." *Handbook of Texas Online.*

Xavier, Sister Mary, IWBS. *Father Jaillet: Saddlebag Priest of the Nueces.* 2nd ed. Corpus Christi, TX: Duval County Historical Commission, 1996.

Yoakum, Henderson K. *History of Texas: From Its First Settlement in 1685 to Its Annexation to the United States In 1846.* Provo, UT: Repressed Publishing, 2013.

Yoakum, H. *Yoakum's History of Texas. First Thus edition.* Austin, 1935.

Young, Elliott. *Catarino Garza's Revolution on the Texas-Mexico Border.* American Encounters / Global Interactions. Durham, NC: Duke University Press, 2004.

Young, Elliott. "Remembering Catarino Garza's 1891 Revolution: An Aborted Border Insurrection." *Mexican Studies / Estudios Mexicanos* 12, no. 2 (1996): 231–72. https://doi.org/10.2307/1051845.

Zamora, Emilio, Cynthia Orozco, and Rodolfo Rocha, eds. *Mexican Americans in Texas History: Selected Essays.* Austin: Texas State Historical Association, 2000.

Zorrilla, Juan Fidel, Maribel Miró Flaquer, and Octavio Herrera Pérez, eds. *Tamaulipas: Textos de Su Historia, 1810–1921.* 1st. ed. San Juan, Mixcoac, Mexico, DF: Gobierno del Estado de Tamaulipas; Instituto de Investigaciones Dr. José María Luis Mora, 1990.

Newspapers

Abilene Reporter
Advertiser (Bastrop, TX)
Alice Daily Echo
Alice Echo
Alpine Avalanche
American Flag (Brownsville, TX)
Aransas Harbor
Austin American

Austin Statesman
Austin Statesman and Tribune
Austin Weekly Statesman
Bastrop Advertiser
Bell Punch (San Diego, TX)
Bellaire Texan
Benavides Facts
Bonham News
Breckenridge American
Brenham Daily Banner
Brenham Banner-Press
Brenham Daily Banner-Press
Brenham Weekly Banner (TX)
Brownsville Daily Herald
Brownsville Herald
Brownwood Bulletin
Bryan Daily Eagle
Chicago Tribune
Corpus Christi Caller
Corpus Christi Caller & Daily Herald
Corpus Christi Gazette
Corpus Christi Star
Corpus Christi Times
Corpus Christi Weekly Gazette
Cotulla Record
Daily Express (San Antonio)
Daily Herald (Brownsville, TX)
Daily Hesperian (Gainesville, TX)
Daily News-Telegram (Sulphur Springs, TX)
Daily Ranchero and Republican (Brownsville, TX)
Daily Tribune (Bay City, TX)
Dallas Times Herald
Dallas Weekly Herald
Denton Record-Chronicle
Duval County Maverick (San Diego, TX)
Duval County Picture (San Diego, TX)
El Demócrata (San Diego, TX)
El Demócrata Fronterizo (Laredo, TX)
El Paso Herald
El Paso International Daily Times
El Regidor (San Antonio)
Evening Tribune (Galveston)

Falfurrias Facts
Floresville Chronicle
Fort Worth Daily Gazette
Fort Worth Gazette
Fort Worth Press
Fort Worth Record and Register
Gainesville Daily Register and Messenger
Galveston Daily News
Galveston Journal
Galveston Tribune
Hallettsville Herald
Hebbronville News
Henderson Times
Houston Post
Houston Daily Post
Indianola Bulletin
Kingsville Record
La Grange Journal
La Libertad (San Diego, TX)
La Verdad (Corpus Christi)
La Voz (San Diego, TX)
Lampasas Daily Leader
Laredo Daily Times
Laredo Times
Matagorda County Tribune (Bay City, TX)
Mercedes Tribune
Meridian Tribune
New Duval (San Diego, TX)
New York Times
Norton's Union Intelligencer (Dallas)
Nueces Valley (Corpus Christi)
Orange Leader
Pleasanton Express
Ranchero (Corpus Christi)
Refugio Timely Remarks
Robstown Record
San Antonio Daily Express
San Antonio Express
San Antonio Express and News
San Antonio Light
San Saba News
Schulenburg Sticker

Southern Mercury (Dallas)
Southern Messenger (San Antonio)
Standard Advocate (Hearne, TX)
State Gazette (Austin)
Sweetwater Reporter
Taylor County News (Abilene, TX)
Taylor Daily Express
Taylor Daily Press
Temple Daily Telegram
Temple Weekly Times
Tribune (Hallettsville, TX)
Upshur County Echo (Gilmer, TX)
Velasco Daily Times
Weekly Corpus Christi Caller
Weekly Telegraph (Houston)

Index

L

Lamberton, Theodore (Theo), 170, 173, 180, 202, 206
Laughlin, Woodrow, 309, 319, 321
Leal, Juan, 206, 320, 322
Levy, John, 37, 40, 61, 85, 95, 210, 221
Levy, L., 210, 221
Lopez, Guadalupe, 270, 292
Lott, Uriah, 72–73, 145, 179, 235, 253, 259
Lotto, F., 256–57, 280, 289
Lovenskiold, Charles, 95, 155–58, 160, 163–64
Lozano, Dolores, 257–58
Luby, James O., 90, 100, 108, 122, 167–69, 202–4, 208, 213, 225, 238
Luby, Kate, 107, 112, 114
Luna, R. F., 289, 302, 306, 317

M

Manges, Clinton, 326
Martínez, E., 109, 210
Martinez, J. C., 118, 172, 290
Martínez, Miguel, 135, 171–72
McDermott, Carlos, 314–15
McDonald, J. L., 316–17
McKinney, John F., 24, 49, 154, 156–64, 252, 265
Mecklenburger, Henry, 94–95
Meek, Walter, Jr., 245, 329
Miguel, Santiago San, 229–30, 243
Moses, J. Williamson, 61, 94–95, 107, 167–70, 203, 207, 212, 219, 221–22

N

Native Americans, xx–xxi, xxiv, 1, 8. *See also* Indians
Navarro, José Antonio, 50, 154, 242, 293, 304–5
Norton, Milton P., 155–56

O

O'Connor, Joseph, 156
oil, xxii, 235, 237–40, 244, 278, 304–6, 313
Oliveira, Jesús, 220, 298–300, 302

P

Palacios, Julián, 197, 203–4, 206, 208, 212–13, 215, 219, 225, 227–28, 230, 234, 242, 244

Palacios, J. V., 256, 261, 280, 298

Parr, Archer, 307, 315–16, 322–24, 326

Parr, Archie, xix, xxiii–xxiv, 74–75, 223, 227–32, 236–37, 242, 247, 251–56, 258, 267, 279, 282–88, 293–97, 299–300, 307–8

Parr, Atlee, 282, 322–23

Parr, George B., xix, xxiii, 279, 284–86, 288, 299–302, 305–9, 311–13, 316–17, 320–26, 328, 333

Parr, Givens A., 258, 263, 277, 282

Peña, Nazario, 224

Peña, Pedro, 128, 130

Peña Station, 70, 72, 75, 112, 185

Pérez, Alejos, 59, 61, 86, 168, 174, 203

Pérez, Anastasio, 74, 218, 227

Pérez, Encarnación García, 59, 86, 90, 94–96, 101, 144–45, 179, 190, 194, 197, 291

Pérez, Mauricio, 60, 271

Pérez, Pablo, 59, 61, 86, 95, 173, 270

Peters, S. R., 77, 134, 224, 226, 229, 242

Pettigrew, George, 91

Piedras Pintas, 69–70, 101, 105, 121, 123–24, 168, 170–71, 178, 182–83, 185, 189, 235, 237–39

Puig, Juan, 147, 203–4, 210, 212–13, 224, 264

R

railroad, 52–53, 55–56, 66, 69–70, 72, 75–76, 104, 139, 145, 177–85, 194–95, 235, 238

Ramírez, Juan Manuel, 31–32, 59

Ramírez, Rafael, 29, 40, 42

Ramírez, Simón, 29, 40

ranches, 18–19, 34, 37–38, 61–63, 65, 81, 83–84, 121–24, 139, 155–56, 184, 187, 326–27

ranching, xx, 61, 79, 91, 191, 235, 253, 297